WITHDRAWN BY
WHITMAN COLLEGE LIBRARY

THE IMPERIAL CANADIAN

CLAUDE BISSELL

The Imperial Canadian

VINCENT MASSEY
IN OFFICE

UNIVERSITY OF TORONTO PRESS

Toronto Buffalo London

© University of Toronto Press 1986
Toronto Buffalo London
Printed in Canada

ISBN 0-8020-5656-3

Printed on acid-free paper

Canadian Cataloguing in Publication Data
Bissell, Claude T. (Claude Thomas), 1916-
The imperial Canadian
A sequel to: Young Vincent Massey.
Includes bibliographical references and index.
ISBN 0-8020-5656-3

1. Massey, Vincent, 1887-1967.
2. Statesmen – Canada – Biography
I. Title.
FC611.M37B56 1986   971.06'092'4   C86-093388-1
F1034.3.M37B56 1986

---

for Christine, Deirdre, and Rob

Contents

Preface ix
Illustrations xiii

1 / The Anglophile 3
2 / Canada Calling 34
3 / Appeaser 72
4 / The Masseys Go to War 107
5 / The Return to Canada 161
6 / The Royal Commission 195
7 / Governor-General 237
8 / *Patriae profuit* 284

A Note on Sources 315
Notes 317
Genealogies 347
Index 349

Preface

The first volume of my biography of Vincent Massey brought the story down to the end of the year 1935, when Massey left Canada to take up his appointment as Canadian high commissioner in London. The second volume spans the years from 1935 to Massey's death on 30 December 1967. He was high commissioner from 1935 to 1946. After his return to Canada, he was chancellor of the University of Toronto from 1947 to 1953, chairman of the Royal Commission on National Development in the Arts, Letters, and Sciences from 1949 to 1951, and governor-general of Canada from 1952 to 1959. From 1959 until his death, he held no official position, but continued an active career as public speaker, patron and philanthropist, and adviser to institutions and the federal government.

The last chapter of the first volume dealt with Massey's term of office as president of the National Liberal Association, which ended triumphantly in the election of 1935 that returned Mackenzie King to power. During the early years in London Massey thought of himself as a political figure on a diplomatic assignment who might be called back to Canada to take up a senior political appointment. In his autobiography, *What's Past Is Prologue*, Massey emphasizes his political and diplomatic role. I have not tried to duplicate his account, but have rather concentrated on particular questions, which he slighted either out of autobiographical modesty or out of a refusal to face a disturbing record. I deal with his anglophilia, his delight in English aristocratic society, and his ardent royalism, all of which exist side by side with a persistent and doughty defence of Canadian rights and a vigorous exposition of Canadian achievements; with his acknowledged position of leadership among the high commissioners of the Commonwealth, and the major contribution he made to the elucidation and launching of the British Commonwealth Air Training Plan; with the contribution of the Massey family to the war effort, the two sons as combatants, Alice and he as founders and organizers of several services for the armed forces; with the complex relations between the High Commission and his minister, who was also the prime minister; and with his acquiescence in the callous attitude of the Canadian government to Jewish immigration.

In the chapters on the London years I emphasize far more than Massey did in his autobiography the role he played as cultural ambassador, and his increasingly important contribution to the development of British cultural policy. Here is the link between the London years and the period from 1949 to 1959, when he was chairman of the royal commission and governor-general of Canada. During the later period, he made his major contribution. More than any other Canadian, he was responsible for the first major movement of the arts and letters from the periphery of national concern towards the centre. It was a notable achievement. It is the underlying theme of this book.

Vincent Massey was not an intellectual, although contemporary commentators invariably described him as such. He was not a scholar, but he admired scholarship, and made use of it in his speeches and books. He was not an artist, but he valued artistic achievement beyond any other. The Massey biographer must, then, venture into intellectual and cultural history, always remembering that his main reason for doing so is to illuminate the man.

Charles Ritchie, who writes about Vincent Massey with characteristic brilliance and sensitivity (particularly in *The Siren Years*, the journal of his years in London, 1937–45 when he was in the high commissioner's office), has made the daunting suggestion that a biography of Massey 'calls out for a Proust, a Canadian Proust.' In the same speculative vein, I have often thought that Vincent Massey would be a good subject for a Henry James fiction. James' characters often oscillate between Europe and America, and the clash between the two allegiances or the choice of the one over the other constitutes the plot. Vincent Massey also oscillated between Europe and America, between the imperial centre and the dependency that had become independent and assertive. Being a Canadian, like being an American, was a 'complex fate,' more complex in many ways, because Canada had two cultures, and the need for keeping a balance between Europe and America was more constant and more pressing.

If Massey saw being a Canadian as a 'complex fate,' it was one that he cheerfully accepted. On his return to Canada in 1946, he wrote a proud little book, *On Being Canadian*, which proclaimed a fervid nationalism. It is an error to think of Massey as an old-fashioned imperialist. The 'imperial' in my title has no political implications. It is meant to suggest his British bias, and also his proconsular manner in expounding his views, a quality in which his Methodist ancestors might have recognized the authority of divine grace.

I follow, for the most part, a simple chronological sequence. But I have, especially in the early chapters, used a thematic approach, and this has often required a temporary return to earlier periods. A biographer must impose a pattern on his material: otherwise it overwhelms both him and his subject. The pattern, rather than any superior, didactic pronouncement, is his interpretation of the man.

The Imperial Canadian, like its predecessor, *The Young Vincent Massey*, is based mainly on manuscript material. I have also talked to, or corresponded with, a number of people. For this volume I am especially indebted to the following: Geoffrey Andrew, Mrs C.A.A. Armstrong, Kirsty Boyanoski, Derick Breach, Mrs Bert Bryant, Esmond Butler, Sir John and Lady Cotterell, Robertson Davies, Kitty de Cheveigné, Archibald Day, Robert Finch, Colin Friesen, Lord Garner, George Glazebrook, Charity Grant, George Grant, Mrs Leigh Gossage, Sydney Hermant, W.C.R. Jones, John Holmes, Robert Hubbard, George and Alison Ignatieff, Douglas LePan, Georges-Henri Lévesque, Norman Mackenzie, Paul Martin, Mrs Lilias Massey, Robert McDougall, Desmond Neill, Carol Ogden, Jack Pickersgill, Timothy Porteous, Charles Ritchie, Graham Rowley, Carl Schaeffer, Charles Stacey, Miroslav Stajanovich, Vincent Tovell, and Peter Waite.

Mrs Audrey Douglas has turned my hand-written manuscript, a puzzle to the generality, into a clear, typed copy. My wife accompanied me on all my research trips to various places in England and Canada, and supplemented or amended my impressions. Despite ten years of exposure to Massey anecdotes and reflections, she retains a lively and sympathetic interest in the subject. In 1983 I was fortunate to win the Jules and Gabrielle Léger Fellowship, administered by the Social Sciences and Humanities Research Council of Canada. The fellowship enabled me to complete my research at the Public Records office at Kew in Surrey, England, to visit Garnons (near Hereford), and to refamiliarize myself with various war-time London sites.

I acknowledge with gratitude the help of staff at the Public Archives of Canada, Ottawa, the Public Records Office at Kew, and the University of Toronto Archives.

I am indebted to Chief Justice Brian Dickson for permission to quote from his letter to Mrs Massey and to Miroslav Stajanovich for permission to quote from his unpublished manuscript about his years with Vincent Massey.

This book has been published with the kind and generous assistance of the Walter and Duncan Gordon Charitable Foundation and of the Social Sciences and Humanities Research Council of Canada; to both of these organizations I express my gratitude.

C.B.
Toronto 1986

All photographs are from Vincent Massey's personal collection, now in Massey College, except for the last one which is reproduced by courtesy of Mrs Gossage.

Howard Ferguson and his wife meet Vincent and Alice Massey, along with Raymond (also BELOW), when they arrive in London in 1935. Vincent is the new high commissioner.

Receiving King George vi and Queen Elizabeth at Canada House

The top staff at Canada House: standing are Lester Pearson and Ross McLean, seated are Georges Vanier and Vincent Massey.

The Duke of Kent opens an exhibition of three hundred Canadian paintings, thirty of them Massey's, at the Tate gallery in 1938.

OPPOSITE

Massey joins the British cabinet to see Chamberlain off on his flight to Munich in September 1938.

The high commissioners meet in the Dominions Office: Massey is on the right of Anthony Eden, for a time secretary of state for the dominions.

With Lionel, injured but repatriated

Alice serving the troops at the Officers' Club

Hart coxed the Oxford boat in 1939.

OPPOSITE

Garnons–the Masseys' convalescent home for Canadian officers; below, the dining room

Mackenzie King became more pleased with Massey's work during the war.

Back in Canada after the war: Vincent's dog carries the queen's purse at Batterwood; Vincent is befriended by a regimental mascot; and (BELOW) Hart, Alice, Vincent, Lilias, and her husband Lionel at Batterwood

Prince Philip, Sidney Smith, Queen Elizabeth, and Vincent as chancellor of the University of Toronto

The governor-general welcomes the queen.

Leaving Rideau Hall to open parliament

OPPOSITE

The imperial presence

With Lester and Maryon Pearson after opening parliament

A 'troika' of governors-general: Massey, Vanier, and Alexander

Scenes from the Arctic tour in 1956

Massey College in the winter sunshine

At home in Batterwood with his family and dogs

Concentration in Barbados

With Mrs Leigh Gossage

THE IMPERIAL CANADIAN

CHAPTER ONE

The Anglophile

On 31 October 1935, Vincent Massey was appointed Canadian high commissioner to London. It was an office to which he had aspired and for which he felt himself eminently fitted. At 48, he could look back on twenty years of public service. As an undergraduate at the University of Toronto he had conceived of a student building that was to be an informal centre for education in the arts and politics, and he had helped to design Hart House, the building that embodied his ideas; and after two years at Balliol, Oxford, and a second degree, he had had an honourable military career, a brief period in the Ottawa civil service in a responsible position, and several years of voluntary work on provincial and federal bodies that were concerned with education. For the last ten years he had exchanged a voluntary for an official role. He had been in succession a cabinet minister, Canada's first minister to the United States, and for the last three years, president of the National Liberal Federation, and a principal architect of the Liberal victory of 1935. He was deeply devoted to Canada. Had fortune favoured him during his brief period in politics – he was defeated in the election of 1925 and failed to get a constituency nomination in the election of 1926 – he would have preferred political life to the diplomatic career to which he was now committed. Although he was immensely pleased by his London appointment, he had not altogether dismissed the idea of returning in a few years to Canada, where he believed his kind of new-deal liberalism had more appeal than Mackenzie King's inscrutable pragmatism, but he now looked forward to being a Canadian in a British setting. In his mind Canada and Great Britain were inseparable. Canada was a European country in a North American environment (and European to Massey meant British, primarily English, with a bracing French infusion), and to be a Canadian was to adapt the European tradition to the peculiarities of the new world, not – as in the United States – to attempt the creation of a glaringly distinct civilization.

Canadian nationalism in the thirties defined itself more by opposition to Great Britain than to the United States, and Massey's pro-British version was suspect. In his allegiance, he leaped over two hundred years of his family's residence in the United States to his Cheshire ancestors, who gave him, he often declared, some strange, enduring affinity with the English soul. To many, his two principal creations – Hart House and Batterwood, his country home near Port Hope, Ontario – were naked English transplants. Hart House, the harsh critics said, was anthologized Oxbridge, and Batterwood was an attempt to establish an English country house on the Ontario strand. Vincent Massey himself was often categorized, especially in newspapers opposed to his politics, as a precious, colonial version of an English gentleman who made up in aristocratic manners what he lacked in aristocratic ancestry. His boyish appearance had now vanished. His features had acquired a sombreness which concealed the playful humour that delighted his family and close friends. His speech was thought to ape upper-class English speech, and to be a conscious striving for superior distinction. Actually, it was a speech mainly characterized by precise enunciation, which was more indebted to the Hart House stage than to the Balliol common room. To sensitive ears, it was, as a British radio critic later observed, 'a plain, robust, pleasant and unaccented voice.'[1]

Vincent's marriage in June 1915 to Alice (Lal) Parkin had strengthened his bias towards Britain. His own family was nine generations removed from England and was staunchly North American and puritan in its attitudes. The Parkins seemed much closer to the mother country. On both sides, Alice's family was New Brunswick loyalist, and her father, Sir George Parkin, had devoted much of his life to imperial causes – first, the movement towards imperial federation and then the Rhodes scholarship system. Alice had spent most of her adult life in England in a country home near Oxford on the river Thames.

Sir George had slender resources but great influence, and the Parkin home was a gathering place for men and women active in public life. Alice had little formal education, but with her striking good looks and warm, spontaneous manners she was welcomed into the society that formed around her father and she learned much from it. She was Vincent's senior by almost ten years and there was a widespread belief that she exercised a dominating influence over her husband. Certainly, their happy relationship was, in part, based on the admiration Vincent had for the Parkin family and the preference he had for Parkin over Massey values.

The Massey's reputation as anglophiles, Vincent's projection of the Balliol 'tranquil consciousness of effortless superiority' irritated a good many Canadians from Mackenzie King down, and no doubt helped to bring his political career to a sudden halt. But, on the other hand, these qualities could be considered an asset to Canada's representative in the mother country. At least, Massey would be thoroughly acceptable to the British; he would not be capable of the initial gaffes of his predecessor, Howard Ferguson, who had announced before his departure that 'I am going to London with the hope that I may be able to do something to remould, or revise, the contemporary spirit of the British people,'[2] a clumsy reference to the non-competitive gospel of British socialism. A good many Conservatives, as well as Liberals, must have echoed J.W. Dafoe's comment, 'I squirm when I think what they say in England about Ferguson – the amused contempt, the resolve to treat him with mock politeness as an oaf, a freak from the outer marches.'[3] Although Ferguson became much more tactful when he reached London, he achieved at his best a reputation only as 'his country's commercial traveller, its best salesman.'[4] Massey, it was assumed, would impress the British simply by being so clearly one of them – indeed, by exuding a suggestion of superiority. The quintessential Massey story rests upon this perception. Two Englishmen of impeccable credentials discuss the new Canadian high commissioner; they agree that he has excellent qualities; then one adds plaintively, 'But damn it all, the fellow always makes one feel like a bloody savage.'

The story survives because it is an exaggeration of a general truth. In the pictures of Massey taken during the discharge of special duties as high commissioner, he stands out clearly in any group – a neat compact figure, homburg hat, double-breasted buttoned coat, striped trousers, gleaming shoes, a rolled umbrella resting casually in one hand, or, on more formal occasions, impeccable evening clothes or full court dress – knee-breeches, elaborately brocaded coat, buckled shoes, a sheathed sword at his side, plumed hat casually tucked under one arm, displaying the trained actor's skill to make the unusual seem the expected. Whatever questions critics might raise about his political or diplomatic skills, there could be no question of the Canadian high commissioner's ability to perform his social duties with confidence and aplomb.

The pre-war years 1935–39 were not a period that would seem to provide a comfortable background for traditional social activity. Today we see these years as a protracted period of crisis. A bare recital of the main international events conveys an overwhelming sense of movement towards climactic disaster. In October 1935, as Massey prepared to leave for England, Italy attacked Abyssinia. In March 1936, Hitler sent troops into the demilitarized Rhineland. In July 1936, civil war broke out in Spain and continued savagely for four years. In March 1938 Hitler incorporated Austria into the Reich. In September 1938, the prime minister, Neville Chamberlain, began a series of conferences with Hitler that seemed to avert war but was actually its bitter prologue. Nevertheless, until the spring of 1939, English society gradually absorbed each calamity and resumed its accustomed ways. In particular the succession of international crises did not greatly alter the social life of the *haut monde*.

The unusually relaxed tempo of English society, given the constant hammering of international events, had a number of sources: the gradual emergence of Great Britain from the economic depression; the apparent achievement of political consensus with the creation of a National Government in 1931 (really a Conservative government, dominated by the Conservative leader, Stanley Baldwin, who became the prime minister in June 1935), and its overwhelming validation in the two elections of 1931 and 1935; and the passionate desire for peace and the refusal to believe that Europe could stumble into another great war. In addition, the four years presented a royal drama of unexampled variety and intensity. It turned the nation's thoughts inward and away from international events. The monarchy became a subject of universal concern, and a particular concern for those whose official positions or social prominence brought them close to the court. If not a full-fledged member of this special group, Vincent Massey was a welcome guest accorded full privileges. During the four pre-war years he was always an enthralled spectator of the royal drama and to his great delight, on occasion, a minor participant. Nothing in his responsibilities as high commissioner gave him more pleasure and satisfaction than his royal associations.

The royal drama began with the celebration of George v's jubilee in May 1935. The Masseys were still in Canada, but their response could not have been greater had they already taken up residence in London. The whole day of 6 May 1935 had been devoted to events marking the royal occasion, most of them official and public; but for the Masseys the real heart of the celebration was a gathering at Batterwood of all the servants in the house and the employees in the surrounding farms, over which Vincent and Alice presided like feudalistic lords of the manor. After the king's death on 21 January 1936, Vincent with the other high commissioners of the dominions was asked to attend the accession council and sign the proclamation. He was deeply conscious of the solemnity of the occasion, and in a letter to his sister-in-law, Maude Grant, drew upon his Toronto and Balliol studies in constitutional history to set the event in august perspective. 'The council,' he wrote, 'is apparently the lineal descendant of the *Witenagemot* of Saxon times and represents the selection of the new King by the wise men. This gathering was a matter of great practical importance in the Middle Ages, because when there was a disputed succession it was important to get as many notable people as possible to back the legitimate King – and quickly.'[5]

Deeply honoured as he was to be asked to participate in this historic event, he had some doubts – shared by other commissioners – about the constitutional appropriateness of his role. Was it in harmony with the Statute of Westminster of 1931 that enshrined the dominions as 'autonomous communities within the British Empire ... united by a common allegiance to the Crown?' Did the act of signing violate that delicate balance between autonomy and membership in the Empire? It was finally concluded to Vincent's relief and constitutional satisfaction 'that the signatures of Dominion representatives on this document meant little more than the names of witnesses in a register of a marriage ceremony.'⁶ Vincent had no such doubts about the appropriateness of the high commissioners marching in the king's funeral procession, despite an initial decision taken in 'high quarters' not to include them. Vincent took the matter up with Sir Alan Lascelles, at the time assistant private secretary to George V, who in turn appealed to high quarters. Vincent recorded with laconic self-satisfaction, 'we marched.'⁷

In the abdication crisis the Masseys were solidly on the side of Stanley Baldwin and sound British opinion. Alice reported retrospectively to Maude Grant that 'we were rather in the know because so many of them are around like Alex Hardinge and Tommy Lascelles – our great personal friends – and they took us into their confidence knowing that we would never breathe a word.'⁸ Ever since Edward VIII's visits to Canada in the twenties as the Prince of Wales, Vincent had been alternately repelled and charmed by him. On the one hand he was 'a decent slightly underdeveloped boy with a natural bent for rather low society.'⁹ As the reigning monarch he seemed bored and restless in the despatch of his routine, social duties. On the other hand, at the opening of parliament early in November 1936, Vincent reported that 'the King made an admirable impression – gleaming regal bearing and a most intelligent and effective reading of the speech.'¹⁰ When by late November the crisis with the king's relationship with Mrs Simpson had been reached, Vincent was in complete sympathy with Baldwin's approach, in which constitutional correctness and moral disapproval were skilfully mixed, although in an interview he warned the prime minister about the king's great popularity in Canada which made it necessary that 'the whole matter should be handled with great delicacy and care.'¹¹ Vincent rejoiced in the final outcome. The affair was like a late Shakespearian comedy in which dark tragedy had suddenly turned into a miraculous rebirth, the winter of bitter discontent giving place to a glorious spring. 'So,' wrote Vincent to Maude (for whom he reserved his most considered reflections), 'what might have been a national and imperial disaster has been turned into a triumph which I really believe has left the monarch and the prestige of the British Commonwealth stronger than ever.'¹²

One result of the abdication crisis was an intensification of Massey's disapproval of Winston Churchill, whom, like a great many both within and without the Conservative party, he looked upon as an irresponsible and disturbing voice on the periphery of events. Now, he thought, Churchill was 'exploiting the crisis for political ends,'[13] by which he meant that he was attempting along with the press lords, Beaverbrook and Rothermere, to launch a popular movement on behalf of the king. When, following Baldwin's presentation of the case for abdication in the House of Commons, Churchill's intervention was shouted down, Massey warmly approved. Churchill, he commented, 'showed his irresponsible, free-booting disposition.'[14]

Vincent's observation that 'what might have been a national and imperial disaster has been turned into a triumph' was brilliantly confirmed by the coronation of 12 May 1937. The choice by the king of 'George VI' as his style and title revived memories of the probity and dedication of his father; and he gladly associated himself with the Archbishop of Canterbury in emphasizing throughout the ceremony the religious and moral mission of the monarchy.[15] To Vincent, this was the ceremony of ceremonies, the opening up of timeless vistas of history:

> *As bugles blow*
> *From Agincourt and Mons and Waterloo*
> *To wake the Lion and the Unicorn*
> *From deep heraldic sleep to new life born.*[16]

The dominion high commissioners carried standards in the procession, and Vincent gloried in this minor role. A month before the ceremony he had been asked to convey a request on behalf of the Canadian government that dress regulations should be relaxed at the coronation, which, in effect, meant that knee-breeches need not be worn. This he did obediently but without enthusiasm. 'I wish to goodness,' he wrote, 'some of my fellow countrymen wouldn't have an almost religious antipathy to knee-breeches.'[17] As for him, he had an almost religious veneration for them. Alice quoted proudly from a letter they had received after the coronation in which it was observed that in the procession Vincent Massey 'looked like a medieval stained glass window.' Alice enthusiastically accepted the appropriateness of the description, and added that 'in his uniform and carrying the standard beautifully he really did.'[18]

Vincent's description was a prose version of Sitwell's poem. Nothing during his ten years in England came near the coronation in its symbolic evocation of Britain's greatness, her blending of the sublime and the human, her firm hold on the verities. He wrote, 'What follows defies all adjectives. No ceremonial could be finer or more moving – this country has a genius for such things because of the combination of essentially English qualities of which English pageantry is an expression, a romantic sense, a feeling for precision without rigidity, a sense of symbolism kept in close check by a sense of humour, a practical sense which relates ceremonial to present-day reality. Pageantry in the English tradition has always stood for pageantry with intelligence and feeling.'[19]

Alice's notes on coronation day are in sharp contrast to her husband's romantic flight. To her sister Maude she wrote as the brisk and competent organizer, a little in the manner of the orderly housewife preparing for a happy but exacting day in the country. They rose at 4.30 a.m. to be in their place in the Abbey at 6.30 a.m. They took with them 'a few sandwiches, a little brandy, and some raisins,' none of which they actually touched. She observed with considerable distaste that, before the ceremony began, there was a good deal of retirement to the lavatory, and went on to comment while 'on this very domestic subject' that 'all of us who had any thought about the day were very abstemious for 24 hours beforehand, and I for one never thought of anything of the kind until I got home about 6.30 that evening.'[20]

The climactic event of the pre-war years was the king and queen's visit to Canada in May and June of 1939. It was an event no less stirring and emotional than the coronation itself. It came at a time when the euphoria of Munich had faded, when faint hope for peace and increasing fear of war were darkly mingled, but at a time when pride and confidence in the strength and determination of the Commonwealth had asserted itself. For both the king and queen, the visit was a final and triumphant resolution of any doubts they may still have had about the tasks they had been called upon to perform. At the Canada Club dinner on 3 July 1939, Vincent Massey said, 'The

Royal Visit to Canada was an event so happy in its conception, so gloriously successful in its achievement, and so fragrant in its memory, that any comment seems both inadequate and superfluous.' This was not the usual oratorical exuberance demanded by a ceremonial occasion. Massey's Canadian correspondents – solemn men not given to emotion – were transfixed in admiration. Norman McLarty, the postmaster general, wrote about the king and queen that 'the general impression in Canada is that their charm is indescribable.'[21] Colonel Osborne, Vincent's associate on the Dominion Drama Festival, wrote that the royal visit was 'a poem.'[22] The governor-general's secretary reported more soberly than the Canadian observers, but his admiration and enthusiasm break through: 'There is no doubt that its success was mainly due to the magnificent performance of the King and Queen themselves, and whether one looks at it from a sentimental point of view or with the critical eye of a hard-boiled official, one is forced to the conclusion that they carried out their exacting task absolutely perfectly. There were, as you may imagine, numerous pitfalls, but they seemed to have an unerring instinct for avoiding them.'[23]

For Vincent Massey, the Canadian tour had a special importance. The proposal had come from Mackenzie King during his coronation visit, but Massey was enthusiastically involved in the arrangements. Most of Massey's correspondence on the subject was with Lord Tweedsmuir, who was more disposed than the prime minister to pay attention to him. Vincent was most concerned about the American visit, made necessary by Roosevelt's personal invitation to the king and queen. He feared that this might be long and overshadow the Canadian visit. 'It would be a thousand pities, of course, if the American visit was in any way allowed to rival the visit to Canada.'[24] Care must be taken even in a short visit to the United States not to give the impression that this was the really important part of the visit. There must not be, Massey warned the governor-general, any conspicuous swelling of the king's staff when he went to the United States. Massey understood the theory: a larger staff was essential when visiting a foreign country. But the Canadian public would not appreciate this, and would sense a national slight.

As the day for the royal departure to North America approached, the Masseys, as Canadian advisers, found themselves agreeably close to the royal household. On 3 February 1939 Vincent had an audience with the king to talk about the Canadian visit. In April they dined at Windsor Castle. 'The King and I,' Alice wrote to Maude with proud sisterly understatement, 'had a most delightful talk, full of indiscretions and frankneses. The table was all gold plate and so was the service, but somehow everything seemed so simple and so absolutely happy in its simplicity.'[25] The great royal event for the Masseys was their own dinner for the king and queen on 2 May 1939. Vincent's diary, usually, in recording social events, confined to the *dramatis personae* with a careful attention to titles, expanded on this occasion into three pages of his small, closely spaced handwriting. He indulged in a few colourful details. Knee-breeches, no longer favoured by the court, were confined to the servants – courtesy, Vincent adds, of Moss Brothers. The orderly at the entrance was a Royal Canadian Mounted policeman, who was 'much more nervous when the King spoke to him than he had been, I am sure, chasing bad men in the north-west.' The talk was so animated that 'the little orchestra on the landing outside could hardly be heard.' The conversation between the queen and Massey, to his great delight, touched on the homely details of the royal domestic economy. Recent state visits of King Carol of Rumania and the president of France had so depleted their resources that they felt 'almost on rock-bottom.'[26]

The succession of royal occasions had inspired a vast array of social events – luncheons, dinners, receptions, ceremonies, balls. In the coronation period from 27 April to 3 June 1937 the Masseys estimated that they had entertained in their home about 2,200 Canadian visitors, and even in calmer periods no week passed without a luncheon, dinner, or sherry party (often all three) at their Hyde Park Gardens home.

12 Hyde Park Gardens, which was to be the centre of the Massey world until war broke out, was not an official part of the high commissioner's establishment. Vincent had hoped that the government, in view of his heavy social responsibilities, would purchase a house for him and his successors. Four months after his arrival in London, Massey raised with King the provision of an official residence. It was difficult, he explained, to rent a furnished house that was suitable for entertaining. They had rented a house at 33 Portman Square, a fine eighteenth-century house built by the Adam brothers, but on a corner

that was 'unbearably noisy' and with a reception room that was 'entirely inadequate,'[27] and there was little prospect of finding one for rent that would answer to the Masseys' concept of the high commissioner's social responsibilities. The solution, he suggested, was the government's purchase of a permanent house. Such a move should be looked upon as a business proposition, and Massey was prepared to see his allowances reduced to cover the interest on the capital investment. Mindful of the storm of protest that the purchase of the legation building in Washington had aroused, Massey assured the prime minister that he was thinking of a comparatively modest investment – about $150,000 as opposed to the Washington $500,000 (which provided both for residence and legation offices). Mindful, too, of the popular Canadian image of Massey as a man of great wealth, he reminded King that 'our resources are not what they would have been had not a large proportion of our family fortune gone into the Massey Foundation with which, as you know, we are trying to do what we can in London.' King did not respond to Massey until over three months later, and then he gave a blunt and uncompromising 'no' to the proposal.[28] Massey did not reopen the question. On 26 August 1936, the Masseys moved to 12 Hyde Park Gardens, a house that they rented from Lord Edward Hay for five years. It was only a short distance from their former residence, but, unlike that house, it was agreeably insulated from the nearest main traffic artery, Bayswater Road. The five-year lease was to cover the pre-war period during which the Masseys were to be most deeply involved in social life.

King warmly approved of the new house, even though he had declined to make it a part of the high commissioner's establishment. After a dinner party at 12 Hyde Park Gardens in October, he wrote that 'the new house is very beautiful, it gives the impression of great refinement, light green tint throughout, is quite pleasing, reception room large and spacious, the other rooms tastefully arranged. A much lovelier house that the one at Washington. It is a quiet part of the city being protected from the road on the front side by a small park.' Then, in a rare mood of enthusiasm for the good life, he added, 'altogether the evening was quite the most enjoyable I have had thus far. One could not but feel that Canada was being represented in an exceptionally fine way in London. I question if any two persons in

Canada could have been found who could do as well, all sides considered, of what the position demands.'²⁹

The Masseys accepted their social responsibilities with alacrity. They liked entertaining, and they liked being entertained. There was satisfaction in feeling part of the *beau monde*. Alice was more concerned than her husband with the complex relationships that developed, when names changed bewilderingly, in accordance with aristocratic custom, or the fortunes of matrimony. Evelyn Waugh might have put this gossipy letter to her sister in the mouth of one of his brittle socialites:

*There was a very large dinner at Lord and Lady Granards'. It will amuse you to know who were there – the Londonderrys whom both of us like very much, the Wigrams, Lady Howe, who was beautiful, Lady Curzon (her real beauty has gone now), and from whom Lord Howe has just got a divorce. I see to-day that he has married some girl in South Africa about half his own age. Her son we are devoted to – he is the present young Lord Curzon (not the Reddleston family) and his wife is one of the most charming girls imaginable. Lord Howe has given them Penn House. Lady Howe is living in a small flat. She is an amusing creature. Scarcely knowing anything of her at all, except for lunching at Penn with a shooting party, she said to me "all I have left is my precious (I forget the name) pekinese.' I sat between Ronald Graham, who used to be ambassador in Rome – a most charming, delightful person – and Lord Bradford, a very nice creature whom I imagine does not do much but look after his own estates. The Bessboroughs were there, and the young Duchess of Westminster, whom I think no longer lives with the Duke. The French Ambassador, M. Corbin – we had a delightful talk together. These are difficult days for him. Lord Granard's daughter was also there – she, as you know, had to leave her husband.*³⁰

Alice Massey obviously enjoyed charting the depths and shallows of English society, having served a helpful apprenticeship in her father's Oxford home. Vincent was less expert, although Balliol had given him a fair start, and frequent visits to England after the First World War had enlarged his range of friends and associations. He was at home in country homes, London clubs, and at formal dinner parties. He was an easy and gifted conversationalist, with no obtrusive obsessions, informed about politics and the arts; and he had a nice dramatic sense, so that he could play his part in drawing-room exchanges that often required more verbal agility than substance – a blending of P.G. Wodehouse and Noel Coward. He had two specific attractions of which hosts were aware. First of all, he knew a good deal about the United States from his three years there as minister. In the pre-war years the United States was an enigma, ambiguous in her attitude to Great Britain, still isolationist; and yet in any war, she would obviously play the decisive role. Vincent Massey was sympathetic to the United States, understood her dilemma, but saw it through British eyes. Canada (although unknown) was not an enigma: as the probability of war increased, she became a great haven of security for children, and, on occasion, for their parents, and the Canadian high commissioner held the key to this haven.

The social world of London in the pre-war years still trailed clouds of Edwardian glory. It was presided over by hostesses with varying interests and preferences, but with a number of indispensable common characteristics: a house, preferably large and imposing, in a fashionable part of London; a wealthy husband who was inconspicuous or invisible; knowledge of the great, skill in detecting those about to become great, and success in capturing both. The Masseys, certainly not among the great, were often only casual guests. They had, for instance, only fleeting glimpses of, perhaps, the most celebrated hostess of the time, Lady Cunard. 'It was in her house in Grosvenor Square,' wrote Sir Henry Channon (always known as 'Chips'), a reclaimed American who rose to heights of snobbery that his fashionable English friends could rarely attain, 'that the great met the gay, that statesman consorted with society, and writers with the rich – and where, for over a year, the drama of Edward VIII was enacted.'[31] The Masseys glimpsed the opening stages of this drama in December 1935, when they attended a sherry party at Lady Cunard's at which the Prince of Wales and Mrs Simpson were present.

With other prominent hostesses, however, the Masseys had close and friendly associations. One of these was Maggie Greville, long a reigning hostess, immensely rich, with a country home, Polesden Lacey, where in 1923 King George VI and Queen Elizabeth (then the Duke and Duchess of York) had spent part of their honeymoon.

Vincent was entranced by her. 'Maggie is very wise and wonderfully well informed as well she might be with a procession of important men talking tête-à-tête, day after day.'[32]

But, for Vincent, the shining hostess of the day, at whose gatherings he and Alice were regular guests, was Sybil Colefax. She had the requisite wealthy husband who, according to Sir Kenneth Clark, confined his conversation to boring summaries of the latest news. But Sybil was much more than a socialite sustained by her husband's wealth. Her family had strong intellectual associations. Her grandfather, James Wilson, was a founder of the *Economist*, and from the sale of this influential periodical to the young entrepreneur, Brendan Bracken, she was one of the beneficiaries. Harold Nicolson, who savagely dismissed Maggie Greville, was a close friend and admirer. She was widely read in literature and the arts, and could, in her letters and conversation, sustain long and detailed analyses of passages in Homer and Proust.[33] But this contemplative side was superseded by her role as the London hostess, which she pursued with all the determination and ruthlessness of a seasoned investor playing the stock market. She was particularly successful in capturing the literary great – local lions like Max Beerbohm, Granville Barker, H.G. Wells, or visiting lions from the United States, like Walter Lippmann and Lynn and Alfred Lunt. Despite declining fortunes, which necessitated a move from a large handsome house on the King's Road to a smaller house on Lord North Street and to her opening a gift shop much frequented by the rich, Sybil Colefax refused to relinquish her social role. During the war, she entertained in the Dorchester hotel, where her guests dutifully responded to invitations to luncheons known as 'ordinaries' and just as dutifully paid for their own meals. The Masseys remained faithful throughout this downward movement in the Colefax fortunes.

Maggie Greville, Emerald Cunard, Sybil Colefax were all, so to speak, professional hostesses. Violet Markham and Margot Asquith attracted like-minded people, and were influential hostesses simply because of their own impressive qualities. Violet Markham had long been interested in social problems and in practical schemes for brightening the lives of workers. She had received a legacy that made her independent. One of the fruits of this was the setting up in her house at 8 Gower Street in London of an informal meeting place for people interested in politics, the arts, and public service. One of the overseas numbers of Violet Markham's group, whose occasional attendance was bolstered by regular correspondence, was Mackenzie King, a friend from the days when he was labour minister in the Laurier government. She was a healthy influence on the idealistic young politician and, later, on the solemn, self-absorbed prime minister, and tried, as she once wrote, 'to direct his mind from the turbid oratory in which all colonial Premiers seem to indulge.'[34] Vincent Massey was not prone to 'turbid oratory,' but he was certainly not as assertive as King about the problems of the workers; still, 8 Gower Street was a healthy corrective to the gossipy speculation of more glittering gatherings. The Masseys had known Violet Markham for a long time; they admired her idealism and social passion, and responded to them. As the probability of war became overwhelming, she wrote to Alice in an intensely personal vein: 'Life and its duties seem to sweep friends so inexorably apart, but ever since that evening years ago which I spent with you and Vincent [a reference to a meeting in the mid-twenties] I have always looked forward to the rare occasion when we are able to meet *à trois* and talk. It's always a joy to catch sight of your faces even in a throng, but the salt and savour of our friendship are not to be found in a crowd. In these dark days when the lamp of the human spirit appears to burn so low, it is more vitally necessary than ever to assert the imperishable nature of the flame.'[35]

Margot Asquith, Countess of Oxford and Asquith, was, like Violet Markham, more friend than hostess. Her husband, referred to by Margot as 'my prime minister,' had died in 1928; she was now living in London, at seventy-one, still fiercely independent, glorying in the past which she recalled with vividness, alert and critical of the present. She was a frequent guest at 12 Hyde Park Gardens. She was now engaged in writing her last book of reminiscence, *Off the Record* (which she, at one time, wanted to dedicate to the Masseys), and her mind leaped from the past to the present, in conversation, as in her book. Vincent recalled an evening when they dined alone with her, and listened to 'a wonderful monologue – recollections of Gladstone, comments on manners, shrewd judgment of contemporary people.'[36]

The rural complement to the London luncheon, dinner, or reception was the week-end in the country house. A network of these houses still existed throughout Great Britain, the most distinctive and the most splendid being the 'great houses,' those that had been associated with one family for long periods. They often owed their establishment to the whims of official favouritism, and their enlargement to the fruits of high office, and judicious marriage with an aristocratic heiress or with the daughter of a wealthy industrialist. In the thirties the transformation was under way from private enclave to public treasure. With the decline in agricultural prices during the nineteenth century, the land economy upon which the great houses were based was undermined; their feudalistic societies had been weakened by the movement of workers to the cities; and the First World War further narrowed their economic base and challenged their very existence. But many survived. Massey describes a week-end in the late twenties at Chatsworth, the principal seat of the Duke of Devonshire, when much of the old feudalistic tradition still remained. Alice was more detailed and more rhapsodic about a visit to Welbeck Abbey, the seat of the Duke and Duchess of Portland, in Nottinghamshire:

Welbeck Abbey, as you can imagine is the most entrancing place, and the Duke and Duchess, two of the most charming people you can imagine. She, I think, is 74, he a little older. She is still extraordinarily good-looking, and to me, even to-day is as beautiful a person as one would want to see. The Sergeant [sic] portrait of her, and four or five different ones by Laszlo show how really lovely she was ... at Welbeck they have created an atmosphere that I found in no other great house in England. Every room is so full with that quality and gentleness and simplicity and beauty of character that pervades them both. The house itself baffles description – I think it is larger than Chatsworth, but looks much more like a great country house not at all as the palatial line of the others. The dining room all Van Dyck pictures – about 10 of them, and all through the house things of beauty that just baffle description. We spent all Saturday morning driving through one part of the property, which, of course, is a part of Sherwood Forest – the stables are all empty, except for a few riding horses, but with great reverence we went into the stable of St. Simon – you will remember the great Derby winner – and also for years one of the best stud horses in England. His stable is kept with fresh straw in it, and the record of his performances all round the wall. It really was touching to watch the Duke as he described his various performances to us – They have built a house on the estate for the Tichfields' (oldest son) which is ludicrously like Batterwood – the same coloured brick, the same shape, almost everything about it even to the electric fittings in one of the rooms which are exactly like the ones in the large Drawing Room at Batterwood, which, as you know, are copies of those at Knowle [sic].[37]

A week-end always included an inspection of treasures: at Alnwick Castle in Northumberland, for instance, it was a Chaucer manuscript that caught Vincent's special interest; at Rockingham Castle, 'an iron bound chest left behind by King John when he went on his last journey to the east coast of England.'[38] At Broomfield, Fife, where the Masseys stayed with Lord and Lady Elgin during an official visit to the Glasgow Exhibition, the most exciting treasure was the stone thrown at their host's ancestor, who, when governor-general of Canada, had insisted on signing the Rebellion Loss's Bill, and thereby asserting the theory of responsible government. 'It was,' wrote Vincent, 'a difficult object for a Canadian to contemplate without emotion.'[39]

A good many of the country houses in which the Masseys were guests did not qualify as 'great houses' in the sense that they were not associated over the years with a particular family. They were recent acquisitions, rural retreats for the affluent. Some could be as splendid as the 'great houses' and a good deal more comfortable, like Sir Philip Sassoon's house in Kent, 'torn,' as Mark Girouard remarked, 'between the standards of *Country Life* and Metro-Goldwyn-Mayer.'[40] Some could be as ancient as the great houses, like Sissinghurst, in Kent, a fragmented ruin of a Tudor castle, which Harold Nicolson and his wife restored. For them it was primarily a rural retreat where each could write, free of distraction. But it was also a place for small week-end parties, one of which the Masseys attended in May 1939, after bidding farewell at Portsmouth to the king and queen, leaving on their Canadian tour. The restorations could be on an elaborate scale, like the medieval castle in Anthony Powell's *A Buyer's Market*, which seemed to the narrator to be 'the Middle Age, from the pages of Tennyson, or Scott, at its most elegant; all sordid and painful elements subtly removed.'[41] Such a country house was Baillif's Court in Sussex, which provided for the Masseys one of a flurry of week-end retreats in the summer of 1939 before, in September, the curtain descended abruptly on the golden life. In his diary, Vincent is poised between admiration of the result and amusement at the laboured ingenuity that brought it about. 'It was,' he wrote, 'a synthetic medieval building – very well done – Henry VI style with George VI plumbing, the medievalisms carried into the costume of the maids, the 2-pronged forks with which one attempts to eat a poached egg at breakfast and the charming *mille fleurs* garden – the best I have seen.'[42]

At one time the country houses had been centres of political power where policy was adumbrated and careers made and broken. The country houses that the Masseys knew and visited were, however, primarily centres of innocuous social activity. Some of them provided both a setting and an agent for a popular religious movement of the decade – 'The Oxford Group,' or, less pretentiously, 'Buchmanism' or 'Moral Rearmament.' The movement flourished most successfully among the affluent and found a natural home in the English country house. Its appeal to self-dramatization provided a moral version of 'charades,' a traditional country house game. Alice's sturdy common sense, not always evident in her dealings with the social world, turned her into a harsh critic. When a friend, Lady Nanton, asked if she could bring Frank Buchman – the founder and spokesman for the movement – to one of her parties, she said 'no,' and went on to explain to Maude: 'It sounds rather rude and intolerant but their method over here this year is to me absolutely disgusting. They have tried to work themselves in everywhere through Lady Nanton's connections, and in doing so boast of the great houses and the great people they have conquered – you know the way they do things. I don't think my blood has got up so much over anything as it has over their way of trying to propagate their special type of religion.'[43]

Some of the country houses were still political, but only in the sense that the hosts had political interests and invited guests whose opinions carried weight in their field. The only country house that achieved a firm political status in the eyes of the public was Cliveden, the principal country seat of Lord and Lady Astor, a short distance from London, a place of 'magnitude and magnificence'[44] presided over by the ebullient and magnetic Nancy Astor. Lord Astor was known to be sympathetic to Germany, as were a number of his guests, and the fiction arose that there was a 'Cliveden set' actively sponsoring appeasement.

On the basis of one recorded visit to Cliveden on 27 June 1936, Vincent Massey has been described recently as 'a fringe member of the aristocratic, largely pro-German and anti-Semitic [Cliveden] set.'[45]

There is an ironic family story in Massey's reputed junior membership of the Cliveden set. A journalist who actively pursued the Cliveden-German association was Claud Cockburn, the editor of an influential, leftist publication, *The Week*. In the fall of 1937, he reported that Lord Halifax (at that time lord president of the council, but shortly to become foreign secretary) had proposed during a visit to Germany that Hitler should be given a free hand in central Europe in exchange for an abandonment of his colonial claims; and that this iniquitous proposal had been 'got into usable diplomatic shape at a party at the Astors' place at Cliveden.'[46] Cockburn became a communist for a few years and fought in Spain in the communist ranks. He had Canadian connections that brought him embarrassingly close to the Canadian high commissioner – he was a brother-in-law of Raleigh Parkin, Alice's brother.

Massey did attend one week-end that was frankly political, but its inspiration did not come from the 'Cliveden set.' It came from the Round Table group, by then a venerable organization of which Massey had been a member since his university days. The Round Table had been concerned initially with establishing an 'organic union' of the Empire, with a great deal of emphasis on the mission of the Empire in maintaining world peace. In the new Commonwealth, it no longer commanded strong support, but its members, who tended to be assertively idealistic, still had a considerable influence. Tom Jones, deputy-secretary to the cabinet from 1916 to 1930 and an intimate of Stanley Baldwin, commented acidly that 'all the Round Tablers are good at collecting any credit there is going, like the Scotch.'[47] The only country house week-end that resulted for Massey in a political declaration – and that at informal one – was held at Lord Lothian's magnificent Elizabethan house in Norfolk, Blickling Hall. Lord Lothian was the Philip Kerr who had been the first editor of *The Round Table*, the movement's official publication. He had been briefly a Liberal cabinet member in Ramsay MacDonald's national government, and he was to serve at the outbreak of war for one notable year as ambassador to the United States. Besides the Masseys, his guests were

Sir Walter Layton, an economist with liberal views, who was editor of *The Economist*, Norman Davis, an American banker and Roosevelt emissary, the Astors, Sir Thomas Inskip, shortly to be appointed minister for coordination of defence (who became dominion secretary at the outbreak of war), Arnold Toynbee, and Tom Jones. During the week-end, in March of 1936, Germany occupied the demilitarized Rhineland Zone and proposed a non-aggression pact for twenty-five years. The event immediately determined the subject of discussion for the party. 'We found ourselves,' wrote Massey, 'during the course of the week-end in extraordinary agreement. Don't get too excited about the technical breaking of treaties, use Hitler's offer as a new foundation of peace.'[48]

Country house week-ends and London entertainments gave the Masseys a wide acquaintance in English society. But these were casual associations, people to be greeted amiably on social occasions, even on a first-name basis, but not friends to be consulted on matters of importance, or to be invited to a small intimate dinner party at Hyde Park Gardens. Friends in this sense went back to early days, particularly to the two golden years at Balliol 1911–13.

Two of Vincent's contemporaries at Balliol – Robin Barrington-Ward and Harold Macmillan – were, when he arrived in England, launched in public careers that were eventually to take them to positions of influence in the Conservative party. They had been his friends in Balliol days, and the friendship had endured and strengthened over the twenty years since they had left the college. Of the two, Barrington-Ward was the more intimate. Their careers at Balliol had been remarkably similar. Both had fared better in extra-curricular activities than in formal studies (Vincent had been more successful; he had got a second in Modern History, Robin a third in Greats). But Robin had risen to greater heights in the undergraduate world. In his last year he was president of the Union, where all Oxford matched wits in debate, and this was just as important for his future career as getting a first in Greats might have been. They worked together in the short-lived Balliol literary magazine, of which Vincent was the founder and Robin the editor.

They both came from middle-class backgrounds, although Robin's family had only the genteel security conferred by careers in school and church, and he did not have the freedom in planning his career that affluence had given to Vincent Massey. The two friends looked alike: both were of slight build, below average height, with a bird-like briskness in movement, and a careful precision in speech. Throughout his years in London, Vincent saw Robin regularly, often at informal dinner parties where they were joined by their wives. They helped each other to reinforce and articulate their views, which were never far apart. Barrington-Ward was in a position of great power. In 1935 he had been deputy editor of *The Times* for a year, and eventually succeeded Geoffrey Dawson as editor in 1941.

Barrington-Ward is best remembered as the man who wrote many of the appeasement editorials in *The Times*. Behind these lay not so much a softness towards Germany as a passionate desire for peace engendered by memories of the First World War, where he had been a front-line infantry officer twice decorated for heroism. After 1939 he was often critical of government policy. He was strongly opposed to sending British troops to Greece in the wake of the retreating Germans, whose task was to clear the way for the restoration of an unpopular monarchy; and he aroused Churchill's wrath. Above all, he sounded early the note of social reform that should arise from the war: 'planned consumption, abolition of unemployment and poverty, educational reform, family allowances, economic organization of the continent.'[49]

Vincent had kept in touch with Harold Macmillan after they had left Balliol. After long, front-line service in the First World War, Macmillan had accepted an appointment in 1919 as ADC to the newly appointed governor-general of Canada, the Duke of Devonshire. The year he spent in Canada was a momentous one: he wooed and married the daughter of the governor-general, a happy union between the predestined head of a major British publishing house and one of the most powerful aristocratic families in England. On a less exalted plane, he renewed, as he himself wrote 'a close intimacy with Vincent Massey which lasted all through the years.'[50] On a visit to England in the early thirties, Vincent had sought out Macmillan to get an idea of the temper of English politics; and no doubt they continued their frank discussion on many occasions during his London days. In those days, Macmillan was still without office, a Conservative MP widely known, but distrusted by party stalwarts as a radical who urged long-range planning and government co-operation with industry and labour. Such ideas were congenial enough to Vincent, who had espoused similar ones during his presidency of the National Liberal Federation; but Macmillan's increasing disgust at Baldwin's and Chamberlain's search for accommodation with Germany must have caused a few strains between the friends until the outbreak of war brought all together in a common mission.

Another Oxford friend, although of an earlier vintage, was Eustace Percy. He and Vincent had become acquainted in the year before the outbreak of the First World War, when Percy was a secretary at the British embassy in Washington and Vincent was a don at the University of Toronto who, in visits to Washington, encountered a group of young intellectuals, of whom Percy was one. Eustace Percy had remained in the Foreign Office until 1921, when he turned to politics. He was elected Conservative member for Hastings and retained this seat until he left politics in 1936. Shortly afterwards, he became rector of King's College, Newcastle, and it was as an academic that Vincent knew him during his stay in England.

Percy, as his autobiography attests, was a philosophical and sceptical Conservative – too philosophical and sceptical to be a success in politics. He was, in the words of a biographer, 'hampered by lacking partisanship.'[51] In the second Baldwin cabinet, he was president of the Board of Education, where he strove to overcome the apathy towards education of his fellow ministers, and was a pioneer in recognizing the need for a co-ordinated approach to technical education. But he did not obtain ministerial rank again until 1935, when he served for a few months as minister without portfolio, resigning in March 1936 out of a general feeling of frustration and an increasing disillusionment with the government's foreign policy. Eustace Percy (Baron Percy of Newcastle as he became) carried his aristocratic lineage with an easy informality. He had a sharp and penetrating mind, and his conservatism had no taint of the reactionary.

Another old friend was Edward Wood, who became Lord Irwin during his years as viceroy of India, 1925–31, then Lord Halifax, secretary of state for foreign affairs, 1938–40, and ambassador to the United States, 1941–46. Massey's first reference to Halifax is in connection with the lectureship that the Massey Foundation had established at the University of Toronto. Massey invited Halifax, just returned from India, to give the inaugural lecture in the fall of 1931. But presumably their association went back a number of years; Halifax's biographer, the Earl of Birkenhead, refers to them at this time as being old friends. (Birkenhead goes on to comment that the lecture, a survey of the problem of India, was 'his longest and most important pronouncement on India since his return.'[52]) Massey thought of Halifax as having the virtues he most admired in Englishmen. Halifax believed that a privileged position in society exacted service to the state; his gentle manners and ironic sense of humour coexisted with a tough mind and unswerving determination; he was a man of affairs who was also an intellectual, the fact indubitably proclaimed by his getting a first at Oxford and then winning an All Souls' fellowship. Other virtues Massey thought of as romantic embellishments that could only be viewed with wonder from a distance: Halifax was a fearless and enraptured hunter, and it was not inappropriate for Goering to invite him to visit Germany in his capacity as master of the Middleton hounds. (Massey's sporting activity was confined to an occasional game of relaxed golf.) Halifax was a devout Anglo-Catholic who loved the ritual of his church and affirmed the need to carry religion into the office and marketplace. (Massey treated his belated Anglicanism with sobriety but did not publicly proclaim his religious principles.)

Three other friends of more recent vintage than Halifax but cut from the same cloth – men of substance and family, who brought to public affairs a sense of duty and minds tempered in one of the two ancient English universities – were Anthony Eden, Viscount Cranborne, and Robert Austin Butler. Both Eden and Cranborne served as secretary of state for the dominions, and were, therefore, Massey's associates in his day-to-day activities as high commissioner. Eden was only briefly in that position. His principal appointment was, of course, secretary of state for foreign affairs, from 1935 to 1938 and then again from 1940 to 1945; and it was chiefly in this capacity that Massey knew him. References to Eden in his diary are uniformly adulatory. A speech Eden gave in the House of Commons on 26 March 1936, on German occupation of the Rhineland and on economic sanctions against Italy, was described by Vincent as having 'dignity, clarity, balance, precision, fine feeling.'[53] A month later, Eden 'has courage, perseverance, and a right instinct.'[54] A year later, Massey experienced a sense of cosy intimacy with the man whom he had hitherto admired from a distance. At a lunch at the Guildhall, he writes, 'I sat next to Anthony Eden and to the neglect of our respective neighbours on either side, we talked busily for the whole lunch – a most interesting and confidential talk about his problem with the reactionary wing in the cabinet.'[55] When Eden broke with Chamberlain and resigned as foreign minister in February 1938, Massey developed reservations about Eden, which, with the outbreak of war, however, disappeared.

Lord Cranborne (invariably called 'Bobbety' by his friends, Massey included) was secretary of state for the dominions for four years, from 1940 to 1942 and from 1943 to 1945, and during those crucial years Massey saw him frequently. He was for Massey, and indeed, for all the high commissioners, their favourite 'chief.' His physical appearance – he looked like a remote and ineffectual don – belied his vigour and incisiveness. A constant source of complaint among the high commissioners was the breakdown in communication between them and the war cabinet, a complaint that the secretary of state also made. Cranborne differed from other secretaries – Sir Thomas Inskip and Clement Attlee, in particular – in that he didn't hesitate to make his complaint directly and unapologetically to the prime minister. Massey greatly admired him, and a close friendship developed between the two men.

Butler – 'Rab' – was a member of an academic family that had produced dons and masters in Cambridge colleges for three generations. He had married a daughter of Samuel Courtauld, the wealthy manufacturer, art collector, and patron, thereby adding affluence to his list of qualifications for high office. When Vincent first became friendly with him he was under-secretary to Halifax, who was serving a brief period as secretary of state for foreign affairs between Eden's resignation and return. Since Halifax was in the House of Lords, Butler had the responsibility of speaking in the Commons on behalf of the government, still clinging to appeasement while embarking on an intensified program of rearmament; and this he did with circumspection and defensive skill. Massey described him after a talk at the

Foreign Office as 'cool and sane.'[56] His admiration grew when Butler served as minister of education in the war cabinet and brought to that neglected area a sympathetic understanding and a willingness to move radically.

Brendan Bracken, minister of information in the war cabinet from 1941 to 1945, whom Massey described as 'a gifted public servant and also a very warm friend,'[57] was a sharp contrast to the classical establishment pattern in the careers of Halifax, Eden, Cranborne, and Butler. To begin with, he was not an Englishman; he kept his background – birth in Ireland and early years in Australia – mysteriously hidden. His physical appearance did not arouse aristocratic associations. 'A very unattractive-looking fellow,' a contemporary described him, 'with a huge shock of thick matted red hair like a Hereford bull, and features like something Cruikshank might have drawn.'[58] But Bracken had, by his own enterprise, fashioned a successful career in magazine publishing, and had become a close confidant of Churchill when he was struggling to awaken the country to the threat of Nazism. As minister of information, he was shrewd in handling the press and sensitive to unnecessary curbs on freedom of expression. Massey admired him for these things, as he did for his interest in preserving the London of the past.

In Canada many of the Masseys' closest friends had been artists – painters like David Milne, Lawren Harris and Alex Jackson, musicians like Ernest MacMillan and the members of the Hart House Quartet. In England the world of arts was too complex and varied to admit the easy entrance of a Canadian diplomat engrossed, by necessity, in the political and social world. But there were a few points of entry. Adrian Boult, who had, in the early thirties, become director of music at the BBC and the first conductor of its symphony orchestra, was an old friend from Oxford days, and he had been immensely helpful in the twenties in easing the way of the Hart House Quartet into the English musical world. A new friend was Kenneth Clark, still in his early thirties when Massey met him, but already director of the National Gallery and, by his own account,[59] a familiar figure in the highest reaches of English society. He came to 12 Hyde Park Gardens to see the Massey collection of Canadian paintings and, no doubt, made some appreciative remarks of a general nature; and he introduced the Masseys to young English painters whom he admired, like Victor Pasmore and William Coldstream, and advised the Masseys on the purchase of canvases for their collection of contemporary English art.

In literature, the Masseys continued their deep interest in the theatre. Carefully preserved playbills indicate that they saw every play of any significance performed in London. But these were lean days in the English theatre. No new playwrights of any importance had emerged. Vincent reserved his most enthusiastic comments for an American play, a bitter comment on the dark international melodrama, *Idiot's Delight* by Robert Sherwood, in which his brother, Raymond, was the star. Shaw was active during the thirties, but Vincent, a Shavian from his undergraduate days, had lost his enthusiasm, as Shaw turned from social comedy to the theatre of the absurd and perceived benign versions of the superman in Mussolini and Stalin. But Vincent recovered his Shavian enthusiasm when he saw *Geneva* in December 1938 – Shaw's final comment on the pre-war madhouse. In that play Shaw brought the dictators (thinly disguised) to trial, and the judge, not 'a worn-out barrister,' as, according to Shaw, he would have been in England, but a professional searching for justice, delivers a final indictment, in Shaw's vaulting and passionate rhetoric: 'Your objective is domination. Your weapons fire and poison, starvation and ruin, extermination by every means known to science. You have reduced one another to such a condition of terror that no atrocity makes you recoil and say that you will die rather than commit it ... I give you up as hopeless. Man is a failure as a political animal. The creative forces which produce him must produce something better.'[60] Vincent, little given to extended critical analysis, simply reported that he found the play 'unexpectedly diverting.'[61]

Vincent knew little of the literary world of London. There is no indication that he read, for instance, Virginia Woolf or Elizabeth Bowen or T.S. Eliot, or heard of a young poet of unusual talent, Dylan Thomas. He met some literary figures at receptions, critics like Cyril Connolly and Desmond MacCarthy, the former a young man in his early thirties who was about to launch the most important periodical of the forties, *Horizon*, and the latter, a senior literary critic of the *Sunday Times*, who exercised a wide influence both among common and uncommon readers.

Vincent Massey's anglophilia was thus solidly based. He had known England since he was a child; he had formed a network of friendships and associations that gave him a wide acquaintance with English life; and now as high commissioner he was consolidating and deepening his knowledge of English institutions. The emphasis was always on England. He was aware of the strong Scottish bias in Canada, and would on official occasions in Scotland refer to the fact that he was that rarity – a Canadian with no Scottish blood in his veins (and there was always a suggestion that he did not look upon this as a serious deprivation). Familiarity and knowledge of England were suffused with a romantic glow that never abated. Early in his autobiography he talks about that romantic view stimulated initially 'by the pictorial England – the ancient villages and the old buildings of London,' later by his association of what he observed to his study of English history. But the romanticism had an instinctive and almost mystical quality. 'I have never felt away from home in England. This cannot be explained by heredity. My ancestors left Cheshire in the seventeenth century, but my feeling for England could hardly have been much stronger if I had emigrated to Canada myself.'[62]

This instinctive romanticism was reinforced by Vincent's sensitivity to physical surroundings and his delight in drama and ritual. Indeed, aestheticism had become for him almost a way of life; the moral fervour that in his childhood home had accompanied the Methodist faith now suffused his perception of form and colour. The supreme expression of the meeting in English life of history, drama, and beauty was the coronation ceremony, but Vincent saw this happy confluence in many lesser events and, indeed, to a great extent, in all of English life. Of the ceremony installing Lord Willingdon as warden of the Cinque Ports, he wrote: 'The old ceremonial was beautifully carried out with that solemnity it merits mingled with gentle humour at appropriate places and now and then deep feeling. I shall not forget the picture of the Archbishop of Canterbury, crozier in hand and mitre on his head blessing the kneeling Willingdon resplendent in his warden's uniform. A wonderful day of colour and history and ancient language and all somehow linked up with the greatness of England today.'[63] The spirit of England found a happy expression in the architecture he most admired – Georgian. In a speech to a group concerned with the study and preservation of Georgian architecture and design, he said: 'whether we are concerned with a great mansion or a modest row of houses in some market town, we are conscious of the same qualities – the smallest building has an essential dignity and grace – the great house has elegance without opulence. The buildings of this great period always suggest in proportion and detail the qualities – balance and moderation, even under-statement, and is therefore almost a reflection of English character itself.'[64]

The England he saw was a carefully circumscribed one, often bathed in nostalgia that arose from his own youthful memories or the revivification of the distant past. There was little place in his England for the depressed world of the industrial cities – the world that had aroused the fiery moral indignation of his brother-in-law, William Grant. It was an ideal world of comfort and of easy equality among an élite: Balliol College 'a pattern, in miniature, of what a civilized western community ought to provide for all';[65] the country house, in Vincent's eye, an informal Oxford college, with picture gallery, library, and public garden;[66] the royal court, symbolic link with the glories of the past, and, at the same time, home of a family that enshrined the fundamental virtues.

There was little room for criticism in Vincent's view of England. When he visited the staff college at Camberley, for instance, he reported that 'like all institutions in Great Britain [it was] full of self-criticism, experience and reform.'[67] An incident told by George Ignatieff (who joined the staff of the high commissioner in 1940 and as Massey's private secretary from 1941 to 1944 was in a good position to observe his chief) shows the extent to which Vincent's romantic love affair with England blunted his critical perceptions. On a visit to Eustace Percy in Newcastle, he launched into an eulogy of the English spirit and outlook during the war. 'The English people were,' he declared, 'the only people in the world who could be entrusted to rule over others.' Percy sharply punctured this soaring fatuity. 'Those sentiments,' he said, 'are the very ones that we are fighting against in this war.'

Vincent, like many sober and learned constitutional theorists, was devoted to the English monarchy. But he often transferred uncritically the splendour of the idea to its human representation. This is a natural inclination. Tom Jones observed shrewdly that 'we invest our rulers with qualities which they do not possess and we connive at the illusion – those of us who know better – because monarchy is an illusion which works.'[68] At times, Vincent's comments on royalty are reminiscent of the aristocratic Montdores in *Love in a Cold Climate*: 'They spoke as though these Princes are so remote from life as we know it that the smallest signs of humanity, the mere fact even that they communicated by means of speech, was worth noting and proclaiming.'[69] An offshoot of this unrealistic attitude towards monarchy was the inordinate value he set on royal honours. The thought occasionally arises that it was the external insignia he valued most, like an actor who becomes the embodiment of his splendid costume.

Vincent's analysis of English politics was more realistic than his general view of English society. He despised the Colonel Blimps, the loud apologists for the old centralized empire. His political friends, as we have seen, were solid, establishment men, but they were also individualists and intellectuals, not enslaved by party, capable of extraordinary deviation from accepted paths. Vincent himself had always been a Liberal – in his Balliol days a supporter of Herbert Asquith, warmly agreeing with the movement towards paring down the power of the House of Lords, and as an active party member in Canada, well to the left in the party, believing in government intervention to achieve social justice. But in England, the Liberal party had withered away, and most of its ideas were embraced by groups within the Conservative party which, by its great number of elected members, controlled the National government.

The romantic anglophilia returned in Vincent's implicit belief that England had solved the great problem in a democracy of finding an élite and giving it power. The key was in the universities (Vincent thought mainly of Oxford and Cambridge) that produced this élite and launched them on their careers. Nothing could have more deeply aroused his love of England than the Oxford ceremony on 21 June 1939, when he was awarded the honorary degree of Doctor of Laws. Of his fellow graduands he knew and greatly admired three: the Marquess of Lothian, Mr Justice Felix Frankfurter, the eminent American jurist, P.G. Wodehouse, the comic novelist. His citation in elegant Latin touched on his period as minister to the United States, his international service, his present efforts towards strengthening the bonds between Canada and the mother country; it ended with a witty reference to his son Hart's coxing the Oxford crew in the recent Oxford-Cambridge boat race. The night before he had been the speaker at the Christ Church gaudy, where, as he pointed out, the new dean, John Lowe, was a Canadian who had been on the staff at Trinity College, University of Toronto, thus introducing 'a new and striking feature in Anglo-Canadian relations.' Vincent recalled that he had been on the committee that had selected John Lowe as a Rhodes scholar and thus had helped to prepare him for his present eminence. It was 'a really memorable evening,' he wrote, 'beautiful in its setting and distinction and warm in its friendliness.'[70]

Vincent's anglophilia may be contrasted with the anglophilia of his old political antagonist, Richard Bedford Bennett, who had resigned as leader of the Conservative party and early in 1939 had arrived in England to take up residence. After the outbreak of war, Massey had a good deal to do with Bennett who was active in the Canadian Red Cross in England, and saw himself as the principal power in the organization of the Canadian war services, an assumption that brought him into sharp conflict with Canada House. But Bennett's main concern was to establish himself firmly and conspicuously in English society. In June of 1941 he acquired all of the official trappings: he became Viscount Bennett of Mickleham, Surrey, and Calgary and Hopewell, Canada; he bought a country house of appropriate grandeur next to that of his great friend and admirer, Lord Beaverbrook. Bennett, however, made little impression on English society. Many in public life remembered his acerbity and blustering aggressiveness at the Ottawa conference of 1932. His censorious, moralistic manner in public and private speech did not win friends. As Beaverbrook observed, Bennett could not discard habits and attitudes he had learned in his native country. 'Canada is a village street, many thousands of miles long. Everyone knows his neighbour and knows him to his disadvantage.'[71] Beaverbrook concludes his little book on Bennett with this elegiac comment: 'England was a legend to him and when he tried to turn the legend into reality he was lost. The romantic was unable to come to terms with his romance.'[72]

England was not a legend to Massey; it was a reality that he warmly embraced. But it did not displace the greater reality of Canada. England was a society similar to the one he had known in Canada, but more mature and self-confident, from which the younger society could learn much.

CHAPTER TWO

Canada Calling

In 1935, when Vincent Massey became the Canadian high commissioner in London, it was the senior position in the expanding system of representation abroad. The other foreign legations – Washington, Paris, Tokyo – were recent establishments, but the high commissionership had a long history. The first high commissioner, Sir Alexander Galt, had been appointed in 1880, and Vincent Massey was the seventh in succession. Its origins in the Victorian era, however, meant that it still carried over some restricting associations. The high commissioner could be thought of by continuing imperialists as a Canadian emissary sent to the seat of Empire to plead the cause of a principal dependency. This, of course, clashed with the new doctrine that the centre and its creations were 'in no way subordinate one to another.'

It was essential now for the high commissioner to think in terms of the new doctrine of equality. He should combine knowledge of and affection for the mother country with a primary devotion to Canada. If, like Vincent Massey, he was well and favourably known in Great Britain, and could walk the corridors of power with assurance, whether they led through Whitehall or through country houses and London mansions, he might seem to have an initial advantage. A representative like Massey, with impeccably uncolonial manners, was assured of a sympathetic audience. But the advantage was illusory unless he thought of all this as preparing the way for his national responsibilities. Massey's predecessor, Howard Ferguson, was aggressive, and even abrasive. Massey was incapable of such an approach even if used as a deliberate political tactic. But there was never any doubt of where he stood; he was a Canadian, proud of his country, determined to maintain its rights, persistent in his enunciation of Canadian interests. For aggressiveness he substituted a stubbornness that, in his dealings with British officialdom, never cracked the smooth surface of his manners but persisted, firm and inflexible.

The stubbornness often showed itself in small matters of protocol or in the assertion of national symbolism. But these were important matters to Massey who was unusually sensitive to external impressions, and knew how these could be rapidly translated into ideas and attitudes. He was insistent, for instance, that the English commissionaire at the entrance to Canada House should be replaced by a constable of the Royal Canadian Mounted Police. On 27 October 1936, he wrote to the under-secretary of state for External Affairs, O.D. Skelton, about this matter in a direct and persuasive way: 'It is important that as far as possible a Canadian atmosphere should prevail in the Entrance Hall of Canada House. This is difficult to establish while the doorkeeper is an English commissionaire.' Dr Skelton, who looked upon Massey as an unprofessional and pretentious upstart in his small and orderly kingdom, discovered that the idea, although sound, was, by reasons of finances and jurisdictional complications, impossible to implement. Massey persisted, further irritating Skelton by a direct appeal to the commissioner of the Royal Canadian Mounted Police and to his minister, Ernest Lapointe. A reluctant agreement finally came from Skelton almost two years later. It was an ironical triumph for Massey, since he was thought to be a thinly disguised British imperialist, and Skelton to be the doughty Canadian nationalist.

On another matter of national definition Skelton and Massey saw eye to eye, and Skelton was grateful for Massey's swift intervention. The first major Canadian event in which Massey participated as high commissioner was the unveiling of the Vimy Ridge memorial in France. It was an event of deeply emotional significance to Canada, and Edward VIII, who had so firmly and romantically established himself in the hearts of Canadians, had agreed to attend and speak. Major Hardinge, the king's assistant private secretary, suggested to Massey that the president of the French republic should be informed confidentially of the king's intention by the British ambassador at Paris. Massey responded sharply. 'I gave Major Hardinge my view that, inasmuch as the King was attending the Vimy Ridge Ceremony on the invitation, and as the guest of the Dominion of Canada, the appropriate person to inform the President of the intending visit was not the British Ambassador but the Canadian Minister at Paris.' Skelton warmly approved. 'As the invitation came from Canada, it was entirely appropriate that the Canadian Legation in Paris should be utilized as the channel of communication. If you had not intervened, this might not have been done, and a good deal of the value of the episode would have been lost.'[1] A small, even petty point, it might be said; but a failure to notice it would have weakened the international recognition of Canadian autonomy, and Massey's punctilious respect for the formal drama of protocol was, in this instance, a valuable asset.

There were a number of other occasions where Massey intervened not as high commissioner but simply as the sensitive Canadian abroad. He noted in *The Times* that Lord Nuffield had made a gift of two million pounds to Oxford in order to bring graduate students from South Africa, Australia, and New Zealand to the Oxford medical school. He immediately wrote to the Oxford Professor of Surgery, Hugh Cairns, to inquire why Canada had been omitted from the list of countries, and was assuaged by a flattering response that 'the scheme is essentially for medical schools remote from the great centres of research' who had not yet 'been throwing up their Bantings, Bests, & Collips.'[2] Another article in *The Times* aroused his Canadian sensitivities. The article described the orchestra that was to play at the coronation ceremony. It was to be a composite body made up of players from existing orchestras, and Massey suggested to the Lord Chamberlain that the orchestra might include one or, indeed, all of the members of the Hart House Quartet, who would happily be in England at the time of the coronation. In the event, the first violinist, James Levey, was invited to play in the orchestra – not a singularly outstanding Canadian event, since Levey had recently come to the Hart House Quartet from the leadership of the London String Quartet.

In all of these interventions Massey had acted from personal prompting, although often in the final stages he had turned to his department for approval and assistance. In another area the personal promptings had a wider range and engaged him far more intensely. This was in the area of cultural activity – in the arts and education.

Here he knew that he could rely on little official assistance. The Department of External Affairs was engrossed in establishing its professional credentials, and the only proper study for a foreign affairs officer was international relations on a severely political and economic plane. The very thought of a cultural attaché would have struck the minister (who, at this time, was the prime minister) and the undersecretary as ludicrous. Massey became his own cultural attaché, a role that was congenial to him and for which he had clear qualifications.

He was convinced that in the projection of Canada abroad,[3] which both he and Alice looked upon as their prime responsibility, the arts and education were crucial. He was aware that he must move cautiously and selectively, for the Canadian *naissance* of the arts, which he would help to initiate, still lay in the future. There was a good deal of painful *gaucherie* on which it would be decent to turn his back – the documentary films about Canada that his office occasionally sponsored, crude, plodding celebrations of agricultural and industrial Canada, the Canadian building at the Paris exposition of 1938, an exclamation mark of dreariness. On the other hand, he did not suffer, like many Canadians, from a sense of inferiority, predestined and changeless, in the presence of an august European tradition.

Vincent Massey's projection of Canada abroad was not, however, to be vigorous or effective in the area of literature. Lovat Dickson, a young Canadian who had established himself in the highly competitive publishing world of London, thought that Massey's arrival as high commissioner was a significant literary event. 'I feel,' he wrote, 'that a powerful triumvirate and one that should be beneficial to the Canadian book trade has come about in the presence of Mr. Mackenzie King as Prime Minister, Lord Tweedsmuir as Governor General and Mr. Vincent Massey as High Commissioner, a coincidence that brings these men of literary tastes and interests to positions of power at this time.'[4] But Lovat Dickson wrote as publisher, not as exponent of Canadian literature, and he had chiefly in mind that Massey 'in the many speeches that he will give and the influence that he will exercise here will persuade English authors and publishers of the importance of the Canadian market and the reasons, both ethical and economical, which make it to their advantage to be aware of its possibilities.'[4] Lovat Dickson had in mind the practice of including Canada as an appendage to the United States when English publishers sold American rights to a book. But Massey took little interest in what was a highly technical matter. Nor did he speak on behalf of Canadian literature. He had never firmly entered the twentieth century as far as poetry and fiction were concerned; he was not sympathetic to recent developments in Canadian literature – to, for instance, Frederick Philip Grove's grim chronicles of the prairies or Callaghan's moral fables of city life, or, in poetry, to Pratt's sea narratives, at once robust and complexly ironic (so harsh beside the charming poetry of Mr Masefield!) At any rate the British public was in no mood to read realistic books about Canadian life: the Canada they knew in literature was romantic and exotic: either Britain transplanted, with North American embellishments, or a primitive and unsullied wilderness, the home of the dauntless explorer or the noble savage. Massey's only public actions on behalf of Canadian literature reinforced the traditional British view.

The first traditional view was embodied in *Whiteoaks*, a play by Mazo de la Roche, which opened in London on 13 April 1936. Mazo de la Roche was at that time certainly the best known Canadian author. In England, particularly, she was widely read and enjoyed. She was published by Macmillan, and Lovat Dickson lists her among the company's most distinguished writers, who then included, among others, Yeats, Sean O'Casey, Hugh Walpole, Margaret Mitchell, and James Hilton. She belonged in this company (as did several on the list) by reason of her popularity rather than by literary merit. Her wide appeal in Great Britain was undoubtedly based on the fact that the life she portrayed had a familiar glint – a touch of the country house, a good deal of the rural squire surrounded by relatives, retainers, and horses. By 1936 she had been living in England since 1929, and her saga of the Whiteoaks family in southern Ontario had already coursed through several widely read popular novels. *Whiteoaks* was a distillation of two of the early novels, with a shameless highlighting of the old grandmother of the family, who was played with enormous relish by the actress, Nancy Price. The play had mixed reviews, and did not attract good houses. It was about to close when a sudden spurt of interest (stimulated by a rave review by St John Ervine in which he shamelessly linked Miss de la Roche with Chekhov) resulted in a continuation in a larger theatre. *Whiteoaks* then ran for three years. Massey did not attend the play until 27 April at which time its fortunes had changed for the better. After the performance he had a dinner in honour of Mazo de la Roche and the cast. He records in his diary that he 'liked' the play, but he was not prepared to hail it as a Canadian triumph. When the play passed its 500th performance, he wrote, not to the author, but to Nancy Price, who was also its producer: 'It is very pleasant indeed, to think that the rather tender plant whose future gave us some concern a year ago has struck such firm root.'[5]

Massey was far more enthusiastic about the representative of the second traditional British view of Canada – the view that saw Canada as an unsullied wilderness and the Indian as a child of nature. The representative was Grey Owl, a Canadian Indian, who, in the fall of 1935, was on a lecture tour in England, speaking to enraptured audiences in all the major centres and arousing so much public interest that, at the high commissioner's official royal interview, he, more than any other Canadian topic, aroused the king's curiosity. Grey Owl was a discovery of Lovat Dickson, who was then struggling to find popular books that would sustain his infant publishing house. In 1934 he had published Grey Owl's book, *Pilgrims of the Wild*. It had been an instantaneous success, and the subsequent tour, undertaken at Lovat Dickson's bold suggestion, had been an even greater success.

In a Britain still groping its way out of a terrible depression, Grey Owl came as romantic balm. In personal appearance he embodied everyone's vision of the Canadian Indian – the hero (or villain) of boys' adventure stories and Gilbert Parker's romances of old Quebec brought vividly to life. 'He came,' wrote Lovat Dickson, 'clad in buckskin jacket and fringed leather pants, wearing moccasins, his long black hair hanging in plaits to his shoulders ... He was over six feet in height, with straight but very spare figure, and he held himself well. His face was ascetic, the skin stretched over his bones ... His eyes were a piercing blue, but the pallor of his face, the black hair, the aquiline nose gave him the look of a fanatic.'[6] His performance on the platform matched his appearance. He was a natural actor, with a deep, resonant voice, and the films he brought with him about the domestication of beaver kittens were beautiful and moving. Encouraged, no doubt, by royal interest, Vincent went, in December 1935, with his secretary and two sons to see and hear 'Grey Owl the Canadian Indian.' He was 'delighted with him.'

In 1937 Grey Owl returned for a second tour, and this time royal interest, which had now spread throughout the family – Queen Mary, the king and queen, and the two princesses – resulted in a special command performance at Buckingham Palace. Vincent Massey accompanied Grey Owl's party and was, according to Lovat Dickson, 'in a great state of fuss,' as he tended to be, when royal protocol was involved. This state was greatly exacerbated when Grey Owl brushed aside a basic rule that the audience and the performer must be seated, awaiting the king's entrance, and then rise at his entry. Nothing could persuade Grey Owl to give up his dramatic entry before a hushed and expectant audience. The great doors to the drawing room in which they were seated would be thrown open by two footmen, and he, not the king and queen, would appear. To his credit, Massey finally agreed to this wayward procedure, as did, presumably, the king. 'The event went off very well,' wrote Massey. 'Grey Owl, clad in his leather beaded suit and moccasins, and with an eagle feather in his long hair, entered very dramatically, stepped with stately tread to the centre of the room, turned and said, "Your Majesties, Your Royal Highnesses, Ladies & Gentlemen"; and then lifting his hand, gave us an Indian greeting, which he afterwards translated. The words were 'How Hola!'[7] Lovat Dickson adds this diverting detail: 'At the end Grey Owl put out his hand to the King, and touched him on the shoulder with the other. "Good-bye brother, I'll be seeing you." '[8]

There is no hint of Massey's response to the revelation made shortly afterwards that Grey Owl, the eloquent spokesman for the oldest native Canadians, was actually Archie Belaney, born in Hastings, England, and brought up by two aunts still living in Hastings and prepared to talk candidly about their eccentric nephew. Perhaps, he concluded, as others did, that this was not an elaborate hoax, that the facts of birth and early upbringing were initially shocking, but ultimately irrelevant, and that Grey Owl was more authentic than Archie Belaney.

For Canadian music and painting, Vincent could act in Britain with an authority that he could not command in literature and the theatre.

The instrument for music was the Hart House Quartet, which had already been well received in England during a visit in 1929, and was now in 1937, during the coronation year, making a second visit of a far more adventurous kind. London concerts (including one at the Canadian high commissioner's home) were central, as they had been in the first visit, but these were now one phase of an ambitious European tour that included Paris, Vienna, Milan, and Amsterdam. The quartet could now expect an enthusiastic response wherever it went, and the Masseys took great satisfaction from its success. It was, in a genuine sense, their quartet. They were founders, patrons, and sympathetic and devoted allies. The close relationship did not cease when the Masseys took up residence in London. Vincent conducted a vigorous correspondence about the quartet with associates in Canada – with Gladstone Murray of the Canadian Broadcasting Corporation, urging more consideration for the quartet in the corporation's musical programme; with the Honourable Mr Justice McFarland, who for years had dealt with the financial details, frequently tangled, of the quartet. And there was a steady stream of letters from a quartet member, Milton Blackstone, chatty and confidential in tone, addressed to Alice, who always found time to reply in a warm personal way. The Masseys were still involved in the quartet's personal problems. Blackstone's wife, who had accompanied her husband in the European tour, had become gravely ill with typhoid when she was visiting her relatives in Wilno, Poland. The Masseys rallied to Blackstone's support: realizing the strain his wife's illness would put on his slim resources, Vincent arranged loans for him, and a small scholarship for his son, then an undergraduate at the University of Toronto. Alice took a motherly interest in the young daughter, Alice, aged ten, at school in southern England, separated from both her parents, and on one occasion sent a visiting niece to comfort the girl in her loneliness.

Had he been a less indulgent patron, Vincent might well have abandoned the quartet after its European tour. Given the dark international situation, he saw that it could not contemplate another European tour in 1939, plans for which were already far advanced; and it was becoming increasingly evident that the quartet could not easily survive financially on Canadian and American appearances. Moreover, a second great internal crisis had arisen. In 1935, the first violinist, Geza de Kresz, had resigned under pressure from his three associates, no longer confident in his leadership, and it had taken a great deal of time and anxious negotiations to secure a fitting replacement. Now Harry Adaskin, second violin, declared his intention of leaving to follow a private career in music. His colleagues found his decision incomprehensible and received it with a good deal of bitterness. The Masseys were even more distressed; Adaskin was the youngest of the quartet members, and they had taken a special paternal interest in his career. But they absorbed the blow, and directed Blackstone to look for a replacement, the only condition being that he should be absolutely first-class. The replacement was Adolphe Koldofsky, born in London, England, of Russian parentage, whose family had come to Canada in 1912. Blackstone wrote with amusing candour to Alice about the failure to find a good violinist of Anglo-Saxon lineage. 'I hoped,' he wrote, 'to find a non-Jew, but it seems that the best violin playing and "Israel's sons" are inseparable.'[9]

Successful as the Hart House Quartet was in Britain, it is doubtful whether it stimulated any great interest in Canada. Quartet music has an intimate and aristocratic flavour, and its audience, although devoutly enthusiastic, is small. The repertoire of the Hart House Quartet was almost exclusively European, confined largely to the masters of the eighteenth and nineteenth century, with an occasional bold move into the music of a twentieth-century composer like Bartok. The members of the quartet were European, too, in name and in their cultural inheritance, and they were received, as indeed they wished to be, as an international group meeting international standards.

But the situation in painting was quite different. In the thirties painting was undoubtedly the most widespread and the most highly developed activity in the arts in Canada. Eric Brown, the director of the National Gallery, who, like so many immigrants to Canada from Britain in the art world, was far more nationalistic than native Canadians, declared that 'Canada occupied the foremost position among the British Dominions in its art development.'[10] The Masseys would have agreed and, indeed, would have given the assertion a wider context. They frequently commented on the greater vigour in Canadian art than in American, and even, on occasion, extended the generalization to a comparison with British art. Moreover, Canadian art was firmly rooted in the country. Eric Newton, the art critic for the *Manchester Guardian*, made this point strongly in a radio talk he gave in the spring of 1937, following a long trans-Canada tour, during which he had sought out and talked to hundreds of Canadian artists: 'I began to realize that Canadian artists, during the last thirty years had been doing the one thing that is really worth while in all art, namely, seeing with their own eyes, standing on their own feet, discovering a style of their own instead of feebly copying the style of Europe.'

The involvement of the Masseys in Canadian art reflected its dominance and centrality. As in music they divided their responsibilities. Alice corresponded with artists in Canada, with A.Y. Jackson, David Milne, Will Ogilvie (who was doing a mural of the Hart House chapel and wrote regularly about his progress), and Pegi Nicol, and with young artists, like Jack Shadbolt who was visiting England. Vincent was the official patron, and here he acted not simply as the head of a foundation with artistic interests, but as a central officer. Since 1925 he had been a member of the Board of Trustees of the National Gallery in Ottawa. He retained his appointment when he went to London; indeed he became the official representative of the gallery abroad, to whom the director, Eric Brown, constantly turned for advice and action. On several occasions, through his art connections in London, especially with Sir Kenneth Clark, he saved the gallery from large expenditures on pictures of uncertain provenance. He also took the initiative in the purchase of paintings, that were events in their own right, with an accompanying air of dramatic excitement. When he secured a picture by Hyacinthe Rigaud, the French portrait painter of the late seventeenth century, he was happy to agree to a news release which, besides mentioning his role in the purchase, emphasized the special significance for Canada of securing an important example of a portrait painter who was 'to Louis XIV what Van Dyck was to Charles I.'

His greatest coup was obtaining the Augustus John cartoon of a battalion behind the lines in France. Towards the end of the First World War, John had been appointed by Lord Beaverbrook as a war artist with the Canadian army, and the chief fruit of his service had been the cartoon, 40 feet by 10 feet, both representative and symbolical in treatment, that was to be the basis of a great painting. When John was doing a portrait sketch of Massey, he mentioned that the cartoon, about one-third painted, was in his country house in very doubtful condition. Massey was impressed by its 'magnitude and distinction,' and made preliminary arrangements with John for its completion and purchase by the National Gallery. Eric Brown raised a number of sound objections, including the unavailability of funds and the likelihood that John would never finish it. In any event it was the cartoon that eventually in 1946 came to the National Gallery, 'rescued' as John's biographer, Michael Holroyd, points out, 'by Vincent Massey.'[11]

An even more dramatic Massey proposal was that the gallery should purchase an Epstein bust of Haile Selassie. Massey saw the work in a dealer's shop and described it in a telegram as a 'magnificent example of Epstein's work.' He went on to point out in the same telegram that 'both artist and subject would make popular appeal and acquisition would give gallery useful publicity.' Eric Brown was, at first, enthusiastic, but then had qualms. The time was December 1936; the Ethiopian emperor had fled from his defeated country, and was popularly regarded in the west as a noble and heroic victim of Mussolini's imperialism. At the same time, the King government had taken a pusillanimous attitude towards the imposition of sanctions against Italy. The prime minister, with his constant fear of arousing the enmity of major minorities, might well see this purchase as a political act that would enrage the Italian community. The Epstein head was not purchased.

Massey's activities in the London art world gave him a chance to talk about Canadian art. For illustrations, he did not have to wait for exhibitions of Canadian art, not likely in any event to occur by British initiative. He had brought over from Batterwood most of his own collection – well over a hundred paintings, with all the contemporary Canadian painters represented and with particularly strong representation of Lawren Harris, A.Y. Jackson, David Milne, James Morrice, Pegi Nicol, Will Ogilvie, Tom Thomson, and F.H. Varley. These were hung, first of all, in their home at 33 Portman Square, then at their more permanent residence at 12 Hyde Park Gardens, dominating the large public rooms in the latter, endowing Georgian symmetry and balance with a dazzle of brilliant colour. The Massey home became the Canadian art gallery in London, and the Masseys made sure that art critics and connoisseurs were given special viewings. Eric Newton's trip to Canada was inspired by seeing the Massey collection, and Sir Kenneth Clark had his first view of Canadian art at 12 Hyde Park Gardens. The collection achieved an illustrated story in the *Sunday Times*, Alex Jackson wrote to Alice about the publicity coup. 'We have just been looking at the Sunday Times with the fine colour reproductions from the Massey collection. It is remarkable work and puts to shame all the rubbish that our Star Weekly turns out.'[12]

In all likelihood, the decision of the Tate Gallery to have a comprehensive show of Canadian painting in the fall of 1938 owed much to Massey's enthusiasm and to the presence in London of his collection. Thirty of the paintings in the show of three hundred came from the Massey collection. The poster for the exhibit reproduced (at Vincent's suggestion) a picture from the Massey collection, Edwin Holgate's portrait of a French-Canadian girl, 'Ludovine.' Massey insisted upon timing the exhibition for the later fall, so that it would come within the full course of the London season, and, in particular, so that it could have a royal launching. His choice was the Duke of Kent, for whom he and Alice had great admiration. On 14 October 1938, the duke opened the exhibit with a little speech that rose gently above the usual level of royal platitudes. Massey also spoke on the occasion; his speech in reply was a good example of the style of dignified raillery of which he was a finished exponent. 'We may hope, Sir, that the strong sun from our Prairies and the winds from our Northern Hills will not have disturbed unduly the classic repose of so historic a place.' Then followed some comments on art education that arose out of Vincent's experience: 'The art room of a school to-day is no longer a sort of penitential institution, but is a definitely popular place. Most of us can recollect grimly the hour or two a week which was devoted in our school days to what was euphemistically called art, when we were given the hardest of hard pencils and asked to draw the dullest of dull objects. Now we find a corresponding period of time devoted to a gay form of self-expression achieved by inexhaustible supplies of tempera lavishly applied to extravagant spaces with brushes of the largest dimensions.'

In a letter to his son, Lionel, who at the time was travelling as the secretary of a commission in New Zealand and Australia, Vincent reported enthusiastically on the Tate exhibition. It was, he said, 'a great success,' with twenty-two thousand people seeing it in the first fortnight. He added a slightly cautionary comment. 'Some of the canvases are pretty strong, occasionally I think too strong.' Happily, the Massey pictures gave a reassuring ballast to the exhibition. 'We never bought extreme ones and this is a considerable contrast between ours and some of the more ultra vigorous paintings from elsewhere.'[13]

In his concept of his cultural responsibilities as high commissioner, Vincent saw the promotion of the arts and of education as inseparable. Vincent thought of Hart House as an important contribution to educational theory and practice, again, like Canadian art, a peculiarly Canadian phenomenon joining local experience with European traditions. He liked to be known in England as the creator of Hart House, and was a little critical of the warden, Burgon Bickersteth, who, despite his vast network of British associations, had not sufficiently emphasized Vincent's creative role. Alice expressed these critical thoughts in a letter to one of Bickersteth's assistants.

You know how devoted we are to dear old Burgon and I know always in the back of his mind he realises and feels intensely the part that my husband played in the creation of Hart House. Of this I am very conscious, but there is one little thing that is bothering me, and that is over and over again people go through Hart House and never have any idea when they return here of my husband's connection with it. Burgon for years has corresponded with Lord Baldwin, and the other day when he was lunching here he was astounded to hear that we had anything to do with Hart House. When I think of the years while he was first at the University of Toronto, and then at Balliol, that Vincent spent in persuading his father that Hart House was the sort of thing the Foundation must do, and when I also think that while at Oxford he thought it out in all its detail, came out and spent one whole holiday with the architects thinking of nothing else, my wifely pride has rather a blow when people come back not knowing he even had anything to do with it.[14]

Vincent's interest in education was not entirely encompassed by Hart House. He had always been devoted to the idea of having young

Canadians with special abilities study in the United Kingdom, preferably at Oxford but, with less enthusiasm, at Cambridge or Edinburgh.

He had established his own system of post-graduate scholarships by diverting money, originally given by his grandfather to a Methodist university in Washington DC for graduates of the University of Toronto wishing to study abroad. The Massey scholarships, as they were called, were a good deal leaner than the Rhodes – the annual stipend for two years was a thousand dollars – but they attracted strong candidates, often men (from their beginning in 1918 there had been one woman) who had missed the Rhodes by falling short of the Rhodes prescription for manliness. This was the golden age for Canadian post-graduate work in Britain, and over the years all but two of the Massey scholars studied at Oxford or Cambridge.

Massey had a special interest in the Oxford students, and became an unofficial visitor for Canadians studying there. He held receptions for them during his frequent visits to his own college, and he (or Alice) was the recipient for their confidence and their problems. Robertson Davies, for instance, who had just left Balliol to work as actor and teacher at the Old Vic, wrote to inquire about opportunities for service in the event of war.[15] Max Patrick, a Massey scholar for 1934–36, wrote long, detailed letters about his gradual evolution into a Balliol man and his European adventures during the long vacation. An opening paragraph of one long letter written as he began his second year at Balliol records his joy in his new life. 'I feel quite incapable of expressing my gratitude to Mrs. Massey and yourself. This last year has been the happiest in my life: that I am to have another, free from worry, and filled with all that Oxford can offer, is more than I can believe. Were I a Greek I should worry lest the Gods might become jealous of my happiness.'[16] Saul Rae, a brilliant student, Varsity tennis player, and a clever composer and actor, who might have become the Noel Coward of Canada, was a great favourite of both Vincent and Alice; he was a frequent correspondent of theirs and a regular visitor to 12 Hyde Park. His Massey scholarship gave him two years at the University of London, which had more to offer in his subject of sociology than Oxford; the Masseys enabled him to get the Balliol imprint by awarding him a special scholarship for an additional year with a stipend of £400, the equivalent of the Rhodes.[17]

The Massey interest in students studying in Britain was not confined to those at Oxford. Vincent wrote to Skelton about the possibility of giving some assistance to a Canadian University Bureau that had been established in London under private auspices. Skelton pointed out that, since education was a provincial matter, the federal government was powerless to act, but suggested the possibility of an external affairs appointment to London who might act as an educational attaché. Massey responded enthusiastically, but the suggestion was not acted upon. As self-appointed cultural attaché, Massey was content to take over responsibilities for education.

There was one tragic incident when Vincent's interest in students coalesced with his general ambassadorial responsibility for the welfare of Canadian students in the United Kingdom. Pat Moss was a young Canadian undergraduate at Balliol. His family, on both sides, had numerous connections with the upper reaches of Ontario society. His paternal grandfather was for many years chief justice of Ontario and vice-chancellor of the University of Toronto; his maternal grandfather, T.C. Patteson, was born in England, educated at Eton and Oxford, and, on coming to Canada, held several influential positions. He established a home and an estate in eastern Ontario of old world amplitude. Joan Patteson, Mackenzie King's companion and hostess, was Pat Moss's aunt. Pat was an attractive young man with, as a memorial volume of letters indicates, thoughtful interests in art and literature. A visit to the Massey home in London had stimulated his interest in Canadian art, and he speculated that 'it would be great fun collecting Canadian pictures in the way the Masseys have done – backing your own taste and getting in at the ground floor.'[18] Suddenly, under mysterious circumstances, he died; his body was found in the countryside a few miles from Oxford beside a half-burnt-out hayrick. Vincent cancelled a week-end invitation in order to attend the inquest, but no light was shed on the tragedy. Pat Moss was an only son, idolized by his mother, grandmother, and an uncle who, after the early death of Pat's father, had played a parental role. Joan Patteson wrote to Alice about the devastating impact of the tragedy on the family: 'I can conceive of nothing more devastating than the manner of Pat's going must be to them all – every human emotion seemed torn – affection, pride, ambition, future hopes – everything swept away in the cruellest fashion by some unknown force ... he was the joy and pride of four broken-hearted people – who will never recover from it.'[19]

The official responsibilities of the high commissioner's office had evolved over the years. Since the days of the first high commissioner, Sir Alexander Galt, who had been Macdonald's first finance minister and a skilled negotiator of trade agreements, there had been a strong emphasis on trade and business relations. Vincent Massey's predecessor, Howard Ferguson, had been squarely in this tradition. He had been actively concerned with preparing the Canadian case for the Ottawa conference of 1932 which relied heavily in its approach and final decisions on the granting of Empire preferences; and much of his time as high commissioner was spent trying to implement agreements that were not always palatable to the British.

Massey could not emulate Ferguson as the spokesman for Canadian business and trade. But he was by no means indifferent to these matters. He had actually had more experience in the business world than Ferguson. For five years he had been a full-time executive in the Massey-Harris company, for the first two years as secretary-treasurer, and for the last three as president. He had left the day-to-day running of the company to the general manager, Thomas Bradshaw, and had concerned himself with broad matters of policy, chiefly with tariff negotiations, with the relations between workers and management, and with, in brief, the political implications of the business. In England, he kept in touch with Massey-Harris affairs through correspondence with James Duncan, who had recently been shifted from broad European responsibilities to become the vice-president and general manager of the company at the head office in Toronto. Massey and Duncan had a friendly relationship, and Duncan's letters to Massey ranged widely through personal comment, details about changes of management in the company on a senior level, and reflections on politics. Another business correspondent who ranged even more widely than Duncan was Floyd Chalmers, the editor of the *Financial Times*, who had turned the paper into an authoritative and respected interpreter of the business world. Chalmers, with no enhancing family connections and without a university degree, had risen by industry, determination, and intelligence, and saw his own success as a witness to the value of the capitalistic virtues. He wrote at great length about the economic climate of Canada, unsparingly critical of deviations from the social centre, whether they were William Aberhart's evangelical brand of social credit in Alberta, R.B. Bennett's sudden embracing of Rooseveltian ideas, or what he believed to be the most dangerous heresy of the age, the American new deal. 'Roosevelt,' he has written recently in his autobiography, 'created an almost completely new social structure for the Western world and in the process almost destroyed capitalism, free enterprise, and individual initiative in the United States and elsewhere.'[20]

Ferguson's ally in his presentation of business and trade interests had been Lord Beaverbrook. In the early thirties Beaverbrook's obsession had been Empire free trade, which, for him, had been chiefly a matter of erecting a trade barrier against the importation of foreign food, thus keeping Great Britain a monopoly for home and dominion agriculture. Massey was not attracted to such doctrinaire ideas; he did not believe that the bonds of Empire required special economic strands. Besides, he did not look upon Beaverbrook as a helpful ally. He no doubt resented the fact that Beaverbrook, despite his long residence in England and his acceptance on the highest level as a force in English politics, nevertheless saw himself (as did most of his associates) as a quintessential Canadian. He was not, assuredly, Massey's concept of the ideal Canadian. Despite his title, and his undoubted affection for his adopted country, he retained, Massey thought, a quality of crude colonial abrasiveness. 'The key to his career,' wrote Massey, ' – or one key – is a social "inferiority complex." His rather sneering reference to a group in New Brunswick to which he was apparently an outsider, his contempt for the English public school and other observations showed that he had a feeling of exclusion which had been followed by an attitude of vindictive contempt and a desire to attain by power what he couldn't get by any other means.'[21] His darkest estimate of Beaverbrook was confirmed by Beaverbrook's alliance with Churchill during the abdication crisis against Baldwin's sober campaign on behalf of morality and constitutional correctness. Still, Massey was not immune to Beaverbrook's charm. When he first met him, he was aware of his extraordinary power 'on certain subjects,' and he commented shrewdly on Beaverbrook's 'artistic temperament applied to politics.'[22] Massey was tolerant enough to realize that Beaverbrook was a great human phenomenon who ranged far beyond his own tidy vision, a mass of contradictions that dismayed a rational observer – a faithful conservative who often embraced ideas congenial to socialists, a tough entrepreneur who spent much of his money to support his friends and to finance his charities, an autocratic press lord who used his papers cynically for his own purposes and yet welcomed dissenting ideas and troublesome journalists provided they had talent.

A more acceptable model for Massey of a Canadian business man in the United Kingdom was Sir Edward Peacock, to whom he turned for advice on a wide variety of subjects – from whom to invite to official Canadian affairs to where to secure the best bargains in wine. Massey's association with Peacock went back to the turn of the century when Peacock was a master under William Grant at Upper Canada College. Now if Beaverbrook was the representative Canadian entrepreneur in residence, always on the verge of leaving for his native land, Peacock was the representative anglicized Canadian man of affairs, who had slipped comfortably into the British establishment. Indeed, there were few native business men who could boast a more impressive roster of positions, some conferring power, all quietly assertive of position and dignity – director of the Bank of England, chairman of Baring's Bank, lieutenant of the City of London, trustee of the Rhodes Foundation, receiver general of the Duchy of Cornwall, chairman of the Imperial War Graves Commission.

Massey's sponsorship of Canadian business and trading interest in Britain had a Peacockian rather than a Beaverbrookian flavour. He avoided involvement in contentious issues, such as the widespread belief of British holders of Grand Trunk debentures that they had been shabbily treated by the Canadian authorities. In a memorandum on a conversation with a representative of the aggrieved group, Massey wrote, in a style that reads like a parody of diplomatic circumlocution: 'I was careful to give him no possible grounds for saying that I expressed any opinion on the issue even by the remotest implication.'

In the major trade campaign that was launched during his tenure of office, Massey took a more vigorous line. The campaign began in

October 1936, appropriately at Glasgow, a city with strong Canadian affinities. The campaign had a poster – a handsome male bucolic figure with open-necked working shirt, doffing his wide-brimmed hat, with an inviting smile that was translated by the accompanying slogan, 'Canada Calling Britain.' The Glasgow papers devoted editorial articles as well as advertising space to the campaign, and aeroplanes flew overhead trailing the messages 'Canada Calling' and 'Buy Canadian Produce.' At a meeting of the Glasgow Chamber of Commerce there was a transatlantic telephone conversation between the lord provost of Glasgow and Canada's minister of trade and commerce, W.D. Euler. Vincent Massey then addressed the audience. The speech was more a graceful tribute to Scottish enterprise and ingenuity than an appeal to buy Canadian goods. The only political note was an innocuous statement 'that Custom duties should only be as high as necessary to maintain in a healthy condition our respective industries.' The Glasgow event was repeated with variations in a number of large urban centres throughout Britain. The Canadian officer most active in the campaign was the senior trade commissioner, Frederic Hudd, whose office was in Canada House, although he was appointed by and responsible to the minister of trade and commerce. He became, in effect, a senior colleague of the high commissioner. Hudd was an Englishman who had joined the Canadian service, a bachelor dedicated to his work. With his interest in the technical details of trade he combined a nice regard for protocol and a facility in devising ceremonial rituals (at the seventy-fifth anniversary of Canadian confederation in 1942, held in Westminster Abbey, Hudd was largely responsible for the 'bidding prayer'); and these were talents for which Massey had a high regard. Hudd acted at various times as deputy high commissioner and provided a note of continuity in an office, exposed to the rapid changes of an expanding international service.

The promotion of trade was, on the whole, a minor concern for Massey. His interests were political, diplomatic, and, in the broad sense, social – entertaining and being entertained, enlarging and brightening the image of Canada, discreetly in private conversations, boldly by deliberate and concerted actions. For this he had two senior officers of unusual talent, each at the beginning of his career of government service, each destined to occupy the highest offices in the country – Georges Vanier, who became governor-general, 1959–67, in succession to Vincent Massey, and Lester Pearson, who became prime minister, 1963–68. Vanier was the senior of the two. He had come to London in 1931 as secretary in the office of the high commissioner, and was the first officer below the high commissioner, responsible for the co-ordination of all the branches, a difficult and demanding task, since the branches were numerous, and many of them had initial responsibilities to the particular government department from which they drew their appropriation. Up until his appointment to London Vanier's career had been in the army. At the outbreak of the First World War, he had helped to organize a regiment made up exclusively of Canadians of French descent – the Royal 22nd, or the 'Van Doos' in the affectionate army vulgarization. He had served in the regiment with conspicuous gallantry; a severe wound had necessitated the amputation of one leg; and, at the end of hostilities, he had remained with his regiment, becoming commanding officer in 1924. Influenced by the governor-general, Lord Byng, who was both friend and revered mentor, he moved into the world of diplomacy, first as military representative on the Canadian delegation to the League of Nations, then as secretary in the high commissioner's office.

Vanier was no ordinary soldier. As a student at Loyola College, and then of law at Laval, his interests had been literary and philosophical. He had inherited a double cultural tradition. His mother was English; English was spoken at home, and his college education at Loyola was in English. Then, he made a conscious decision to embrace his French inheritance. Under the influence of a retired professor, who was a passionate francophile, this inheritance, both in language and as cultural outlook, took on a pronounced transatlantic bias. France, and Paris in particular, became for him the centre of civilization. He wrote his mother from France: 'It is hard to believe that there are people in Canada who dare criticize the French; if we were more like them in Canada we would be a nobler, a better race.'[23]

Vanier was an obvious choice to become the first minister to France, and his appointment to London was looked upon by the deputy minister, Skelton, as a transition to the higher office. In 1933, he had assured Pauline Vanier, George's wife, that 'George ought to have

Paris, and I am doing all I can to say so, and to further the idea.'[24] No doubt Massey knew about this plan, of which Vanier and his wife warmly approved, but the relation between the two men, always friendly and untroubled, was never intimate. Vanier's wife, independent and high-spirited, was not at ease with Alice Massey, who could, on official occasions, assume an imperious manner. If Alice was a daughter of the famous Sir George Parkin, Pauline Vanier was the daughter of a distinguished judge and, on her mother's side, a direct descendent of Charles de Salaberry, hero of the War of 1812.

Massey and Vanier differed fundamentally in temperament and attitude. When Massey was first spoken of as high commissioner in London, Vanier agreed with Lord Byng that he was 'too Balliol' for the job, and that 'he was the least typical of Canadians.'[25] Vanier was not himself a typical Canadian. Both he and Massey were strong individuals who adhered to no national norm. Although they were both humanists, with primary interests in literature and the arts, they emphasized different values. Vanier was a romantic, with a vein of poetic mysticism, who saw life, even the terror and filth of trench warfare, in a religious light. Massey was an aesthete who saw life as a drama that demanded sensitivity and self-awareness as the price of comfort, and religion was part of that drama, not a transcending experience. Vanier's francophilia was also a stumbling block to Massey. Massey had always had a warm and sympathetic attitude towards French-Canada and had advocated bilingualism long before it was widespread enough to be an issue. But he was severely critical of modern France, of its unreliable political leaders, and its stubborn adherence to the letter of the Treaty of Versailles.

Massey's relations with his second officer were far closer. He had known Lester Pearson since the days before the war when Pearson was an undergraduate at Victoria College in Toronto and he was the dean of the men's residence. In 1921 when Pearson decided to forsake business for the academic life, Massey had chosen him as one of the foundation fellows. Pearson had followed in Massey's footsteps: two years studying history at Oxford, followed by five years in the history department at the University of Toronto. Then, in 1928, he wrote the examinations for the Department of External Affairs, about to begin a remarkable period of expansion, and looking for young men of conspicuous talent. Pearson ranked first in the examinations, immediately accepted an appointment, and began a career that moved smoothly upwards. When he joined the high commissioner's office in London in October 1935, he had already had eight years of varied experience that regularly brought him close to the centre of policy-making. During the Ottawa conference he had been in charge of press relations and information; he was secretary to the Canadian delegation to the ill-fated world conference on disarmament that began its sessions in Geneva, in February 1932, and then secretary and adviser to the Canadian delegation to the assembly of the League of Nations that agonized for almost a year over the question of sanctions against Italy.

Pearson's appointment to London was a peculiar one, since it bore no official title and was concerned with an area that the Department of External Affairs did not look upon as an essential part of the high commissioner's duties. He was to be concerned with political affairs, and this meant liaison with the British Foreign Office and political and diplomatic reporting to the Canadian government. Both the minister of external affairs, Mackenzie King, and the deputy minister, O.D. Skelton, were determined to keep relations with the British government firmly under their control. The high commissioner's duties, they thought, lay in the area of trade and publicity; and this policy was especially to be emphasized during Vincent Massey's regime, since he was doubly suspect – as a crypto-imperialist, and as a student of foreign affairs and a diplomat, who had been trained in an exacting school in Washington. Possibly Skelton thought that by assigning diplomatic and political matters to a junior officer, Massey's role in those vital areas could be minimized. The opposite took place.

Massey and Pearson saw eye to eye on the political function of the high commissioner's office. Pearson produced a memorandum on the 'activities and organization of the Political Section.'[26] That was the obvious basis for the high commissioner's memorandum of 31 January 1936, containing 'observations with regard to the organization and conduct of what might be termed the political or diplomatic activities of the office of the High Commissioner for Canada in the United Kingdom.' Both the memorandum and the letter plead for giving to the high commissioner's office the central place in the exchange of information of a political and diplomatic nature between the British and Canadian governments, and for a policy of informing the high commissioner's office of any development in Canada that might bear upon British-Canadian relations. Pearson also wrote an influential memorandum on 'Canadian Publicity in the United Kingdom.' It was difficult, he argued, for Canada to establish a favourable image in the United Kingdom. 'It is not easy to convince the Englishman that a British-American is anything but in transit from the "British" to the "American", and already rather more than half-way there, yet Canadian publicity in these islands must show that this picture is false. We must emphasize our conviction that Canada can, to put it another way, work out her national American destiny as a British state within the Commonwealth.' At the same time, publicity must be based on differences between Canada and the United Kingdom, from small matters of custom and habit, to major questions of national outlook. 'We should base Canadian publicity in these islands on Canadian nationalism.' No doubt these observations arose in discussions with Vincent Massey, who endorsed all of them.

In a letter to her sister Maude, Alice Massey, with typical exuberance, expressed her husband's satisfaction with Pearson's work. 'You simply can't think how much in the intricacies of things large and small Mike Pearson meant to Vincent. Mike has a magnificent brain, and he and Vincent think very much in the same lines.'[27] When Pearson was approached in 1936 to be director of public relations for the Canadian Broadcasting Corporation, Massey immediately wrote to Skelton recommending that Pearson be made 'counsellor,' a senior appointment above first secretary. Skelton demurred at making the immediate appointment, but agreed to it two years later. After the war, when Pearson occupied positions of ascending authority in government, he was a supporter of Vincent as he too moved upward. His comments on Massey in his autobiography, however, are a little muted in tone as if he were delivering a formal eulogy arising more from respect than from admiration. He was 'an understanding and considerate chief, a skilled professional in diplomacy, and one whose cultivation of mind and broad knowledge commanded respect. He was exceedingly conscious of his position as the representative of his country, and careful to surround it with dignity, and when necessary with formality.'[28] About Massey's friendship with aristocrats and members of the royal family, Pearson couldn't resist a typical stylistic touch of facetious exaggeration: 'Mr. Massey seemed to know every duke by his first name.'[29]

Alice's assessment of the relation between Pearson and Massey may well have reflected her natural buoyancy and optimism. 'Mike' was the most genial of democrats who savoured the role of the discerning colonial in the land of pomp and circumstance. He lacked the sardonic bite of his friend and close associate in External Affairs, Hume Wrong, who had joined the department at the same time and had worked with the Masseys in Washington, but he no doubt smiled appreciatively at Wrong's satiric portraits of the Massey style. He wrote to Pearson congratulating him on his appointment to London: 'If Vincent Massey goes there, I think he will prove a great deal easier to work with than he was in Washington. He will be interested in the show-window and social aspects of the job (Alice in particular will be seeking to break into the inner ranks of Society), and these activities will concern his staff far less in London than they did in Washington. Remember that Vincent is always the intelligent actor, ever conscious of his audience, always trying to impress them, and ready to change his tune at any time in order to suit the audience.'[30] After Pearson had been with Massey for a short time, Wrong continued in the same tones: 'How are you getting on with Vincent – and Alice? I imagine that they are having a lively time, and are wearing themselves out in their efforts to attain an appearance of effortless perfection in their public performances. Does Vincent still write all his speeches at least three times and rehearse his impromptus carefully? Does he take himself *very* seriously as a delegate to the Naval Conference?'[31] Wrong's observations have a shrewd base in fact, particularly the emphasis on Massey as self-conscious actor, but like all satirical observations, they are generously laced with malevolence.

The third member of Massey's inner group in the high commissioner's office was Ross McLean, whom Massey had selected as his personal secretary. He was, like Stephen Cartwright, Massey's personal secretary for a brief period in Canada, a former Rhodes scholar. When Massey appointed him he was secretary of the Canadian Clubs. McLean's career in London came to a sudden end early in 1938. A few months before he had been attending meetings of the League in its new modern building in Geneva. Leaving a meeting suddenly, in a hurry to fulfil another obligation, he failed to recognize that an exit was not an open space but a plate-glass door and suffered, in the ensuing encounter, a long, deep gash in his forehead. The unhappy incident, occurring in a conspicuous spot and at the conclusion of a tense, packed meeting, helped to bring on a mental depression that necessitated McLean's return to Canada. While recuperating at home in Manitoba, he wrote long, chatty letters to Massey, who replied in kind, with affectionate solicitude for McLean's health and prospects (after the war, Ross McLean filled senior posts in the National Film Board and the administration of radio and television). Vincent Massey's treatment of Ross McLean was not atypical. With the young men who worked with him, and whom, in many instances, he had chosen, he had a friendly relationship. They would often become intimates of the Massey family, now, more even than in Canada, united and closely knit.

Vincent Massey presided over a strong and effective group of senior officials. The philosophical and temperamental difference between him and Vanier did not in any way prevent their easy co-operation on an administrative level. Among the more junior officers, James Spence, in charge of press relations, was directly involved in the carrying out of policy, especially in the frantic coronation year of 1937. He was a man who prided himself on formal elegance in his letters and memoranda. At the end of 1938, he sent Massey a letter in praise of his publicity program. Writing from the Savage Club, he considered that the subject called for a literary touch. 'I have felt, if I may say so, the efficient thrum of a new publicity axis – to use a totalitarian phrase in a far-from-totalitarian connection – of which I have been the frail end, cast in light alloy, but revolving at least in concert with this higher extremity.'[32]

Vincent no doubt appreciated this tribute, but he would have recalled that the year had begun harshly. Towards the end of 1937, there were scattered complaints that Canada House had not dealt either efficiently or consistently with Canadian pilgrims. Some journalists were especially irritated by their treatment. A former political agent of Massey during his election campaign exploded in a long letter of a bitter complaint. He complained about favouritism in the assignment of seats for coronation occasions, and added that 'it is the general opinion that nobody gets anywhere with you unless they have a university education – irrespective of brains and ability.'[33] Massey gave him a soft answer. 'Thank you for your letter of 28th January. I am a believer in the candid expression of opinion, and I am glad to have the views you discuss.'[34] He then called attention to a memorandum enclosed that explained the administrative guidelines that had been followed. Such private complaints from a disgruntled newspaperman who had presumed on a former acquaintance were not disturbing. But when they reached the public press in Canada and were linked with a more serious charge, Massey was aroused. The serious charge emerged from a preliminary report of a government committee from the Department of Agriculture that the recent publicity program to stimulate Canadian trade in the United Kingdom had been far less successful than similar campaigns conducted by other dominions, and that the money allotted to such publicity – $350,000 – should be shifted from Canada House to the Department of Trade and Commerce. A newspaper story about the report originating in Ottawa was picked up and widely used by the Canadian press. It carried the implication that some of the money had been used by Massey for his own entertaining.

Massey was initially despondent about the attack. He wrote to W.E. Rundle, president of National Trust, the firm that looked after his finances, that 'there is irony in the fact that two jobs in the last two years which people have been good enough to say have been really successfully accomplished – the advertising campaign and the Coronation hospitality – have now been branded as failures in the public mind.'[35] Rundle wrote to King about the insinuation that Massey had misappropriated government funds for his own entertaining. 'As you are perhaps aware, my official position makes me fully acquainted with our friend Massey's finances. I know what it cost him personally while at the Canadian Embassy in Washington and also while he has been in London as High Commissioner. I can therefore assure you that personally he has been out of pocket tens of thousand dollars a year during the years referred to. The rates granted Massey by Parliament for salary and expenses have been far short of the money he has expended in doing what he considered should be done at Washington and London in the interests of Canada. Consequently he dipped deeply into his private purse.'[36]

Massey took up his case in two firm, factual letters to King, the first detailing the arrangements made for the coronation and the second criticizing the publicity report as being a preliminary version full of error and misrepresentation, that 'naturally shocked the morale of the staff concerned and bewildered members of the business community here whose confidence and co-operation are so essential in the marketing of Canadian goods.'[37] King dealt with this promptly in the debate on the Speech from the Throne, and roundly defended his high commissioner. King had already dismissed the complaints about the handling of the coronation visitors. 'My understanding was that they all did a wonderful job. They were under great pressure at Canada House during the Coronation and I thought they handled the situation remarkably well.'[38] The statement in the House concerned the more serious charge of inefficiency and fiscal irresponsibility. The prime minister said that the publicity report did not refer to Massey's advertising campaign, which had been done 'effectively and efficiently' and that the shift of the publicity money to trade and commerce had been done with the compliance of the high commissioner, who would continue to be the chairman of an inter-departmental committee responsible for all publicity in the United Kingdom. The prime minister then concluded, 'I desire to refer to an insinuation made by one newspaper correspondent that money voted by this parliament for publicity purposes had been used by Massey, the High Commissioner, for entertainment and social purposes. I deny that statement emphatically and totally. I wish to add that if more statements of that kind appear in the future, the Government will not hesitate to institute prosecution of those responsible for them.'[39]

Whatever private doubts Mackenzie King entertained of Vincent Massey, he always supported him in public with vigour and apparent conviction. Vincent was grateful, as he was for the governor-general's concluding words in a long letter to him about the state of the nation. 'One private word in your ear. There seems to have been some foolish criticism of your work, especially at the Coronation, of which echoes have strayed into the Canadian press. Don't pay the slightest attention to that. The unanimous opinion here is that you did the Coronation superbly and are doing everything else magnificently.'[40]

The attacks on Massey were successfully countered, but the incident did not leave him unscathed. Doubts and suspicions voiced in the press helped to develop an impression of a self-centred snob contemptuous of the common man – an impression that was eagerly absorbed by the jaundiced populism with which Canadians assess their public figures. But the unpleasant experience did not blunt Vincent Massey's deep devotion to his native country. His projection of Canada in Britain was accompanied by a studied support of his many Canadian projects.

Vincent and Alice planned to return to Canada once every year. They were able to make a Canadian visit in 1936 and 1937, each year in the early fall before the London 'season' was fully under way. The Munich crisis in September forced the abandonment of their plans for 1938; and by late spring of 1939 it was apparent that any return to Canada must be put off indefinitely. In their visit of 1937 – four days in Toronto, two in Ottawa, one in Montreal, preceded by two in New York – they seem to have had a premonition that this was the end for the time being of free movement back and forth. The days were consumed in a systematic attendance to all their Canadian interests. There was a meeting of the Massey Foundation. Vincent attended meetings or saw officials of all the organizations in which he had continued his interest by correspondence or direct action: the University of Toronto and Hart House in particular, Upper Canada College, the Toronto Symphony Orchestra, the Art Gallery of Toronto and the National Gallery, the Dominion Drama Festival, the Canadian Broadcasting Corporation. He and Alice saw old friends – George Wrong, now long retired as head of the history department at the University of Toronto, the inspiration of his youth and his academic mentor; David Milne, the artist, who made a special trip from his cabin in the woods to see Alice and him; Norman Lambert, with whom he had worked in the Liberal Federation; Brooke Claxton, a rising Montreal lawyer who was a Massey admirer and had just written a flattering article on him for the *Fortnightly Review*. There were, also, a series of official talks in Ottawa, an unsatisfactory one with the prime minister, a business-like interview with O.D. Skelton, a long and friendly chat with the governor-general, and a series of talks with some cabinet ministers.

After the visit of October 1937, Vincent relied on correspondence and the occasional visitor to fuel his knowledge of Canada. A particularly welcome visitor was Paul Martin, whose political career Vincent had helped to launch. The young man, rapidly moving upward in the political world, never forgot his early indebtedness to Vincent, and was in his later, influential years to acknowledge that indebtedness actively and generously. Martin, now a Liberal member of parliament, arrived in London on his way to attend the League of Nations assembly in Geneva in September 1938. Vincent wrote in his diary: 'We were delighted to see him, and found him growing in capacity all the time – also in girth.'

Personal letters from home were continuous, detailed, and instructive. It was as if the writers thought of themselves as correspondents writing intimate supplements to their official despatches to a wise and sympathetic editor. Brooke Claxton was the most regular and informative correspondent. He still thought of Massey as a potential political leader. 'I do hope,' he wrote in his first letter after Massey's departure in 1935, 'that you will pay frequent visits to Canada so that the movements about which you were keen in Canada may have the support of your continued interest and your friends and followers may have the advantage of seeing you both.'[41] As late as April 1938, he is still hinting of a possible Massey return: 'There is moreover, a growing feeling in well informed circles in Ottawa that King must give way to a more vigorous leader if Confederation is to be saved. I would not be surprised if that was the view of several members of the Cabinet to-day; it is certainly the view of people who are usually well informed.'[42] Claxton's general themes were the growth of French-Canadian nationalism and the increasing corruption of Quebec political life, the early problems in the enunciation of a policy for public radio, and increasingly, the drift to war (about which he was more pessimistic and realistic than Massey).

T.L. Macdermot, principal of Upper Canada College, moved in his letters beyond college administration to give a remarkably incisive and prescient account of Canadian separatism:

French Canadian separation is simply another, and perhaps because of its nationalistic sinews, the most obdurate and divisive form of disintegration, that threatens the Dominion as a whole: inevitable, true, but dangerous if it goes much further.

... at present there seems little prospect of anyone rallying the national forces of Canada against the provincial. And of course our constitution and the Privy Council have done their best to crystallize, even to petrify the situation ... of this I am sure that if there is any truth in the tonic power of patriotism – that is, of a sense of devotion to a large social unit, whose size and unity are worth preserving – it is difficult to hold up the truth to young people where it is plainly flaunted on all sides by a local patriotism so small and self-seeking and uninspiring that even youth sees through it.[43]

George Smith, a close friend from early years at Balliol and in the history department at Toronto, now on the staff of the University of Alberta, wrote about the inscrutable movement of the Alberta premier, Aberhart, who combined religious fundamentalism and social credit economic doctrine. Alan Plaunt kept Vincent informed of the activities of the Radio League, an informal association of various national groups, concerned with unified government control of all radio broadcasting in Canada. Herbert Bruce, just resigned as lieutenant governor of Ontario, sent a detailed account of how the provincial premier, Hepburn, an unpredictable mixture of populist and petty tyrant, had arbitrarily closed Government House.

There was a steady stream of letters from the warden of Hart House, Burgon Bickersteth, some of them long, detailed accounts of every event in Hart House, whether it was the problem of finding the right place for a coronation chair given by Vincent, or the relationship of Hart House to the central administration. After spending most of 1937 in England on convalescent leave, Bickersteth found his Hart House duties increasingly onerous. He was not on good terms with the president, Henry John Cody, who, he thought, did not understand the nature of Hart House. Indeed, his attitude to the whole university was taking on a gloomy cast: 'The whole character of the University has changed in the last 10 years and it is difficult for you to realize it because of your long and almost continual absences. Whereas formerly it still had a certain leisurely, almost small-town atmosphere, now it is a huge city institution. Women students are a far more potent influence in the men's lives than they were. There is a general restlessness and also an even increasing pressure on the men's time. Simple pleasures no longer please. Everything must be bigger and better.'[44]

In London Massey saw a good deal of two governors-general whom he had known in Canada, Willingdon and Bessborough. But the governor-general whom he knew best was John Buchan, Lord Tweedsmuir, who arrived in Canada just as Massey was leaving for London, and whom he was to see only on a few occasions before Tweedsmuir's sudden death in 1940. His friendship with John Buchan went back to the twenties. On their first visit to Canada the Buchans had stayed at Batterwood. He had pleased Vincent by his enthusiasm for Hart House, and Alice and Susie Buchan, who came from a London family of means and gentility, had a friendly relationship.

In his letters John Buchan touched upon matters that he knew would be of interest to Vincent. He commented at length, for instance, on the swift termination of the appointment of the new principal of McGill University, A.E. Morgan, who had succeeded Sir Arthur Currie. Morgan, an Englishman from the University College of Hull, had been a victim of the familiar clash at that time in the Canadian university system of governance between a powerful board and an academic head with strong views. Buchan was sympathetic to Morgan, but reported in his letter to Vincent that 'I have told Beatty [Sir Edward Beatty, chairman of the McGill board] I am very much against any attempt to bring an Englishman out to succeed him, and that they must have a Canadian who, at the start at any rate, will accept this theory of a principalship, and will not rub up people the wrong way by what they think English arrogance.'[45] We do not have Massey's reply, but he would have agreed with Buchan's judgement. His fondness of the English character did not blind him to its limitations in an unfamiliar setting.

There were some striking parallels between Buchan and Massey in upbringing and general cast of thought. Buchan had shaken off (although never entirely denied) his Calvinist childhood in a Scottish Presbyterian manse. By the twenties he had become outwardly the complete upper-class Englishman, living in a manor house in Oxfordshire, travelling daily to London on legal and literary business. Vincent Massey had also shaken off a similar, although less doctrinaire, childhood, and his credentials as English gentleman were no less explicit. Both had arrived at similar political outlooks: Buchan had grown to despise the sanctimonious liberalism that flourished in Scotland, and had become a tory, having a romantic reverence for ancient families with chequered pasts, although a tory capable of radical deviations. Vincent was an active, partisan Liberal in Canada, but in England, where the Liberal party was in rapid decline, he was at ease with Conservatives, especially if they were intellectuals and occasional dissenters. Both Buchan and Massey were 'careerists' – men who carefully plotted their future course, and fixed their eyes on high positions for which they felt themselves well qualified. Buchan found compensation for his failure to reach a position of genuine political power in his prodigious creative talent as novelist and biographer. Massey had no comparable compensation, but he had a broader familiarity with the arts and combined this successfully with a sharp political sense.

Massey's admiration for Buchan was not absolute. When consulted by Mackenzie King about a successor to Bessborough, he expressed his preference for Lord Halifax over John Buchan. Massey was not yet prepared to accept a commoner as the king's representative in Canada (the elevation to Lord Tweedsmuir came only after Buchan's appointment as governor-general.) He agreed, for instance, with palace bureaucrats who criticized Buchan for speaking too frequently, and with an unplatitudinous directness not appropriate for the official mouthpiece of royalty. In some obscure corner of his mind, Massey may have been expressing jealousy of a rival who had anticipated what he intended to do (although there is not a hint in any letter or document that Massey had begun to think of himself as a future Buchan successor). Buchan retained royal protocol in Ottawa, but combined it with an easy democratic approach in his travels. His speeches were opportunities to talk about matters of general concern, and he spoke with a brevity and a cogency that sharply contrasted with the interminable woolliness of the Mackenzie King school of oratory. In these respects, Buchan pointed the way to what Massey himself seventeen years later would strive to do.

During the Masseys' trips to Canada, there were few family visits and in their correspondence few family exchanges. The reason for this was that the family they valued most were already in London – their two sons, Lionel and Hart, and Vincent's brother, Raymond; and three of the four children of Maude and William Grant, Charity, Alison, and George, came at various times to stay in England. (Maude Grant had become the head of Royal Victoria College, the women's residence at McGill, in 1937 and could make only a short visit to England before the outbreak of war, but she and her sister Alice, corresponded regularly; Margaret, the fourth Grant child, had married Geoffrey Andrew, a master at Upper Canada College.) To his own family, outside of his brother and his children, Vincent maintained a steady indifference. As a youngster he had spent a good deal of time at Dentonia Park, the rural home of his remarkable uncle, Walter Massey, who had died in 1901 at the early age of 37. He had formed a close attachment to Walter's oldest child, Ruth, and in later years greatly admired her work as an art historian. But in general the relations between Walter's surviving family and Vincent had been strained, in the main because of differences over grandfather Hart's will. Denton, the youngest and most visible of the four children, had aroused Vincent's wrath during the election campaign of 1935. An increasingly influential Conservative spokesman, he had characterized Vincent in the darkest colours as 'a man supposedly cultured, a man of education, and the Dean of a University, a man of diplomatic training. Yet that man blindly followed his leader to the extent of making statements which he knew, he must have known, were utterly untrue.'[46]

Only once during the London years did Vincent's Massey relatives break the silence. In January 1936, he received a letter from Arthur Massey, son of his uncle Charles Albert, who had died before Vincent was born. He asked Vincent to give his daughter a job in Canada House. She was coming to London to wait for an English divorce and would need to earn her support. She had no special qualifications, but had, her father assured Vincent, a general knowledge 'of the shops and better places of entertainment in London.'[47] Vincent replied with icy politeness that he would be happy to see Arthur's daughter, but there was no possibility of a job in Canada House. A month later Vincent received a telegram from Arthur's son, Arnold, saying that his father, disconsolate about misappropriation of mortgage money entrusted to him, had shot himself, and inquiring whether Vincent, to avoid disgrace to the family name, could cover the amount of the misappropriated sum from the Massey Foundation ($450,000). Vincent cabled promptly, expressing his regrets at Arthur Massey's death, and curtly refusing the impossible request. Arnold subsequently wrote a polite letter, explaining that he was simply acting on a suggestion that his father had left in his papers, and indicating that he knew the futility of the request. When Arthur's daughter wrote a 'Dear Vincent' letter renewing her late father's plea for assistance, she received only a discouraging note signed by the secretary to the high commissioner.

When Vincent and Alice had arrived in Waterloo Station on 13 November 1935 to begin their official duties, the small welcoming party included Vincent's brother, Raymond, a resident in England since 1922. The two brothers differed greatly both in appearance and in temperament. Vincent resembled his mother, who was a small, vivid brunette with delicate features. Raymond was unmistakably a Massey, the stern, romanesque appearance of father and grandfather softened by a suggestion of romantic melancholy. In temperament, however, Vincent was more the Massey, with a good deal of the sobriety and canniness of his puritan ancestors. Raymond was sentimental and emotional, with an easy, out-going manner that won him quick acceptance. Raymond was nine years younger than Vincent, and, from early years, they had gone their separate ways. Raymond had enlisted in the army in 1915 at the age of 19 and had spent the next five years in England, France, the United States, and Russia, whereas Vincent's military service had been entirely on the home front. Since 1922, when he had boldly launched himself as an actor in London and had steadily risen to the top ranks of the profession, he and Vincent had met only briefly when either was on a transatlantic visit. By 1935 Raymond was at the height of his career, and during the next four years was to appear in three of his most famous roles – the title roles in *Ethan Frome* and *Abe Lincoln in Illinois*, and as Harry Van in *Idiot's Delight*. After an unhappy first marriage, he had married Adrianne Allen, a fine actress herself, and the marriage had been a success. They lived in style and affluence, with a town house in London and a country house in Sussex. During Mackenzie King's visit to London in 1936, Vincent had taken the prime minister to see a play in which Adrianne was appearing, and they had gone afterwards to a reception at Raymond's home. In the taxi with the Masseys and Mrs Anthony Eden was, King noted, 'a famous young movie star, Ingrid Bergman.' Despite this engaging prologue, King was not pleased by the general atmosphere of the party. 'After taking off coats and before supper, the waiter asked which one would have, champagne or whiskey. There was no suggestion of plain water ... Raymond Massey looked to me to be pretty tired and worn.' He concluded solemnly 'one sees how clearly the "whole upper set" is going on with a sort of extravagant and frivolous life which preceded the great wars and revolutions of the past.'[48]

King's comment, an unduly sombre reflection to arise from the occasion, had some relevance to Raymond's personal life two years later. He and Adrianne separated and then agreed to a troubled reconciliation. Alice and Vincent were now deeply involved, since they were fond of both Adrianne and Raymond, each of whom trusted them. Alice wrote to Maude on 17 May 1938: 'All our spare moments have been taken with the most tragic problem of keeping Raymond and Adrianne together.' Their sympathies were on the side of Raymond, a triumph of brotherly affection over dispassionate judgement. Raymond fell in love easily and frequently. When he was in New York in the fall of 1938, playing in *Abe Lincoln*, he sent telegrams imploring Adrianne and the children (Daniel and Anna, their two children, and Geoffrey, the child by Raymond's first wife) to join him, although he freely admitted to the continuation of a love affair that had started in England. He was torn by the emotional conflict. He wrote to Vincent and Alice. 'I am near the end of my tether. I'm the biggest acting success in the smash hit of New York and I'm on the brink of tears all the time.'[49] They urged him to persevere in his attempt to have Adrianne join him. 'Up to you darling. Just be the real Abe. God bless you,' they cabled in reply.

The outcome was happy and melodramatic, worthy of a Noel Coward play (Adrianne had starred recently in *Private Lives*). Raymond and Adrianne each turned to a new love (by an ironical twist, Adrianne's new love was the ex-husband of Raymond's). A divorce, as Raymond observed in his autobiography, was 'amicably' arranged,[50] and Raymond married for the third time.

Raymond's new wife, Dorothy Ludington Whitney, was very different from the deeply emotional Adrianne. She was an astute business woman, a graduate of Vassar and the Yale School of Law, who had made her name in a firm devoted to legal problems of the theatre. She was a woman of wit and determination, with strong political views, firmly and combatively to the far right – views that Raymond, to his brother's horror, warmly embraced. From this time on, Raymond became an American actor and eventually an American citizen. Having played the archetypal American hero in Abe Lincoln, he in a sense repeated the role in the popular television serial, 'Dr Kildare,' where he played Dr Gillespie, an elderly Lincoln with a stethoscope.

Raymond, who had lived an intercontinental life, had no difficulty in adapting himself to the American environment. But for the other members of the London family that would have been an impossibility. The three Grant children who had come to London at different times and for different purposes – Alison in 1936 to continue her art studies with a scholarship provided by the Massey Foundation, Charity in 1937 with an extended stay in Germany to learn German, George in 1939 as an Ontario Rhodes scholar – had also been warmly received into the Massey home (George Grant observed that 'Uncle Vincent treats our family as if they really were their own'[51]). All the Grants were, in their various ways, Canadian nationalists for whom living, studying, and working in Britain was part of the preparation for Canadian careers.

This was true of Lionel and Hart as well. Both were at Balliol with the intent of reading history as their father had done before them. Neither prospered academically. Lionel failed to pass his preliminary examination, and finally settled for a diploma course in economics and political science. Hart fared better, but his history tutor found his essays 'conventional with hardly a trace of his shrewdness.' 'I must,' he added, 'get the twinkle in his eye on to the end of his pen.'[52] Both flourished non-academically. Lionel was a member of the Bullingdon Club, devoted to horses and revelry, and spent much of his time competing in point-to-points and steeplechases. Hart, following an operation at the age of six years that saved his eyesight but inhibited growth, was at eighteen the size of a boy seven or eight. But he had been brought up to ignore his disability and to participate fully in peer activities. Quickly recognizing that rowing was Oxford's basic religion, he set himself to become a cox. He eventually achieved his

Varsity blue, and coxed the Oxford boat in the Oxford-Cambridge race of 1 April 1939. Although Oxford lost, Hart was the hero of the occasion, celebrated in newspaper stories all over the world. Even the Oxford orator in presenting Vincent for his honorary degree inserted in the citation a reference to Hart's accomplishments. 'Who at Oxford does not know the "little Julus", who like "the steersman Palinurus himself on his high poop" recently came in next to, but alas! a long way behind, the Cambridge cox?'

The truth is that neither Hart nor Lionel were prepared for or wanted a pure liberal arts education; they were studying history at Oxford because it was pleasing to their father, and he believed it would be good for them. Both had practical interests that could best be developed elsewhere. Hart was an able artist, with a talent for caricature, demonstrated in a set of political cartoons he did while observing a meeting of the assembly of the League of Nations that were reproduced in the influential Canadian periodical, *Saturday Night*. By the fall of 1938 he had decided that his real interest was architecture. A Canadian architect recommended that he would find a long and demanding course ahead of him if he did his preparation in Canada, and that he would find it less difficult to follow the English prescription. Hart could not begin his studies in architecture until after the war. Then he unhesitatingly chose to return to Canada, and enrolled in the Faculty of Architecture at the University of Toronto. Lionel had always taken a keen interest in the Batterwood farms, and after leaving Oxford in 1938 spent some months in New Zealand and Australia studying their agricultural economy. This he did while a member of the secretariat of the Institute of International Affairs, where he demonstrated an aptitude for administration and public relations. In the spring of 1939 when Lionel returned to England, he had made up his mind about what he wanted to do. He wanted to return to Canada, and to enter a business firm – preferably not the old family firm.

The pre-war years in London were a particularly happy time for Vincent and Alice. There was, of course, the constant undercurrent of fear bred by the international situation, but, for them, the fear did not become a gnawing concern until the spring of 1939. Vincent could fully realize his idea of the Canadian nationalist, who was all the more nationalistic for being British. He and Alice could pursue their Canadian concerns with just as much vigour in London as in Toronto or Ottawa. They could, for Britain, clarify the Canadian outlook and achievement. Through visits and correspondence they retained a lively consciousness of Canadian affairs while, at the same time, enjoying the pleasures of Britain – the week-ends in the enchanting countryside, which was at once cosy and storied, the constant reminder of an ancient past that had not been obliterated, the brilliant theatre, the superb museums, the sense of a high debate that went on in university common rooms, the House of Commons, and, at times, in the newspapers and drawing rooms. They were closer to their immediate family than they had often been in Canada.

Secure and happy in London, Vincent yet felt close to the Canadian scene and aware of the various prospects that awaited him on his return. If war did not break out, they might return to Canada very soon. At the conclusion of his article on Massey in the *Fortnightly Review*, Brooke Claxton had speculated about future possibilities: 'Vincent Massey's appointment to London has already raised the question as to what lies before him. Only forty-eight, experienced in the public life, generously endowed by nature and good fortune, what does the future hold for him? Some day he might become Minister of Foreign Affairs in Canada (since 1912 that post has been held by the Prime Minister) or principal of a great university, even enter other services abroad.'[53] Of these alternatives, the university head seemed at the time the most probable. Claxton, judging by the terminology he used, had in mind his own alma mater, McGill. The greater likelihood was Toronto. The only hint of any speculation on Vincent's part was a note in the diary on 27 June 1939: 'Call from Sanderson (Toronto Public Library). Said I was being talked about as Cody's successor.'

Vincent's pre-war years in London were so happy that he found it difficult to believe that civilized and rational man could deliberately destroy what he so deeply enjoyed and valued. He held to this doggedly until the ugly facts demonstrated that reason and civilization did not go hand in hand.

CHAPTER THREE

Appeaser

During his presidency of the National Liberal Federation from 1932 to 1935, Vincent Massey had, at times, essayed a political role. His emphasis had been on domestic problems, particularly on methods of curing unemployment and arresting economic depression. Mackenzie King had resented these incursions, particularly since Massey had moved perilously close to the views of the new radical party, the CCF. But firmly established in power in the election of October 1935, his moderate views handsomely vindicated by the electorate, King could forget Massey's lapses into insurgency. Massey was, however, contemplating another bold departure. The position of high commissioner in London would, he thought, give him a platform for the presentation of his views on foreign policy. He had already elaborated these views in a book, *Canada in the World*, but had decided against its publication once his appointment had been officially announced.

Vincent Massey had some reason for thinking of himself as one qualified to speak on foreign policy. Certainly his credentials were sounder than those he had in the field of social policy, where his ideas were drawn shadowily from American progressivism and the emerging structure of the Rooseveltian new deal. Few Canadians, for instance, had had his opportunities to travel in Europe. Ever since a young boy he had gone abroad regularly, first as a member of an affluent family, then as student, young man of affairs, business man, and government representative. The main goal of his travels had usually been an extended stay in Great Britain, but he had, from time to time, moved outward in Europe, particularly to France, Italy and

Spain. His presidency in the early twenties of the family firm with its world market enjoyed an international outlook. He had gone on business trips to eastern Europe and was one of the early visitors to communist Russia. In Washington in the late twenties, as Canada's first minister to the United States, he had had a sense of agreeable proximity to the world of high international affairs. The American secretary of state, Kellogg, discussed with him his hopes for a new world order. He relished his part in welcoming the British prime minister, Ramsay MacDonald, returned to power in the election of 1929, proclaiming in America his gospel of a world of peace to be achieved 'by the strenuous action of good will.' He was chairman in 1931 of the Canadian delegation to the Institute of Pacific Relations, which met in China just as Japan invaded Manchuria and thereby issued the first in a series of fatal challenges to the authority of the League of Nations. Finally, as we have seen, Massey had friends in the United Kingdom who held, or were shortly to hold, positions of national authority. Massey's expectation that he would play an important role in the shaping of Canadian foreign policy was understood and respected in the United Kingdom. Norman Archer, the British high commissioner in Ottawa in 1936, wrote to a colleague in the Dominions Office that whereas Massey's predecessor, Howard Ferguson, was thought to be 'rather uninformed,' Massey was 'capable and intelligent,'[1] this sharp contrast being based upon the perception of Ferguson as a provincial politician and Massey as the cultivated internationalist with a special understanding of British affairs.

There was, however, an essential ambiguity in the conception of the office of the high commissioner that was to confound Massey's spacious expectations. The high commissioner was clearly a business and trade agent for the Canadian government, a super-agent who consolidated and directed the work of a great number of government officials in the United Kingdom. He was also clearly an interpreter of Canada to the United Kingdom, striving to eliminate misconceptions about his country, and to create in the minds of the British public an impression of Canada that was both colourful and attractive, without being inaccurate. But although the high commissioner was the senior representative abroad, he did not paradoxically have an official diplomatic status. In the theology of the Commonwealth he was appointed by the Crown, and the Crown could not appoint a representative to itself. Massey, who was versed in the theology of Empire and Commonwealth and enjoyed expounding it to the uninitiated, did not think in this instance that Commonwealth theory need stand in the way of common sense. The high commissioner could be given diplomatic status if the prime minister so decreed. The subject had come up for discussion at the British Commonwealth Relations Conference held in Toronto in 1933, and the conference had resolved 'that, where Dominion Governments so desired, the status of the High Commissioners in London should be raised so as to enable them to discharge diplomatic duties if they were so instructed. Further, that High Commissioners of the new status should communicate freely with the Foreign Office directly, so as to receive personally information on foreign affairs.'[2]

The Conservative government of R.B. Bennett that appointed Howard Ferguson was sympathetic to the findings of the British Commonwealth Relations Conference. In spite of being 'rather uninformed' Ferguson played an important diplomatic role in a major crisis. On 3 October 1935, Italy launched its long-threatened attack on Abyssinia. With Lester Pearson as secretary and W.A. Riddell as permanent advisory officer, Ferguson headed the delegation to the meeting of the League of Nations assembly in Geneva. He and his Canadian associates were shocked by instructions from Skelton, the under-secretary of state for external affairs, that Canada should refrain from voting on the motion branding Italy as aggressor, thereby condemning the country to join a small group of Mussolini's lackeys. The argument was that an affirmative vote would imply an agreement with the imposition of sanctions, to which Canada had not committed herself. Ferguson reached Bennett, then in the final stages of his election campaign, and got his permission to bypass the bureaucrats, and to cast an affirmative vote. Buoyed up by this victory, Ferguson, now made a member of a committee to consider what sanctions should be imposed, cut through an interminable procedural wrangle, and made a statement that, for a Canadian diplomat, had a cauterizing bluntness: 'The sole problem before the Committee was to decide what sanctions the delegations could all agree upon that afternoon and put them into action immediately. Let them show the world that the League was no longer to be laughed at, but that it meant business'[3].

Mackenzie King would have disapproved sharply of the substance of Ferguson's action: he looked upon the League of Nations as a conciliatory body, and not as an active instrument for enforcing international law. Moreover, he would have disapproved of the whole procedure: the high commissioner had no diplomatic status; he had no business even raising foreign policy issues with the prime minister, let alone enunciating a national policy publicly. King spelled out his 'high and dry' theory to Massey. He was to look upon himself as 'the agent of the Government in London just as Floud the British High Commissioner in Ottawa was the agent of the British Government in Canada. [There was] no diplomatic service within the Empire ... the Governor General represented the King in Canada and the King represented Canada in England.'[4] King was more blunt and explicit in a telegram he sent to Massey (the telegram was sent by Skelton, but a draft in King's handwriting indicates that King was the author):

My colleagues and I very strongly of the opinion that any important communication between British Govt. should be direct in form of communication from P.M. to P.M. or between Sec. of State for Dominions and Sec. of State for External Affairs as has been customary in the past and should not be through High Commissioner. This is the only way in which we can possibly have opportunity required collectively to consider a state attitude and policy and which will insure full responsibility of British as well as Cdn. Govt. with respect to any statement of policy or position and avoid all possibility of misunderstanding as to what has been said or meant in any verbal communication.[5]

King insisted on extending his austere doctrine of high commissioner innocence to Massey's associations with his fellow high commissioners. There were four others – representing Australia, New Zealand, South Africa, and, somewhat anomalously, the Irish Free State. Malcolm MacDonald, who had become secretary of state for dominion affairs just before Massey arrived, revived a custom that had existed in the twenties of regular meetings of the high commissioners. With the explosive rise of Hitler in Germany, and Italy's reckless pursuit of a new Roman empire in the Mediterranean, MacDonald believed that the dominions should be kept informed and that their opinions should be sought, on the understanding that discussions would be informal and non-binding on the participating countries. But King had always been opposed to such meetings and had been responsible for their discontinuance in the twenties. They constituted, he believed, an imperial cabinet in the making, providing opportunities for the British government to develop an imperial policy without direct negotiations with the dominions. They were all the more dangerous since Australia and New Zealand were willing participants. Conscious of their vulnerability in a remote area, yet much closer in spirit than Canada to the mother country, they did not see a conflict between close consultation and autonomy. Indeed Stanley Bruce, the Australian high commissioner since 1932, could be described as an Australian minister for British affairs resident in London. But for King, autonomy could not risk such open associations, especially when he was not in charge. In international affairs Canada should be like Stephen Daedalus' artist, 'invisible, refined out of existence, indifferent, paring his fingernails.'

Massey was aware of King's fears, and in an early letter he set out to placate him. He began circumspectly, emphasizing, at the beginning, that he had been 'much concerned with the problem of wheat' (a proper priority for a Canadian high commissioner). When he came to the delicate question of high commissioners meetings, he attempted to forestall King by recognizing his fears as legitimate, but in this instance rendered groundless by their common devotion to Canadian autonomy within the Commonwealth. 'A regular conference of High Commissioners might unconsciously develop characteristics contrary to the spirit of the Commonwealth as it has been accepted and exists. I am always conscious of the principle which you, as a matter of fact, expressed in our last conversation in Canada, that the individual entity of the Dominion must be zealously preserved not only in its extra-imperial but in its intra-imperial relations. This truth, I feel, is entirely accepted in official circles here, although one occasionally meets the diehards amongst retired people or in the commercial community whose conceptions of the Empire is still suggestive of the 19th century.'⁶ King was not moved by such blandishments. His reply came in a telegram sent again by Skelton, who warmly shared King's views.

*I desire to repeat that in any case where British Govt. desires to consult Canadian Govt. on important matter of policy, communication should be direct to avoid possibility of misunderstanding & to give Canadian Government opportunity to consider & state its attitude. Meetings such as referred to in despatch under reference convey disturbing & erroneous impression in Canada & will make it necessary if question is raised in House for us to state our position clearly. Consultation between Foreign Secretary & all the High Commissioners together is further liable to implication of collective decision. We could not agree to the development of an Imperial Council on Foreign Affairs, sitting in London.*⁷

In his diary Massey permitted himself an unusually lively protest.

*A rotten day begun by long cables from Ottawa assuming from irresponsible press despatches that I had concurred and participated in 'consultations' with F.O. as to foreign policy and condemning me unheard without any effort to ascertain the facts which were contrary to their apprehensions. Ottawa is apparently panic-stricken and seeks to protect itself by an ostrich-like policy of not even wishing to know what is going on. I agree with the principles of Dominion autonomy in all things as much as any other Canadian but not in my experience has there been the slightest risk of its being violated or any intention on the part of responsible people to violate it. Sometimes I feel that Ottawa really wishes its H.C. to express himself by (a) dignified inactivity (b) an active distrust of British policy. However patience and tolerance are important qualities to cultivate in public life.*⁸

This outburst, modulating at the end towards a mood of suffering resignation, becomes in his official reply a dignified assertion of innocence: 'Gravely disturbed. Conversation simply for infm. You will agree that this is no cause for uneasiness arising out of conversations in question and that important principles on which you rightly lay stress have in no way been prejudiced.'⁹

In a bitter, confidential account of his relations with Ottawa that Massey wrote in the midst of the Munich crisis, he reported that 'I scrupulously followed their instructions [the 1936 instructions about meetings with the high commissioners and the Dominion secretary], although this involved a ridiculous application of nationalistic theory – incomprehensible to sensible people & often very embarrassing to me. It was also very unfair to overworked ministers with whom I had to have a special solitary appointment to hear what the other High Commissioners had heard as a group.'[10] When he wrote his account, Massey had decided that he could no longer 'scrupulously' follow instructions. The great surge of events, any one of which might have precipitated war, ruled out his special treatment by Malcolm MacDonald. In a telephone conversation, the first that he had had since his arrival in England, he 'told Skelton that I was going to the meetings, having let them know I must use my own judgment. I take reasonable precautions, however, against stupid things being said in the press, and I approach MacDonald's room, if there is a crowd of reporters outside, either by the Home Office corridor or the Clive steps in the quadrangle of the Colonial office. It all sounds incredibly silly.'[11]

Having reduced Massey's daily diplomatic activities to that of a nervous eavesdropper at high commissioner meetings, King took care to deny him a platform at official international meetings. He was accorded a brief appearance on the world stage at the meeting of the assembly of the League of Nations in July 1936, where he delivered the official Canadian speech (written no doubt by Skelton), in which he spoke of the failure of economic sanctions against Italy without regret and without any indication of a desire for their revival. He must have had reservations about the tone and substance of what he said, but at least he had the satisfaction of being a visible participant. In his diary, he reports, no doubt with satisfaction, that 'the speaking was done by Te Water, [The South African High Commissioner], myself, Eden, Litvinoff [the Russian foreign minister].' About the difference between his defeatist remarks and Te Water's aggressive defence of continued sanctions, he commented, in the spirit of a critic observing a dramatic performance, that 'Te Water & I took dramatically opposite lines thus showing the flexibility of the Empire.'[12]

But at the more important meeting of the assembly of the League of Nations in the following September, which James Eayrs describes as marking 'the disappearance of the League of Nations as a force in international affairs,'[13] Massey was confined to the periphery of discussions. 'The choice of committees left to me,' he observed mournfully, 'fell between Committee No. 5 (opium, Child Welfare etc.) and Committee No. 4 (Budget and League Administration).'[14] King did not appoint him as a delegate to the imperial conference held in May and June 1937 – another crucial conference at which Chamberlain took over from Baldwin as its chairman and piloted through a resolution that endorsed 'the settlement of differences that may arise between nations ... by methods of cooperation, joint inquiry, and conciliation.'[15]

Even if King had been more generously inclined towards his representative in the United Kingdom, it is doubtful if Massey's expectations would have been realized. The processes for passing on information and determining policy, in both Canada and Britain, were slow and untrustworthy. During a trip to Canada in the summer of 1939, Pearson sent back a depressing report on the state of the Department of External Affairs. 'The department, in one crude phrase,' he wrote, 'is in a mess.' The burden was carried at the top by Skelton and Norman Robertson, and there was little delegation of responsibilities, and little expertise in the lower ranks even if delegation had been carried out. The chief source of the malady was 'the fact that the P.M. is our minister – with the best departmental organization in the world this would make for confusion and delay.' Add to this 'a queer ministerial doctrine of direct contact – based partly on theory and partly on personality.'[16]

In the United Kingdom, the flow of information and the discussion of policy were apparently accelerated by the creation in 1930 of an independent Dominions Office with a secretary of state for dominions affairs. But this recognition of the special status of the dominions did not strengthen the position of the high commissioners. Indeed they often found themselves confined to a backwater, cut off from direct access to the dominating Foreign Office, dependent on ministers who looked upon their appointment as temporary and even demeaning. When Anthony Eden was appointed dominions secretary in September 1939 (he held the office for only eight months), his recent biographer comments, 'surprisingly Eden accepted this humiliating office.'[17] To Sir Thomas Inskip, who succeeded Eden briefly, Chamberlain remarked 'It is not a very absorbing department. You will be available for committees.'[18] Attlee, who held the office for one year 1942-43, was busy with other tasks, in particular the chairmanship of a cabinet committee on India. Fortunately there were two strong secretaries, one at the beginning and one in the final years of Massey's tenure of office – Malcolm MacDonald (1935–39) and Viscount Cranborne (1943–45) – but they were both relatively junior, and they spent a good deal of this time in arguing with their superiors in the cabinet about the importance of the dominions.

As high commissioner, Massey soon discovered that he had little impact on the making of Canadian foreign policy. He represented the senior dominion, yet he was virtually powerless in this vital area. With regret and with envy, he would have agreed that Bruce was expressing a basic truth (although in a flamboyant way) when he declared that during the war and the years preceding it 'Australia was invariably better informed on international affairs, and had far more influence on the U.K. Government and its policy, than all the rest of the Empire put together.'[19] But Massey never lost his personal concern for foreign affairs. Joe Garner, who was Malcolm MacDonald's assistant private secretary, thought that 'Massey's interests were almost exclusively in foreign affairs.'[20] Feeling cut off from Canada and bitterly resentful of the treatment he received, Massey saw international developments through English eyes. Anglophilia temporarily triumphed over his Canadian nationalism. His diary provides an outline of the evolution of his views. At first foreign affairs is a thin stream meandering through the pleasant English meadows; by the fall of 1938 it has become an encompassing torrent.

In the twenties and thirties, foreign affairs had not been widely discussed in Canada. Mackenzie King was conscious that an open debate in the House of Commons on foreign policy would arouse strong and disparate opinions that would increase the danger of sectional disaffection. He was constantly steering between clear-cut attitudes, searching for a compromise that would be inoffensive and vague. There were three main attitudes that he had to take into consideration. The first was the least worthy of serious consideration, since it seemed now to belong to the past. It was an uncritical acceptance in Canada of British leadership in foreign affairs, often accompanied in the

United Kingdom by an assumption that greater experience and superior wisdom sanctified such leadership. The turning point had come in the summer of 1922 as a result of a diplomatic exchange between London and the dominions about what seemed like an imminent war between Britain and Turkey. The Turkish army, having defeated the Greeks, were threatening the town of Chanak, which was under international control and a key position in preserving the international status of the Dardanelles. Winston Churchill, then secretary of war in the Lloyd George coalition, drafted a telegram inviting the dominions to send troops. He invoked memories of past imperial sacrifices: 'Not only does the Freedom of the Straits for which such immense sacrifices were made in the war involve vital imperial and world wide interest, but we cannot forget that there are twenty thousand British and Anzac graves in the Gallipoli peninsula.'[21] A positive announcement in London about dominion participation was made before the dominion prime ministers had even received the telegram. (In the event the diplomatic initiative of the British commander at Chanak enabled Britain and Turkey to reach a peaceful compromise.) Coming in the first year of his long tenure as prime minister, the incident left a lasting impression on King. Despite official proclamations of complete equality between the dominions and the mother country, old imperial ideas, he believed, still lingered on and even dominated the mind of powerful figures like Winston Churchill.

The other two attitudes demanded more serious attention. They were widely held by influential spokesmen in the universities and public life, and they were both based on a recognition of complete Canadian autonomy. From this common basis they went on to reach sharply opposed conclusions. One was isolationist. Canada, an independent country, blessedly removed from the chaos of Europe but constantly tortured by her own difficulties in achieving unity and economic security, should turn inward and look to her own well-being. The other was aggressively internationalist. Autonomy, far from blessing self-absorption, carried with it an obligation to play an active part in the solution of international problems.

Vincent Massey's attitude in foreign affairs was often thought to be close to the first and widely discredited attitude. The *Canadian Forum*, in the issue of December 1935, greeted the announcement of his appointment as high commissioner with gloomy foreboding. 'The Canadian Government is going to be subjected to constant pressure from London during the next few years to get it committed to the support of British foreign policy; Mr. and Mrs. Massey may be predisposed to accept the British point of view already.' And Mackenzie King, in the comfort of his diary, would meditate sourly on Vincent's passion for aristocratic society. Massey's first London speech, King observed, had an 'imperialist ring' and displayed 'sycophancy to P. of W. etc.'[22] But these were only surface glints of Massey's anglophilia. Officially he was an autonomist and an internationalist.

At the Port Hope conference of 1933, which Massey had conceived as a forum for liberal ideas, the exposition of 'A Foreign Policy for Canada' had been given to P.E. Corbett, the dean of the Faculty of Law at McGill and a prominent member of the Canadian Institute of International Affairs. Corbett took a vigorous, uncompromising view. Canada, he argued, had done her best to undermine the authority of the League of Nations by attacking the concept of collective security as embodied in articles X and XVI of the covenant – the recognition of aggression and the steps to be taken to check it, economic and, if need be, military. 'Our moral and economic influence should always be aligned against aggression, and no alliance or sympathy, foreign or imperial, should detain us from condemning, in the proper place, acts or policies which all the world knows to be illegal and unjust.'[23] Massey's approach in 'Canada in the World' followed Corbett, but in a more measured and politic tone. 'Perhaps,' he wrote, 'we are learning to feel that peace can only be secured by our willingness to take risks.'[24] We must face the possibility of going to war to preserve peace. 'The application of Article XVI of the Covenant means the likelihood of war between the members of the League, of which Canada is one, and the recalcitrant state.'[25] Massey, much more than Corbett, places his internationalism in a Commonwealth context. Autonomy means a release into an adult world, not a reversion to adolescent self-absorption. 'We shall show our political maturity best by the active use of our new status rather than by any unreal fears that the status is in jeopardy.'[26] In the Commonwealth, Canada should not be content with a silent influence. 'She should formulate her views on foreign policy and convey them to the government of Great Britain.' He then adds, however, in the cautious style of his political master, a restrictive clause: 'in so far as it is appropriate to do so.'[27]

Both the isolationist and international points of view favoured disarmament. For the isolationist arms were unnecessary; for the internationalist, necessary only as a contribution to a League of Nations force. 'Negatively we prove our intelligent pacificism by our freedom from burdens of armaments,' wrote Corbett.[28] There was a widespread belief in the thirties that the unrestricted growth of private armament firms exacerbated nationalistic tendencies and was a principal cause of wars. In the last speech that Massey gave in Canada he called upon his country to support the League of Nations unreservedly and to 'put an end to the manufacture for private gains of weapons for the destruction of human beings.'[29] Massey was enunciating ideas that were widely held at the time. Blair Neatby reminds us of the popularity in the thirties of such books as *Merchants of Death: A Study of the International Armament Industry*.[30] Soon after Vincent arrived in London, he saw a performance of Robert Sherwood's *Idiot's Delight* – a passionately anti-war play which enjoyed great popularity. In an early scene a French radical socialist attacks the international armament manufacturer, who is a fellow-guest at an Italian hotel: 'he is a master of the one real League of Nations – the League of Schneider, Creusot, and Krupp, and Skoda, and Vickers and Dupont. The League of Death.'[31] When, in a later scene, Italian planes return from a bombing mission against France, the tycoon's mistress congratulates him warmly: 'all the great, wonderful death and destruction everywhere, and you promoted it.'[32] The play appealed to the widespread cynicism in Great Britain about the nature of nationalistic wars, which went hand in hand with a faith in the League of Nations as international arbiter. Such ideas were congenial to Massey, and formed the basis of his early stand on foreign issues.

Stanley Baldwin had succeeded Ramsay MacDonald as prime minister on 7 June 1935, and had overwhelmingly confirmed his mandate in the election of 14 November 1935. It was a National government in name but a Conservative government in fact. Baldwin, responding with characteristic skill to the mood of the country, had conducted the campaign on a platform of adherence to collective security through the League and a modest armament program. Hitler had become chancellor of Germany on 30 January 1933. But, as yet, the Nazi rise to power had not aroused deep apprehension. Anthony Eden, the young parliamentary under-secretary at the Foreign Office, had visited Hitler in February 1934, to discuss a proposed disarmament convention among the great powers. He reported that 'I find it hard to believe that the man himself wants war.'[33] Hitler had an uncanny skill in assuming the tone and in mimicking the key phrases of those whom he wanted to deceive. Some of his early speeches as chancellor sounded like extracts from a high-minded pacifist of the British Labour party. 'It is in the interests of all,' he declared in the Reichstag on 17 May 1933, 'that present-day problems should be solved in a reasonable and peaceful manner ... The application of violence of any kind in Europe could have no favorable effect upon the political and economic position ... The outbreak of such unlimited madness would necessarily cause the collapse of the present social and political order.'[34] The Anglo-German Naval agreement of 1935 seemed to give assurance that Britain could live with Hitler's Germany. Its main provision was that Germany would be permitted to build a navy 35 per cent as large as the British. The agreement was negotiated without consultation with France, which seemed at the time to be a stubborn impediment to any understanding with Germany.

The more immediate and disturbing problem in the autumn of 1935 was caused by the other dictator, who had launched his attack on Abyssinia. This immediately raised the question of League of Nations sanctions against a flagrant violation of the Covenant. After its strong endorsement of the League in the election of 14 November, the government suddenly reversed itself and proposed, in concert with France, to end the war by giving Italy the fertile plains of Ethiopia and providing Abyssinia, as compensation, with an outlet to the sea. This was the Hoare-Laval plan, worked out by Sir Samuel Hoare, the British foreign minister, and Pierre Laval, his French counterpart. The plan was bitterly attacked, and Sir Samuel Hoare, abandoned by the cabinet that had originally approved of his action, resigned. The high commissioners, Vincent reported, were 'all with the exception of Bruce disturbed over its terms and said so clearly.'[35] A few days later Alice and Vincent attended the Commons debate on the Hoare-

Laval plan. Vincent's theoretical disapproval was not strong enough to smother his sympathy and respect for an English statesman of the old gentlemanly school. Hoare's speech, he said, 'was a fine, dignified, magnanimous and moving effort.'[36]

For the next few months, the question of continuing and expanding sanctions against Italy dominated government discussions. Vincent, uninstructed from Ottawa, asserted his own autonomist, League-of-Nations stance. When Malcolm MacDonald asked if the dominions 'were ready for the more unpleasant implications of sanctions,' Vincent replied 'that such queries should come from Geneva rather than London having in mind a certain crisis in 1922.'[37] And when the new foreign minister, Anthony Eden, asked Vincent 'about possible military support to Great Britain in case of a mad-dog act by Mussolini,' Vincent reiterated his stand: 'necessity of approach from Geneva rather than London.'[38]

The question of sanctions became increasingly unreal as Mussolini's army, preceded by a pillar of poisonous gas, stepped up the speed of its advances and, with the fall of Addis Ababa on 5 May 1936, completed the conquest of the primitive and abandoned country. At the assembly of the League of Nations in September 1936, both sanctions and the League were piously interred. Vincent, who was a pallbearer at the funeral, may have reflected that from now on he was, in matters of foreign affairs, completely on his own, his modest edifice of international ideas shattered, the voice from Ottawa either inaudible or, briefly, shrill and admonitory. From now on he was, in matters of foreign affairs, a temporary Englishman with privileged access, on a high level, to news, gossip, and informed debate.

The Italian problem dominated the year 1936. Eden believed that, on a scale of deceit and moral ambition, Hitler ranked considerably below Mussolini. Hitler, after all, had some justice on his side: his country had been savagely dealt with by the allied victors, and he was now trying to restore its fortunes by following the sound Wilsonian doctrine of national self-determination. Besides, in his dealings with foreign statesmen, Hitler was persuasive and low-keyed, whereas Mussolini was an arrogant braggadocio. Hitler's first major move towards the reconstitution of Germany – the sending of troops into the demilitarized Rhineland on 7 March 1936 – did not elicit any sharp

British rebuke, although the move was in complete violation of international agreements. French fears of German aggrandizement were reawakened, and France was prepared to take action initially through the League of Nations. Hindsight observes sadly and knowingly that had Britain joined with France in a disciplinary action, Germany, still in the early stages of its rearmament program, might have quickly withdrawn, Hitler would have been declared a dangerous mountebank by the German army and removed from office, and Europe's story would have taken another, and possibly, happier course. But Eden's policy, supported by the cabinet, discouraged French action and sought to reach 'as far-reaching and enduring settlement as possible while Herr Hitler is still in the mood to do so.'[39] Vincent Massey warmly agreed. He had been a member of a week-end party at Lord Lothian's country home that had come to the same conclusions as Eden. A week later while attending as a spectator a special session of the council of the League of Nations at St James Palace, he criticized the French delegates for 'concentrating on the legalistic interpretations of the crisis in the traditionally Latin manner with no effort to conciliate German opinion.'[40]

Hitler's move into the Rhineland and the Italian conquest of Abyssinia aroused deep concern, but not the passionate division inspired by the Spanish Civil War, which broke out in July of 1936. To leftist thinkers, this was a clear-cut, ideological war between fascism and democracy. To the British government there were more important issues: first, the need to keep the Spanish war from expanding into a world war given German and Italian intervention on the side of General Franco, leader of the fascist insurgents, and Russian support of the loyalists; second, the possibility that the revolutionary radicalism of the loyalists might spread into France. The British government elected for non-intervention, and presided over a committee on which even Russia, Germany, and Italy sat with smug hypocrisy. To left-wing critics this was simply a polite, official way of making a Franco victory certain. Orwell, who fought for the loyalists in the field and in his books, wrote: 'By a combination of meanness and hypocrisy that would take a lot of beating, Chamberlain and his friends have allowed the Spanish Republic to be slowly strangled.'[41]

Massey left no record of his political attitude towards the Spanish war. After Franco's government had been recognized by Great Britain in February 1939, he became an admirer of the elegant Spanish ambassador, the Duke of Alba, a solid Franco supporter, but, according to Massey, a firm believer in the British cause who worked to maintain Franco's independence from his fascist allies. His only comment during the course of the civil war has an emotional tone that he rarely permits himself in his Diary. 'Got into a mental "tail-spin" over the international situation arising from the Spanish crisis. What can come of it but a general explosion. How wearing it is to be sitting all the time on a powder keg which someone is pushing steadily nearer the fire!'[42] It is reasonable to assume that Massey agreed with Anthony Eden, his *beau ideal* for his first three years in London, who was, according to Carlton, 'certainly more favourable to the Spanish [Republican] government than many of his colleagues.'[43] Perhaps some of Massey's left-wing liberal sentiments were aroused when his favourite niece, Alison Grant, took part in protest marches against British policy in Spain.

The year 1937 was happily free of external events that aroused wide public apprehension. At the beginning of the year Britain, relieved by the happy resolution of the Mrs Simpson affair, looked forward to the coronation of George VI. Until that event on 2 May and for several weeks afterwards, Vincent and Alice were joyfully absorbed in preparations and celebrations. Stanley Baldwin, having displayed in his handling of the royal crisis, so Vincent thought, the full range of his virtues – 'sanity, magnanimity, common sense, simplicity and honesty'[44] – retired as prime minister and was succeeded on 26 May by Neville Chamberlain. Baldwin had little aptitude for foreign affairs and had taken no initiative in this area. Chamberlain, although his interests lay primarily in domestic problems, had strong views about the conduct of foreign affairs. A conflict between him and Anthony Eden soon developed. The conflict arose in part, from the foreign secretary's resentment at incursions into his special field. But it went beyond this to a difference in methods of dealing with the dictators. Chamberlain believed that, by patient negotiation, specific differences between Britain and Italy and between Britain and Germany could be resolved. Eden was now pessimistic about both Italy and Germany. Germany had superseded Italy as the major threat.

Eden advocated an attitude of 'unheroic cunctation' variously described as 'supine delay,' and 'carping hesitation.'[45] 'We must keep Germany guessing as to our attitude. It is all we can do until we are strong enough to talk to Germany.'[46] The conflict finally led to Eden's resignation on 18 February 1938. Churchill saw Eden's action in a heroic light. 'He seemed to me at this moment to embody the life-blood of the British nation.'[47] Massey, recording his impressions of the House of Commons debate in the resignation, took a different view. Eden's resignation was 'a high-minded but rather quixotic act. Chamberlain's was the most effective speech of the three [Viscount Cranborne, the under-secretary of state for foreign affairs, resigned at the same time as his minister], badly delivered but to my mind more convincing than the other. It was clear that his mind and Eden's approach the subject of foreign affairs very differently.'[48]

From now on until the declaration of war Massey was firmly and unshakeably on the side of Chamberlain. Eden, for the most part, silent as a back-bencher, still exerted great influence as the unofficial head of a group of National government supporters, numbering some thirty, who were critical of the government's handling of foreign affairs. This group, along with a few more radical dissidents around Winston Churchill, brought increasing pressure on the government. Vincent's admiration for Eden suffered a brief eclipse. He listened sympathetically to R.A. Butler, under-secretary of state for foreign affairs, 1938–41, who thought that 'the disloyalty' towards the government with which the F.O. is seething was 'a legacy of the resignation of Anthony Eden.'[49]

The note of apprehension in Massey's comments on foreign affairs, briefly present when the Spanish Civil War was raging, now became more pronounced. After Hitler's occupation of Austria on 13 March 1938, he wrote, 'the whole world is now full of tension over the rape of Austria. For the first time since coming to London there is a note of very real apprehension everywhere.'[50] He terminated a brief late-summer holiday in France that year to return to London. On 14 September he heard that Chamberlain was flying the next day to Germany to see Hitler, and commented: 'a very brave thing to do.'[51] Throughout the next three weeks, during which Chamberlain met three times with Hitler, the last taking the form of a conference at Munich where he was joined by Daladier, the prime minister of France, and Mussolini, Massey was in favour of each successive concession to Hitler: 'so long as there is no real surrender of principle it is worth taking every sharp corner to get past this crisis and save civilization as we know it'[51] – a sentence that embodies the confusion and self-contradiction of the Munich spirit.

There exists a revealing photograph taken at the airport as Chamberlain is about to leave on his flight to Munich.[52] Chamberlain is by himself in the foreground, his homburg raised high above his head as if acknowledging the cheers of millions of unseen well wishers. Behind him is a first row of senior colleagues: Sir Kingsley Wood, secretary for air, Lord Hailsham, the lord chancellor, both short, stout, and benign, smiling broadly; then Sir John Simon, chancellor of the exchequer and Lord Halifax, the foreign secretary, towering above the first two, their smiles a little subdued. Behind them is a row of lesser cabinet lights: one of them, Duff Cooper, shortly to resign in protest against Chamberlain's policy, has lowered his head, as if he were attending the funeral of a colleague with whom he was only on moderately good terms. According to the caption, three high commissioners also saw the prime minister off. The only high commissioner in the portrait, however, is Vincent Massey, who stands beside Lord Halifax in the first row, homburg in one hand, rolled umbrella in the other, his expression sombre, as if he were uncertain of the real spirit of the event.

The euphoric relief at Chamberlain's apparent success in avoiding war was followed swiftly by a realization of the enormity of the concessions about the Sudetenland he had made and by a widening conviction that Hitler could neither be trusted or appeased. The House that had received his announcement of the Munich meeting, as if it were a divine intervention, quickly grew captious and critical. Vincent listened to the critical speeches with sullen impatience. 'Most of the speeches off the point – much talk about the wrongs at Czechoslovakia but little about the decisions which Chamberlain made and thereby saved the world from war which would have destroyed the Czechs and civilization as we know it.'[53] This attitude survived even the savage pogrom launched against the German Jews in November. He wrote to Maude Grant in an attempt to still her doubts about Chamberlain's policy. 'I am satisfied that the great bulk of the population here is behind Chamberlain, although their support is often a silent one. There is great moral indignation over the technique of Berlin, and that is natural. And there is widespread sympathy for those who have suffered from an inevitable alteration of boundaries in Central Europe. A capacity for moral indignation and chivalrous sympathy is probably the finest thing in the English character, but it is dangerous when unaccompanied by constructive thinking. When it takes the practical form of Mansion House Funds for Czech refugees it performs a meritorious service. When it results in a vague clamour for a preventive war which would have multiplied and intensified the sufferings of the Czechs a thousand times over in the process of destroying civilisation, it doesn't make sense.'[54]

Two weeks later, he wrote to Mackenzie King explaining that 'appeasement' is not 'a very happy choice of words, for what the Government here is endeavouring to do: ... real friendship between the Governments of the United Kingdom and Germany is hardly possible.' All we can hope for is 'an agreement based on self-interest ... Chamberlain will not be deflected from the course which he has set himself to obtain a European settlement.'[55] In March 1939 German troops occupied Prague and the dismemberment of Czechoslovakia followed. In a speech in Birmingham on 17 March Chamberlain repudiated the policy of appeasement; Hitler's bad faith had made a mockery of it. Massey agreed. 'Hitler's rape of Czechoslovakia ... has outraged opinion all over the world.'[56] Massey now approved of Chamberlain's new policy of resisting further German aggression by giving a guarantee to Poland, next on Hitler's timetable for absorption, and by even, although without enthusiasm, entertaining the possibility of a Russian alliance. Massey wrote on 16 May 1938: 'I continue to have great confidence in the policy of Chamberlain's Government, and if war can be averted the world's debt of gratitude will be chiefly to Great Britain.'[57] But by August it was clear that the price for peace was too high even for Chamberlain. The Nazi-Soviet pact of 23 August gave Hitler a free hand in eastern Europe. On 1 September Germany invaded Poland, and on 3 September, after the expiration of its ultimatum, Britain declared war on Germany.

'Appeasement' has now become a rhetorical term used to discredit or demean. It connotes a notable list of moral vices, including betrayal, hypocrisy, and self-deception. These connotations arose out of the bitter assessment of the significance of the Munich agreement. Yet the word, before then, had had an honourable history and had been used to describe a central British policy in foreign affairs that was widely respected and admired. In essence, it was a belief that through negotiation and concessions conducted in good faith two strong nations could maintain their security and guarantee the general peace. Gilbert Martin reminds us that 'every Prime Minister between the wars accepted this policy and pursued it. Appeasement was the cornerstone of inter-war foreign policy. For twenty years it dominated all arguments and blessed or bedevilled all policies. Lloyd George cautiously, Ramsay MacDonald enthusiastically, Stanley Baldwin doggedly and Neville Chamberlain defiantly pursued it throughout their premierships.'[58] As Gilbert's summary suggests, there was a gradual decline in the strength of the belief in appeasement. That decline followed a gradual waning of sympathy for Germany and of a trust in the good faith of her leaders. Even that decline, swift and shattering after Munich, did not altogether kill appeasement. If concessions to Germany meant a betrayal of allies and a surrender of principle, war with Germany meant a world war that would, in all likelihood, destroy all that was valuable in society. Vincent Massey was one of a group (not few in numbers or ill-informed) who clung most tenaciously to the concept of appeasement.

When Massey arrived in London in 1935, sympathy and respect for Germany had not yet been seriously lessened by the two years of Hitler's rule. Bloody internal purges in the Nazi party and Nazi complicity in the murder of the chancellor of Austria, Engelbert Dollfuss, had aroused disgust, but not yet apprehension of German imperial designs. Hitler could still effectively play upon the German sense of grievance at the harshness of the Versailles treaty. Here he could count upon the sympathy of liberal opinion in the west. At the Canadian Institute of International Affairs Vincent had heard much of the perfidy of the 'war guilt' clause in the treaty. It was not true, according to the new school of historians, to say that the war had been 'imposed' upon Britain and France 'by the aggression of Germany and her allies.' It was more accurately an accidental war, for which all nations must share the responsibility. In *The Economic Consequences of the Peace* (1919) John Maynard Keynes had attacked the stupidity of forcing Germany to pay vast reparations that would cripple her and undermine the world economy; and, in *Peacemaking*, published in the same year, Harold Nicolson, a young diplomat present at the making of the treaty, revealed the vindictiveness and shoddy haste that lay behind many of the allied proposals.

The harsh post-war policy towards Germany was pursued with peculiar vindictiveness by France, and it aroused anti-French feeling. Massey, as we have seen, shared this anti-French feeling, which made him sympathetic to Germany and, for some, helped to explain the rise of Nazism and, by implication, justify it. But his sympathy for Germany was political and had no deep personal roots. His European trips as a young man had rarely included Germany. During the pre-war years, he took frequent holidays in France, either in Paris or in country retreats, but avoided Germany. During these years his single visit to Germany in 1936 was an accidental part of an extended Scandinavian tour. 'The atmosphere is strangely different from the tranquillity and contentment of Scandinavia. Marching, counter-marching, restlessness and a feeling of self-consciousness everywhere.'[59] The only important German he knew was Joachim von Ribbentrop, who had arrived in London as ambassador in August 1936, although he had been known there for a year or so before as Hitler's itinerant propagandist and privileged messenger. Vincent reported shrewdly that 'he is very second rate – she I think genuine.'[60] Alice was more effusive about Frau von Ribbentrop. 'I had a most interesting talk with her. She adores the Fuhrer, and is most frank talking about him.'[61]

Von Ribbentrop had issued a general invitation to Massey to visit Hitler, and Massey clearly wanted to go. He would have followed a succession of British visitors to Hitler in 1936 and 1937 – setting out like pilgrims to visit an unorthodox monk in his mountain retreat, rumoured to use strange rites, but known to exercise a potent influence over his followers. The visitors had included Lord Lothian (making his second visit), the eminent historian Arnold Toynbee, Lloyd George, George Lansbury, former leader of the Labour party, and Lord Halifax. Despite the wide variety of political allegiance represented by this group, they were all favourably impressed by Hitler, convinced that he did not want war, and that Britain would find it possible to come to an amicable agreement with Germany. Lloyd George, grossly flattered by Hitler as Britain's great war leader, returned the compliment threefold. Hitler, he said, is 'the greatest German of the age.'[62]

Vincent's opportunity came when he had a long interview in June 1937 with Mackenzie King, just after the imperial conference. King announced that, at the invitation of von Ribbentrop, he was leaving immediately for Berlin where he would meet with Goering, von Neurath, the German foreign secretary, and Hitler. Vincent's request to go with him was brusquely brushed aside. This would be King's great day, and he alone would savour it. 'This,' he wrote in his diary, 'would seem to be the day for which I was born.'[63]

Of all the innocents abroad, King was the most innocent. Whereas his British predecessors had refrained from praising the Nazi regime, King sounded, in his summing up, like a disciple of Oswald Mosley. Hitler, he thought, was creating a new and virile nation. The opposition to Germany arose 'from position and privilege' in nations not yet touched by revolutionary fervour. 'It is impossible,' he concluded, 'to see the idealism that underlies efforts in the direction which they are being exerted and think that the German people are reverting back into any materialistic attitude towards life.'[64] As for Hitler, he was not merely a man capable of reasoned reflection: he became a liberal saint worthy of taking his place beside William Lyon Mackenzie, Laurier, and Gladstone.

My sizing up of the man as I sat and talked with him was that he is really one who truly loves his fellow-man, and his country, and would make any sacrifice for their good. That he believe himself to be a deliverer of his people from tyranny ... His face is much more prepossessing than his pictures could give the impression of. It is not that of a fiery, over-strained nature, but of a calm, passive man, deeply and thoughtfully in earnest ... There was a liquid quality about the eyes which indicates keen perception of profound sympathy ... He has a very nice, sweet and [words indecipherable] one could see, how particularly humble folk would come to have a profound love for the man ... as I talked with him I could not but think of Joan of Arc. He is distinctly mystic.[65]

To his credit, King did not raise with Hitler a common argument propounded by those who took a soft attitude towards the Nazi regime – that, whatever its brutalities, it was still a bastion against bolshevism (a point that Hitler regularly made to his British visitors, and doubtless made to King). Stanley Baldwin's statement before a parliamentary deputation is typical of the argument. Hitler 'has come out with it in his book, to move east, and if he should move east, I should not break my heart ... If there is any fighting in Europe to be done, I should like to see the Bolshies and the Nazis doing it.'[66]

Vincent Massey never used this argument to justify his support of appeasement. He was not susceptible to the anti-Russian phobia that was current especially among right-wing conservatives. He had visited Russia in the early twenties and may have retained some sympathy aroused at the time by the comparatively idealistic stage Russia had reached in the development of the communist state. He knew Ivan Maisky, the Russian ambassador in London since 1932, 'a scholarly little man, with a quiet, often humorous way,'[67] a respected and popular member of the diplomatic corps. But he visited the Russian embassy rarely, and in the summer of 1939 when conversations were proceeding languidly between the Russians and the British, he showed no enthusiasm for a positive outcome.

An influential figure for Massey in determining his attitude to Germany was Lord Lothian. He had known Lothian ever since he had edited the *Round Table*, which was launched in 1910 and became one of the young Massey's enthusiasms. The *Round Table* was a political journal that was the organ of the 'Milnerites,' the young men who had worked with Lord Milner to reconstitute South Africa as a part of the Empire after the Boer War. The *Round Table*, with its strong Empire orientation, saw events in an international context. Britain could not afford to concentrate on Europe; she must be sensitive to what happened in the middle and the far east. Her attitude towards a resurgent Germany must be influenced by her wide international commitments. Lothian thought that Germany had genuine grievances and that, if these grievances were satisfied, she would fit into the European balance of power. He made two visits to see Hitler, in January 1935 and in May 1937. From the first he returned with the conviction that there was 'no immediate prospect of war' and that 'a frank discussion between Germany and Great Britain could produce a political settlement';[68] after the second visit, he reported that the situation was 'both more dangerous and more soluble.'[69] When Vincent sent Lothian an academic document setting out the policy of encircling Germany by alliances, Lothian replied with heat:

These Professors who rely entirely on the written word and do not establish sufficient human contacts to realise that most men are human beings and not devils plotting war are really more dangerous than the gangsters themselves for the reason that they set out to build up a thesis that another nation cannot be trusted at all. So we have got to be wary. If we really accept the thesis that the Germans are entirely sui generis *and consist of nothing but Ludendorffs, the sooner we exterminate every German the better. The root of the present difficulty is that the Germans have got a case, but nobody is willing really to make the concessions necessary to meet their claims. They therefore take refuge in saying that every motion taken by a nation to equip itself to secure by* Machtpolitik *what it ought to be given by justice is evidence of the kind of infamy which is unknown among the self-righteous.*[70]

Lothian began to abandon his conciliatory position at the time of the Austrian *Anschluss* and he was strongly opposed to the Munich settlement. It is possible that Massey came to a despairing conclusion about Germany earlier than Lothian. He was, for instance, greatly impressed by a book written by an Australian professor, Stephen H. Roberts (later vice-chancellor of the University of Sydney), called *The House that Hitler Built*. Roberts did his best to find a few encouraging signs in Nazi Germany. There was 'a striking eagerness for friendship with Great Britain,'[71] and Hitler had an attractive poetic, dreaming side. But, in the end, Roberts came to believe in the inevitable drift to war, given the Nazi ideas and aspirations. He emphasized, in particular, the terrible unanimity on the Jewish question. Neville Chamberlain read the book early in 1938, and commented: 'if I accepted the author's conclusions, I should despair, but I don't and won't: never the bleak doctrine of inevitable war.'[72] The Masseys selected the book as their principal Christmas present to Canadian friends, especially to friends in positions of public responsibility. (Mackenzie King did not make the literary list; he was given cuff-links.) If, then, it is a fair assumption, that Vincent accepted Roberts' interpretation and conclusion, why did he cling to his appeasement ideas so stubbornly?

The short answer, as Massey's comments on Munich indicate, is that he believed that any settlement was preferable to war. It was better to be stoic than heroic. Throughout the thirties, statesmen representing a great variety of views sounded a doomsday note. Baldwin was an early prophet of world disaster. In a speech in the House of Commons in 1932 he predicted that the mastery of the air would mean in war-time the wiping out of European civilization.[73] Churchill's early campaign for rearmament was based on a conviction that this was the only way to preserve peace. He wrote to his wife on 8 March 1935, after an appeal to Baldwin and Chamberlain for action, that 'if the Great War ever resumed, – for that is what it would mean in two or three years' time or even earlier – it will be the end of the world.'[74] Chamberlain, in the debate on Eden's resignation, asked: 'are we to allow these two pairs of nations [France and Britain versus Germany and Italy] to go on glowering at one another across the frontier, allowing the feeling between the two sides to become more and more embittered, until at last the barriers are broken down and the conflict begins which many think would mark the end of civilisation?'[75] Imagination feeding on Mussolini's use of poison gas in Abyssinia and the bombing of Guernica during the Spanish war evoked a vision of annihilation in war that the nuclear age can now precisely document.

Massey's appeasement was less flamboyant and less persistent than that of his prime minister in Ottawa. The Munich settlement was for Mackenzie King an occasion for devout thanksgiving. The British high commissioner thus described the post-Munich celebration presided over by the prime minister:

The relief displayed by Mr. M.K. at the agreement reached at Munich was most marked. He rose from his sickbed on Friday, the 30th September, to pay a round of congratulatory calls on the representatives in Ottawa of the countries which had played a leading part in the negotiations preceding the agreement, though his visits failed to include one to this office. He also personally organized, on the afternoon of the same day, a ceremony at the Canadian War Memorial which is now nearing completion, when the figures of Peace and Freedom were placed in position by him in the presence of a small gathering of Cabinet Ministers, foreign representatives, the acting High Commissioner for the U.K. and officials. The P.M. stated publicly that he had arranged this ceremony in order to associate Canada in some degree with the rejoicing felt throughout Europe that war had been averted, and the cordiality with which he greeted at the ceremony the German Consul, who had just returned from Germany, was particularly marked. (I regret to have to report that in many quarters this whole proceeding was regarded as slightly ludicrous).[76]

The Massey celebration was of a less splendid nature. 'Lal and I, Tom Harvey and Hart who had come up from Oxford for a few days went to a joyously vulgar show at the Palladium to celebrate the new hope of peace. Afterwards L & I went to Westminster Abbey for a few minutes.'[77]

By early summer of 1939, Massey had abandoned all hope of a settlement with Germany. King never gave up hope until events shattered it. In his letter of 16 July 1939, Pearson wrote to Massey: 'Dr. Skelton tells me that King is not in sympathy with recent British policies, and prefers Chamberlain the appeaser to Chamberlain the avenger.' James Eayrs documents the last two intercessional messages that King despatched, the first on 25 August designed for Hitler but, at the suggestion of the German consul-general, sent to the president of Poland, and the second and last on 26 August sent to Chamberlain, with a suggestion that the king issue a statement 'in the interests of humanity as being above all nations,' and if need be, become the agents [he now added the queen] of appeasement.'[78]

Massey's views on appeasement were not, of course, enunciated formally in public speeches. They were private views confined to his diary, personal correspondence, and to conversations on relaxed, social occasions or in his meetings with fellow high commissioners. He encountered no strong opposition in Canada House or in the Dominions Office. Lester Pearson, who was responsible for the political despatches to Ottawa, had reservations about Munich and Massey's attitude. He wrote to Skelton early in 1939 about Massey's continued hope for a settlement with Germany. 'True, as Mr. Massey often tells me, there are seventy-five million decent Germans, who love peace and apparently revere Chamberlain. They may eventually, with the help of friendliness and restraint on our part, cast out their own evil spirits. That's a hope, I admit. But though I am on the side of the angels, in Germany the opposite spirits are hard at work, and I have a feeling they're going to do a lot of mischief before they are exorcised.'[79] In the Dominions Office Massey did not hear even this kind of worried doubt. Joe Garner writes that 'the settlement, distasteful as it was, was welcomed by the senior staff of the D.O. – as throughout the country as a whole – with all but unanimous relief.'[80] Massey's fellow high commissioners were solidly behind the Munich agreement (although the New Zealand government, as it had been on the question of sanctions, was opposed. Its high commissioner, however, did not register his opposition at the meetings of high commissioners.) At a meeting on 26 September 1938, even before Chamberlain had obtained some minor concessions, Stanley Bruce moved 'that the U.K. ought not to get involved in war on the present issue,' and all supported Bruce. At the meeting on 29 September all the commissioners agreed to take a firm line with Dr Benes, the Czechoslovakian president. 'Mr. Massey said that the latest expression of the Czech Government's objections confirmed the suspicion that the Czech government had, in fact, been adopting a deliberately dilatory policy.'[81]

Among his London friends Massey could not count on the comforting unanimity of the Dominions Office. Robin Barrington-Ward, who wrote many of *The Times* appeasement editorials, and Rab Butler, who spoke in the House for the government on foreign affairs, were strong allies, and helped to shape and strengthen Massey's views. But at least five of his friends, all formidable antagonists, were on the other side. Anthony Eden and Bobbety Cranborne were the leaders of the so-called 'glamour boys,' about thirty in number, who, since Eden's resignation, hovered menacingly on the flanks of the government. Brendan Bracken was a Churchill intimate who had faithfully supported Churchill throughout his bitter campaign against government inaction and indecision. Harold Macmillan and Harold Nicolson belonged to a group (dubbed 'the insurgents' by Chips Channon) that was closer to Churchill than to Eden.

Massey records only one exchange with an anti-appeaser. It was with Harold Nicolson, whom he greatly admired, and who later on was to write about Massey with warmth and understanding. They met at the entrance to their club the day after Chamberlain made his first flight to Germany. Massey gives this report: 'He said, "It's pretty gloomy, isn't it?" I agreed, but asked whether he was pessimistic about Chamberlain's visit to Hitler. He said "We'll have to pay too big a price to keep Hitler in check". He said "War". I said "I don't believe in preventive war". He spoke about the danger of letting the dictators get away with it. I countered by saying that it is one thing to give a man an inoculation against smallpox, even if you do make him temporarily ill, and quite another to expose him to smallpox in the hope that *if* he survives it will avoid his being equally ill later on *if* he should get the disease". Nicolson agreed and said that this was putting the other case rather forcibly.'[82] (Massey's metaphor is not transparently clear. I take it that 'inoculation' means British placation of an aggressive Germany and 'exposure to smallpox' means war.) Nicolson's version is briefer and quite different: 'Met Vincent Massey at the Club. I say, "Well, are the Government going to give way?" He says, "It is better to have smallpox three years from now than at once". I say "Yes, but if we have it now, we shall recover; if in three years, we shall die".'[83] At least, both men were convinced they had won the argument.

Had Massey been in Canada during the pre-Munich years, it is likely that his attitude would have been different. It would have been shaped by feeling comfortably removed from the probable scene of war and by the reflections of his friends with advanced liberal views. Writing as the Munich discussions began, Brooke Claxton expressed vigorous 'hawkish' views. 'At this distance, it looks as if there were at least ten occasions on which the British government could have put an end to this kind of thing by flatfootedly telling Hitler that he had to stop. That would have ensured peace, and so far as I can see, it was the only way to ensure peace. Now the policy of peace at any price is step by step strengthening Germany and destroying the unity and moral integrity of those who oppose her.'[84] Claxton went on, in a friendly, conciliatory way, to say 'I know that you do not go as far as that.' Massey did not reply; a reply would have unsettled Claxton's view of him as a left-wing liberal.

Massey's personal views on Munich did find their way back to Canada and exerted some influence on opinion, at least in southern Ontario. The intermediary was Floyd Chalmers, who had gone on an extensive European trip in the summer and early fall of 1938. In London he had seen a good deal of the Masseys and had discussed the international situation at great length. On his return to Toronto, he spoke at the Canadian Club to 'an overflow audience, the largest we have had at the club in six years.' 'I knew you would be interested in all this,' he wrote to Vincent, 'because it has been very much under your own inspiration and guidance that I have been able to coordinate the conflicting views I heard in the Old Country and weave them together to a positive pattern of interpretation.'[85] Chalmers thought that he had helped to arrest Canadian doubts about British policy at Munich.

Chalmers enclosed two news stories of his speech, one from the *Globe and Mail*, one from the *Evening Telegram*, and a long and enthusiastic editorial from the former paper. He had presented Munich as a triumph of a tough, realistic British policy that had forced Germany to back down. Moreover, Chamberlain's resolute leadership had had a popular response in Germany and had driven a wedge between the German people and their leaders. Britain had not let Czechoslovakia down. 'Czechoslovakia would have been the Flanders Field of any war fought to defend her, instead of being given the opportunity to become a peaceful and prosperous neutral State on the model of Switzerland.'[86] 'Mr. Chamberlain is being hailed as the new Pitt, the new Fox of European democracies. He is the spiritual field marshal of the army of moral forces now arrayed on the side of peace in Europe.'[87] But Munich was not, Chalmers concluded, a guarantee of peace. We must increase our armaments, and unite behind Britain; and the *Globe and Mail* editorial added some sharp criticisms of the slowness of the King government to increase armaments and their failure to give strong support to British policy.

Appeasement in action meant negotiations with Germany on international treaties, on, for instance, the status of German colonies surrendered to the allies and on the reconstitution of boundaries determined at Versailles. Discussion of internal affairs was avoided. The abandonment of democracy in many countries and the rise of a generation of dictators led by Stalin, Mussolini, and Hitler may have been deplored in Britain, but there was no disposition to question the legitimacy of anti-democratic governments. Indeed, at the beginning of the early thirties, when Stalin and Mussolini were the dominant dictators, they were praised from both the left and the right. In the preface to *Too True to be Good* (written in 1931), George Bernard Shaw wrote: 'Stalin and Mussolini are the most responsible statesmen in Europe because they have no hold on their places except their efficiency; and their authority is consequently greater than that of any of the monarchs, presidents, and prime ministers who have to deal with them.'[88] Two years later, in the Preface to *On the Rocks*, he referred to the 'dictatorships which are springing up all over the world as our pseudo-democratic parliamentary institutions reduce themselves more and more disastrously to absurdity.'[89]

But the close association of dictatorship and anti-semitism in Germany introduced a factor that was more difficult for well-wishers to absorb. Still, in the early years of Nazism, its anti-semitism was played down or ignored, certainly in official comment. None of the visitors to Hitler from 1935 to 1937 seem to have raised the issue. Some of them no doubt sympathized with Nazi anti-semitism, which, like their own, often arose from resentment at the great success of Jews in the intellectual and cultural life. (Roberts in *The House that Hitler Built* pointed out that, although the Jews in Germany were a small minority of less than one per cent of the total population, they provided 50 per cent of the lawyers, 48 per cent of the doctors, and 30 per cent of the professors. Twenty-three of twenty-nine theatre managers were Jewish, and Jews were dominant in the press.[90]) Others thought that official anti-semitism was a rank, early growth that would wither away. 'The extirpation of the Jew as such,' wrote Shaw in 1933, 'figured for a few mad moments in the program of the Nazi party in Germany.'[91]

Two other views, held by some appeasers, were inspired by what were considered realistic perceptions of the political situation. One was enunciated by Walter Lippmann, who wrote a column in the New York *Herald Tribune*, widely read and influential on both sides of the Atlantic. He was a frequent visitor to London, where his informants included Vincent Massey, whose work as Canadian minister in Washington he had greatly admired. Lippmann, from a wealthy German

Jewish family, believed that Jews should actively seek for assimilation into the countries of their adoption. He wrote about anti-semitism in Germany with a cool disinterestedness. Persecution of the Jews, he explained in a 1933 column, helped to keep the Nazis in check. 'By satisfying the lust of the Nazis who feel they must conquer somebody and the cupidity of those Nazis who want jobs, [repression of the Jews] is a kind of lightning rod which protects Europe.'[92] Vincent had encountered this surprising idea in a comment by a University of Toronto undergraduate during a Hart House discussion in October 1933. Obviously paraphrasing the Lippmann comment that had appeared shortly before, the undergraduate said 'that the Jews were performing a service in directing Hitler's attention from extensive aggression.' Massey quoted with approval the reply of Rabbi Eisendrath, the eloquent and influential rabbi at Holy Blossom Synagogue in Toronto, the Canadian home of reformed Jewry: 'It's noble to die a martyr's death for a cause; it is not a noble thing to be killed for the shape of one's nose.'[93]

Massey never expressed, or endorsed, Lippmann's point of view. But a second point of view, that strong external protests against Nazi treatment of the Jews were making it more difficult to negotiate with Hitler, seemed to Massey to be more realistic, certainly less unctuously hypocritical than the first point of view. In 1936 Lord Lothian expressed this second point of view with a degree of sober restraint. 'I believe,' he wrote to H.G. Wells, 'that Germany would now be willing to come to terms with the Jews if the external pressure and denunciation were relaxed.'[94] But by 1938 the statement of the point of view had taken on an hysterical edge, as Nazi anti-semitism became more brutal and more open, and as determined appeasers feared the breakdown of negotiations and a rapid decline into war. Lord Astor's comments had a blunt anti-semitic bias. 'The attack on appeasement,' he wrote, 'is largely due to intensive and widespread anti-German propaganda being conducted by Jews and Communists. Newspapers are influenced by those firms which advertise so largely in the press and are frequently under Jewish control.'[95] Massey's comments are more balanced and compassionate but make the same point. He wrote to Mackenzie King: 'Everyone who believes that a war is inevitable and says so or acts as if it were, makes Chamberlain's policy so much more difficult and makes war more likely. Jewish opinion is not helpful.

The Jew, to-day, not unnaturally, feels very passionately about the sufferings of his own race in Nazi Germany and regards any agreement with Hitler as unthinkable. This keeps him from sympathising with Chamberlain's effort to arrive at a constructive peace, and Jewish influence is now noticeable in certain sections of the press and in various other ways.'[96] In short, sympathy for the Jews, natural and justified, must not be permitted to interfere with the pursuit of peace.

After Munich, British response to Hitler's anti-semitism became a question of deeds, not words. Hitler's triumph at the negotiation table was followed almost immediately by a campaign against the Jews, sweeping in its extent, and brutal in its implementation, even by previous Nazi standards. The Jews in Germany, in newly annexed Austria, and in doomed Czechoslovakia sensed that the prison doors of Europe were about to close upon them. Ever since Hitler came to power there had been considerable movement of Jews to other countries, particularly to the USA, Britain, and Palestine. But the outbreak of war would make movement difficult, if not impossible. Even without war, it was doubtful whether hospitable countries would continue to welcome more Jewish immigrants. Already, the one country where the Jews had been assured of a safe haven was in doubt. A British White Paper on Palestine, issued in May 1939, restricted future Jewish immigration to 10,000 a year for the next five years. What about countries that had not responded – European colonies (especially Africa, as Walter Lippmann urged) and the British dominions, sparsely settled by European standards, with vast stretches of unused land? Canada, for one, replied categorically in the negative.

The Canadian response was led by Charles Blair, director of the immigration branch of the Department of Mines and Resources, whose minister, Thomas Crerar, viewed immigration as a minor responsibility to be left to the director. Blair was an inflexible bureaucrat who took satisfaction in the strict application of the Canadian immigration laws by which Jews had a low priority. Moreover, admission was contingent on demonstrating willingness to go on the land and an aptitude for farming, and Blair believed that Jews were essentially city people. That provision was especially important in the thirties with high unemployment in the cities. A powerful reinforcement for Blair's stand was the general French-Canadian suspicion of Jews, enemies, it was believed, to their religious faith, and supporters of revolutionary political causes – an attitude that was powerfully presented by the senior cabinet minister from Quebec, Ernest Lapointe. Arching over all these factors was a general feeling that Jewish immigration would intensify existing anti-semitism, in itself a hypocritical form of anti-semitism. Irving Abella and Harold Troper, in their corrosive account of Canadian policy with respect to Jewish immigration from 1933 to 1948, conclude that by 1939 'an unofficial, unholy triumvirate had been forged with the Immigration Branch, the cabinet, and, to a lesser degree, the Department of External Affairs opposing the admission to Canada of refugees in general and Jewish refugees in particular.'[97]

It would have taken a man in London who was both incautious and heroic to go counter to this formidable and dedicated bureaucracy. Vincent Massey was not such a man. In a letter to Mackenzie King, he expressed sympathy with the Jewish plight and advocated a common solution. 'Debates and discussions on foreign policy during the last week or so have been dominated by the repercussions of the anti-Jew outbreak in Germany. I wish that energies could be directed more successfully to the task of finding new homes for the unfortunate German Jews and less to the rather futile business of expressing moral indignation at public meetings. When feelings on this subject are expressed in words rather than deeds it makes possible rather an easy rejoinder from the Nazis. But where are the Jews to go? In most countries – our own included – I should think too many Jews would create an anti-Semitic movement. Probably settlement in French and British colonies would represent the most that can be done, and that cannot be very extensive.'[98]

On Canada's role, he advocated a policy that would show generosity to the refugees, but at the expense of the Jews. It was in brief: admit 3,000 Sudeten Germans, which 'put us in a much stronger position in relation to later appeals from and on behalf of non-Aryans.'[99] Massey followed this telegram with a lengthy explanatory letter to King:

What I want to mention, however, are the two major refugee problems: –
a) non-Jewish Sudeten Germans
b) German Jews from the greater German Reich.
I ventured to send a cablegram a few days ago suggesting that if Canada

could make a gesture in declaring her willingness to receive an appropriate number of refugees in the former category – Sudeten Germans – we should be in a better position with regard to the far more difficult problem presented by Jewish émigrés. A number of those who have been forced to leave Sudetenland and are now in Czechoslovakia would qualify for admission to Canada in the ordinary course. That is to say they are experienced agriculturalists, and if they could bring the requisite amount of capital which can possibly be provided from some of the funds which have been raised for relief purposes, they would come within the four corners of our existing Immigration Regulations and the Colonisation Departments of the two Railways could take charge of their settlement next year.

The Jewish problem, of course, bristles with difficulties. There are, I gather, very few Jewish refugees who have been following agricultural pursuits and they would naturally swell the already substantial Jewish population of our larger cities, with the inevitable risks of an anti-Semitic feeling developing.

I don't know the view you will take on this problem, but it did occur to me that it would be easier to refuse to make a substantial increase in our admissions of Jewish immigrants if we had made what contribution we could to the problem of placing the political refugees from the Sudeten area.[100]

When he wrote this nine months before war broke out, Massey, like most observers in the west, was not yet aware of the enormity of the Nazi policy towards the Jews. Certainly his attitude was not shaped by anti-semitic views. He had been brought up, it is true, in a society that accepted anti-semitism as an undeclared assumption, rarely, however, given an explicit public statement. In his own personal relations, however, he demonstrated an independence of the society in which he had been reared. He was attracted to intellectuals and artists, and a high proportion of these in any western country were Jews. In Washington the Americans he admired most were Jews – Walter Lippmann (who was, however, accused of being anti-semitic), Felix Frankfurter, and Louis Brandeis. No group was closer to him and Alice than the Hart House Quartet, and, at any stage in its long existence, the majority of its members were Jews. In London, he had actively supported Lionel Gelber, a young Jewish Rhodes scholar from Toronto, who was having difficulty in obtaining a Canadian appointment. In the correspondence Massey vigorously confronted Canadian anti-semitism. In a letter of support to the federal minister of labour, Norman Rogers, he wrote: 'Gelber is a Jew, and no doubt anti-semitic prejudice has been one of the factors responsible for his failure to find an opening but he is far too generous to admit this, which makes me all the more anxious to help him.' Close friends in Canada – George Wrong, Sir Robert Falconer, B.K. Sandwell – all protested against harsh Canadian restrictions on Jewish immigration, and, had he remained in Canada, it would be difficult to think of him as remaining aloof from such a protest.

But in London, in the pre-war years, the Jewish problems seemed remote compared to the imminent threat to his beloved England; and in the upper-class society he frequented he was not likely to hear impassioned protests against Nazi anti-semitism. Before the war, he submitted passively to the King-Blair-Lapointe policy of obstruction. After war was declared, and most of Europe became a heavily guarded prison camp, it was too late to arrest the Nazi savagery.

CHAPTER FOUR

The Masseys Go to War

Vincent and Alice Massey were in London throughout the entire war. Vincent was indignant when, during a period of heavy bombing, a story appeared in the Canadian press that the Masseys had left the city to take up residence in a country house. He cabled immediately to Maude Grant: 'Please cable collect when and where did press report appear of our having taken country home which is not true.'[1] He and Alice spent week-ends and occasional holiday breaks at Garnons, the convalescent hospital for Canadian officers near Hereford that they had founded, which was within two hours' drive from London, yet remote from the battle. But the city was their home, and they were proud to be known as Londoners.

With the concentration in London of the major government departments and military headquarters and of an ever-growing number of allied governments in exile, and with the ceaseless ebb and flow of troops from a dozen countries, the city was the forward command post of the war. For two extended periods it was in the front line of battle. The first was a period of eight months, from early September 1940 until mid-May 1941, the period of mass bomber attacks by night, of raging fires, endless devastation, and heavy casualties. The second period lasted eleven months, from mid-June 1944 until April 1945, the period of the V–1s or pilotless planes and the V–2s or rockets. During the first period, known as the blitz, London was the front line. In the preceding weeks the line had been in southern England, where the objective of the Luftwaffe had been to destroy the RAF and its airfields. Now, it moved north to the capital, where the objective was to devastate London and to kill the civilian will to resist an imminent German landing. Elizabeth Bowen recalled how 'that autumn of 1940 was to appear, by two autumns later, apocryphal, more far away than peace. No planetary round was to bring again that particular conjunction of life and death; that particular psychic London was to be gone forever, more bombs would fall, but not on the death city.'[2] It was a city of omnipresent death. 'The dead, uncounted, continued to move in shoals through the city day, pervading everything to be seen or heard or felt in their torn-off senses, drawing on this tomorrow they had expected – for death cannot be so sudden.'[3]

Initially, the blitz had been concentrated in the east end of London and the houses of the working class had suffered most. This was, in part, inevitable, since the houses were near obvious bombing objectives – docks and warehouses. But concentration on working-class districts was also a deliberate policy, one that was followed with grim alacrity by the allies; it was thought, mistakenly by both the Germans and the allies, that such a policy would be most shattering to morale. Soon, however, the German attacks moved westward, and the long list of devastated buildings began to include historic churches, public buildings, hotels, popular west-end restaurants, and night clubs. When the war had begun in earnest on 10 May 1940, with the German invasion of Holland and Belgium, the Masseys had abandoned their imposing house at 12 Hyde Park Gardens and moved to rooms in the Dorchester Hotel. (The Hyde Park residence became a supply headquarters for the various hostels and service clubs that came under Massey supervision.) The Dorchester, astride Park Lane, with Hyde Park on the west and Mayfair on the east, combined solidity with a sober air of affluence. A modest oval reception hall opened into a long, narrow lounge, with a marble floor, classical pillars decorated in gilt, the whole suggestive of the senate chamber of imperial Rome. The Dorchester had attracted diplomats, like the Masseys, cabinet ministers, affluent aristocrats, and distinguished visitors. It had the inducement of a private air-raid shelter in its deep and heavily reinforced basement. A short distance away, people from the bombed-out areas spent night after night stretched out in closely packed rows on the platform of tube stations. At the Dorchester, a night in its air-raid shelter was, Massey observed, 'rather like a fantastic fancy-dress ball organized by some eccentric hostess.'[4] One evening he recognized among his fellow refugees Lady Halifax, Lady Oliphant, Richard Tauber, Diana Duff Cooper, and André Maurois.

The residents of the Dorchester were not exposed to the full rigours of the blitz. Charles Ritchie, Vincent's secretary and a brilliant diarist, described the Dorchester as being 'like a luxury liner on which remnants of London society have embarked in the midst of the storm.'[5] But even luxury liners hit icebergs, and bombs fall without discrimination on the rich and the poor. The Dorchester did not, however, suffer a direct hit. But there were, certainly for Alice, 'terrible nights,' as she recalled later, 'when the lights went off and the whole place shook,'[6] and she was sure that disaster was imminent.

For everybody in London, there was always the continuous ordeal of sleeplessness at a time when the days demanded steady nerves and quick responses. Hyde Park was a natural concentration point for anti-aircraft guns and there was a battery a few hundred yards from the windows of the Massey rooms. 'We have acquired the habit,' wrote Vincent, 'of sleeping on the floor on mattresses in our little entrance hall to get away from windows and escape both noise and the danger of shrapnel.'[7]

The Masseys themselves escaped any of the brutal blows of the blitz. Others close to them were not so fortunate. Alice's sister, Grace Wimperis and her husband, Harry, a scientist retired from a senior position in the air ministry, were bombed out of their London flat. Charles Ritchie, on an overnight trip with Vincent to visit Canadian troops at Aldershot, returned to find his flat a heap of rubble, and was given 'snug safety' in the Dorchester by his chief. Every heavy air raid brought news of death and injury among the staff of Canada House or of the various services in the city.

In the midst of death and destruction, the air raids could bring a sense of exultation. A cool observer might distance himself from the event, and see it as a great apocalyptic display. Thus Evelyn Waugh described a night bombing in London: 'The sky over London was glorious, ochre and madder, as though a dozen tropic suns were simultaneously setting around the horizon; everywhere the searchlights clustered and hovered, then swept apart; here and there pitchy clouds drifted and billowed; now and then a huge flash momentarily froze the serene fireside glow. Everywhere the shells sparkled like Christmas baubles.'[8] In his diary Massey records from time to time visits to bombed-out areas but is sparing of descriptive detail and laconic in his expression of emotion: 'It was a disturbing picture of destruction. I went to bed feeling oppressed by it all.'[9] 'A grisly scene of destruction on all sides with fires blazing in every direction.'[10] He reserves his most extended entries for panoramic views of the night raids from an observation point on the roof of the Dorchester. He is like a journalist determined at great risk to give his readers a first-hand account of a natural disaster: 'Up on the hotel roof during an air-raid in the morning – this time was fortunate in seeing some real drama. For a time all was quiet with the occasional drone of planes in the fleecy clouds which dotted the sky. Then we saw a succession of bombs dropped along the river bank across from Battersea – then individual planes appeared in the sky above us – very high and in a moment we saw a fighter (I'm sorry to say, as we heard later, was one of ours) drop like a stone to the ground across the park (the pilot I'm glad to say had baled out). Then a German bomber circled down in flame, its wings and tail shot off and coming separately, incredible things to be seeing over Hyde Park on a quiet Sunday morning.'[11]

If Massey's sense of the sublime and the picturesque was aroused by the air raids, it was also dampened by their destructiveness. When one night of a heavy raid Hart and Charles Ritchie made their way to the Dorchester through the din of the anti-aircraft guns, the rattle of the flack, and the scream and thud of bombs, Vincent upbraided them for their chattering excitement. 'You seem to be pleased at what is happening,' he said, 'I do not understand you. The places that are being destroyed are irreplaceable – to me it is like a personal loss.'[12] In the meetings of high commissioners Massey expressed concern about the destruction of works of art and important records during the blitz, and was indignant when he saw valuable paintings still hanging in London homes and public records not yet removed for safekeeping. He thought priority should be given to cleaning up bomb-damage sites since they had a depressing psychological effect.[13] Bill Jordan, the New Zealand high commissioner, a hearty man of the people, an ex-London policeman who persisted in his cockney speech and tastes, was irritated by Massey's emphasis on problems of morale and the preservation of works of art and scholarship, and, like Hotspur on the battlefield upbraiding the delicate lord who came to demand his prisoners, protested indignantly against what he took to be Massey's indifference to human misery.

When the V–1s and V–2s arrived, the end of the war was in sight. The allies were moving out of their bridgeheads in France and the Russians had turned a stubborn defence into a triumphant pursuit. An attack on London was now an act of desperation, the offspring of an illusion in Hitler's mind that secret weapons could miraculously turn defeat into victory. And yet, as Winston Churchill wrote, 'This new form of attack imposed upon the people of London a burden perhaps even heavier than the air-raids of 1940 and 1941. Suspense and strain were more prolonged.'[14] In the midst of the V–1 attacks, Alice wrote to Maude, 'I don't think I have ever longed for the "all clear" more than I do now.'[15] Although Canada House was close to a 'doodlebug alley' and had several near-misses, Vincent did not dwell on the attacks. But he sensed, along with others, the significance of the V–2s for future warfare. 'The present use of rockets by the Germans,' he wrote to Norman Robertson, 'apparently represents only the preliminary experimental stage in the development of a weapon which may become a major instrument of aggression.'[16] Germany, having driven out her best scientists, was far behind in the nuclear race, but she had taken the lead in devising the technology of long-range delivery of explosives. The V–2s came with incredible swiftness, carried a heavy weight of explosives, and confounded any defence. They were messengers of a nuclear doomsday.

By reason of their good fortune, the special privileges conferred on diplomats, and their own courageous and imperturbable attitude, the Masseys endured the attacks on London and, at times, were even stimulated by them. But there was another testing of a more grievous kind. Like thousands of other Londoners, they had members of the family serving abroad; and the news from abroad during the first two years of the war was, with a few exceptions, unrelievedly bad – a series of defeats and evacuations – France in May 1940, Norway in June 1940, Greece in April 1941, Crete in June 1941.

The war had begun for Vincent and Alice on 2 September 1939, a day before the official declaration, when Vincent accompanied Lionel to the War Office to complete the technicalities for his obtaining a commission in the British army. (The stern, competitive attitude towards commissions had not yet arrived.) Vincent heard with dismay that Lionel's regiment, the King's Royal Rifle Corps, might be going abroad very soon, in all likelihood, to the middle east. Although he was relieved to hear that training in England would take five or six months, he 'couldn't help being terribly depressed by all that it means.'[17] Lionel left England on 10 November 1940. He had spent his last leave with his parents, during which Vincent had bought him an advance birthday present – a landscape by the English painter Tristram Hiller that Lionel had greatly admired. (Painting had become a major interest to Lionel, and he had begun a collection of contemporary artists and of books on art.) Vincent and Alice were proud of his success with the regiment, whose officers, from the commanding officer down, were mainly permanent force. He was now adjutant, with his captaincy in the offing. 'A great achievement for a young amateur from Canada of 24 years,'[18] Vincent observed. On the day of his embarkation, Vincent and Alice telephoned him. It was 'agonizing to us both – knowing we wouldn't see him before he sailed nor hear his voice for so long.'[19]

Vincent and Alice did not hear about Lionel's whereabouts until 15 April 1941. Sir John Dill, chief of the Imperial General Staff, who had just returned from Cairo, reported that Lionel's unit was in Greece. This was bad news. The sending of British troops to Greece had been a political act, undertaken in the full knowledge of its hazardous nature. As long as Greece had to contend with the Italians, there was no great military threat. The Italian army, deaf to Mussolini's rhetoric of imperial invincibility, had crumbled in Africa and was making no headway against Greece. But early in April the Germans took over the subjection of the Balkans; they moved south, crushing Yugoslavia savagely, and overwhelming the Greek defences in the north. The campaign for the British became a retreat towards embarkation points in the south, constantly harassed by German dive-bombers, who had complete control of the skies.

The Easter holiday in mid-April 1941 'was overhung with a black cloud of anxiety both personal as well as general.'[20] In Libya the Germans under their new commander, Rommel, had taken over from the hapless Italians and had driven the British back. On the night of 16 April, there was a particularly devastating air raid that destroyed many public buildings, including the Victoria League Hostel, where there were several Canadian casualties. But, above all, was the bad news from Greece. At Garnons, where Vincent and Alice went for a short break, they thought of 'nothing else than the desperate fight Lionel's battalion was having in Greece.'[21] Alice did some desultory fishing in the River Wye. Vincent, no fisherman, stayed with her, and they had a desolate lunch, by the beautiful river now aglow with spring 'resurrection fever.'[22]

It was a month before they got final word. On 23 April came an enigmatic telegram – 'would love to buy a Rouault if there is a good one' – from which Vincent and Alice extracted the comforting message that 'all is quiet and Lionel is safe and evacuated.' Definite word came on 12 May. Lionel was wounded and in German hands. Some details came on 16 May when they went to have lunch with Queen Mary in Badminton and were met at the door by her secretary with a telegram telephoned from London. Lionel had been wounded in the leg and was in hospital in France. He had actually been wounded severely in both legs, and, in the hospital and later in German prison camps, this was to require a series of operations.

Subsequently, it was learned that Lionel had taken over command of the battalion from the commanding officer, who had collapsed under pressure. Later on Anthony Eden sent the Masseys a first-hand account of the action that he had received from one of Lionel's fellow-officers. He wrote: 'We lost Lionel Massey in Greece. I think he is alive all right, in the hospital which was left in Athens. Never has any man shouldered more responsibility, acquitted himself better and remained more calm and bright than he did in the critical days of the Florina Gap battle.'[23]

Lionel returned to Britain on 27 May 1944 as one of a group of exchange prisoners, after a long and circuitous trip, from his prison camp in Bavaria to Berlin, then by train to Marseilles – three and a half days sitting up on bare benches – from Marseilles to Barcelona, then to Algiers, and finally by boat to Belfast. Vincent went to Belfast to meet the ship, and the family reunion – Hart had 48 hours compassionate leave – took place in London on 30 May. In a long, exulting letter to Maude, Alice gave an account of the meeting in Belfast where the governor of Northern Ireland gave a dinner to Vincent and his son:

They were all sitting talking in the drawing room when this charming man burst open the doorway, not saying anything to H.E., or apologizing, and just shouted at the top of his voice, in true naval fashion, 'Lionel, your mother is on the telephone!' At my end, the telephone bell rang and the first thing I heard was; 'It is the censor – be careful what you say.' Then a voice said, 'This is the private secretary of the Governor of Northern Ireland speaking, is that Mrs. Massey,' and then the next thing I heard was, 'Hello, Mom.'

He really is in grand form, although pretty lame, but that we all think can be cured ... His face, of course, is thinner, but he is just the same dear old Lionel, with no mental wounds from his prison life – in fact, this is extraordinary – I don't quite know how to explain it – perhaps the best way to say it is spiritual and intellectual growth, and, as usual, always thinking of others. I don't think there is a mother, wife, or sweetheart, whose belongings he knew in the camp, that has not had a telephone message, a telegram, or a letter, or a long talk with him about their own men.[24]

Lionel spent a recuperation period in the Canadian hospital at Basingstoke, then, to ease his way back into 'a normal life,' lived for a few months in a furnished cottage in Dorset, where a 'coloured maid ... valeted him with immense care and pride.'

Within a few months, Vincent and Alice faced another crisis, this time with the second member of the family on active service – Hart. Hart, too, had been given a commission shortly after the outbreak of the war, as a pilot officer in the RCAF. The skill and determination he had recently demonstrated as cox of the Oxford crew no doubt helped to win him acceptance in the services, and the same skill and determination, along with a keen mind and a cool, relaxed attitude towards his physical shortcomings rapidly assured him success in his new career. As talk of a second front in France grew, Hart became increasingly excited by the role his squadron would play. He commented ruefully to his father that he 'would be in rather a fix if he had to jump off a landing craft into six feet of water.'[25] But then, in serious vein, he would describe how his size could be a great boon in emergencies, when, for instance, a crippled returning aircraft crashed: 'it is a queer feeling when you see a machine all smashed upon the ground, when you feel and know that there is something warm inside, and you say to yourself "How can I go to it, what will I find," and then you forget everything in your effort to get out what is inside, and then when you find a human being is alive and alright you can't imagine what it feels like.'[26]

He served, initially, as intelligence officer of a squadron, and his only concern was that he was 'threatened' with a promotion that would take him away from close association with a combat unit. He avoided this undesired recognition, and went to France in the fall of 1944 in his original capacity, with wider responsibilities. On 2 January 1945, late in the evening, Vincent received a telephone call from Air Chief Marshal Breadner that Hart had been seriously injured in a New Year's air raid on his airfield.

The air raid was the last phase of the final German offensive on the western front, an attempt to repeat the breakthrough of May 1940. For a few days it achieved great success, particularly disquieting at a time when the allied armies were poised for a sweep into Germany. But the offensive was contained, and by New Year's day had lost its momentum. The air raid was a 'violent low-level surprise attack on all our forward airfields. Our losses were heavy.'[27] Hart was at an advanced airfield in Holland, near Tilburg, and the casualties on the ground were numerous and severe. Vincent got an account of how Hart was wounded: 'Hart apparently was standing in the door of his hut when he was hit, and walked about for an hour afterwards refusing to have anything done for him and insisting on helping to look after the other casualties. He crawled back into bed and was discovered some time afterwards having lost a frightening amount of blood, and was placed among other casualties in the first-aid post in the airfield. When Johnson [Major Johnson, army liaison officer working with Hart] and the M.D. came to him, the latter said: "I can't do anything for him, he's too far gone. I must look after the others." Johnson said "That's the High Commissioner's son and I am a friend of the High Commissioner" (which as he said was a reasonable fiction at the moment) and we must do what we can for him. So he was permitted to take Hart to the hospital in his car, the ambulance being fully occupied. He was in a very dangerous state of shock which alarmed the doctors considerably. Transfusions and other means brought him round, however, after a few hours. He was flown back to England, where he was operated on immediately. The metal fragments which had penetrated his head were removed, and the haemorrhage which was feared would take place was overcome by the use of some wonderful new substance which serves as an astringent.'[28]

Hart recovered rapidly, and the injury left behind no permanent impairment. Parental pride in their younger son redoubled. Alice wrote to Maude about a tribute to Hart from Sir Arthur Salter, Oxford professor and senior civil servant: 'He felt Hart was one of the great heroes of modern times, having conquered all that he has conquered, with all his disabilities,' a judgment that Alice accepted with a motherly qualification: 'As a mater of fact, I never think of anything in connection with Hart as a disability – he so superbly rises above everything.'[29]

Two of Maude's children were in London during the war. Alison had come in 1936 and remained throughout the war. Vincent and Alice were devoted to her, as she was to them. In a letter to Uncle Vincent she recited her shining list of indebtedness: 'You have given me presents, sent me on holidays, lent a patient ear to endless problems, enthusiasms, and gossip (very dull), provided a background to me in London.' 'Background' was accurate. Alison was not part of the official entourage and affection for her aunt and uncle did not dampen her talent for cool appraisal. For a short time, at the beginning of the war, she was with an ambulance unit, then worked briefly at the Beaver Club, the centre for Canadian soldiers, and, for the rest of the war, at the War Office. On 3 December 1941, Vincent wrote to Maude: 'We see Alison every few days and always enjoy a glimpse of her. She is very modest about her work at the War Office, but putting two and two together it is quite clear that her work is growing rapidly in importance and that they regard it highly.'

George Grant, the youngest of Maude's children, had been chosen an Ontario Rhodes scholar at the end of his undergraduate course and set out (apprehensively) for Oxford in September of 1939. His mother wrote to Alice, 'he has been through a most difficult and heartbreaking time – the impact of the war on him has been dreadfully hard.'[30] In the spring of 1940, George, who was a conscientious objector, left Oxford and throughout the blitz served as air warden in the most devastated areas in the east of London. Alice gives a vivid discussion of George's war experience in this letter to her children's 'nannie.'

I want to tell you about George Grant. I simply cannot tell you what that boy has gone through, and how magnificent he has been over everything. He never spared himself through all the bombing last year, and if ever anyone deserved the George Medal, he did! Always where the danger was greatest – always! The men and children and the little children in that part of London in which he was working simply adored him, but, dear thing, he has now had to pay the price of endless nights of sheer hell, I would say – because he really did get the reaction that many get in that sort of work, doing it as intensely as he did. Many a time he gave up his own meals for others, and he has come into my office in the morning, black in the face with smut and dirt of all the hours' work he had gone through, wet boots, wet clothes, and even then it was hard to persuade him to go up to Hart's flat and rest, but we did always manage to make him dry himself and get a wash-up. I think he always had the feeling that he had no right to have soap and water and a certain amount of comfort when so many he had seen suffering or killed did not have it.

Then, as you know, he made up his mind to go into the Merchant Marine, and we let him go and saw that he was warmly clothed, but really feeling that he was not well – with the result that, after working on the Docks for weeks, the doctors simply made him go on to a farm and get back his health. He is now looking quite a different person, but I do not suppose anyone will ever know how much comfort and help that dear, tall, calm person gave to so many through those awful days. I have never seen anyone so calmly and quietly, without saying a word to anyone, so live the Christian spirit that is in him. How proud his father would have been, and how proud his Mother must be. He has never shirked danger, he has never shown any fear and he has gone on quietly doing this without a word to anyone. We have had to drag everything out of him, and then have heard of much from the others with whom he worked. We are very much hoping that we can finally persuade him to go home to really recuperate, although he is much better and we do feel he is feeling quite a different person now, we do feel he needs this. Imagine going into a shelter, seeing about forty people sitting there, and then finding that none of them were alive – all of them having been killed by blast![31]

His decision to go into the Merchant Marine was based on his feeling that 'he would be among the sort of people he has got to know in the East end, and would be less regimented than those in the navy.'[32] But he never recovered from his 'blitz' experience and was sent back to Canada in the spring of 1942. When he recovered, he got a job in adult education work. The director, E.A. Corbett, reported enthusiastically about his work. Corbett, wrote Maude to Vincent, 'gave George the encouragement he needed after his illness, just as you and Lal helped him through his difficult time in England by your faith and encouragement.'[33] At Vincent's insistent advice he returned to Oxford in the fall of 1945. He had been far more severely tested by his war service than had been most of the members of the armed forces. The same moral imperative that determined his war-time choices would operate strongly in his later philosophical writings that were to have such a profound influence on a new generation.

Despite the family anxieties, and the constant shock of sudden human loss and insane destruction, Vincent and Alice were happier during the years of war than they were during the four pre-war years. The years from 1935 to 1938 had been, in many ways, diverting and satisfying. The Masseys had enjoyed a life spent in a colourful, cosmopolitan society, peopled by politicians, diplomats, influential journalists, artists, writers, and fashionable hostesses. But they had always recognized that their primary duty was to interpret and expound Canada, and a love of England had not weakened their robust Canadianism. For Vincent, however, it was not easy to speak for Canada. The official Canadian voice was muted and indistinct. The prime minister as his own minister of external affairs, to whom Vincent Massey was responsible, saw Europe as a source of complex and mysterious evil from which Great Britain was excluded only in his moments of sentimental patriotism; and the under-secretary of state for external affairs, O.D. Skelton, had similar views unsoftened by sentimentalism. They thought of Vincent Massey as a man easily ensnared in the toils of the British Foreign Office. When they were not maintaining a cool distance between External Affairs and the high commissioners, they were making it impossible for the high commissioners to play the role of a diplomat. Massey, as we have seen, could not take an official part in the meetings of the Commonwealth high commissioners, of which he was, by history and precedent, the senior member.

The Johnsonian dictum about the prospect of hanging can be extended to the prospect of war: 'it concentrates the mind wonderfully.' In the changed atmosphere, Massey's position was clarified and strengthened. Even Mackenzie King, whose transatlantic shadow in pre-war days hung heavily and menacingly over Massey, now seemed almost benign. In the early years of Massey's London appointment King had taken his most malevolent view of Massey. He saw him as a corrupt force threatening the moral universe of which he, King, was the centre, and of which his rebel grandfather, his grandmother, his parents, and the great Liberal saints, Gladstone and Laurier, were the guardians. Massey represented everything that was antithetic to this world: inherited wealth, an effete aestheticism, a burning zeal for self-advancement, and a servile attitude towards the English upper classes. Massey would long remember the extended meeting he had had with King on 17 June 1937, just before the prime minister had set off for his rendezvous with destiny in Berlin. King had charged Massey with aspiring to displace the prime minister in foreign affairs, with hounding him continuously with questions and requests, with succumbing to 'sinister British influence.' Massey, who even in the shelter of his diary rarely indulged in personal attack, exploded in this instance, and, in a passage omitted from his own account in his autobiography, savagely analysed the psychological basis for King's attitude.

> *I was struck throughout this most disagreeable hour by the unpleasant – almost sinister – expression which was created. It was almost as if he was possessed by something evil. He referred to everything in terms of disparagement. Everybody's motives were given the most unfavourable interpretation. He seemed to have, if not a 'persecution complex' at least a conviction of neglect – lack of appreciation. I am certain that there is a pathological interpretation of this appalling mood. But although it only occasionally happens that the controls are off and he speaks his mind, unfortunately the ideas are always locked up behind a façade of sentimental unrealities which does not conceal them from anybody who knew him well.*[34]

No such interview marred the war years. King's other attitudes towards Massey prevailed – an almost cloying assertion of deep personal friendship, coupled with official declarations of support. Massey responded happily, and his comments on the prime minister are those of a devoted officer about his respected chief. During King's visit to Britain in August and September of 1941, Massey was in constant attendance and reported enthusiastically about the visit. King had already sounded a note pleasing to Massey in a preliminary statement in which he sharply criticized proposals for an imperial war cabinet and 'stressed the value of the function of the Canadian High Commissioner in London and paid tribute to the work performed by Mr. Massey and his staff.'[35]

The visit began inauspiciously at Aldershot when the prime minister, attempting to speak to about five thousand Canadian troops packed in a grandstand watching a sports program, was greeted by a mixture of boos and perfunctory cheers. 'It was,' Massey wrote, 'a very uncomfortable and embarrassing episode.'[36] But King's speech a few days later at the Mansion House was a great success and obliterated the unfortunate Aldershot début. His speech was about the need for full participation in the war by the Americans. 'He was the only man who could have said it,' observed Massey, 'and he said it well and at the right moment.'[37] When King left for home, Massey was his sole companion on the train to Edinburgh. This time there were no recriminations. They covered a wide agenda, and Massey even managed to raise amicably the question of a Canadian honours list, a project dear to him and usually anathema to King. The happy relations continued until the end of the war. In a telegram to Vincent at Christmas 1943, King fused all his benign *personae*: paterfamilias, spiritual counsellor, fulsome eulogist: 'You and Alice have performed your tasks magnificently. From every side, I hear only the highest praise of the position you have won for yourself and for Canada at the heart of the Empire. May you continue to be given the strength, vision, and wisdom so greatly needed in these times by all who bear responsibilities such as yours. God bless and keep you all.'[38]

King's second visit in the spring of 1944 to attend a conference of Commonwealth prime ministers inspired another round of Massey compliments. He praised 'King's gift for conciliation' in a preliminary discussion with Cranborne. He was enthusiastic about King's speech to Parliament, in which his 'tribute to the Empire reassured those who regard W.L.M.K. as lukewarm on the subject.'[39] In a reflective letter to King on the prime ministers' conference, which King had dominated, Massey wrote: 'It seems to me that one of the big things that the meeting did was to lift the British Commonwealth out of the realm of controversy for the time being at least, and as far as the rest of the world is concerned it should do a great deal to make the Commonwealth better understood'[40] – a reference to King's contention that the Commonwealth was not an economic or political bloc, but a group of autonomous nations voluntarily associated.

Massey, however, never forgot the tongue-lashing of June 1937. In all likelihood, he reflected, it was the expression of King's real attitude and the halcyon period would endure only as long as war forged its stern bonds of unity.

The improvement in Massey's relations with his minister was repeated on the departmental level, particularly after Skelton's death early in 1941 and Norman Robertson's succession as under-secretary of state for external affairs. The relations between Skelton and Massey had been characterized by icy propriety or thinly controlled irritation. Skelton espoused a passionate nationalism in which there was no room for Massey's anglophilia. Norman Robertson was devoted to his old chief. Like Skelton, it was 'his occupation to be plain.' Shortly after his appointment in 1929 as a third secretary to Department of External Affairs, he wrote to his parents about the initial appointments to Canadian ministerial posts: 'He [H.M. Marler, minister to Tokyo] is a member of our slim and select silk hat brigade; of Massey's stamp but perhaps not even Massey's calibre – these millionaire *amis du peuple* affect an acquired elegance that rubs me the wrong way.'[41] Three years at Balliol as a Rhodes scholar had left him immune to Balliolatry, and early experience as a trade negotiator with both Britain and the United States left him with an American bias. He wrote to his immediate contemporary in External Affairs, Mike Pearson: 'Our direct negotiations with the U.S. are the least of your worries right now. We can cope with them but not with God's Englishmen and the inescapable moral ascendancy over us lesser breeds.'[42] These were youthful observations and some of the acerbity disappeared from Robertson's comments after he became under-secretary. When Robertson accompanied the prime minister to England in the summer of 1941, he and Massey had a long talk, about which Massey wrote with relief and satisfaction. 'Found him refreshingly objective. I could detect no prejudice. His mind is of course first class. His outlook less academic than I had thought.'[43] From the outset of the war, Robertson had no qualms about the need for full Canadian participation, and this eased Massey's role in Britain. Letters to the under-secretary changed from 'Dear Dr. Skelton' to 'Dear Norman.' A certain aloofness to each other remained, but it never created problems in official communications and it was laced, on each side, with a basic respect.

Norman Robertson brought order and a measure of unity to a department that had known neither. Robertson shared responsibility with two colleagues, actually senior to him in point of service – Hume Wrong and Lester Pearson, both of whom Massey knew well. He had appointed Wrong, the son of his revered history professor at the University of Toronto, George Wrong, as his first secretary when he went to Washington in 1927 as minister. Wrong, whose talent for unbuttoned invective and personal disparagement covered a wide front, turned sharply against his minister. He resented being left in charge of the dull minutiae of the legation, while the minister was off giving speeches of an instructional and inspirational nature, and meeting the quality of the land. Massey was no less disenchanted with Wrong, although he always recognized and valued his sharp and penetrating intellect. They were together briefly in London where Wrong was posted as special economic adviser after the outbreak of war. Massey was concerned about fitting him into his establishment, not an easy task since Wrong placed great emphasis on the seniority conferred by his last posting as Canadian representative to the League of Nations: 'To take advantage of his first-class mind I made all the concessions I could,'[44] Massey wrote magnanimously.

No such personal problems marred Massey's relationship with Pearson. They had worked together harmoniously in London, and Pearson's recall to Ottawa in March 1941 (he actually left London two months later) was a great blow to Massey. But Pearson, in the midst of new and complex responsibilities in Ottawa as Robertson's chief associate and, after January 1942, as minister-counsellor in Washington, always kept in touch with Canada House. He wrote to Vincent, 'Canada House in general and yourselves in particular will always have a staunch supporter and friend as long as I am here.'[45] It was not just a polite declaration. Pearson wrote long personal letters, with sharp comments on the Ottawa scene ('C.D. Howe is of the Lord Beaverbrook type and causes confusion while he secures results') and undiplomatic assessments of the activities of the American State Department. Vincent commented on the improvement in official despatches and correspondence from External Affairs. 'I can assure you that the correspondence from External Affairs since you arrived has been met with cheers from all concerned in this office. It is a good thing to have someone in Ottawa who understands our problems here but above and beyond all that we are delighted to see your touch applied to the letters and despatches which emanate from the East Block.'[46]

Early in 1945, Pearson was appointed ambassador to Washington. During his visit to Canada and the United States in February and March 1944, Massey had seen Pearson in Washington. The ambassador [Leighton McCarthy] gave the impression of moving vaguely on the periphery of the institution. The mission was sustained, Massey concluded, by Pearson's 'infinite tact' and 'productivity,' although 'there are many things that he would like to do that only an ambassador can do – and doesn't.'[47] On his return to Ottawa, Massey reported to the prime minister on Pearson's excellent work, and warmly supported his appointment as McCarthy's successor.

Massey's connections with Ottawa were further strengthened by the appointment of Malcolm MacDonald in May 1941 as British high commissioner in Ottawa. His predecessor, Sir Gerald Campbell, had been outspoken and vigorous, with a tendency towards the indiscreet and the precipitate in his despatches; and he had found Mackenzie King baffling. Malcolm MacDonald seemed to understand King, was fond of Canada and Canadians, and made numerous friends in all parties. Before the outbreak of war he had been briefly secretary of state for the dominions, and he knew the difficulty of giving proper regard to dominion autonomy at a time that called for Empire unity. He and Massey knew each other well, and at occasional meetings during the war years kept each other fully and frankly informed.

With an outwardly benign minister, a deputy who was considerate and undogmatic, close personal ties with Lester Pearson, who was moving rapidly upward in the Department of External Affairs and establishing himself in international circles, and with Malcolm MacDonald, who had the respect of both the Canadians and the British, Massey felt a freedom and a confidence in his work in London that before the outbreak of war he had never enjoyed. That freedom and confidence are apparent in the part he played in the regular meetings of the dominion high commissioners. The minutes of the meetings, although sparsely recorded, indicate who raised the main questions and shaped the discussions. Certainly Massey was a principal and influential participant.

There were four high commissioners eligible for membership; the high commissioner for Eire was now eliminated by reason of his country's declaration of neutrality. The South African high commissioner was a minor voice. There were a succession of appointments during the war, and no one was strong enough to make an impression. The New Zealand high commissioner, William Jordan, was blunt and outspoken, with a warm emotional approach to problems, rarely buttressed by an understanding of the issues. 'His shoulders,' Alice wrote to Maude, 'are just covered with chips.'[48] He was a popular figure, a refreshing variation on the diplomatic stereotype, but it is doubtful if he was taken seriously by senior officials. Joe Garner recalls Lord Cranborne's Freudian slip at a farewell dinner. 'When Bill Jordan got up to speak in the League of Nations, it was like a breath of hot air.'[49]

Stanley Bruce, the Australian high commissioner, was a formidable figure. He was completely at home in Britain. He had gone to England in 1902, when he was nineteen, had taken his degree at Cambridge (where he was a famous oarsman), had been called to the bar in 1906, and had practised in England until the outbreak of war. After the war, during which he served with great distinction as a front-line officer, he had returned to Australia to take over the family importing business. He became a wealthy man, and his business career provided training in close, hard-fisted negotiations. He had entered politics in the Nationalist party, and had been prime minister from 1922 to 1929. He had gone to London in 1932 as resident minister, a position that gave him access to the highest levels of British policy; he had been appointed high commissioner the following year. He had the confidence of the Australian government, whether Labour or Nationalist. In 1942 he was given a seat in the British war cabinet, in view of the high Australian stake in the far east. Bruce was a big, handsome man, with an imperturbable and icily polite manner. He had no great gift of eloquence, but was always sure of what he wanted to say and simple and direct in saying it.

Bruce and Massey respected each other, but differences in attitude and style ruled out any intimacy. Between them, they dominated the agenda of the high commissioners' meetings, and rescued them from the atmosphere of querulous complaint or inconsequential gossip that threatened to descend.

The meetings of the high commissioners were not designed to be formal bodies with specific powers. They were essentially an administrative device whereby important information could be passed on to the high commissioners, and the high commissioners could be given the opportunity to comment on policy and raise issues of concern to them. Much depended on the secretary of state for the dominions, his closeness to the ultimate source of power – to, in short, Winston Churchill – his sympathy to the problems of the dominions, and his willingness to press their case on Churchill. Not until Lord Cranborne took over during the last two years of the war did the high commissioners have a secretary of state in whom they had confidence. Anthony Eden, who served briefly in the opening year of the war, was impatiently waiting to move on to higher things. His successor, Viscount Caldecote (formerly Sir Thomas Inskip) was treated with ill-concealed contempt by the high commissioners: about Caldecote's appointment Massey wrote 'not the kind of office to be given as a consolation prize to a retiring politician.'[50] Clement Attlee, who was secretary of state for less than a year, had seniority; he was deputy prime minister and a member of the war cabinet. But both Bruce and Massey found Attlee dull and taciturn. 'Talking with Attlee is a little like a conversation with a bronze Buddha except for the monosyllabic ejaculations which he utters occasionally.'[51]

Between Caldecote and Attlee, Cranborne had a brief period in office. He lost no time in making clear to Churchill that he must be able to keep the high commissioners fully informed. In a minute to the prime minister he wrote: 'I find that what the Dominions value most is the sense that they are taken into the full confidence of His Majesty's Government.'[52] Apparently this condition was not met, and at the end of the year Cranborne returned to the attack with a good deal of heat. A Cecil was not disposed to bend before any man, not even before the great warlord himself. Liaison, he wrote, 'has become increasingly defective. For one thing I do not know what is going on. Many of the most important discussions and decisions of the Government are taken at meetings, at which I am not present. Moreover, most of the important telegrams are exchanged by you personally either with Heads of States or with Dominion P.M.'s, and these I am not empowered to show or even mention to the High Commissioners ... if the High Commissioners want secret information, they tend more and more to go, not to me, but to other sources which apparently talk more freely ... In such circumstances the position of the Dominion's Secretary becomes a farce.'[53]

Churchill did not find it easy to preside over a free Commonwealth at a time when action had to be taken quickly and, often, secretly. He still lived in the days of the old Empire that moved instinctively as a single unified whole, bound together by romantic attachment to British ideals and pride in British accomplishments. In the thirties, he had opposed the Statute of Westminster, and he was willing to sacrifice his political career to arrest constitutional advances in India. Churchill's unwillingness to take the high commissioners into his confidence may have had personal, as well as theoretical, sources. They were not unclouded witnesses to his wisdom and omniscience. This was particularly true of Vincent Massey, who, in pre-war days, had shared to the full the common belief, both inside and outside the Conservative party, that Churchill had lacked 'judgment,' that he had (in Massey's words) 'an irresponsible, free-booting disposition.'[54] In the crisis of May 1940, however, Massey welcomed Churchill as a war leader,[55] but never lost his doubts about his soundness. He was not alone among the high commissioners in this view. In April 1942, after a series of British disasters – the sinking of the capital British ships, *Prince of Wales* and *Repulse*, the fall of Singapore, Rommel's advance in Africa – Massey and Bruce discussed 'the apparent planlessness of the war on the allied side, the falling stock of the "Headmaster" [Massey's critical term for Churchill], the rising star of Cripps and the need for his clear head and disinterested energy.'[56]

The high commissioners never discussed high strategy in the conduct of the war. Indeed they were often not informed of decisions – in the early years, for instance, the decision to attack and destroy the French fleet – and they constantly complained about being kept in the dark. By necessity, as well as by natural inclination, they emphasized questions of publicity and propaganda, of how the British case could be presented most effectively to the world. As high commissioners, they were all concerned with the projection of their countries abroad, so that the shift to a bigger client and a wider public was easy and consoling. Massey and Bruce had long established international interests. Bruce had spent much time at the League of Nations, and Massey was recognized as the expert on the United States.

The United States was a dominant theme in their discussions – down to December 1941, a potential ally to be cajoled and won over, and, after that date, the dominant power on the allied side, the ultimate guarantor of victory. At an early meeting of the high commissioners Massey immediately raised the centrality of the United States. 'Vincent Massey referred to the desirability of keeping the U.S. Government fully informed as to our general position and aims and suggested that the possibility of giving the U.S. Government the greater part of the information sent to the Dominion Governments on these questions might well be considered.'[57] With the end of the 'phony' war and the fall of France, the publicity problem with the United States became enormously complex, something quite different from 'keeping her fully informed.' The United States must be convinced that, although Britain's plight was desperate, it was not hopeless; that she was doing everything in her power and that with immediate, and the prospect of continued, aid, she could eventually triumph.

The high commissioners doubted whether the British position was being convincingly presented. The American ambassador, Joseph Kennedy, was a shaky intermediary. He had doubts as to whether Britain could survive – doubts indeed as to whether Britain's entrance into the war was justified. (When Vincent delivered the Canadian proclamation of war to the King, the King reported a recent talk with Kennedy: he 'had been struck by the fact of his materialistic outlook, deploring the loss of money which would be entailed. "He always thinks of money," added the King.'⁵⁸) Lord Lothian, the British ambassador to the United States, was ideal; he was fond of the Americans, and skilful in expounding the British point of view. But he died suddenly in December 1940, and his successor, Lord Halifax, aroused disturbing associations with appeasement and aristocratic aloofness. 'I wish I could think *he really liked* the Americans,' commented Vincent, who knew that for the British liking did not always come easily.

If the problem of persuading a neutral United States to come in on the side of Britain was difficult (until it was solved by the Japanese attack at Pearl Harbour), the problem of dealing with the committed ally was far greater. Now that Britain was not in immediate peril of collapse, some of the old, traditional American suspicions of the 'Empire' began to emerge. Vincent reported a disturbing discussion among the high commissioners of the American attitude towards the British Colonial Office. 'There is no doubt that a legend of British exploitation and incompetence has developed and will become increasingly hard to eradicate unless something is done to remove American illusion.'⁵⁹ No clear distinction was made by Americans between Empire and Commonwealth or between colony and independent dominion. American troops moving in large numbers into Australia and New Zealand in preparation for the assault on Japan asked their hosts 'if they are going to be "free" from England after the war.'⁶⁰ The American criticism was often so densely wrong-headed that it aroused the anger of a liberal internationalist like Violet Markham, Mackenzie King's confidante and Massey's friend. She declared that after listening to American attacks, 'she felt like having her under-clothing made of Union Jacks.'⁶¹

Unfortunately, the British were not good at meeting criticism and expounding their own case. A nation, Massey remarked, that went in for understatement was not good at propaganda. In its news broadcasts the BBC still maintained its remote and unemotional tone. Perhaps, Massey reflected, Canada could help in this situation. She was a self-governing member of the Commonwealth, aware of the movement within the colonial empire to greater autonomy; she had a natural sympathy for the American point of view, and she now had a publicly controlled radio system that had demonstrated a special interest in educational and political broadcasting. Specifically, Massey thought of his friend, Leonard Brockington, who had been the first chairman of the Canadian Broadcasting Corporation. Before that he had been solicitor for the city of Calgary and counsel for the North-West Grain Dealers' Association at Winnipeg – positions that seemed to proclaim his Canadianism. Brockington was actually a Welshman who had studied and taught classics before coming to Canada, and was better known as a broadcaster and orator than as a lawyer and businessman. Indeed, he was an orator in the great classical tradition. He could, however, join high rhetoric with a light, colloquial touch, and set his words to an enchanting Welsh lilt. He came to England late in 1941 to give a few radio speeches to Canadians about the British war effort, and Massey conceived of a greater role he could play. Brendan Bracken had become minister of information in June 1941, and Bracken and Massey were friendly. Bracken, moreover, as Churchill's old and faithful ally, had great influence. Massey suggested that Brockington should be given a post in the ministry of information as adviser on Empire affairs. Bracken agreed. 'Brockington would be a tower of strength and would give to our Empire publicity organisation the inspiration which we all agree they have hitherto lacked ... as a speaker and broadcaster he scarcely has an equal.'[62] Early in 1943 Brockington was dispatched on a speaking tour in Australia and New Zealand, where he was a great success. He was not content with a defence of the *status quo*. When, at Massey's invitation, he appeared before a commissioners' meeting, he argued that we 'should take a more aggressive line in defence of our ideals. The field of idealism was being left to U.S. politicians.'[63]

The high commissioners became increasingly doubtful as to whether American motives had a generous idealistic basis. A sharp critical note began to dominate their comments on the United States. Vincent Massey, once an understanding and generous friend and interpreter of United States policy, now became the sharpest critic. Although, he explained, the hostility to the concept of Empire 'appeared to have an idealistic inspiration, it also went hand in hand with high speed American commercialism. In fact, the danger of the war would not be from American isolation but from American Imperialism.'[64] This was clearly evident, Massey pointed out, in the American preparations for the international control of civil aviation. The United States 'had come to regard the air as something created by divine providence for them to dominate. We should rudely disabuse them of this illusion.'[65] At the Chicago conference on civil aviation in January 1945, Massey commented cynically on the role of the American chairman, Adolf Berle, who, he said, was simultaneously an American propagandist and worked in close association with the South American delegates, several of whom were employees of Pan-American Airways.[66]

Many of the meetings of the high commissioners in the final years of the war turned into a chorus of anti-Americanism. The United States suffered, it was alleged, from Russia-phobia, Americans were taking over control of liberated Paris (where, Massey said, 'infiltration tactics were practised by American business men in uniform.')[67] The American army used harsh disciplinary methods ('The American attitude,' said Massey, 'was based on the belief that you could pour discipline into men, and took no account of other methods, such as the encouragement of self-discipline'[68]). American soldiers in Britain acted like an army of occupation and did not adjust to British society. The chorus of specific charges always ended with general disapproval of the demeanour and conduct of the American soldiers in London.

For a year after Dunkirk, the commissioners were much concerned with attitudes towards Vichy France. Here again Massey was a leading spokesman and briefly, although at a comfortable remove, an active participant. He was attached to France emotionally and culturally; next to Great Britain, it was the European country he knew best, and during his pre-war period in London, he and Alice spent a holiday almost every year in France. He had always been a strong partisan of the French presence in Canada, and had been one of the earliest supporters of biculturalism and bilingualism. But he was, at the same time, sharply critical of French foreign policy. He thought that France, long before the advent of Hitler, had been legalistic and vindictive in her attitude towards Germany, and had thereby helped Hitler to win power within Germany and a good deal of sympathy without. Vincent, with Norman Rogers, the minister of defence, and Harry Crerar, the senior officer at Canadian Military Headquarters in London, had visited France after the outbreak of war. They had been taken by the Canadian minister, Georges Vanier, to meet Premier Daladier and the French 'Generalissimo' Gamelin. Vincent took a poor view of Gamelin – 'he was living in a fog that ought to have stifled the palm placed beside his chair, and he was sloppily dressed'[69] – a view that, however superficially formed, was amply justified by events. When, after the fall of France, Madame Vanier arrived in London from France, following a harrowing voyage, she was full of the pity and the terror of the tragedy she had witnessed, and she bitterly resented Massey's suggestion that this was not heroic tragedy but contemptible farce. 'I inadvertently aroused Pauline Vanier's morbidly pro-French sensibilities and for a few moments she was very difficult.'[70]

Now, with the establishment of the Vichy régime under Marshal Pétain, the British had still not lost their hope in a mild resurrection of their great ally. Underneath every external indication of increasing tension between Britain and Vichy, there still existed, it was thought, some possibilities of reconciliation.

Here, Massey provided a helpful link. He was aware of the fact that French Canada had a benign attitude to Vichy. A regime that proclaimed its devotion to *travail, famille, patrie* had more appeal to the traditional, church-centred French-Canadian society than did one that exalted *liberté, égalité, fraternité*.[71] He thought of an able French-Canadian diplomat, Pierre Dupuy, who had been a member of the Canadian legation staff in Paris and was now in London as 'chargé d'affaires in France, Belgium, and Netherlands' – under the circumstances, an empty title. Massey 'felt that a Canadian chargé d'affaires could get information and express a point of view on behalf of His Majesty's Government here (but without saying so) which would be more helpful to the Foreign office.'[72] The British government agreed and obtained Canadian approval. 'Little does Ottawa know,' Massey wrote with obvious self-satisfaction, 'that Dupuy's journey to which they reluctantly assented was my idea.'

Dupuy made three trips to Vichy, and became briefly the only Canadian diplomat close to high international policy. Charles Ritchie relished the irony of the situation: 'Pierre Dupuy came to pay me a visit. What an enjoyable war that little man is having! He exudes high politics and dark diplomacy ... From being a dim little diplomat he has become an international figure – the only Canadian except for the prime minister whose name is known in Paris and Berlin political circles and in the inner circles of London.'[73] Dupuy was the guest of honour at a dinner given by Churchill at Chequers (a distinction never attained by Massey); Churchill expressed his gratitude and urged Dupuy to continue his efforts to detach Vichy from Germany.[74] At a number of the high commissioners' meetings, Dupuy was the star witness, and Massey proudly watched his man perform. But now Ottawa became alarmed at the uncharacteristic prominence of a Canadian diplomat. Massey felt personally affronted: 'As soon as any representative shows either imagination or initiative he calls down the displeasure of the powers that be in External Affairs. The ideal diplomat belongs to Mme. Tussaud's waxworks.'[75]

Dupuy made three trips to Vichy, but by September 1941 it was apparent that a Vichy-British reconciliation was impossible, and Dupuy's turn in the international spotlight came to an end. Massey and the other high commissioners turned their attention to Charles de Gaulle, whose egotism and arrogance they did not find an attractive alternative to Vichy pusillanimity.

The commissioners occasionally touched upon the dark and lowering question of the German policy towards the Jews, now extended by conquest to almost all mainland Europe, as well as to vast areas of Russia. When in 1938 Vincent Massey had recommended that Canada should take Sudeten Germans in preference to Jews, he thought that the question was one of providing an escape from persecution, not from annihilation. As the war progressed, cruel persecution turned into carefully planned and coolly executed genocide. At first, there was reluctance to accept the fact: it soared beyond any idea of the wildest teutonic infatuation with death and annihilation. But by the end of 1942, the evidence was irrefutable. On 17 December, Canada joined the allied nations in condemning 'this bestial policy of cold-blooded extermination' and in warning that 'those responsible for the crimes should not escape retribution.'[76] A few months later, the commissioners received a report on German morale from a Foreign Office spokesman. The report, which had a good deal of detailed speculation, concluded with this terse statement: 'There were few Jews left in Germany at all – the policy of deliberate extermination had done its work.'[77]

Following the 1942 statement of Nazi atrocities, the 'Nazi persecution of the Jews was made a central theme of the British propaganda to Europe.'[78] But the British made it clear that little could be done for the Jews in Nazi-occupied Europe, other than to bring about military victory as quickly as possible. When Mackenzie King made a comprehensive statement in the House about the Jewish plight, he concluded that 'there is nothing that the allied government can do to save these hopeless people except to win the war as quickly and as completely as possible.'[79] Long-term strategy must not be altered in favour of the Jews. Britain was particularly sensitive to the political balance in the middle east. If the restrictions on Jews entering Palestine were relaxed, the British would incur the enmity of the Arab world. Massey had doubtless been briefed on the subject by Anthony Eden and Malcolm MacDonald, who both upheld a strict observance of the White Paper of 1939 restricting the movement of Jews to Palestine. At a meeting of the high commissioners he 'drew attention to the bearing of the Jewish problem on the situation in Iraq ... he had been given to understand that our failure fully to implement the White Paper policy was influencing Arab opinion generally against us.'[80]

If the millions of Jews caught within the Nazi net were doomed, the small group – a pitiful remnant numbered in a few thousands – who had escaped to neutral countries, particularly to Spain and Portugal, could be saved. But the allies were not responsive. They spent a great deal of time organizing futile conferences and manoeuvring to shift responsibilities to each other. In this sad charade Canada was a principal player. The old triumvirate of Prime Minister's Office, External Affairs, and Immigration Office still operated and was adept at producing reasons for inaction – shortness of shipping, absence of immigration offices in Europe, the possibility of Nazi infiltration among the refugees, the failure of most Jews in Europe to meet the rigid immigration laws still giving heavy priority to 'an agriculturalist having sufficient means to farm in Canada,' and above all, a sullen wave of anti-semitism widespread in Canada, with a bitter, inflexible headquarters in Quebec.

In such an atmosphere, it is doubtful whether any initiative from London could have had much effect. Separate schemes for rescuing refugees foundered or were abandoned. In January 1941 Massey wrote to King about Allied refugees – Czechs and Poles of whom a number were Jews – in countries not yet overrun by the enemy, pointing out that 'their fate if they fall into German hands, does not bear thinking of,' and urging that Canada should accept some of them.[81] The Canadian cabinet agreed to accept a thousand, but made it clear that it did so only on condition that the allied governments accepted responsibility for the cost of transportation, the repatriation of the refugees after the war, and a strict limitation on the number of Jews. In discussions at a high commissioners' meeting, Massey 'expressed concern that the attitude of the Treasury was likely to upset the scheme to which his Government had agreed for sending allied refugees to Canada.'[82]

In the summer of 1944 an unusual opportunity suddenly opened up for rescuing Jews from Nazi-controlled Europe. Hungary, aware of the probability of German defeat and anxious to negotiate favourable surrender terms, offered to release their Jews, who had so far escaped 'the ultimate solution.' But the Germans moved in quickly and immediately began their satanic work of liquidation. At one point, there was some possibility that the Germans would exchange some Jews for civilian goods. But the Hungarian opportunity, really a mirage, disappeared. It was solemnly discussed in the intergovernmental committee of refugees, on which Massey now sat as Canadian representative. The allies were alarmed at the magnitude of the opportunity suddenly placed before them, and each manoeuvred to shift responsibility to others. Massey reported on the discussions to the high commissioners. By this time, their suspicions of American designs had been deeply aroused, and they relished Massey's linkage of the realities of American politics with the formulation of American foreign policy: 'The U.S. apparently wanted the Jewish vote without taking in more Jews, because if they allowed more Jews in they would lose the R.C. vote.'[83] Massey didn't add that he could have made exactly the same observation, with some slight adjustments, to the attitude and actions of his own country.

Ironically, the only war-time scheme that resulted in the coming to Canada of the kind of Jewish refugee of whom Massey would have warmly approved – the artist and the intellectual – was the result of a blunder in which the office of high commissioner was involved. In

July 1940, at the height of the hysteria over a presumed German invasion, Canada agreed to accept from Britain, German internees and German prisoners of war. At the last minute, to make up an agreed quota, about two thousand young German refugees, technically internees, but actually young men who had escaped from concentration camps or the prospect of being condemned to them, were included in the group sent to Canada. Massey twice complained at a high commissioners' meeting 'that harmless refugees had been placed with dangerous Nazis amongst the internees sent to Canada.'[84] For the young refugees this meant a long period of prison-like confinement. But release finally came, and Canada was the happy beneficiary. Among the refugees were scholars, musicians, and artists who would greatly strengthen the cultural life of Canada – among them, philosophers, Gregory Baum and Emil Fackenheim; scholars and writers, David Hoeniger, Kurt Levy, Kaspar Naegale, Henry Kreisel, Erick Koch; musicians, Helmut Blume and John Newmark.[85]

If the high commissioners found the Jewish question too vast and terrifying to deal with either as a practical problem or an incitement to idealism, they did not flinch from speculating in spacious terms about the nature of the post-war world: from their first war-time meetings they had emphasized the necessity of looking beyond the war and the destruction of Nazism. In September and October 1939, when Hitler had paused after the crushing of Poland to proclaim his desire for peace and for the preservation of the British Empire, the high commissioners had urged Chamberlain not to reply in a purely negative way and to seize the opportunity to set before the neutral nations Britain's concept of a stable, peaceful world. When Chamberlain appeared before the high commissioners to discuss the proposed reply to Hitler, Massey spoke for them 'pointing out that the suggestion that we had in mind had been put forward by four Dominion Governments without consultation and as individual opinions which in itself was very impressive. I had in mind but did not express the fact that these Governments represented one third of the white population of the Empire at present at war with Germany and 4 out of 5 of the governments ... it would have been well to have given rather a stronger touch in the statement of what we least expect as a result of the peace treaty which must come at the end of the present war. One should give a hint of the "brave new world" in order to reassure neutral opinion and strengthen our own resolve.'[86]

At this stage of the war, the high commissioners' attitude might have been seen as a re-emergence of an appeasement policy that the government was anxious to bury. But when even the faint hope of a peaceful world in which Hitler would continue to exist vanished utterly, the high commissioners returned to their emphasis on peacetime goals, now with explicit economic and social objectives. In July 1940, Bruce distributed copies of a memorandum on war aims that he had sent to the government, in which he declared that 'we make it abundantly clear that we stand not only for liberty but for economic and social justice.' This, he argued, will give us 'every chance of mobilizing a revolutionary movement in Europe behind the ideals of the British Empire and its friends.' Subsequently Churchill met with the commissioners, and a debate ensued between him and Bruce, 'the latter for some organized consideration of the new world we were fighting for; the former against anything which might divert our attention from the supreme object of winning the war.'[87]

Massey took no strong initiative on this front, although his sympathies were clearly on the side of Bruce. His diary records frequent meetings from 1941 onwards with Robin Barrington-Ward, who, in his *Times* editorials, was constantly urging a radical post-war policy. He wrote to Vincent in 1945 enclosing a copy of 'a Declaration of Principles' that he had sent on to the government, 'knowing,' he added, 'the part you and your colleagues have played in endeavouring to secure a statement of war aims.'[88] The crucial principle was a co-ordinated economic policy through international partnership 'to secure equality of economic opportunity and of economic security for all nations and for all classes within the nations.' Alice no doubt reflected Vincent's views in a characteristically warm and emotional outburst to her sister, Maude: 'The thing uppermost in people's minds is that every one should get hold of the vision of a new world, and this time a real one, not one of mere words, so that everyone has his chance.'[89]

On these broad issues – the attitude towards the United States, France, and the persecution of the Jews – the meetings of the high commissioners were mainly meetings of a debating society. But, on occasion, they could launch specific actions. Of these, the earliest and the most important was the British Commonwealth Air Training Plan, which at its height supplied 11,000 pilots and 17,000 aircrew every year. 'There had never been an effort like it in the world before,' wrote Eden, 'and its contribution to victory was capital.'[90] The idea of the plan came up at a meeting of the high commissioners on 16 September 1939. The minutes read 'Mr. Massey and Mr. Bruce suggested that consideration should be given to a scheme whereby Canadian, Australian and New Zealand Air Forces should be trained in Canada on planes to be specially built in Canada or the U.S. and should then be sent to the front as distinctive Canadian, Australian, and New Zealand air forces. The Secretary of State undertook to look into the proposals.'[91] On 23 September the secretary of state for air, Kingsley Wood, 'announced a scheme of staggering proportions for the training of pilots ... Canadian, U.K., Australian, and New Zealand,' 'I was delighted,' said Massey, 'at the imagination which lay behind the scheme and its impressive magnitude. It actually involves training establishments in Canada as against G.B. I hope Ottawa will receive it with equal imagination for this plan seems to offer the best chance of our getting definite air superiority within the next year.'[92]

Mackenzie King did accept the concept. It was not a new one, although it had now evolved in a way that appealed to King. Previous approaches by the British government, going back to 1936, had had, for King, a disturbing colonial caste, since they implied recruitment in Canada for the RAF and they had been ambiguous about Canadian control. Now this objection was swept aside, and King saw the proposal as a means of establishing a clear primary commitment that would providentially reduce the necessity for a large expeditionary force and thereby appeal to Quebec. Massey was asked to edit Chamberlain's telegram to King, and added a paragraph of his own composition, cunningly phrased so as to sound like an echo of King's innermost thoughts. After the war King read in an article by Anthony Eden of Massey's role, and was retrospectively enraged. 'I was much surprised and disturbed to notice that he [Eden] stated that it was Massey and Bruce, between them, at a meeting which he, Eden had called as Foreign Minister, without any conversation with the Government here, proposed the air training scheme. It was given as an example of the help to Britain to have foreign representatives taken into confidence in London. The outrageous part is that Massey, as representative of the government, should not have made the suggestion to the administration here in the first place.'[93] No doubt, Massey realized that at the time a direct appeal from him to his minister would have been received with suspicion and delay, if not with contemptuous dismissal.

After the war, a brisk controversy arose as to who was actually responsible for the idea of the air training plan. The Air Ministry proposed that the conception be attributed to Massey and Bruce. Massey was agreeable, but Bruce refused. 'Our respective attitudes,' Bruce wrote, 'were not unlike those of the two mothers in the Judgment of Solomon. I was convinced that the conception of the scheme was mine, and I was not prepared to be a party to my child's being cut in half.'[94] But the metaphor is not appropriate; the scheme was not an infant in September 1939; it was an adolescent looking for direction. Clearly both Bruce and Massey had thought about a specific scheme and had discussed it with various officials in the government prior to the formal proposal on 16 September. Harold Balfour, the under-secretary of state for air, in his rambling, anecdotal autobiography, *Wings over Westminster*, gives exclusive priority to Bruce, ignores Massey completely, and combatively attacks a claim never made by Anthony Eden that he was the father of the scheme. Anthony Eden favoured Massey as the prime begetter. At the farewell dinner for Massey by the Canada Club at the Savoy, Eden, in supporting the toast to the guest of honour, 'referred to early meetings of Dominion Ministers, at one of which Mr. Massey said that the most imaginative use should be made of our resources in the air. As a result of his suggestion an approach was made to the Air Ministry and thus was evolved the great Empire air training scheme.'[95]

A second scheme that bore a strong high commissioner imprint was the evacuation of British children to the dominions and the United States. Canada played by far the major role in the scheme. By the end of 1942, 14,000 children had been evacuated, of whom over 7,000 went to Canada, with 3,000 going to the United States, 1,900 to South Africa, 1,500 to Australia, and 500 to New Zealand. There were two types of evacuees: children who went under an official scheme and were distributed to various volunteer hosts who received a weekly stipend of five shillings for each child, and children who went out on the invitation of friends and relatives, for whom the government took no responsibility. The official scheme came to a sudden end in September 1940 when a ship carrying evacuated children was torpedoed with considerable loss of life. The evacuation continued under private auspices, but was then confined to those who were going to the homes of friends or relatives.

The scheme never had Churchill's blessing, who looked upon it, especially as Britain prepared for a Nazi invasion in the summer of 1940, as a concession to defeatism. He thought that a young correspondent struck the right Churchillian note when he wrote to him: 'I would rather be bombed to fragments than leave England.'[96] Early in July, the war cabinet had decided to bring the scheme to an end, but a protest from the high commissioners' meeting on 8 July 1940 prevented its immediate execution. The minutes read as follows: 'The High Commissioners all expressed disappointment at the decision and were in favour of sending the children in unescorted ships if necessary; Mr. Massey in particular pointed out that the Canadian Government had taken the proposals very seriously, and had enthusiastically made large-scale preparations, and he was afraid that the disappointment thus would be intense.'[97]

Vincent Massey was particularly concerned about the second category of children evacuees – those going under private auspices to homes of relatives and friends. He saw this as a covert form of immigration whereby Canada would acquire citizens 'of the best possible kind,' and he attempted to persuade Treasury, 'that temple,' he said, 'of high-minded pedantry,' to relax the strict currency laws so that Canadian hosts would not suffer financially.'[98] *The Times*, no doubt in the person of Robin Barrington-Ward, also saw the evacuation as an imaginative act in the strengthening of transatlantic ties. 'The transfer of British children to distant countries of North America possessed by their own race – somewhat like Alice going surprisingly through the looking-glass she had so often contemplated – will fashion now links of mutual understanding.'[99] Massey's approaches were summarily dismissed. The children's Overseas Reception Board in the UK addressed a peremptory telegram to the British high commissioner in Ottawa: 'Question of remittance by persons sending children outside the scheme has been raised by Massey. It has been explained to him that it will be quite indefensible if in addition to facilities under the scheme, which applies to all classes of children, further facilities were given outside of it by which individual parents and children could escape the existing financial dollar restrictions. To do so would be to grant an exclusive and discriminating privilege in respect of such persons and nothing would be so likely to cause ill feeling and public dissatisfaction here.'[100]

The high commissioner's meetings were an essential part of Massey's war; he was a major participant and he helped to launch a number of co-operative Commonwealth schemes. But his main work lay with Canadians and with the exposition of national policy. In war-time London with the rapid build-up of the Canadian armed forces (in March 1944, the overseas forces numbered approximately 300,000, exclusive of the navy), the Canadian colony became a small nation abroad, with the various military headquarters constituting what amounted to a separate and distinctive government. As Canada's senior representative in Britain, Massey was closely associated with that temporary government and was the principal liaison officer between it and the government in Canada. If his status among the high commissioners had been legitimized and strengthened, his status in the Canadian community in Britain – both civilian and military – was acknowledged to be central.

During the war Massey's primary responsibility continued, of course, to be with the Department of External Affairs. But an increasing amount of the day-to-day business of the high commissioner's office was with the Department of Defence in Ottawa, and its principal administrative arm, the National Defence Headquarters (presided over by the chief of the general staff), and with the two centres in the UK, the Canadian Military Headquarters (CMHQ) and the Senior Field Headquarters, which became, in early 1942, the Headquarters First Canadian Army. In this quasi-military extension of his duties, Massey worked chiefly with three men: J.L. Ralston, who, following the death of Norman Rogers in June 1940, became minister of national defence; General A.G.L. McNaughton, the commander of the Canadian forces in the theatre of war; and General H.D.G. Crerar, at first the senior officer at CMHQ, then during 1941 chief of the general staff in Ottawa, finally in December 1941 commander of the First Canadian Corps, and eventually McNaughton's successor as army commander.

With Ralston and Crerar, Massey had good relations. Ralston was a successful lawyer who had gone into politics, first in his native Nova Scotia, then in the federal House, where Mackenzie King had quickly picked him out as a likely cabinet member. He had not run in the election of 1935, but King had persuaded him to return to politics as minister of finance. He had a reputation for probity and soundness, the virtues that provide a ballast for the occasional bursts of utopianism in the Liberal party. He was also known for his punctilious attention to detail, a natural tendency strengthened by his legal and business experience. This could be an irritating virtue, as Massey sharply observed after an initial meeting. 'He was difficult to work with,' wrote Massey, 'because he acts as his own secretary, clerk, draughtsman etc. etc.'[101] But these were minor irritations to be endured more by officers in the high commissioner's office than by Massey himself. Massey no doubt remembered a warm letter Ralston had written to him after an early official visit to London. Ralston had enclosed a copy of a letter he had written to Mackenzie King when in 1930 King was considering the London appointment: Ralston wrote, 'Obviously if Massey can be spared from Washington and wants this position I feel that to choose him would be ideal. He's the sort of man who would comfort our British friends by making them feel that we are not out of sympathy with this perplexed country, and, at the same time he is clear headed and practical and would avoid the jingo Imperialist attitude which dies hard.'

Ralston had commanded an infantry battalion during the First World War, had been wounded, and awarded the DSO. His military experience gave him confidence in dealing with professional soldiers as well as a nostalgic taste for combat. He was, like many Canadians at the time, impatient at the lack of battle experience of the Canadian army, and disposed to think that action would be an excellent therapy for the long, uneventful vigil in England.

Massey was much closer to General H.D.G. Crerar than he was to Ralston. (He soon became 'Harry' to Massey; Ralston never became

'Layton' to Massey or, one suspects, to any other contemporary.) During the first months of the war, Crerar and Massey were close neighbours. Crerar was establishing and organizing the Canadian Military Headquarters in the Sun Life building adjacent to Canada House, and Massey, who was often consulted, found him 'sensible and easy to work with.'[102] In his outline of army administrative structure, Crerar assigned an important role to the high commissioner. 'The channel for communication on policy [to the minister of national defence] will be through the High Commissioner for Canada in the United Kingdom, who will be advised in military matters by C.M.H.Q. as required. Similarly, on matters of policy, the channel of communication between the Minister of National Defence and the G.O.C. 1st Canadian Division is through the High Commissioner.'[103] After Crerar returned from Canada in December 1941 to command the second division, he and Massey met frequently and informally. They quickly established an easy relationship. 'Crerar says,' wrote Massey, 'that we [Massey obviously includes Alice] are the only people to whom he can let himself go.' The persistent subject between them was Andy McNaughton, 'his virtues and faults.'[104] Crerar became more and more critical of his chief. He disagreed with him about army reorganization, resented McNaughton's treatment of him (no details were given), but, nevertheless, Massey concluded, remained loyal. Massey, for his part, abandoned his discreet air of impartiality and came down solidly on the side of Crerar. 'I'm sure Crerar is a sounder soldier than McNaughton.'[105]

In appearance and manner, Crerar and McNaughton provided a sharp contrast. With his prominent nose, long narrow face, and saturnine expression, Crerar looked like a renaissance prince and later, in his headquarters in Europe, lived like one.[106] McNaughton looked like a highland chieftain and often acted like one. (Ralston referred to his 'black Highland blood.') He had a sombre, brooding face, but his manner belied his appearance. He was direct in speech, with a warm, democratic approach to people and problems. He had become the archetypal Canadian soldier, the leader who aroused confidence and gave assurance of victory. He had been tested in battle during the First World War; he was a scientist who had altered army doctrine on the use of artillery; he was an effective speaker and an indefatigable and humane administrator; above all, he was a passionate nationalist who believed that the Canadian army united under Canadian leadership was 'a dagger pointed at the heart of Berlin.' Moreover, Canadian control of her own forces was, in a remark that McNaughton made and Stacey carefully noted, the 'acid test of sovereignty.'[107] Early in the war, when the allied front in France was in hopeless disarray, he had been asked by the British to make a dangerous and crucial reconnaissance to see whether Canadian troops could be sent through Calais to Dunkirk. Massey saw him briefly on his return from this venture, and his description evokes a vivid picture of the warrior-leader, completely unconcerned about appearance, absorbed in the immediate problem. 'On coming away from the Map Room at the War Office just after six I met McNaughton in front of the admiralty waiting for his car, a picturesque figure – steel helmet a little on one side, web equipment and revolver holster – uniform in dissaray and with a twenty-hour beard.'[108]

McNaughton in conference was not to Massey such an attractive figure. Massey's comments are sharp, with a touch of uncharacteristic venom. 'Generally has his mind made up on the matters he wishes to discuss, and cooperation with him is a bit like cooperation with an Act of Parliament.' 'I'm afraid he's rather a spoiled darling with a prima donna complex – despite his great ability.'[109] Massey's reference to McNaughton in *What's Past Is Prologue* as an 'old friend' was obviously an empty flourish by which the autobiographer self-indulgently blurs the past. Pearson remarks that during his days at Canada House, McNaughton preferred to deal with him. 'Their temperaments [referring to Massey and McNaughton] were at the opposite poles and neither felt at that early stage very comfortable and relaxed with each other.'[110] Douglas LePan, who worked closely with both McNaughton and Massey, is more emphatic and considerably less gentle to Massey. To him McNaughton was a man cast in a heroic mould and Massey was a plenipotentiary without substance.[111] All judgements of character and ability aside, it is clear that Massey, the English gentleman in search of rational compromise, was not at ease with McNaughton, the Scottish chieftain, full of passionate conviction.

In the dispute that arose in 1942 and 1943 about McNaughton's fitness to command the Canadian army in the field, Massey played a discreetly cautious role. In many ways he was sympathetic to McNaughton's insistence on preserving the integrity of the Canadian army and maintaining its Canadian leadership. But he was under an obligation to present the case approved by the Canadian war cabinet for the commitment of part of the army to the invasion of Sicily and Italy. McNaughton was unhappy about any Canadian participation in this campaign, but at least he hoped that the Canadians would return after Sicily to rejoin their comrades in England in time for the real second front in France. His attitude did not endear him to the British military hierarchy – Sir Alan Brooke, chief of the imperial general staff and General Sir Bernard Paget, commander in chief of the home forces. They finally concluded, no doubt with some cause, that McNaughton was unfit to lead the Canadian army in the field: he had been ill for three months in the latter part of 1941; he had made some mistakes during a major scheme in the spring of 1943; he was worn out, they concluded, by four years of the intense and troubled task of organizing and training the Canadian army. When in November 1943 Ralston informed McNaughton of the intention to relieve him of his command, McNaughton reacted savagely. He despised Ralston who, he believed, was determined to get rid of the man who stubbornly resisted the break-up of the Canadian army. Massey was helpful in placating McNaughton and avoiding a public controversy, a goal that he knew would be close to the prime minister's heart. The method was to shift the onus for the decision to drop McNaughton from Ralston and the chief of the general staff, General Stuart, to the British high command, a shrewd move, with a good deal of factual warrant.

The problem of maintaining a distinctive Canadian entity was even more difficult for the air force than for the army. When Massey and Bruce made the original proposal for the Commonwealth Air Training Plan, they envisaged graduates who would 'be sent to the front as distinctive Canadian, Australian, and New Zealand Air Forces.' But the Canadian government had not thought through the process of achieving a 'distinctive' Canadian air force, and by delaying until January 1943 the assumption of full financial responsibility for its airman in Britain it lacked the essential prerequisite for implementing the national policy. Air Vice Marshal Edwards, who became in November

1941 the senior officer overseas, pursued the policy of 'Canadianization' (the ugly term that was generally used) with rigour and persistence, but with indifferent results. In five meetings Massey had with Edwards during the year 1942, the subject was always the same – the slowness of the 'Canadianization' process and the resistance to it in the British air ministry and among many of the Canadian airmen themselves. Edwards complained that even the creation of an RCAF headquarters was looked upon by the RAF as 'a piece of nationalistic window dressing.' Massey listened sympathetically, but took no action to support Edwards. No doubt, he was influenced by Hart, who was strongly opposed to the policy and valued his service with 'mixed squadrons' drawn from the whole Commonwealth.

If, on the broad question of the Canadian identity of the army and air force, Massey put strategic necessity ahead of national sensitivities, on specific issues he was the persistent Canadian. He was following the 'functional' nationalistic policy of Robertson, Pearson, and Wrong in External, and he was doing so with an élan and a conviction that went far beyond the call for diplomatic consistency. At almost any time during the war, he was engaged in a protest against some aspect of British policy or action, protests delivered in polite, diplomatic language, usually reinforcing, but occasionally initiating, action by Ottawa. In March 1941 the protest was against the leasing of Newfoundland bases to the USA, which was done without consultation with Canada ('a sacrifice on the altar of Anglo-American cooperation').[112] Repeatedly throughout 1942, there were protests against failure to be informed of important decisions that affected Canada.

In October 1942, in the aftermath of Dieppe, Massey protested against the unilateral decision of the British to shackle German prisoners in response to the alleged tying of the hands of Allied prisoners; he took the Canadian case to a meeting of the high commissioners, arguing that British policy would lead to a 'contest of reprisals,' and urged the calling of the neutral protecting powers to resolve the crisis. He and his associates in Canada House drafted the telegram sent by King to Churchill, and he was pleased by the final acceptance of the Canadian solution. As to Dieppe itself, he made no protesting remarks, other than to comment astringently on the undue publicity given to the minor American participation. But he must have had some doubts about the tragic affair after he heard Louis Mountbatten, the commander-in-chief of combined operations, admit that 'the original intention had been to land strong forces on either flank and to strike at Dieppe from the rear, but this was changed for the plan of making a frontal attack on the town.'[113] When the Canadians took part in the invasion of Sicily, along with British and American troops, Massey contends that the inclusion of Canada in the official announcement on 10 July 1943 'was largely due to efforts made in the last two or three days from this office.'[114] In view of the fact that Lester Pearson also claims credit for the announcement as the result of an interview with Roosevelt arranged by King, Massey's assertion is clearly an exaggeration; his role was probably contributory and not decisive. At the same time, he voiced Canada's protest against her omission from anti-submarine communiqués, fruitlessly, as it turned out, since Churchill was adamant against any reference in the communiqués to individual members of the Commonwealth.

As victory came in sight, Massey emphasized this special case for Canadian representation in the shaping of the post-war world. He reinforced Pearson's more powerful representations in Washington that Canada should have full membership in the United Nations Relief and Rehabilitation Administration, and was pleased to hear from Norman Robertson 'that we are going to be tough about it.' He was equally displeased when he heard 'that the War Committee of the Cabinet had felt obliged to withdraw their claim to full membership, and had accepted the compromise of representation (albeit the Chairmanship) of the subsidiary committee concerned with supplies.'[115]

All of Massey's war-time activities I have mentioned so far were in the line of duty as Canadian plenipotentiary in the United Kingdom. There were two others which lay outside of a strict interpretation of official duty, but that were, nevertheless, the most important contributions that the Masseys made to the war effort. These were the establishment of a war artists' program and the launching of a number of services for the forces. Each involved close co-operation between Vincent and Alice, and drew upon enthusiasms that they shared – for Canadian painting and for imaginative and generous hospitality.

Canada had had her war artists during the First World War. Max

Aitken (not yet the more familiar Lord Beaverbrook) had managed to get the Canadian government to approve of his vague appointment as Canadian emissary overseas, and among his multiple activities – historian, publicist, negotiator – he set up a Canadian war memorials fund that commissioned artists to record the Canadian war effort. The group of artists blended public fame with creative genius; initially they were all British. They included Wyndham Lewis, Muirhead Bone, William Orpen, C.R.W. Nevinson, and Augustus John. (We have seen how Massey had rescued for Canada one of John's major war-time canvases.) By 1917, a Canadian initiative directed by Sir Edmund Walker, chairman of the Board of Trustees of the National Gallery, added a number of Canadian artists, among them Varley and Milne. But these had no official government status.

Now Massey set out to make the war artists' program in the Second World War an exclusively Canadian enterprise. A beginning had been made in Ottawa. The director of the historical section of the general staff was Colonel Archer Fortescue Duguid, an engineer and an artillery officer in the First World War, whose style of administration had, like his name, a quality of pompous formality. Duguid appointed a private, E.J. Hughes, who had been a painter in civilian life, to record, under his explicit direction, activities of the Canadian army. But Duguid had a grimly narrow concept of the function of art in the services.

In London Massey had begun a campaign to establish a war artists' program that would use Canadian artists of recognized standing and would have as its goal the vivid recreation of the nature and spirit of the activities of the Canadian forces. In Ottawa, his chief ally was H.O. McCurry, director of the National Gallery. Massey remained a trustee of the National Gallery and was in regular correspondence with McCurry about gallery policy and European acquisitions. Early in 1940 he had written to McCurry about war artists; this he saw as an enterprise that should be initiated by the gallery. When the project was finally launched, McCurry became the chairman of the Canadian committee. In London his chief ally was General Price Montague, who succeeded Crerar as senior officer in CMHQ and eventually became chief of the general staff. In civilian life Montague was a judge of the county King's Bench in Manitoba; he was the senior Canadian army legal officer overseas. He was interested in art and sympathetic to Massey's project, although a little uncertain in the presence of the artist. Massey recalls an encounter between Montague and Henry Lamb, an English artist (best known for his superb portrait of Lytton Strachey), who was working as a British war artist, but spent much of his time portraying the activities of Canadian troops. 'Amusing talk between my red-blooded general and the shy and retiring artist who was rather afraid of him. Great desire on both sides to please.'[116]

Together Massey and Montague tried to capture the minister of national defence for their cause. They took Ralston to the National Gallery to see the work of the British war artists, hoping that he would be inspired to emulate the British achievement. Ralston, who was unfortunately colour-blind, could summon up only polite interest. But the most valuable ally in Britain was Colonel C.P. Stacey, who thought that art should be part of the historical record and not an instructional tool or a recruiting gadget. He assumed responsibility for the first Canadian war artist, Will Ogilvie, not in the first instance officially appointed, but simply relieved, through Massey's intervention, of his military duties as a private, to work for a time as an artist.

Stacey was Massey's indispensable associate when the scheme became official and a substantial establishment was approved. But official approval came slowly. In August 1942, there was no decision from Ottawa; indeed, there were indications of a sullenly negative attitude. In September Massey described his discussions with Stacey as a 'conspiracy' and was still working to create a favorable atmosphere for action. One device was to take Canadian journalists to see the British war pictures in the National Gallery, in the hope that they would write articles in Canadian papers about the need for a similar Canadian venture. Then in the spring of 1943, the authorization came through and soon all three services had their war artists. As founder and patron, Massey now presided over the whole program.

Election to the board of trustees of the National Gallery in London in June 1941 and his appointment as chairman in April 1943 gave him an unusually prominent position in the art world of London. He could now get the help of the director of the National Gallery, Kenneth Clark. Clark served as critic and judge, and eased the way for a series of exhibitions of Canadian war artists in the National Gallery. When in August of 1946 the Art Gallery of Toronto mounted an exhibit of Canadian war artists, there were almost thirty represented, among them artists – Colville, Nichols, Ogilvie, Comfort, Lawren Harris Jr., Holgate, Schaeffer – who would dominate the Canadian art world of the forties. The Massey project had turned into a major cultural movement.

In the development of the Canadian artists' program Vincent was the officer in command devising the grand strategy, determining when and where specific attacks should be launched. Alice was a senior headquarters officer in charge of intelligence and morale. Carl Schaeffer recalls gratefully the role played by Mrs Massey in his own career as a Canadian war artist. He had arrived in England in 1943 with the rank of flying officer, but the RCAF did not seem to comprehend the artists' program and he was left to fend for himself. Charles Comfort, an old friend who was working happily and fruitfully as a war artist in the army, suggested he come to London, and go to 'Mother Massey's Hash House' (the affectionately disparaging way by which members of the forces referred to the Canadian Officers' Club) and ask for Mrs Massey's intervention. As soon as they arrived, Alice, who was as usual behind the counter serving the long line of officers, recognized them (although she had met both only briefly before), left her post, and embraced each with great warmth. They were immediately invited to come to dinner that evening at the Dorchester, where they could talk over their problems with Vincent and, incidentally, meet Kenneth Clark and a group of prominent English painters who were also coming to dinner. That evening greatly altered Schaeffer's outlook. When later he became seriously ill, he owed his repatriation to the Masseys' intervention.[117]

In the broader area of services to the Canadian forces, Alice Massey took over the command post, and for six years devoted most of her time and energy to her work. For her, 'auxiliary services,' to use the condescending military term, had a precise and personal meaning. It meant providing the comforts and the pleasures of home, or as many of them as possible, 'home' conceived of in her own exalted way. At the centre was always the provision of good food, never an easy matter in war-time Britain, especially since she insisted that it have a Canadian flavour. She delighted in her own prowess as a cook. She liked to tell the story of how 'years ago, my father said we all had to have something at our fingers' ends that we could do. I loved painting and I loved music, but could do neither of them well, so hied myself off to Edinburgh, where I studied cooking at Athol Crescent. For this training I have been grateful all my life.'[118] Food, she believed, must be served in surroundings that were colourful and harmonious, and this must be true of all the areas where soldiers relaxed from their duties; and there must be provision for games, the casual book, music, and conversation. In short, Alice set out to found a number of little Hart Houses in war-time Britain, all of them a far cry, of course, from the original, but one of them rivalling it in the splendour of its physical surrounding and the variety and elegance of its services.

In the early fall of 1939, before the arrival in late December of the first contingent of the Canadian army, the preparations for services to the forces was a matter of voluntary effort. At first, Alice addressed herself to directing the Canadian Women's Club, of which she was the honorary president, to war-time tasks. She organized a 'War Emergency Committee,' of which she was chairman. The emergency committee enrolled over four hundred women, most of whom were volunteers, and established a number of divisions, each directed to a separate task. Then complications arose. R.B. Bennett had become chairman of a London advisory committee for the Canadian Red Cross Society and was going about his duties in a magisterial way. Vincent had never forgotten Bennett's revocation in 1930 of his appointment as high commissioner in London, and he was not happy in the official relations that Bennett's residence in England thrust upon him. Alice, who never forgave anybody who slighted her husband, did not attempt to conceal her dislike of Bennett. A conflict between Bennett and the Masseys was bound to arise, now that Bennett was moving into territory that Alice thought of as peculiarly her own. Bennett resented the wide latitude in the operations of the Women's Canadian Club, especially since at an earlier period the club had offered to establish an information bureau under the general direction of the Red Cross. Alice, with dubious authority, wrote to Bennett, stating peremptorily that 'the war work of the Canadian Women's Club has developed to such an extent that we feel we are no longer free to assume the responsibility of maintaining an Information Bureau under the Canadian Red Cross, which we originally offered to do ...'[119]

Bennett replied in a heavy, legalistic letter, as if he were presenting a brief before the Privy Council, challenging Mrs Massey's right to speak on behalf of the club, and then in a subsequent letter, referring to 'the unwarranted attacks you make upon me personally.'[120] In the dispute both Bennett and Alice Massey acted arrogantly, but Bennett was technically in the right. At any rate, the executive of the Canadian Women's Club decided to follow Bennett and the Red Cross, and to disband Alice's war emergency committee. The result was an ugly confrontation that Vincent described with disgust and some relish. 'The executive behaved like a rather foolish clique in a girls' school club ... They descended on the offices in the Sun Life Building to demand all the furniture, equipment and files ... They behaved rather more like fishwives than ladies ... 5 or 6 women like harpies went rushing about the room, collecting everything they possibly could, sending it upstairs out of reach of Lal ... The whole thing is a disgusting episode.'[121]

The outcome of this unpleasant event was, for Alice, a happy one. 'Women's organizations, especially social ones, are not the easiest to work with, and perhaps I was too much of an autocrat,' she wrote to their close Montreal friend, J.M. McConnell; and to an English friend, she wrote philosophically, 'My own work must be on broader lines.'[122] The 'broader lines' were quickly outlined and, just as quickly, translated into action.

The Masseys were deeply involved in the founding and management of three institutions, to at least one of which almost every member of the Canadian armed forces serving abroad had reason to be grateful. The most important of these was the Beaver Club, which was for non-commissioned members of the Canadian forces (and was open also to men from the other members of the Commonwealth). It was the Massey response to the threatened hegemony of R.B. Bennett. At various celebratory events that marked the progress of the club, a member of the royal family would usually be present. The club came to symbolize the Canadian war effort. Vincent presided over a representative committee of men drawn from various organizations and interests, and Alice presided over a group of women volunteers ('the nicest and prettiest women I can find,'[123] she declared), who worked in four-hour shifts in the Club. Funds were raised from a variety of sources, often directly from individuals – from, for instance, Lord Beaverbrook and J.M. McConnell.

Alice was responsible for the selection of the quarters for the club. She wrote, 'One day going down the passage way to Spring Gardens, opposite Canada House and Admiralty Arch, we saw that the old London County Council building was vacant. We finally got into it. It was very dirty and very gloomy. Immediately I dashed down, with Vincent's permission, to see the London County Council people, those in charge of the buildings and pleaded the cause.'[124] The Masseys arranged for the rehabilitation of the building, and Alice chose the furniture, the china and glass, and worked out the colour scheme. This, like Hart House, was to be an intimate building that could, on a daily basis, absorb large numbers (an average of a thousand meals were served each day, and in the first year about a quarter of a million men had made use of the club.) The building could not have been more happily situated – convenient to Canada House and a stone's throw from Trafalgar Square. At its opening in February 1940, Gregory Clark in the Toronto *Daily Star* gave it with bold over-simplification, a royal setting: 'At one end of the Mall is Buckingham Palace, at the other Beaver House [sic], the Canadian home-from-home for the boys on leave.'

The Beaver Club was a great success, its history, for the most part, being one of steady progress and harmonious co-operation. But there were, especially during the first year, vexatious problems of a broadly political nature. The Bennett–Red Cross–Canadian Women's Club imbroglio left behind a smog of misunderstanding and resentment. Vincent's diary records his strong personal responses. He finally directed his anger against the whole Canadian community. 'The Canadian community here is full of complexes, jealousies, and ambitions, fantastically hard to please. Most diplomats regard their local colony as a perennial problem, and I wonder if any of them have difficulties comparable to those created by the Canadian colony here – the more you try to do the more you incur rancour and jealousy.'[125] Vincent had his doubts about giving a warm welcome to the various official services, even to the YMCA that eventually became the club's main sponsor. 'It's very hard,' he complained, 'to keep the whole soul-saving tract-pushing tendencies of the YMCA personnel from getting out of hand.'[126] But by July of 1940, all Vincent's complaints cease; the bickering, the malicious gossip, the struggle for power vanish, consumed in the success of the club and the necessity for hard work that that demanded. Periods of unrest would come again, but they would be the result of inevitable differences between management and the volunteers, not of fundamental clashes about policy. Providentially the club escaped serious damage during the blitz. In the heavy raid of 16/17 April 1941, the large room for parties and dances was destroyed, but a generous gift enabled the club, by adaptation of the remaining space, to continue its regular program.

The Canadian Officers' Club was small and limited in its objectives by comparison with the Beaver Club. It had two rooms and a kitchenette in space made available by Cunard White Star in its building on Cockspur Street, and its function was to serve luncheon to Canadian officers. It was a Massey enterprise, financially supported by them, and in its management completely free of any democratic complications. Alice referred to it with good cause as 'my little institution.' She had determined the décor (walls green, curtains orange, furniture cover bright chintz), did the cooking with the aid of a maid, and served the luncheons (with the aid of volunteers). There were few officers serving abroad, from the lowest to the highest, who didn't at some time go to the club. The food was appetizing, usually an ingenious blend of standard war-time rations and a few Canadian delicacies, served at half the cost of an average meal in a London restaurant. Alice Massey stood beside the counter, serving the main course, a vivid red apron covering her plain black dress, a large black hat worn at a jaunty angle. She talked to each man as he moved by – finding out where he came from, suggesting shows to see in London or shops for special purchases, reporting on her two sons in the services. And there was special concern for those who had just come through a trying experience – survivors, say, of a Russian convoy, who had been in the water for hours; airmen who had escaped from prisoner-of-war camps, or who had come down in the Channel after a strike in German-occupied France, and after 6 June 1944, the convalescent wounded and those on one brief leave from the western front.

The two clubs – the Beaver and the Officers' – were close to the day-to-day activities of the services. They were heavily used by the army which was concentrated in the southern counties, and they could be reached in an hour or so by men on a short leave. Garnons, the country house turned convalescent hospital, was something quite different. It was 150 miles to the west of London, in Herefordshire, a county that had escaped any enemy action and that had no heavy concentration of troops. During the entire war, only four bombs fell in the county, and these were dropped by enemy planes returning from a mission elsewhere, and eager to lighten their load. Garnons was a hospital only in name. It was technically part of the medical establishment; a medical officer was appointed by central command, and the residents were admitted from the hospitals where they had been patients. But, in effect, Garnons was a private institution financed by the Masseys through the Massey Foundation and conceived and operated by them. To those who stayed in Garnons, the hospital was invisible, and during the average residence of two or three weeks, even the consciousness of being a combatant faded. The atmosphere was that of a country house, where a large house party was constantly in progress. There was a principal hostess to preside, and three assistants, young ladies carefully chosen by Mrs Massey, whose task was to give style and feminine grace to the life of the house and to assist the men in their brief return to civilian life. Residents were officers of any rank in any of the Canadian services.

Garnons was an actual country house leased from its owner and occupant, Sir Richard Cotterell, who was serving abroad with the British army. It looked very much like a baronial mansion or a Norman castle, and young Canadians seeing it for the first time may well have thought of it as having been built centuries before as a defence against the marauding Welsh. Actually, it was a nineteenth-century creation begun in 1816 and completed on a grand scale in 1860. In general Garnons fulfilled the vision of the eminent landscape architect H. Repton, who in 1791 first described the building that he thought would be appropriate for the setting he had been asked to design. He wrote that 'a house which is the seat of Hospitality, and where according to the custom of Herefordshire, not only neighbouring Families but even their servants and horses may receive a welcome, must necessarily form such a mass of building as will give an air of Greatness to the general appearance.'[127]

The interior was as impressive as the outside. Suddenly, beyond a great Tudor hall, more or less in harmony with the exterior, Garnons became a Georgian mansion, with high ceilings, unleaded windows, Doric pillars, Grecian mouldings on the doors and ceilings, and spacious symmetrical public rooms – dining room, drawing room, and library. According to the authority Niklaus Pevsner, the greater part of the house was 'georganized internally' about 1907. Lieutenant Robert L. McDougall, Canadian Seaforth Highlanders, thus described the library in a letter to his mother:

It must be fully forty feet long, about twenty-five or thirty feet wide and twenty feet high. Nearly the whole of one side is taken up by three tremendous windows which stretch from floor to ceiling and open onto a stone flagged courtyard and a croquet lawn. At each bay formed by these windows is a writing desk. There are huge fireplaces at each end of the room, both with high and impressive mantlepieces of white marble. Above each of these fireplaces hang enormous oil paintings in heavy gilt frames. The remaining wall space is taken up with book cases, which, like the windows, reach from floor to ceiling. The rest of the furnishings complete a colourful picture: a thick, red floor carpet, heavy green drapes, deep sofas and easy chairs, a large mahogany card-table. Certainly a lovely room, exuding wealth, good taste, and comfort.[128]

'The enormous paintings in heavy gilt frames,' to which Lieutenant McDougall refers, looked down on all the public rooms. It was not a distinguished collection – dark landscapes (two by Ruisdael), architectural studies in the manner of Canaletto, a portrait by Lely, and a number of portraits of the more recent members of the Cotterell family by the obligatory artist for the socially prominent, Laszlo.

The Garnons estate had impressive dimensions. The fifty-room house was set in six thousand acres that included the large home farm, tenant farms, a number of small villages, each with a church (the 'living' was initially in the gift of the reigning Cotterell), a large wooded area from which the average yield of the shooting each season was 220 partridges, 1,000 pheasants, and 100 hares, and fishing rights for several miles along the River Wye. When the local train still ran, Sir Richard would send a servant to the station a short distance away to get his copy of *The Times* and a piece of fresh fish (this latter, despite the fame of the salmon fishing in the Wye). The Cotterells, like their house, had risen to prominence in the nineteenth century. The first baronet had been created in 1805, and the incumbent at the time of the Canadian invasion was the fifth baronet. But the estate was set down in a district whose history could be clearly traced back to Saxon times. Remains of the dyke built by Offa, King of Mercia, in 870 AD mark the boundary with Wales and could easily be identified a short distance from the house. The grave of Owen Glendower, the heroic Welsh warrior of the fifteenth century, was reputed to be in a churchyard a few miles from Garnons. Hereford, the principal centre of the county, was seven miles to the east. Its magnificent cathedral rose on the banks of the Wye 'half house of God, half fortress against the Welsh'; its fine choral tradition had been strengthened by the presence in the city of Elgar, who wrote much of his best music there at a time (1904–1912) when the city still retained a good deal of its medieval tranquillity and colour.

Above all, Garnons was in a countryside of great natural beauty. It was a countryside of vistas, of broad fields in variegated colours, of gentle hills and distant mountains. It was the countryside of the Reverend Francis Kilvert whose late nineteenth-century diary vividly recalls the rural life of Victorian England and captures forever the beauty of the scenery. The heart of Kilvert country lies some fifteen miles to the west in the rugged Welsh borderland, but Kilvert knew the more gentle landscape immediately to the east, and for the last two years of his life he was the vicar of Bredwardine, a little village on the outskirts of Garnons. Here is a passage that might have been written from a Garnon's lookout: 'How beautiful is the descent into Bredwardine from Brobury. Especially as I saw it this afternoon, the lovely valley gleaming bright in the clear shining after rain, the thickly wooded hillsides veiled with tender blue delicate mists through which the brilliant evening sun struck out jewels of gold where he lit upon the upland slopes and hill meadows, while the poplar spires shot up like green and gold flames against the background of brown and purple woods and the river blazed below the grey bridges with a sparkle of a million diamonds.'[129]

Garnons was superbly sited to afford views such as this. It was built at the base of a hill, which rose gradually behind it to a height of 700 feet, and it looked out on a vast, encompassing field that sloped gradually to the main road, a half a mile or so away. A short distance beyond the road was the valley of the Wye that, at this point, twists and turns placidly through the countryside, and in the distance were the Black Mountains of Wales that changed with the shifting light, now dark and menacing, now bright and verdant. Those who came in the spring caught their first glimpse of Garnons garlanded by flowers – pale yellow primroses, white and blue violets, yellow and white daffodils.

No doubt the Canadian officers were charmed by the countryside, and some of them sought out the historical sites. The Masseys made available a short historical sketch of Garnons and a brief guide to the historical sites. The former was prepared and written by Kitty Earp, one of the hostesses, who was a graduate of Cambridge in modern languages and an artist with a lively interest in art history.[130] The latter, entitled 'Sight seeing at Garnons, or what one can discover in a series of short walks,' was the work of a resident officer, a brief document, hortatory in tone, a little like an army lecture to the troops on the maintenance of morale. But for most of the officers, the countryside and the historical sites existed as a vague, pleasant background to a life of games – croquet, billiards, golf, bridge – visits to the nearest pub, trips to Hereford, a succession of excellent meals that, for the time being, banished the taste of service fare, a wine cellar of dizzying size and variety, parties, improvised skits, periods of complete, uninhibited relaxation – playing, for instance, with an electric train that Vincent brought down one day from London.

One Garnons guest wrote to Alice Massey that 'it was like returning to civilization after years in the jungle.' But all was not paradisic in this Eden. Inevitable tensions and misunderstanding arose among staff and hostesses, and Vincent would occasionally report that Alice was engaged in a major reorganization at Garnons. Some officers would not take kindly to the country house atmosphere and would seek an alcoholic retreat in their own rooms (Vincent thought that bedroom drinking was a result of the crabbed Canadian liquor laws). No doubt, the hostesses, young and attractive, found it difficult at times to draw the line between camaraderie and involvement. They came directly under the supervision of Alice, and she took pains to emphasize that they did not have a soft billet. They had long hours; they could not withdraw from the social round because of an onset of tedium or indisposition. Every dinner was a formal affair when the men wore their service dress and the hostesses wore long gowns. Each was assigned a specific task in addition to the general concern for the welfare and happiness of the guests. These included the writing of a daily report (these exist as a thick mass in Alice Massey's papers, and are, for the most part, dull repetitions of trivia) and the gathering of flowers, copiously available in the garden and conservatory, to soften the grandeur of the common rooms. For Kitty Earp, who had worked in handicrafts, there was the setting up and running of a room that could be dignified as 'occupational therapy.' She found, after two and a half years as a hostess, during which 1,500 officers had passed through Garnons, that she could no longer face her duties with a light heart. She wrote to Mrs Massey about her decision to leave. 'Do you understand if I say it's as if my heart won't go on stretching? I believe this work to belong very much in the realm of the heart, meaning nothing sentimental by that. Its mostly just a here-and-now friendship we can give people, but it does need to be real.'[131]

No doubt those who worked at Garnons and some of the patient-guests had moments when they questioned the very idea of the place. Wasn't this oasis of genteel luxury absurdly removed from the austerity of service life and the democratic ideals to which they were dedicated? At one evening party a dramatic skit was presented in which the hostesses played the girls and Alice the madame. The irreverent thought may have occurred to both the players and the spectators that this was a fantasy with some roots in reality.

But if this idea arose, it vanished quickly. Garnons was a charmed place. It was a war-time service, limited in its scope (a battalion of 2,500 or so passed through compared to the army at the Beaver Club), but its fame spread widely and it left a deep impression on those who stayed there. The Masseys received hundreds of letters of thanks from

Garnons graduates, and most of them rose above polite notes.[132] Garnons for the Masseys also became their country house, an English Batterwood on a larger and more exuberant scale. It took the place of the country house week-ends that had brought so much satisfaction to them in pre-war days in England. They could now be the hosts on week-ends or for longer breaks from their unrelenting official chores. They would preside at the cocktail hour, the dinner, and for a social hour afterwards, Vincent rarely holding forth, but listening intently, asking questions (a technique, Alison Grant slyly suggested to Kitty Earp, that he learned from the Duke of Kent, whom he much admired). It aroused anew his deep love of English rural life, its abiding sense of the past, the flourishing of the individual, despite the rigid stratifications of society. One summer week-end Charles Ritchie was a guest. He and Vincent wrote comments in their diaries that echoed each other. Ritchie wrote, 'Mr. M. and I are both bitten with this place. We cannot escape the charms of the past. These institutions were made for men and women human in scale.'[133] Vincent wrote, 'Lal and I love Garnons. We feel as if we had lived there all our lives – a happy house with friendly ghosts and the most lovely countryside in England.'[134]

Garnons, like the Officers' Club, was primarily Alice's responsibility. She was in daily touch by telephone and on week-ends she looked closely at the administrative arrangements. In London she was busy each day, in the morning preparing and serving the luncheon at the Officers' Club, in the afternoon dictating endless letters, most of them to Canadian relatives of men she had met at either of the two London clubs and increasingly as the war gained in tempo, to the relatives of the wounded and killed. When the Masseys went to war, Alice and Vincent, as always inseparable, marched resolutely together and shared the burdens and dangers. Violet Markham wrote to Alice about their war work: 'When I look at you and Vincent and the way you turn your back on all rest and pleasures and recreation I feel what a slack and selfish creature I am. You have written a noble page in the war. When I passed a Massey harvester on a farm yesterday I wanted to stop it and shake "hands." '[135]

Of the two, Alice was the more resolute, the more persistent in pursuing her goals. Lester Pearson wrote from Washington: 'It remains a never-ending source of amazement to us both that she can do so much and do it so well.'[136] Undoubtedly, as a result of her war work, she undermined her health. 'She wore herself down in the war by hard work for Canadian servicemen in England,' wrote Charles Ritchie, who was in a position to know. 'I see her plodding along Cockspur Street laden with provision for the Beaver Club ... or at her desk writing hundreds of letters to the relations of Canadians serving abroad.'[137] Her best memorial is the plaque placed by Vincent in Grosvenor Chapel, where they worshipped during their years in London. On walls covered with plaques chiefly commemorating in solemn prose eighteenth-century worthies, it stands out by reason of its simplicity and grace both in form and message. It reads:

To the dear memory of Alice, wife of Vincent Massey, P.C. C.H., sometime High Commissioner for Canada in London, and daughter of Sir George Parkin K.C. M.C. She was born in Fredericton, N.B., and died at Batterwood near Port Hope, Ontario 27 July, 1950. Her name lives in the hearts of all who felt the glow of her friendship.

CHAPTER FIVE

The Return to Canada

On 7 May, 1945, at one of their last meetings, the high commissioners were informed that the 'German High Command had signed the Instruments of Surrender at 2.41 a.m. and that the surrender would take effect at one minute past midnight on May 8.' The Masseys celebrated VE day in a quiet, domestic manner. Alison joined them for dinner; they listened to the King's speech, and then Vincent, Hart, and Alison sallied forth to see the town – first to Buckingham Palace where an immense crowd waited for the King and Queen to make an appearance, then down the Mall to Trafalgar Square stopping en route at the door at the Beaver Club, where Vincent, above the din of celebration within, smilingly asked the corporal on duty whether all was quiet.

When the jubilation died down, the war-time routines without the war-time excitements and expectations returned. Food rationing and long queues continued, and the great scars from war-time bombing remained. The Masseys, like everybody else, felt the prolongation of war-time restrictions. More important, they felt the cessation of war-time pleasures, in particular the gradual fading away of the three service clubs that they, in large part, had created. The Beaver Club and the Officers' Club had ceremonial closings. The closing of the Beaver Club on 19 February, 1946 had a royal glow. Queen Mary was the guest of honour, and Alice rhapsodized: 'You simply cannot imagine how regal and wonderful she looked. She had a long, dark purple velvet coat over a long purple dress, beautifully fitting, beautifully slim with a little fur around her neck, a small toque, with her wonderfully groomed hair, and enough jewels (including a spray of gold and jewelled maple leaves given her in Canada when she came out as Duchess of York) to add to her queenly look.'[1] The Officers' Club had no such ceremonial closing. Alice wrote to Hart sadly about its demise. 'My little club, which I started one month after war was declared, and which has carried on through fair and foul weather – blitzes and victories – is no more.'[2] The Beaver Club closing had an anti-heroic note, since Canadian soldiers no longer flocked to London. Four hundred were imported for the occasion from outside the city, most of them recent arrivals in England who had a low patriation priority. Most melancholy of all was the passing, gradually with no dramatic end, of the Masseys' proudest creation, Garnons, its war-time inhabitants back in Canada or lying in foreign fields. Garnons seemed like a dream, to which the Masseys had given a brief and colourful life. The insubstantial pageant had faded, leaving not a rack behind ...

The end of the war did not bring a respite from official duties; if anything, the tempo increased. Vincent wrote to Mackenzie King about his multiplicity of duties: 'Commonwealth Air Transport Council, Telecommunications meeting, shipping problems in relation to the repatriation of our forces, questions concerning demobilisation and post-war rehabilitation, the repatriation of our prisoners of war, the War Crimes Commission.'[3] The list sounds more impressive than it actually was. The first two meant little more than keeping a watching brief at meetings, since there had been no explicit direction from Ottawa. The remaining items were the responsibility largely of the office staff, which had been greatly expanded and worked efficiently – not a belittlement of Massey's contribution, but rather evidence of his firm organizational grasp and sensitivity to the interplay between individuals. All this business was anticlimactic. Most of the responsibilities were residues of the war, the sad, untidy aftermath of brave ventures. What he was now concerned with was important to a great many people, but not exciting in itself. Early in 1946 Massey began to think that the time had come to leave his post and that his tour of duty was coming to its natural end.

He had now served ten years as high commissioner. From February to March 1944 he had been in Canada for the first time since 1937, and there had been a subsequent trip, this time with Alice, from August to October in 1945. He had re-established his various interests in Canada, and he was reasonably confident that new opportunities would arise there. But if nothing attractive presented itself in Canada, he could foresee other possibilities. When, just before the announcement on 12 March 1946 of his resignation, he went to see the new prime minister, Clement Attlee, and his dominions secretary, Lord Addison, he said to them: 'If I cannot find work to get my teeth into in Canada and come trotting back here to ask for a job, will you give one to me?'[4] The question was, he said, posed half-jokingly, but he was delighted when both of them took it seriously and replied in the affirmative. At the end of his ten years as high commissioner, he was widely known as a Londoner who could, if he chose, remain in England and continue there his career of public service.

In England Massey first established for himself a reputation as an able and effective speaker. This was not a small achievement in a country where Churchill's Augustan oratory was, in the early years of the war, Britain's principal weapon. As a diplomat, Massey spoke only on formal ocasions, where the atmosphere was friendly and uncritical, and tolerance for the obvious was at its highest. But he handled the obvious with simplicity and dignity; he did not aspire to Churchillian rhetoric (although one American critic, in an uncritical flight, referred to him as a Canadian Churchill);[5] like Iago, as he remarked once, he avoided a style 'horribly stuffed with epithets of war.' Occasionally, a modest epigram emerged: speaking of the dominions, he said 'out of the last war emerged their status, out of this one their stature'.[6] Occasionally, he moved beyond the descriptive to the hortatory. In a speech to the Royal Empire Society in March 1942, at a time when a growing confidence was not matched by accomplishments in the field, he struck a note that was much applauded in the press, as in this report in *The Times*: 'Now was the time for a mental offensive. We were always in danger of something he ventured to call "maginotism" of the mind – mental inertia and a passive attitude – a posture which, like that sad fortress-line in France, could be outflanked. Our ideas must match the momentum and the thrust of our weapons in the field. There could be no better time than now to reaffirm our faith. Now was the time for new breath to quicken the pulse of democratic peoples everywhere.'[7]

Massey always prepared his speeches well in advance, rehearsed them, and delivered them from a manuscript, without, however, giving the impression of being slave of his text. He had, observed one English commentator, 'the attractive gift of making a speech sound like an earnest, almost vehement conversation.'[8] He was, in short, an accomplished actor with a voice attuned to the music of the language. Another English commentator declared that 'he has humour and the family histrionic talent, which shows itself in an unexpected turn for mimicry.'[9] Given these virtues – directness, simplicity, a feeling for the language, and a sense of the dramatic – he was a first-class broadcaster. Many of his best efforts were what the BBC called postscripts, brief impressionistic reports to mark a special day. The 'critic on the hearth' in the *Listener*, the BBC's official publication, was rhapsodic about the broadcast on Dominion Day 1942: 'of the pure original postscripts the best I can remember for ages ... this sense of wireless composition was matched by a sincere, virile, and wholly unaffected voice, its purity of tone warmed by the pleasant kind of Canadian accent.'[10]

Before he went to Britain, there is no indication that Vincent made use of speech-writers. Certainly, the professional speech-writer had not yet become an accepted member of a political establishment, and public figures had not yet exchanged their own styles, good or bad, for the glossy products of the public relations industry. In London, however, Massey had assistants whose writing talents it would have been a pity not to use. Charles Ritchie and Douglas LePan, for instance, were primarily men of letters who happened to be officers in External Affairs. Both wrote, or helped to write, some of Massey's speeches; they were the first of a group that would be, in vice-regal days, considerably enlarged. Charles Ritchie recorded in his diary the secret delight of the speech writer as he hears his words lifted from the page and given public utterance. 'Last night I wrote a speech for Mr. Massey to deliver to Canada on the general theme of "the darkest hour before the dawn," "British spirit is unbreakable," "The nightmare of horror and destruction that hangs heavy in the air in these lovely days of English spring." Mr. Massey delivered it. It was a great success.'[11]

As he had during his term as minister in Washington, Vincent published a selection of his London speeches under the title of *The Sword of Lionheart and Other Wartime Speeches*. The title was inspired by the statue of King Richard outside Westminster Hall, which was slightly damaged in a bombing raid. The crusader's sword held aloft by Richard had been bent by the force of the explosion, and Vincent was moved to express in verse his hope that it would remain forever in this condition:

> *So let it stand, a people's sign and token*
> *Figured in bronze, for all free men to see –*
> *The Sword of Lionheart though bent, not broken,*
> *In this new warfare of God's chivalry.*

The lines were much quoted and praised, presumably on the grounds that any signs of creativity in a public figure are to be applauded. Vincent's pious wish was not respected. In the House of Commons Major Maurice Petherick replied in a quatrain more finished than Vincent's:

> *Would not King Richard casting with scorn away*
> *A crooked weapon blunted in a fight*
> *Fiercely have shouted 'Back into the fray*
> *Bring now a sword worthy of England's might*[12]

The slim little book of 102 pages sold 5,000 copies. Perhaps this was a reflection of the scarcity of new books in war-time London, although the *Times Literary Supplement*, not given to puffery, thought the success was achieved on merit. Its review elaborated on the nature of the book's appeal: 'It is difficult to say again with any freshness those things that have been said to and about us since the war began, but it has been accomplished here. Mr. Massey avoids that hortatory note of which the public ... grows increasingly weary. He is not an orator in any grandiose sense of the term; his speeches are simple statements of fact and feeling – descriptions of what he has seen going on around him, interpretation to each other of two countries which he knows well and loves equally. [The speeches have] the virtues of simplicity and sincerity, and [are] free from the too well-rubbed small change of platitudes about freedom and democracy, which, as handled by some speakers, have lost a good deal of their original high value.'[13]

Massey's accomplishments as a speaker were generously recognized and praised. He was consistently reported in the newspapers, usually at considerable length, especially in *The Times*, over which his close friend Robin Barrington-Ward presided. But it was in the arts and education that he made his greatest impression in Britain. Here he was accepted as a cultivated layman who could move easily among professionals. Massey was the only diplomat who arrived in London with his own carefully selected collection of paintings. He remained an active trustee of the National Gallery of Canada, and pursued suggestions with professional acuteness for the acquisition by it of old masters. Above all, he rapidly became known as a collector and connoisseur of English painting, and early in his tenure of office decided, as a project of the Massey Foundation, to make a collection of modern English painting which would be presented to the National Gallery in Ottawa. Shortly before the Masseys left for Canada, on 14 April 1946, the result was exhibited at the Tate Gallery. It was a twentieth-century collection, from artists like Philip Wilson Steer and Walter Sickert whose roots were in the Victorian era, to contemporary artists like Graham Sutherland and Victor Pasmore, to whose work Massey had been introduced by English friends. The British collection was a complement to his own Canadian collection, and each was meant to be an introduction to one country of the art of the other. Eric Newton wrote in the *Sunday Times*, 'Canada will have reason to be grateful to Mr. Massey for a gift so comprehensive and so carefully selected, and Britain should be equally grateful to know that its best painters will, at last, be properly represented in Canada.'[14] The collection was a mirror of Vincent's taste (which also meant Alice's); it avoided extremes, the staid Royal Academicans at one end, abstract painters at the other.

Massey's appointment as a trustee of the British National Gallery in May 1941 had not been a polite diplomatic gesture. The board consisted of ten men of wide influence with an attested interest in the arts, and Massey was considered to be an obvious selection. Kenneth Clark, the director, wrote that 'it is a brilliant appointment, the best that has been made for years.'[15] Two years later Vincent was made chairman. Alice wrote proudly to Maude: 'Yes, some months ago Vincent was chosen and appointed by Mr. Churchill Chairman of the National Gallery. I was sorry at the time that they didn't make a little more of it in the Canadian Press – not from the point of view of any bombast, but I do think it is an honour to Canada that he should have been asked to do this.'[16] The chairmanship was for a two-year term, but he was asked to stay on. Arthur Lee (Viscount Lee of Fareham) wrote on behalf of his fellow trustees: 'There is really no one at the moment who could take your place at all adequately, and, after some preliminary soundings amongst our colleagues, I am strengthened in my conviction that it would give great and general satisfaction if you could be persuaded to continue in the chair for a further term.'[17] Vincent was persuaded, and remained as chairman until his departure for Canada.

Massey's chairmanship coincided with preparations for the reopening of the gallery. The pictures had been stored in a Welsh quarry, safe from bombing, but not safe from serious accidents. Massey's first task was to assure the co-operation of the Ministry of Works, which was responsible for the safekeeping of the pictures but nursed a bureaucratic grievance that it had not been properly consulted in the initial decision. This was a minor irritation beside the question that, as the return of the pictures became imminent, dominated the meetings of the trustees: should the National Gallery concerts be continued? These concerts had been held daily, except on Saturdays and Sundays, since 10 October 1939. They had been introduced as a wartime measure, a means of strengthening morale; they had been something much more – a witness to the indestructibility of the arts and the imperturbable spirit of war-time London. They had become powerfully identified with Myra Hess, who served the concerts both as organizer and as artist. With the end of the war, solid practical reasons were advanced for their continuation: they met a proven need; there was no other hall in central London that could be used for concerts of this kind; and the crowds who came to hear the music would stay to see the pictures. The trustees were sceptical about the last argument. With some dissension, they agreed first to a three-months, then to a year's extension. Myra Hess pleaded for a final decision. She was of two minds: eager to see the concerts continued, yet aware that continuation depended on a permanent administration to which she could not, without sacrificing her career, give leadership. It was Vincent's responsibility to convey to Dame Myra the final decision of the trustees to bring the concerts to an end in April 1946. He wrote: 'It is mainly the condition of the building – the fact that we can put less than half our rooms to their normal use, and that in this we must let the Ministry of Works get on with their repairs – that led us to the decision that the concerts must come to an end now. It was a most unwelcome decision to have to make, and we have been careful to draw up our resolution in such a way as to leave the door open for music to return to the Gallery when we have command of all our building again. So you have not only brought music to the Gallery but you have given us a great idea for the future and you have shown that it can be carried out.'[18]

Vincent presided over two important gallery events in the transition from war to peace. The first was the reopening of the gallery on 17 May 1945. About fifty of the great masterpieces had been brought back and placed on view. Before the general public was admitted the king and queen and a number of guests were invited to view the pictures. Lord Keynes, a trustee, proposed a ceremonial touch to which Vincent warmly agreed. Lord Keynes was about to meet, as he put it, 'for some continuous discussion of various outstanding matters' with a Canadian party, consisting of the governor of the Bank of Canada, Graham Towers, and two senior civil servants, W.L. Mackintosh and Hector McKinnon. He asked that they be invited to the royal prologue: 'This would be all the more suitable in view of your being Chairman of the Trustees. We could offer them this little ceremony on their arrival as a symbol that some things, at least, have come to an end.'[19]

The second event was more crucial to the future of the gallery. Kenneth Clark had been director for twelve years, having received two extensions of his original appointment so that he could see the gallery through to its reopening. Clark was a combination of scholar, connoisseur, and social lion. About his successor Massey wrote, 'The

National Gallery is now full of life and interest but I do not think that the tradition which K [as Clark was known by his intimates] has established will continue on its own momentum. The place may well step back into conventional lines unless we have a man who is receptive to new ideas and can produce some himself.'[20] Massey suggested Philip Hendy, who was eventually appointed.[21] He had met Hendy, who was director of the Leeds Art Gallery, during an official visit to that city, and Hendy's dossier – it included previous employment as curator of paintings in the Museum of Fine Arts, Boston, and Slade Professor of the History of Fine Arts, Oxford – reinforced an initially favourable impression.

As the result of his chairmanship of the National Gallery, Massey served on two national committees with broad terms of reference. Of one committee concerned with the 'preservation and restitution of art treasures appropriated by the enemy,' he was vice-chairman, and as a result of the illness of the chairman, Lord MacMillan, became in effect chairman. He addressed himself to establishing a realistic basis for the committee's discussions by forming a firm liaison with the Foreign Office and with the parallel committee working in Washington. The second committee, of which he was chairman and which, like a later Canadian report, came informally to bear his name, was 'appointed by the Chancellor and the President of the Board of Education to examine the functions of the National Gallery and Tate Gallery, and, in respect of paintings, of the Victoria and Albert Museum, with special reference to their relations with one another and to the fuller representation of British Art.' This committee, which included the directors of the three institutions referred to in the terms of reference, concentrated on the anomalous position of the Tate, which had been established as the national gallery of British art, had acquired an ill-defined additional responsibility for modern foreign art, yet enjoyed no administrative autonomy and was denied any official government support. The recommendations of the committee were far-ranging and really comprised a national policy in art. The core of the report was the sharp delineation of the nature and function of the Tate: while retaining its traditionally close association with the National Gallery, it should be an independent institution; it should have an annual grant from the government and the effective control of a major private fund, hitherto in the unsteady hands of the Royal Academy; and it should have two distinct collections, one in British art, one in modern art, each with a keeper working under a director.

When the report came out in May 1946, *Country Life* observed that 'the Massey report ... will serve as an admirable and characteristic memorial to the retiring High Commissioner for Canada.'[22] It was also a prologue to what would be his principal Canadian accomplishment – in Britain, a program for the distribution of rich cultural resources, in Canada a strategy for preserving and expanding resources, modest and underdeveloped.

In the field of the arts Massey was a cultivated amateur; in education – particularly higher education – he had some claims to being a professional. This was the most likely field where, if he decided to stay in England, he could with some confidence expect a permanent appointment. There was no question of a pure academic appointment, and he would have been the first to scotch such an idea. His brief term as a teacher of history on a university level lay far in the past, and his subsequent career had smothered any pretensions he may have had to scholarship. He had continued to read widely, but it was reading dictated by the fluctuations of contemporary taste rather than by any systematic pursuit of a subject. But he had an interest in education that did not need to be sustained by scholarly reading, and in England that interest was concentrated on his old college, Balliol. From the day he landed in Britain, he had kept up close ties with Balliol, and he (in association with the other two Balliol men in the family and with Alice, 'a beloved mother of the house') had furnished a banquet room 'where the students may eat and disport themselves.'[23]

Now, as the college prepared for the return of veterans, it was apparent that all was not well. Vincent was one of a number of influential Balliol men, eventually their unofficial chairman, who met to discuss the plight of the college. It was not attracting the best men from the schools, as it once had, and as a result its academic reputation had suffered. More important, the college spirit, whether expressed as 'a tranquil consciousness of effortless superiority' or as a simple determination to excel for the glory of Balliol, had suffered an alarming decline. There were a number of reasons for this state of affairs, most of them reflecting changes in Oxford ways – particularly a livelier competitiveness among the colleges. But there was one reason that affected all others and that could profitably engage the interest of old Balliol men – the character of the current master, A.D. Lindsay. At a dinner of Massey's group on 1 November 1944, there was general agreement on a list of defects – Lindsay's 'obsession with outside things, his lack of real interest in the life of the college, his bad judgment of men, his lack of contact with undergraduates.'[24]

The heart of the indictment was in the first item. Lindsay was a social activist (not in itself a bad trait, his critics admitted), but unlike his predecessor, A.L. Smith, whose social interests grew out of a primary interest in the college, Lindsay was thought to be making the college a platform for his projects and campaigns. Moreover, Lindsay was a left-wing activist with a strong identification with the Labour party. His political aggressiveness and his insensitivity to the college came together, his critics said, in his desire to appoint a prominent left-wing economist, T.H. Balogh, as a fellow. Balogh was believed to be an acerbic person who would not adorn the Balliol common room, and he was known to be a powerful and influential opponent of the government's support of the recent multilateral trade agreements reached at Bretton Woods. Lindsay responded heatedly and, as Vincent admitted, effectively to the attack on Balogh. He wrote to Vincent about a critical assessment that had been sent to him: 'What your fellow says amounts to saying that Balogh belongs to a heretical school, and I do not think a College, or a University, ought to pay any attention whatsoever to that sort of criticism. If economics is going to be tainted with a sort of *odium theologicum* it will be a bad business.'[25] After Labour won the election of July 1945, Lindsay became Lord Lindsay of Birker, and it was assumed that he would soon relinquinsh his mastership. Massey was talked of as his successor.

The Labour victory had not disillusioned Vincent about the future of Britain, and he did not experience any of the sense of panic that arose in some Conservative circles. His Conservative friends – Harold Macmillan, Rab Butler, Robin Barrington-Ward, 'Bobbety' Cranborne, all on the left wing of the Conservative party – thought that it was 'on the whole a good thing to rebuke the diehards in the party and encourage the progressives.'[26] Certainly Oxford would adjust easily to the new political climate. On an overnight stay at Balliol, despite a bed of 'concrete-like rigidity' and a succession of disturbances, he felt a resurgence of his deep allegiance. 'The gardens looked untroubled by the war and the architecture simply sang.' The prospect of returning to his old college was alluring, and it could now in time be a reality.

The immediate decision about which there were no doubts and hesitations was 'to return to Canada.' Alice was firmer about this than Vincent, and as the time approached to leave London her letters to her sister Maude were full of a happy anticipation of their return. By early spring of 1946 both sons were in Canada. Hart had accompanied his parents when they visited Canada in the summer of 1945 and had stayed to prepare for his entrance to the faculty of architecture in the University of Toronto. (He complained good-naturedly that, after a Balliol degree and five demanding years in the air force, he was now reduced to the status of a school boy struggling with basic mathematics.) Lionel had become engaged to a Canadian girl serving with the Red Cross in England – Lilias, daughter of the late Senator Thomas Ahearne of Ottawa – and the marriage was planned for the summer of 1946 in Ottawa. He had gone to Toronto in April to take up a position with the old family firm. Vincent and Alice, after a succession of farewell dinners and official leave-takings beginning with a dinner given by the king and queen, finally left for Canada on 23 May 1946.

They could not yet look forward to a specific appointment to, as Alice wrote, 'an arduous and a strenuous and a real job.'[27] Vincent was no doubt aware of Canadian newspapers' discussion of the possibility of the appointment of a Canadian to succeed the Earl of Athlone as governor-general and of the speculation that he would be nominated. There is no mention in his letters and diary of this speculation, nor was he aware that Mackenzie King had actually moved to make a Canadian appointment. In September 1944, King had asked General McNaughton, now returned to Canada, to become governor-general, and McNaughton had accepted. But King, agonizing over the conscription issue, then came to the conclusion that McNaughton could be more useful to him politically as minister of defence. McNaughton, who believed that conscription was not essential for victory, responded to King's 'call to duty' and gave up the governor-generalship. King had also considered Massey and Vanier for the position, but now abandoned the idea of a Canadian appointment. He asked Massey to see C.M. Trevelyan, the distinguished historian and Cambridge master, and inquire if he would take on the job. Trevelyan declined on grounds of his lack of political or diplomatic experience. Massey thought this 'wise and realistic.' Shortly after, Field Marshal Sir Harold Alexander accepted the appointment. Massey welcomed the choice and observed that 'his regime should be a great success.'[28]

By the time Massey announced his retirement as high commissioner, King had abandoned the thought of high office of any kind for him. Vincent must have read the final paragraph of the prime minister's unctuous letter in response to his resignation as a polite but firm dismissal. 'I am glad your missions abroad have been not only so helpful to us all, but so rich in experiences to yourself. I have no doubt you have in mind recording much of what you have known and experienced at first hand. That, of itself, should afford ample material for literary work over the next few years.'[29]

On 19 May King arrived in London for Commonwealth meetings just four days before Massey was scheduled to depart for Canada. For Massey they were anxious and disturbing days. On 8 May he had been informed by the king's secretary that the king proposed to make him a Companion of Honour, a member of an order of high renown limited to the king and fifty others. This would be the climax to his term as high commissioner. Royal awards were to him the ultimate symbolism, holy and transfiguring. But he could not accept it without the permission of his prime minister and that permission had not yet come. In the preceding weeks, King had been thinking a good deal about Massey, and his ruminations were consistently dark. He had, for instance, taken a grimly critical view of Massey's gift of English paintings to the National Gallery of Canada, partially, no doubt, because he anticipated that the pictures would be 'modern' and outside the parched range of his own artistic taste. He described the gift as a kind of 'self-glorification,' and then ranged back in his mind to what he considered the ultimate source of the gift – high prices 'exacted by the Massey interests from the farmers.'[30] King recalled a dream. 'I was in a room with Vincent Massey, who was sitting at a desk, and in my presence, dictating to one of my staff. He seemed to be ignoring my presence completely. I finally took a chair from another part of the room and sat almost immediately opposite to him letting him see I intended that I would have to do with my own affair and that I resented his attitude.'[31]

The resentment and the feeling of inferiority that the dream transparently reflects surfaced in King's attitude now. The one clear 'sansculottish' remnant King retained from his grandfather's radicalism was a detestation of all honours. When a proposal for a Canada medal and a Canadian order had come before cabinet several weeks earlier, King told his colleagues he 'had never experienced more pain and anguish over any public matter than I have on anything that has to do with decorations. I said that personally I was all against them upon conviction; for honours that were done one, multitudes were ignored who were more worthy.'[32]

When he arrived in London, King was not disposed to make an exception for Massey in this universal disapproval. He was not impressed by the argument advanced by senior advisers that the royal proposal was unique and did not, therefore, constitute a precedent for the future. Indeed, he found the proposal a particularly sinister undermining of sound Canadian values and a witness to Massey's perfidy. 'It shows all of what is back of his public service – vain glory; desire for Royal recognition; preference of another country, as Bennett did, to his own instead of remaining with the country that had honoured him with the position of High Commissioner.'[33]

The palace had arranged for the CH to be presented to Massey by King George at a special ceremony on the evening of 22 May. On the morning of the twenty-first, Sir Alan Lascelles, the king's secretary, phoned to say that 'Attlee's recommendation to the king that I should be made a C.H. had not received W.L.M.K's approval – so it was off.'[34] King came to see Massey in the evening, and Massey 'found his manner definitely unsympathetic' despite the conventional compliments. He abandoned hopes of the honour.

That night, King had a change of heart. (He himself thought that he 'received some direction from Beyond.') He telephoned Louis St Laurent, who was presiding over a cabinet meeting, subsequently received a telegram from St Laurent giving the cabinet's approval of the CH, then went to the Dorchester to announce his agreement to Massey. There followed a highly emotional scene in which each vied with the other in expressions of joy and satisfaction. King thus describes the scene. 'He said to me: "O Rex this means so much. There is nothing I would rather have than this. I cannot tell you how deeply I feel or how grateful I am to you." I said: You have nothing to thank me for, Vincent. You have had a great record here; done a great work and I am pleased it has been recognized. It has given me pleasure to have to do with its recognition.'[35]

At 10 p.m. that evening Vincent and Alice went to Buckingham Palace. Lascelles greeted them with Wellington's famous remark about Waterloo: 'It was a damned near thing.' They were received by the king and queen and Princess Elizabeth. 'There could never have been an investiture so intimate and charming. It left with us a precious memory of that half hour which will never fail.'[36] Late that evening King, who was staying in the Dorchester near Massey's rooms, went down to congratulate Vincent and Alice. The scene had a Shakespearean glow, Vincent as Richard II with his crown magically restored. 'The order of the Companion of Honour,' King wrote, 'was on the arm of a chair and Vincent had been looking at it, if not worshipping it. This was, of course, the apex of Vincent's ambitions and career. It was amazing to see the change."[37]

King interpreted his reversal as evidence of his own intrinsic goodness of heart. His wish to bring happiness to Massey had triumphed over his deeper political convictions. Moreover, he thought, Massey 'will return with kindly feelings towards myself.' A less prejudiced observer might have concluded that the episode showed King enjoying sadistically the exercise of power, first humiliating a dependent, then restoring him with protestations of affection and high regard.

Massey had no illusions about the nature of King's feelings towards him. When he returned to Canada, he waited for three months to hear from Ottawa. Then on 14 October he received a phone call from King offering him the lieutenant-governorship of Ontario. King knew that Massey would find the invitation unwelcome. Several months before leaving England, Massey had heard that King might make this proposal. Alice wrote to Maude: 'Imagine our thinking of such a job as the Lieutenant-Governorship. I would rather live in a two-roomed cottage for the rest of my life.'[38] Vincent wrote to Hume Wrong urging him to bring pressure to bear on the prime minister to drop the idea, and Wrong assured him that 'The P.M. would not make such an offer, as he would realize that it would not be welcome.'[39] King's decision to do so was both a calculated political move and a personal affront: he could say with great sincerity that he had offered Massey a high office and had been turned down, but he knew that he was actually telling Massey that there was no place for him in the national or international field where Massey believed his talents could be most shiningly displayed. Denied the kind of recognition from the government he desired, Vincent turned to another area where he had expectations of a favourable response.

When, at the end of 1944, Vincent became interested in Balliol affairs, he was at the same time engaged in a lively correspondence about a possible appointment at the University of Toronto. If he had some doubts about his qualifications for the mastership of Balliol, which had hitherto required scholarly achievement and often scholarly eminence, he had few doubts about two positions of his first alma mater. The first was the presidency, which, like the mastership of Balliol, had traditionally made scholarly demands he could not meet. But that was no longer a fixed principle. Sir Arthur Currie, with no academic qualifications whatsoever, had been a successful principal of McGill, and the current president of Toronto, Dr Henry John Cody, had been a famous preacher and an occasional politician before he had assumed office in 1932. Moreover, Vincent Massey had been favourably mentioned as a candidate when Cody was appointed, and his name had come up regularly when a successor to Dr Cody was being discussed. The other appointment, that of chancellor, was more likely and more appropriate. It customarily went to a man eminent in public affairs with an interest in higher education, and Vincent Massey fitted the prescription perfectly.

Vincent's interest in an appointment at the University of Toronto came as an old entrenched regime was passing. Dr Cody and the chancellor, Sir William Mulock, had each held office so long as to become patriarchal figures in appearance and in manner. Sir William, tall, bearded, with a deep sepulchral voice, a chief justice in his later career, evoked memories of political crises and triumphs that went deep into the nineteenth century. Dr Cody looked and acted like the Anglican bishop he might easily have become; he had a genially dominating manner and an unparalleled facility for public discourse, these qualities strengthened by a sturdy, slightly rotund figure, strong features, and a powerful, persuasive voice. Cody had been chairman of the university's Board of Governors from 1925 to 1932 before he moved into the presidency, and he had continued to be the dominating voice in the board.

There were three occasions between 1930 and 1947 when Vincent appeared as a candidate for either the presidency or the chancellorship, the first two ending with his withdrawal, the last with his appointment. In each case he found himself arrayed against Cody, at first shadowily, at the end directly and bluntly. He had known Cody since the twenties: each viewed the other with polite respect. Cody was an active Conservative, who had served for a year as minister of education in a provincial Conservative government, and in the twenties and thirties Massey's aggressive Liberalism led to some tensions between the two men. But now Cody had long since abandoned a strong party stance, and was, if anything, out of sympathy with the provincial Conservative government. Massey as well now thought of himself as a professional diplomat and not as a party man; his difficulties with Mackenzie King had dampened the ardour of his Liberalism. Their opposition in the 1940's arose, not from politics, but from a clash of interests between two men of determination and unquenchable ambition. Cody was in a strong, entrenched position. But Massey had powerful allies among those who were resolved to bring Cody's long domination of the university to an end.

Three of these allies occupied key positions in the Ontario political scene. One was George Drew, the leader of the provincial Conservative party, who had defeated the Hepburn Liberals in the election of August 1943 to become premier of Ontario. He had come to England in December 1943, and Vincent had a number of discussions with him about Ontario activities in London. Drew, a tall, impressive man, whose good looks were almost excessive, was buoyant and charming, and Vincent 'found him a delightful fellow to have anything to do with.'[40] He was especially impressed by Drew's decision to be his own minister of education and by the educational ideas he expounded. The second ally was George McCullagh, the publisher of the most influential morning paper in Canada, the *Globe and Mail*, who was another visitor to London in 1943. McCullagh was full of passionate and formless convictions on a number of subjects, but certain in his belief in the British Commonwealth and in a strong attachment between Canada and Britain. The third ally, Herbert Bruce, was an old friend with whom Vincent had kept up a steady correspondence. He was a distinguished surgeon, austere and aristocratic in appearance, but often direct and controversial in action and speech. He had been lieutenant-governor of Ontario in the thirties and was now, in 1944, a Conservative MP. All three were deeply interested in the University of Toronto. Drew as premier and minister of education had a special concern for the provincial university, which drew its support primarily from the provincial government. Bruce and McCullagh were both members of the Board of Governors.

In February 1944, during the first war-time visit Vincent made to Canada, Herbert Bruce came to talk to him about the university. He showed him a letter held for his arrival in which Bruce 'and other influential members of the Board of Governors wished him to accept the presidency.'[41] Bruce indicated that, although it was not a formal invitation, he had no doubt that, once Massey said 'yes,' the formal invitation would follow, with the understanding that Massey would take up the position when hostilities ceased. Massey expressed interest and said he would reply from London after consulting Alice. A reply never came. On May 9 Bruce wrote to Massey informing him that Sidney Smith, the president of the University of Manitoba, had been appointed principal of University College and executive assistant to the president, with the right of succession to Cody, who would retire on 30 June 1945.

Bruce, of course, had had no authority to make the offer. The incident illustrates the instability at the time of university government, with strong members of the board acting independently of both the chairman and the president. Whether or not Cody knew of this subversive move, he acted with equal daring and questionable authority in making the proposal to Sidney Smith. His action was eventually legitimized by the board after some worried delay.

Had Bruce's offer been sustained, Vincent would most likely have replied in the negative. Alice, who had been enthusiastic about the presidency for Vincent in 1930, was now doubtful, and her doubts, as always, reinforced Vincent's. Vincent had no doubts, however, about a proposal that Cody himself made when he wrote Vincent an annual 'state of the union' letter a short time after the announcement of Sidney Smith's appointment. Cody's letter ended as follows: 'I have long desired to see you elected as Chancellor of your Alma Mater, and I should gladly use whatever influence I possess to bring that to pass.'[42] Two months later Bruce wrote making the same proposal, saying that it was supported by both McCullagh and Drew. Massey was delighted to accept the invitation; he would have his name placed in nomination for an election by graduates in September. There was now no problem of timing as there was with the presidency. The chancellorship was essentially an honorary post. His chief responsibility would be presiding at convocation, and this he could do even if prolongation of the war beyond June 1945, the date at which the chancellor took office, should make it impossible for him to resign as high commissioner.

Then, in a way known only in academic communities, a simple proposal was burdened with Byzantine complications. The dissident board members and George Drew attributed the complications to the actions of Cody. They had some cause, although perhaps they and Massey simply did not realize that Cody's stated enthusiasm for Massey as chancellor referred to a comfortably removed period in the future. In the meantime Cody acted as if to ensure the immediate succession for himself. A by-law passed in 1939 proclaimed that in the event of the death of the chancellor, the president would succeed for the balance of the term. Sir William Mulock, the present chancellor, was a hundred years old and ill health made him for all practical purposes unfit to serve another term. If, however, he were to express a wish to continue in office, there could be no opposition to the grand old man. Cody went to see him and reported back that Mulock wished to die in harness. All that was needed now was Massey's withdrawal. Mulock would be automatically elected, and, in a very short time, Cody would succeed. Accordingly a telegram was dispatched to Massey by the registrar, A.B. Fennell, after consultation with Cody, that virtually made it necessary for Massey to withdraw his name. The telegram pointed out (1) that anybody nominated could refuse the nomination; (2) that 'Sir William has been informed of your nomination but as he wishes to die in harness he has stated that he will be a candidate'; (3) that 'the Act provides that no person shall be eligible for election as chancellor unless he is a resident of Ontario.' The third point, vaguely threatening in tone, raised a technicality of no substance, since diplomats do not abandon their Canadian residence when they serve abroad. But the statement and Sir William's intentions were crucial. The telegram had its intended effect. Massey withdrew his name from nomination. Sir William was duly elected by acclamation, and died a few days later. Cody then proposed that the senate, the academic government of the university that would normally appoint the president as chancellor for the balance of the term, should instead meet as a body and make the election, and a new statute was drawn up to this effect.

The friends of Massey now saw a second chance to secure his appointment. Before the date of the election, 17 November, could not the senate be persuated to make the election by the graduates at large? Massey's nomination could be resubmitted and there was a fair chance that in an open election he would triumph over Cody. Stanley McLean, a prominent industrialist, active in the cultural life of Toronto and a member of the Board of Governors, organized a petition calling for an open election that was signed by three hundred graduates from across Canada.[43] The proposed new statute was, however, defeated by the senate, and Cody, as the only nominee, was declared elected for a four-year term.

The board was bitterly divided by this sequence of events. The dissidents saw Massey as the victim of cynical political manoeuvring, and they contemplated a counter-attack. The premier could be counted on to give substance to it. He had followed the whole affair carefully, and had concluded, as he wrote in a letter to Massey, 'that Dr. Cody has come to look upon Toronto University as his own private property to be dealt with according to his own wishes.'[44]

The reply finally came in an act of the provincial legislature, passed early in 1947 and embodying the proposals of a joint committee of board and Senate. The chancellor was to be elected by the senate and the Board of Governors upon the nomination of a special nominating committee composed of representatives of the board, the senate, and the alumni federation. This seemed like a sensible, orthodox procedure. But the catch came in that the act declared the term of chancellor to be three, instead of the previous four years, the new arrangements to begin a few months later, on 30 June 1947.

Dr Cody's term would be cut short by a year. The nominating committee brought forward the name of Vincent Massey, but the senate turned it down, not because it was antagonistic to Massey, but because it was sympathetic to Cody. A special meeting of the senate was called at which the president, Sidney Smith, explained that the university solicitor had declared that both the senate and the board had only a formal role in the election of a chancellor and must accept the nomination brought forward by the committee.

This final phase of the Cody-Massey entanglement erupted in violent controversy in the press. The first phase had largely gone unnoticed since the maneouvring was private, but the entrance of the provincial government suddenly enlarged an academic dispute into a political issue. Moreover, there was now clearly a victim, a man ripe in years who had served the university faithfully and well during his long career and was now being treated shabbily. Massey, who had returned to Canada the previous summer, seemed, especially to many academics, to be playing a dark role. Was it not probable that the new act had been tailored to meet his needs? There is no evidence that he had insisted upon the date of 30 June 1947, but he was not a man to wait patiently in the wings, and in the absence of any sign from the federal government he was no doubt anxious to have an alternative appointment that would give him a recognized public position. Besides he may well have reflected that Cody's ambiguous conduct during the first phase of the affair merited the implied rebuke in the government's legislation.

The affair inspired lively, detailed newspaper reports, black headlines, and a general tendency to sympathize with Dr Cody. Massey was not attacked; the general line was that he was a fine choice as chancellor, and it was a great pity he had to make his entrance to such a cacophony of controversy.

Between his arrival in Canada in May 1946 and his election as chancellor a year later, the Masseys quickly moved into the Canadian mainstream. Batterwood had been virtually abandoned for eleven years; on the last war-time trip home they had 'camped' in the house for a few days. Now new servants had to be found so that they could reassume the role, polished anew by the long residence in England, of host and hostess of a hospitable country house. They were fortunate, at this time, in gaining the services of a couple who were, for the next fifteen years, to give the Massey ménage a happy stability. Miroslav Stajanovich had been an officer in the Yugoslav army, and his anti-Tito views had decreed emigration. On coming to Canada, he and his wife Anna accepted domestic posts with the Masseys, and adjusted happily to the new and unaccustomed life. Miroslav (or Mircha, as he was always known) had dignity and presence combined with a sensitivity to the needs of those he served; he performed his duties as houseman and valet with pride and care. He was not a servant, but a gentleman who had decided to serve others. His wife was a superb cook who satisfied Alice's high standards. They were devoted to the Masseys, as the Masseys were to them; and after they left their service, Mircha wrote a long, detailed, and affectionate account of his life at Batterwood and Rideau Hall. To his valet, Vincent Massey was a hero.

The immediate family was now reunited. Hart was a student in the faculty of architecture, where, at long last, he was doing academic work in which he delighted and at which he excelled. Lionel had not found the kind of work he desired – an appointment in industry concerned with agricultural development, preferably in Montreal. He had been compelled to settle for an office job in the Massey-Harris head office in Toronto. His marriage had occurred shortly after his parents returned to Toronto. He had wanted a minimum of formality, a wish shared by Lilias, who was forthright and impatient of the social conventions. But Lilias was also, as the Ottawa papers duly noted, 'the grand-daughter of the late Right Rev. Trever Lewes, Bishop of Ontario, grand-daughter of the late Sir Collingwood Schreiber.' The marriage took place in All Saints Church, Ottawa, and acquired the solemn status of an Ottawa social event.

Raymond had been a resident of the United States since 1936, and, as he pointed out in a letter to Vincent, a public figure, popularly thought of, not, first of all, as an actor, but as a reincarnation of Abraham Lincoln and a spokesman for the Republican virtues. In the spring of 1944 he had become, despite Vincent's disapproval,[45] an American citizen. Possibly a brief and unhappy war-time experience as an officer in the Canadian army had hardened his decision to change his allegiance. With Vincent's warm approval and influential support, he had, early in 1943, accepted a Canadian commission and had presented himself in Ottawa for assignment. But no appropriate assignment was made. By August of the same year he was back in the United States in civilian life, 'completely humiliated and frustrated in the Canadian army.'[46] He wrote to Vincent bitterly about the ineptitude and bureaucratic rigidity of Ottawa's military establishment, and the dulness of most of its representatives. The final blow was the refusal of the Canadian ambassador to the United States, Leighton McCarthy, to accept Raymond as a military attaché in Washington, on the grounds that he was an actor and therefore a man of inadequate substance for the high calling of diplomacy.

This Canadian farce did not disturb the happy relationship between the brothers. When, during his Canadian trip in 1944, Vincent stayed briefly in New York with Raymond and Dorothy, he found that they were at the centre of a society whose members exhibited 'quick intelligence, charm of manners, cultivated background.'[47] Recalling the visit, Raymond wrote to Vincent and Alice: 'once again I cannot tell you two what a great joy it was to have Vincent with us. Please let the four of us never miss a chance of being together. I don't want to sound pompous and I always am with a pen, but there is with us a real understanding and companionship and it's very precious.'[48]

Two events in this first summer of 1946 dramatized the Massey contribution to the cultural development of Canada. The first was the farewell concert of the Hart House Quartet. Almost a quarter-century had passed since that electric evening in Hart House theatre when Vincent, sensing the extraordinary impact made by the infant quartet in its first formal concert, appealed to the audience for financial support, and later placed that support on a continuing basis with an annual grant from the Massey Foundation. Twenty-three years is a long life for a quartet, in which the delicate balance of the music must be accompanied by an equally delicate balance in the temperaments of those who play it. The Hart House Quartet had survived a succession of emotional crises, withdrawals, and intricate reorganizations, and at each crisis the Masseys had been there to give financial support, encouragement, and patient advice. Now, in its final concert, only one of the original four remained – Boris Hambourg, the least volatile of the four originals. The quartet belonged essentially to the twenties and thirties; it had achieved an international reputation in an area where mere survival was a triumph; and it had aroused great pride in a country that had thought of musical greatness as existing only beyond its borders.

The second event was a showing of Canadian war artists at the Art Gallery of Toronto. It was an event in which the Masseys could take considerable personal satisfaction. The original idea, which they had helped to shape and to translate into reality, had encompassed a whole generation of painters. The impression of those who saw the exhibit was that of plentitude, of a great number of vigorous and talented artists, who would now, in the post-war world, move on to great things. The final concert of the Hart House Quartet was the end of an era; the Canadian war artists show was the beginning of another, richer and more ample, and the Masseys could reflect that they had helped to inaugurate both.

But Vincent had no intention of returning to private life, of settling down in the comfort and isolation of Batterwood with an occasional descent on Toronto to attend a meeting or a formal dinner. While he was still high commissioner in England, he had sounded out Norman Robertson about returning to Canada in his official position and delivering to the Canadian people a formal account of his stewardship. The idea received an icy reception; Mackenzie King, still the minister of external affairs, immediately perceived another Massey intrusion into the political arena and another Massey summons to be appointed to high office. He was aware, as was Vincent, of frequent suggestions in the Canadian newspapers that the highly visible high commissioner should be considered for positions where he could have a more immediate impact on policy: a cabinet post as a full-time minister of external affairs, or, failing that, under-secretary of state for external affairs; externally, the director-general of the newly created United Nations, or an eventual return to his old post in Washington. Louis St Laurent's appointment as the first full-time minister of external affairs was obviously a temporary posting for a man destined to succeed King, and Vincent may have entertained the hope that he would succeed St Laurent and re-establish the happy relationship with Lester Pearson, who had now returned from Washington to be under-secretary of state for external affairs. As for possible foreign appointments, Vincent wasn't interested. Canada was his first choice. A return to England was the one possible alternative, but only if he were rebuffed in Canada and denied the chance to exercise national leadership.

From the fall of 1946 until the end of 1947, Massey followed an exacting, self-imposed schedule of speaking, a national tour of the Canadian clubs providing a basic structure for his program. In the early stages he sounded like the seasoned diplomat who had formed some solid conclusions about the trend of events and felt called upon to deliver a message of mingled hope and warning. His first and dominating point was that Great Britain, although naturally depleted by the war, remained a world power, sustained by her traditional inner resources, both spiritual and material. No country, he maintained, was more important to Canada: she knew Canadian qualities and needs, and her advice was sound, her help indispensable. A second point of emphasis in these early speeches was a warning against Canada's joining the Pan-American Union, a persistent but minor question that had been periodically raised ever since the union was launched in 1890, but rarely with any sense of forceful relevance. Massey's position in his speeches was that joining the union would needlessly extend Canada's external commitments, not a convincing argument from one who had always stoutly opposed Canada's isolationism. His real argument appeared in his book, *On Being Canadian*, published in the summer of 1948 – that joining the Pan-American Union would magnify American influence in Canada. The union, he argued, was an American creation, and in its 'grandiose building' in Washington the bust of George Washington cast an imperial shadow on the lesser national effigies. As a member of the Pan-American Union, Canada, he believed, would lose its special place vis-à-vis the United States and would be indistinguishable in a swirl of satellites.

Massey was invariably polite and considerate in his public reference to the United States. He remembered that he was a former Canadian minister to that country who must always avoid remarks that would give Americans offence. He remembered the civilizing influence of the New York theatre and galleries on the young man reaching out beyond the little world of Toronto, and he valued the friendship of American intellectuals like Walter Lippmann and Whitney Shephardson. But his years in England had made him, at least in his private remarks, an anti-American: it may have been the impact of an abrasive and insensitive American ambassador like Joseph Kennedy or the complacent self-satisfaction of visiting American movie stars and politicians;[49] this tendency must certainly have received an impetus from the over-glorification of the American military role in Europe and American over-assertiveness in Newfoundland and northern Canada.

Audiences listened to Massey's eulogy of the British ways and his dismissal of the Pan-American Union with polite attention. But these were not subjects of great moment. His comments on the USSR aroused a quick response both in his audience and in the press. The cold war had now begun in earnest. The heroic ally of the war had become a mysterious and malevolent dictatorship so obsessively concerned with its own security that it pursued a domination of countries touching on its border with a Nazi-like brutality. Canadians, who had recently been immersed daily in the story of a Russian spy ring as revealed by the Russian defector Igor Gouzenko, felt in their marrows the cold, bleak wind that swept out of Russia. Massey, although he took care to distance himself from the Soviet system, did not join the chorus of righteous condemnation. He distrusted ideas based upon emotion, especially if they were inspired by a prophetic fundamentalism. As a young man in the early twenties, he had seen the Soviet in its youthful stage, receptive to the avant-garde in the arts, proclaiming its devotion to goals of human betterment. During the war, he had, like all of Britain, rejoiced in Russian military successes, and, like many Britons, had read (or reread) *War and Peace*, seeing in it comforting parallels to modern times. This was not a time, he thought, to invoke the failure of appeasement with Nazi Germany and to proclaim holy war. Appeasement had failed with a country that had chained itself to a plausible madman, but it need not fail with Russia. His comments on the Russian situation were widely quoted.

What can we do to break down these illusions that menace our relations? Free contacts would help, but these we are not allowed. There is no short way out, but I am convinced there is one quality we must show above all else. It is patience. However we are provoked and irritated, however hard it may be to arrive at anything that can be called understanding, we must be patient. I am not forgetting firmness. That is a primary need, but patience is more difficult. Everyone who talks provocatively about Russia feeds Russian suspicion and makes the task of statesmanship just so much harder. The Soviet system is poles apart from ours. Their ways are not our ways, but we have no desire to interfere in their domestic affairs. The two systems – theirs, ours – can exist side by side with mutual forbearance. If Russia can be brought to believe this and to share our attitude of live and let live with non-interference on both sides, then we can dwell quietly alongside each other on this planet no matter how different our ideologies. That must be our goal and it lies at the end of a long road and patient effort. But there is no other way.[50]

The international note at first so vigorously sounded faded gradually away. Perhaps Vincent realized that his future no longer belonged in the field of diplomacy, that with the increasing professionalization of External Affairs and the great increase in numbers of foreign service officers, he no longer commanded a position of eminence; and Pearson's appointment to the cabinet as minister of external affairs in September 1948 (of which he warmly approved) put an end to any political aspirations. The speeches of 1947 and 1948 now look inward. They may initially proclaim an international note, but they rapidly become sermons on the national state. 'Foreign Policy Begins at Home', one of his titles, could have been used for all of them. They preach a strong nationalism. 'Canada can never have too much national feeling,' he declares. 'We are one of the countries which can indulge in it without danger to anybody, and without it we will lose that cohesive force we need.'[51] The full gospel appeared in his book *On Being Canadian*, which was written in the spring and summer of 1948 and published that fall. In it, he drew a picture of a new Canada, a born-again Canada that, not surprisingly, was an embodiment of Massey's own idea and prejudices.

Canada, he believed, was then a country awaiting the full recognition and celebration of its distinguishing characteristics. These distinguishing characteristics he saw optimistically and buoyantly in the light of his experience during the war, and his book begins with an idealized (but not inaccurate) picture of the Canadian serviceman in England: self-confident, purposeful, quietly proud of his country. These characteristics spring from national qualities, of which two are emphasized. The first is a sense of stability, a sense of tolerance, an inclination to be moderate, a quality attributed to the dominance of people from northwestern Europe – the British isles, northern France, Scandinavia, and (surprisingly) Germany. The second is a passion for freedom – the French-speaking insistence on freedom for their faith and language; the United Empire Loyalists' pursuit of freedom to live as they pleased; the Canadian initiative in creating the British Commonweath, 'that monumental conception which has given the world so great a pattern of political liberty.' The portrait of Canada is a portrait of the individual type whom Massey most admired, and of which he might have confessed himself to be an example – a man of moderation and reason, devoted to the arts of peace.

But this positive quality of Canadian nationalism, the argument continues, has a negative shadow. Canada has done little to articulate its own virtues or to proclaim them to others. The answer is to develop those arts of peace to which her nature summons her: literature, painting, music, scholarship, education, good in and for themselves, and the best means by which to project her national image. The book turns into a gentle lament over the anaemic state of Canadian culture – the lack of federal initiative, the failure to keep her own scholars, the absence of a major national art gallery and a national library. There is a note of urgency here, for at his back Massey always hears the steady approach of the great southern neighbour. The fear of American influence is expressed with admirable tact, worthy of a former, respected ambassador to Washington. It is a question of size: sheer bulk intensifies the tendencies that he deplores – 'the standardization of life ... the uncritical acceptance of the second-rate' – and 'we in Canada are increasingly exposed to this influence.'[52]

To articulate and to give body to this cultural nationalism, Canada needed a leader with a program of action. Massey saw himself increasingly as such a leader, but one who must wait for a summons from the centre of power, the federal government. In the meantime he would work zealously in an important field where circumstances had given him a strategic position – the chancellorship of a major university.

The chancellorship of the University of Toronto was a post that Vincent maintained he had not actively sought but that, once obtained, he greatly relished. It was a return to his early interests. Harold Tovell (who was a college classmate and had married Vincent's favourite cousin, Ruth) recalled, in a letter of congratulation, that their freshman class had been assigned an essay by their English professor on 'How to do or make something' and that Vincent had elected to write on 'how to run a university.' Eustace Percy, who had also left diplomacy to head a university, hailed his old friend who had returned to his 'first love' and had joined him in the groves of Academe. Brendan Bracken, observing that 'it is harder to find first-rate heads of Universities than it is to discover adequate Prime-Ministers,' recited the qualities that Vincent would bring to the post: 'wisdom, tolerance, love of beauty and infinite experience of men and affairs.'[53]

Bracken was, of course, mistaken in his implication that Vincent was the head of the university. Vincent was perfectly aware of the nature of the post. He was the largely ceremonial head of state and the president was the prime minister. But at the same time he believed that, as chancellor, he could exercise influence and shape decisions. He had been encouraged in this by early conversations in England with George Drew, who suggested that Massey could give a leadership that had not been conspicuously present in the immediate past. In his reply to Eustace Percy he observed astutely that 'providing one has good relations with the President of the University and the Chairman of the Governing Body, there is a wide field for useful effort.'[54] These good relations quickly developed. He had some preliminary doubts about Sidney Smith. His own restrained public manner was in sharp contrast to Smith's, who was as genial and exuberant on the public platform as he was in private life. But he came to admire Smith's belief in the first priority of the humanities – a belief quickly translated into action that aroused tensions with a board devoted to the advancement of the professional faculties. Vincent already knew Eric Phillips, the chairman of the board. As one of Canada's leading industrialists, Phillips had played a prominent part in Canada's war effort, and his work had taken him to London and inevitably to meetings with the high commissioner. Phillips had a powerful and incisive mind; his opinions were expressed with a deceptive sense of tentativeness, and always with great urbanity and style. Few could resist the combination of toughness, intelligence, and charm. He and Massey had a wary respect for one another.

For the first two years of his chancellorship Massey devoted all his time and energy to the university (with a subsidiary but deeply concerned interest in Upper Canada College, where he took a leading part in selecting and appointing the new principal, Rev. C.W. Sowby). His installation on 21 November 1947 was an impressive affair, carefully planned and rehearsed with a coronation-like attention to detail, and the central ceremony and Massey's speech were accompanied by a procession of honorary graduands who represented the chancellor's principal interests.[55] Vincent's speech was a major effort. It was a warning against the dangers that lay ahead and were of particular moment to his alma mater, which had grown from the small, intimate community of three thousand or so that he had known in his undergraduate days to seventeen thousand, much of it in a sudden postwar expansion. The two lions in the way were now 'the curse of bigness' and 'irrelevant expansion.' 'Mass education,' he said, 'is surely a contradiction in terms.'[56]

Vincent Massey's warnings were received as exhortations of an appropriate nature for ceremonial occasions – general, theoretical, and irrelevant. The Board of Governors, with a number of new appointments from the business world, was concerned with immediate and specific problems of administration. Its members reasserted their responsibility for financial control, a responsibility that had not been carefully observed under the previous chairman. One of their concerns was Hart House. It had a tradition of independence: it was a gift from Chester Massey; it had been the creation of Alice and Vincent; and a separate fee paid by all male students gave it a high degree of self-sufficiency. But it still required a substantial subsidy from the university for physical maintenance, and its administration came under the scrutiny of a special committee of the board. Several members of the board thought that the chancellor looked upon Hart House as his special fiefdom, and resentment of this bred two administrative clashes that deeply affected Massey's attitude towards the university's central administration. The first clash was over the appointment of a new warden.

Bickersteth had been on leave of absence from 1940 to 1944, first as personal assistant and adviser to General McNaughton, then as director of army education for the British army – the latter, in particular, a demanding and exhausting job. On his return to Hart House, he quickly decided that he did not have the energy, or indeed the understanding, to deal with a new generation of students who seemed to him to come from a more abrasive world than the one he had known before the war. At the end of the second academic year after his return, he and Vincent agreed to recommend George Grant as his successor, to take over early in 1947. Grant had returned to Oxford after the war, and was working towards a doctor of philosophy degree in theology, but he was willing to accept an appointment before he completed his degree. Sidney Smith had interviewed Grant and was in favour of the idea. When, however, the appointment came before a committee of the Board of Governors, objections were raised because Grant had not served in the military. He had in fact served with heroism on the London front-line, but he had not had actual war service and had, moreover, asserted his position as a conscientious objector. The recommendation was turned down, and both Massey and Bickersteth were incensed. Bickersteth wrote to Massey: 'I don't think I have ever felt more depressed. Here have I slaved away at this House, which is infinitely precious to me, only to have its future endangered by the narrow, vicious and ignorant opposition of a few governors who do not understand and never have understood what Hart House stands for or what the ex-service men are thinking about.'[57]

A second and much more grievous clash between Vincent and the board occurred when Bickersteth retired. He had given twenty-five years' service to the university (and there could be no doubt about his devotion to his work and the affection and respect he had aroused), but under the policy then in force no one was eligible for a pension until after thirty-five years of service. If he had pleaded physical disability, he would have been eligible for a lesser pension, but this he refused to do. At first, the board decided on an *ex gratia* pension of $1,500 (the pension after thirty-five years would have been $2,000). Then at the end of the academic year, 1949, 'by a large majority, the Board of Governors after extended discussion decided that as a matter of principle no such allowance could be made.'[58] If the decision about Grant could be defended as a public relations act, this decision, Massey felt, was completely indefensible. Massey wrote to Henry Borden, a recent board appointee, arguing that 'there are a good many cases in which allowances have been paid – quite justifiably – to members of both the administrative and academic staffs of the University in lieu of or in excess of pensions which makes the Board's decision in connection with Bickersteth all the more indefensible.'[59] The board finally recanted; early in 1956, nine years after he retired, Bickersteth was informed that 'the Board of governors have approved of the payment of an annual allowance of $1,200.00, this sum in no way to be considered as guaranteed for future years.'

Massey found that his role of chancellor was confined to matters outside administration. He was entrusted with a program to revive alumni interest in the university and with the direction of a financial campaign. For the latter he had little relish. On one day he recounted that a visit to a possible major benefactor was preceded by a painful session with his dentist. He found the dental appointment much more agreeable.

Vincent was careful to observe the administrative boundaries set for the chancellor. In one instance his desire to strengthen the university's connections with Britain led to a mild indiscretion. He received a letter from Lord Reith, the shaper of the BBC and a friend from London days, in which Reith, depressed by his post-war prospects, indicated that he intended to settle in Canada and would be grateful if Massey could suggest a possible Canadian opening. Vincent replied promptly and enthusiastically, suggesting that Reith, who had an engineering degree, would be an ideal person to succeed the retiring dean of engineering at the University of Toronto. Reith was delighted and began to think of the possibility as an opportunity he should embrace. Vincent reported to Sidney Smith and Eric Phillips, who were encouraging but advised discussions with senior members of the board who had graduated from the university in engineering. These discussions brought negotiations with Reith to a halt. He was seen as too old, a candidate who would not have time to make his mark before the compulsory age of retirement. (This, at least, was the reason given to Reith.) Although, technically, he had made only a tentative approach, Vincent was distressed. 'I think,' he wrote to Reith, 'I must assume a large share of responsibility. My desire to bring you, with all your great qualifications, into our university community led me to do a very impulsive thing. It would have been better to have discussed the matter here before approaching you. However, there it is. I do hope you will forgive me.'[60]

When, in October 1948, Vincent went to England for a three-month visit, he may have had some doubts about his Canadian mission. Certainly, the chancellorship of the University of Toronto had not turned out to be a firm platform from which to launch a crusade for cultural nationalism. In England the old happy associations crowded in on them as he and Alice moved from one country house to another, and renewed their numerous London friendships. Now the offer of the mastership of Balliol was made official by the college's Visitor, Viscount Herbert Samuel, at a Balliol dinner. Vincent must have reflected on the differences between the small, élite college, with its host of old accepted traditions and its settled ways, and the Canadian university, young by British standards, now exposed to the pressure of an impatient and clamorous age.

Lester Pearson, who saw Massey in England in November, was deeply concerned that the government might lose him both as a supporter and as an agent in the carrying out of Liberal policy. He wrote to Jack Pickersgill, King's private secretary and influential adviser, who was clearly destined to play the same role for King's successor, expressing his concern about the government's failure to satisfy Massey's desire to have a continuing national responsibility.

What I particularly wished to write you about at this time is a conversation which I had on Monday last with Mr. Massey. Very confidentially, he had been asked whether he would accept the Mastership of Balliol if it were offered to him and naturally he was attracted by it, but he told me frankly that he was very reluctant to leave Canada if there is anything he can do in his own country. He is somewhat restless and does not find the Chancellorship of the University much of an outlet for his energies. He is also disappointed that he has not been able to secure other and more interesting activities.

I think it would be too bad if he left Canada for good, but I think it would be equally unfortunate if we did not try to secure him some useful employment which would make him friendlier to us than he has been. He himself is, of course, quite receptive to any approach and professes to be very anxious indeed to help Mr. St. Laurent or the government in any way that is possible. I think that he is genuine in this desire. Recalling our talk in Ottawa when you put forward a very interesting suggestion indeed, I expressed the hope to Mr. Massey that he would not make any final decision on the Balliol matter until he had returned to Canada, which will be in about ten days.

What I have in mind is that you, on behalf of Mr. St. Laurent, might give him a call in a fortnight and ask him to come to Ottawa for a chat. Even if nothing concrete resulted I think it would be a very good thing if Mr. St. Laurent could have a few words with him. The Royal Commission idea which you mentioned seemed to me to be an imaginative and excellent one and Massey would, of course, be admirable for that work.[61]

Pickersgill acted promptly. He arranged for Massey to see the prime minister. The subject for discussion would be the 'imaginative and excellent idea' that he had mentioned to Pearson.

CHAPTER SIX

The Royal Commission

On 6 January 1949, shortly after his return from England, Massey was asked to go to Ottawa to see the prime minister. St Laurent made the formal request that he 'take the chairmanship of a Royal Commission, the relation of Government to the cultural field, coordination of existing institutions, radio, television, UNESCO.'[1] Massey did not respond immediately in a positive way, despite the fact that for some time he had suspected that such a request would be made and realized that it well might be the national opportunity for which he longed. But he sensed a dry reserve in St Laurent's approach, an inadequate appreciation of the scope and centrality of the task he was asking Massey to undertake. Vincent commented in his diary: 'Important and interesting, but will the one or two years' work reach fruition and actual legislation? Much uncertainty involved.'[2] He was not reassured by the presentation on 27 January of the commission in the Speech from the Throne, and by the prime minister's brief, low-keyed exposition in his opening remarks.

But although he delayed giving his acceptance for several weeks, there was never any doubt about what his final reply would be. He quickly discovered that behind St Laurent's unimpassioned presentation was a strong commitment within the cabinet. The most outspoken member was Massey's friend and admirer, Brooke Claxton. In April 1946, when Mackenzie King was still firmly in control, Claxton had proposed in a memorandum to King that Massey, on his return from England, should be made a general overseer of the various government agencies concerned with the arts and communication

– 'The Film Board, Canadian Information Service, the C.B.C. or an assortment of these.'[3] King's reply (never put into a written form) can be easily imagined. He had no intention of giving Massey an important responsibility and he had no interest in strengthening activities that he thought of as irritating accretions imposed on government by special interests. Claxton persevered. He regretted that a proposal for a commission on the arts, sponsored by the Canadian University Liberal Federation at the National Liberal Convention in August 1948, had been ignored, and he subsequently made the proposal himself, adding that Vincent Massey should be asked to be chairman. He had every right to observe in a letter to Massey, expressing his delight in Massey's acceptance of the chairmanship of the royal commission, that 'having had something to do with the origin of this, I believe that it is a very important activity which may have a great and useful influence on our national life.'[4] Mike Pearson was an equally enthusiastic supporter of the commission and of Massey's chairmanship, and, as St Laurent's former deputy and now as his successor as Minister of external affairs, he had more influence than Claxton on the prime minister. In several long discussions with Massey following St Laurent's offer, he gave assurance that the cabinet 'meant business' and would look to the commission for guidance on specific legislation. He was responsible, along with Jack Pickersgill, special assistant to the prime minister, for formulating the terms of reference. They gave the bland words of the Speech from the Throne a national setting and an urgent ring. The commission became the Royal Commission on National Development in the Arts, Letters and Sciences, and the prologue to the statement of specific responsibilities declared 'that it is in the national interest to give encouragement to institutions which express national feeling, promote common understanding and add to the variety and richness of Canadian life, rural as well as urban.'

By the middle of February Massey had concluded his exploratory talks and was prepared to accept the appointment. He had discussed the commission with members of his family (or, more accurately, Alice's family) – Maude Grant and Jim Macdonnell – and with national spokesmen in the arts and literature – Harry McCurry, director of the National Gallery, and B.K. Sandwell, editor of *Saturday Night*. He had talked at some length with George Drew, who had become the new leader of the federal Progressive Conservative party and had alarmed Massey by his sharp comments about the proposed commission during the debate on the Speech from the Throne. Drew complained about the commission's 'vagueness, uncertainty, and lacking any limitation on its scope,' about the anti-private emphasis in the projected introduction of television and the disregard for provincial rights in the implicit concern of the commission with education 'which, in my opinion, is the most important way of enriching our national life.'[5] Presumably Massey reached an understanding with Drew, that the latter would cease his attacks until the commission had made its report. There was, fortunately, a reserve of good feeling between the two men – during his London days, Massey had seen Drew several times, had been impressed by him, and had contemplated with satisfaction the possibility of Drew's moving into federal politics and becoming prime minister; and Drew had worked actively to secure the chancellorship for Massey – and Massey had recently accepted an invitation to give the eulogy at a Toronto dinner in Drew's honour.

Now that his initial doubts about the commission had been dissipated, Massey contemplated his task with confidence and enthusiasm. He had every right to agree with the common assumption that he was the ideal man for the chairmanship. His career had made him either a patron or an informal critic of every institution and activity that would come under scrutiny. In some areas of the arts – in Canadian painting and modern drama – he was by way of being an expert. Perhaps the only area where he was deficient in knowledge and understanding was contemporary poetry and fiction. As a young man in the twenties he had begun inauspiciously as a patron of literature by organizing a public tribute to Wilson Macdonald, a Canadian poet who enjoyed a brief notoriety for his social criticism and occasionally engaging lyricism but had rapidly drifted into pretentious doggerel.

Earle Birney tells a distressing story about Massey's more mature literary taste. Shortly after Birney arrived in England as an officer in the Canadian army, he had visited the Canadian Officers' Club. On the troopship crossing the Atlantic he had written a long, elegiac poem, 'For Steve,' a tribute to Stephen Cartwright, who had been Massey's secretary in the early thirties, had enlisted in the RCAF after the outbreak of war, and had been killed in action. It is a long poem written in stanzas of a traditional form, the language passionate and bold but never difficult or obscure. Birney thought that Vincent Massey would like to see this tribute to his young colleague, and entrusted his manuscript to Alice. He returned to the club a few weeks later and inquired about his poem. Alice drew the manuscript from her handbag and said, 'Mr Massey thinks there are several good lines.' No comment could have more distressingly combined condescension and insensitivity. It is charitable to think that Alice forgot to show the poem to Vincent, and was hurriedly producing a comment for a Canadian poet who, she assumed, was a fumbling beginner. But Massey's insensitivity to modern poetry, whatever its degree, was not a deficiency that seriously impaired his chairmanship of a committee concerned with judgments of a general and judicious nature. Moreover he was sensitive to good prose, prose that was clear and precise and purged of clichés and pompous generalizations; and he knew that the impact of a report 'on the arts, letters, and sciences' would be peculiarly dependent on the clarity and incisiveness of its prose.

Vincent's ten years in England had reinforced his lengthy and extensive Canadian experience in dealing with the arts. No Canadian had ever served before on the boards of the two senior British galleries and observed at first hand the interrelationship between the arts and government in a highly sophisticated society and had, indeed, helped to direct national policy. He had seen and admired the high regard with which the arts were held in Britain during the war, when they were looked upon not as frills but as essential for the maintenance of morale, and he saw in the emergence of the Arts Council in 1945 a model that Canada could and should follow.

In Canada, too, there had been a resurgence of the arts. It was confined initially to official bodies of artists that were self-centred organizations concerned with their own professional welfare, but the war atmosphere was beginning to generate a wider sense of social responsibility. First had come a movement towards bringing the public, the consumers of art, into closer association with the artists, the producers. In June 1941 a successful conference had been organized by André Bieler at Queen's University, where Bieler was professor of fine arts (supported as such activities invariably were in the colonial stage of Canadian cultural development by the Carnegie Corporation). It led to the formation of a more inclusive society and the founding in the following year of the Federation of Canadian Artists, which brought together professional artists (chiefly painters), amateurs, and interested laymen. Then followed in 1944 a federation of all the Canadian bodies concerned with the arts, sixteen in number, chiefly made up of practitioners of the visual arts, but now embracing musicians, writers, and workers in the theatre. The federation was inspired by the prospect of presenting a brief to a special committee of the House of Commons concerned with post-war 'reconstruction and re-establishment.' Miraculously the sixteen bodies agreed on a common brief and sent a strong delegation to the capital (an event subsequently elevated in the arts mythology to 'the march on Ottawa'). Greatly encouraged by this demonstration of unity and by the sympathetic reception it met on Parliament Hill, the federation became in 1945 a formal body, the Canadian Council of the Arts. Its official status was recognized when its president, Herman Voaden, a playwright, and the chairman of its foreign relations committee; Elizabeth Wynwood, a sculptor, were appointed as two of the eight Canadian delegates to the first convention of UNESCO.

From these activities had emerged a political ideology of the arts. Lawren Harris, the activating force for the Federation of Canadian Artists, linked the cultivation of the arts with the national concern with war-time unity. He wrote in the federation's prospectus: 'This country cannot be pulled together by politics, by economics, or by any one religion, but it can be greatly aided towards a unity of spirit by and through creative life and activity in the arts.' The new apologists were dead-set against the concept of the arts as 'frills.' In its brief to the parliamentary committee, the federation took an Olympian view of the place of the arts in the economy. 'Manufacturing is as dependent upon design as upon capital, labour, and raw materials. Construction, which is possibly the greatest single source of employment, is dependent upon the architectural arts. The printing and publishing services are dependent upon journalism and illustration. The radio ... can function only because of literary, musical, and dramatic talents.'[6] The brief had two other major proposals – a central governmental body that would make grants (there was disagreement as to whether this should be a ministry of culture or an independent body funded by the government), and a series of community centres in small towns and rural areas throughout the country that would provide facilities for drama, music, and the visual arts.

Vincent was aware of this mild resurgence of the arts in Canada. He had seen something of it at first hand when he was in Canada in the spring of 1944. He had, for instance, participated in the discussions that led to the establishment of the Canada Foundation, which evolved from the Canadian Committee, a body originally charged with informing RAF men training in Canada about the country's society and culture. The Canada Foundation, under the quietly effective leadership of Walter Herbert, preserved its original informative emphasis but took on a wider mission: Herbert, for instance, gave good advice about the artists' brief to the parliamentary committee, and warned enthusiasts about the pitfalls of a cultural ministry. Vincent also knew most of the leaders in the Council of the Arts, and had kept in touch with them during his years in London. Lawren Harris and he had been friends since early student days; Sir Ernest MacMillan, one of the most vigorous and best informed delegates at the Ottawa presentation, was Vincent's principal source of information about the Canadian musical world; A.Y. Jackson kept him briefed about developments in Canadian art and advised him on his Canadian purchases. When he accepted the chairmanship of the commission, he thus knew that he could count upon faithful allies and could draw support from groups who had learned how to articulate their ideas and present them to a wide public.

Vincent was thus not only admirably fitted for the task of chairman but came to it when popular interest in the arts was increasing and finding vigorous leadership. Above this, he had an almost messianic sense of the importance of the commission. He saw himself as following in a long tradition and completing the work of distinguished predecessors. Hitherto that work had been a vice-regal responsibility. In *On Being Canadian* he recorded the contributions made to Canadian cultural life by governors-general. 'The Royal Society of Canada and the National Gallery at Ottawa were founded by Lord Lorne whose efforts also led to the formation of the Royal Academy of Arts ... The Canadian archives were greatly strengthed and developed as a result of the initiative of Lord Minto ... to Lord Bessborough we owe the

Dominion Drama Festival. It was Lord Tweedsmuir's keen interest in Canadian letters which led to the establishment of the Governor-General's annual Literary Awards during his régime at Ottawa.'[7] His own work, Vincent reflected, might also follow in this royal procession. Lord Alexander's term of office as governor-general would come to an end in 1950. In an era of confident nationalism, sustained by the magnitude of Canada's contribution to the war effort and by the country's enhanced international status, it seemed increasingly likely that the next governor-general would be a Canadian. It was widely accepted that Vincent Massey would be the choice. Indeed, while he was still working on the manuscript of the commission's report, Vincent was asked in February 1950 by Pearson, on behalf of the prime minister, if he would consider the vice-regal appointment of Governor-General of Canada and he replied that he would consider it 'very seriously.' Alexander's term of office was twice extended, however, and Massey did not in fact succeed until 1952. But, in a sense, the chairmanship of the commission was his first vice-regal task, providentially removed from the protocol and restrictions of the office, yet giving him in the years following the submission of the report the opportunity to keep a discreet but authoritative watch over the implementation of the commission's findings.

Once he had made up his mind to accept the chairmanship, Massey moved quickly to appoint administrative officers and fellow commissioners. The office of secretary was his first and, in may ways, his principal concern. During his career he had always thought of secretaries and personal assistants as men to whom major responsibilities could be delegated, not mere administrators organizing paper and arranging meetings and travel but active participants in policy and the enunciation of it. The last point was particularly important: the secretary of a royal commission on the arts, letters, and sciences would have to be a scholar, and should be able to write with style. He thought first of Douglas LePan, who had taken over increasingly important areas in the high commissioner's office. LePan was now in Canada. He had won a Guggenheim fellowship (for which Massey had given him strong support) in 1948 and was now working on a second book of poetry, dealing mainly with the Italian campaign in which he had served as a gunner in the Canadian army. LePan declined the job, though he sensed the importance of the commission and the probability that the report would be of permanent value to Canada. 'On the other hand is the chance, the hope only, of producing a book which in its own small way might contribute towards making us articulate and conscious of ourselves.'[8] Vincent replied, 'I am sorry I have not been able before now to send you a line to tell you how entirely I understand your decison on the rather disturbing proposition I put before you a few weeks ago. I am sorry if I appeared to apply undue pressure. I only did so because I know what a splendid job you would have done and because I would have enjoyed greatly having you in this important post on my team.'[9]

Other possible candidates were John Robbins, who at that time was executive secretary of almost every national body concerned with scholarship and education, and Hugh MacLennan, whose first two novels had brought excitement and poignancy to the dramatization of national themes. There is no record of any active discussions or proposals with either, however. Massey finally settled on Archibald Day, who had joined the Department of External Affairs after the war, during which he had served at CMHQ and at Canadian Army HQ in London, with, at the end, the rank of lieutenant colonel. Massey didn't know Day but accepted him on the basis of three recommendations: one from Pearson; one from Gilbert Norwood, the great classicist, who had known Day as an undergraduate at the University of Toronto and later as a member of the Toronto staff in classics (he had subsequently taught at McMaster and Queen's); the third from Terry Macdermot, who was now a colleague of Day's in External Affairs. Macdermot's recommendation was the most persuasive. He wrote that Day was one of the ablest and certainly one of the most popular officers in the department: 'He writes well; has a great gift for conversation; a very civilized sense of humour and considerable drive and organization power.'[10] Day justified Macdermot's praise. In particular, he worked on the final editing of the report and was no doubt responsible for the uniformly high quality of the writing.

The membership of the commission was announced on 8 April. The selection was the chairman's responsibility although during the process he kept closely in touch with the government. The Very Reverend Georges-Henri Lévesque, a prominent member of the Dominican order, founder and dean of the faculty of social sciences at Laval University, was chosen by a process agreed to by the prime minister and Massey. Each drew up, in order of preference, a list of French-Canadians who might be considered: Father Lévesque stood at the head of each list. He in turn recommended the associate secretary, who would be responsible for the French version of the report. He was René Garneau, graduate of the University of Montreal, Laval, and Paris, a former assistant librarian of the Parliamentary Library of the Province of Quebec, a member of the Wartime Information Board, and a writer and critic of increasing authority. A second member from Quebec was Arthur Surveyer, an engineer and business man, who had already served on government commissions. He was the choice of the prime minister and the representative of the world of affairs, known to have an interest in broadcasting. From the far west came N.A.M. Mackenzie, who had become president of the University of British Columbia after the war and was directing with skill and panache the growth of that institution in numbers, buildings, and academic distinction. Hilda Neatby, the fourth member, was an associate professor of history and acting chairman of the department at the University of Saskatchewan.

The Maritimes had no representative, but 'Larry' Mackenzie, who had been born in Pugwash, Nova Scotia, attended Dalhousie, served in a Nova Scotian unit during the First World War, and had been president of the University of New Brunswick from 1940 to 1944, clearly had strong maritime credentials, including a Scottish name and a highland bearing. Quebec, with two commissioners, had the largest representation. No doubt this was deliberate government policy, to which Vincent Massey, always a friend of French Canada, readily agreed. Both St Laurent and Massey were aware that Father Lévesque was a controversial appointment, regarded by the implacable premier of Quebec, Maurice Duplessis, as a political appointment to a body that was, in any event, an unconstitutional affront to provincial autonomy. To Duplessis, Lévesque was a member of the political and clerical opposition and therefore an enemy to be crushed. In the summer of 1949, as the commission was getting under way, Lévesque gave support to the workers in the long strike at Asbestos,

Quebec, and Duplessis, who had broken the strike violently, redoubled his efforts to rid himself of this turbulent priest.

Norman Mackenzie was a relaxed commissioner, with an attitude that usually seemed to hover between the benign and the amused. But when his special subject, the financial plight of the universities, was being discussed and he encountered uninformed opposition, he would change dramatically, the eyes flashing, the voice rising, the gospel enunciated in measured and emphatic phrases.

Father Lévesque also seemed benign and amused, more so even than the relaxed Mackenzie. The friendly, generous face would light up, the eyes would sparkle with good humour but with a pleasantly distracting hint of irony. The appearance proclaimed the generosity of spirit, but it concealed the crusading ardour that, like Mackenzie, he possessed in abundance. The priest who seemed the very embodiment of pastoral cordiality was also an impassioned social reformer who proclaimed in a speech he gave a few months after he joined the commission: 'The true anti-communists are those who build the new society with justice and love ... nothing will stop us, neither slanders nor threats, no matter whence they come.'[11]

Hilda Neatby was the junior member of the commission both in age (she was in her mid-forties) and in position. Shy and rather stern in appearance, she was content to play a minor role in the sessions with delegations. But she was influential in the shaping and writing of the report. She was also the only commissioner to write a background paper, and it, entitled 'National History,' is one of the best of an impressive collection of studies.

Arthur Surveyer, the oldest member of the commission, took a lively interest in problems of organization and urged the employment of special librarians who, he pointed out, had been used by banks and various industries to summarize and codify opinions and facts on relevant subjects. He was initially a vigorous member of the commission, persistent in his pursuit of facts, but he was inclined to grow weary, as he wrote to the chairman, when it was 'debating questions which were not familiar to me,'[12] and his business commitments and frail health prevented regular attendance.

The commission was largely an academic body, overwhelmingly so if the chairman, as an active chancellor of the University of Toronto, were to be admitted to the fraternity. They were all members of what John Porter would call the clerisy, identified in the public mind with the exposition and defence of established institutions, particularly with institutions that were highly valued by a cultural élite. But the commission could not be accused of preciosity or artiness. Lévesque and Mackenzie were social scientists who had tested their theories in action. If anything, the choice of commissioners could be criticized for slighting the arts. Massey was at ease with artists; he thought that civilization reached its highest expression in their work, but he felt also that there had to be a constant accommodation between the aspirations of the artist and the daily satisfactions of society: artists should be circumscribed by more sober citizens. The absence from the commission of an artist – a poet, painter, sculptor, dramatist – was a typical act of Canadian caution. When Dorothy Livesay, the poet, wrote to him recommending the appointment of Alan Crawley, the editor of *Contemporary Verse* – a sound suggestion since Crawley, as she pointed out, had maintained 'the highest standards of peotry' and 'probably knows more of the poets personally, and their problems, than anyone else,' – he replied curtly that the west already had two representatives.[13]

The members of the commission worked together amicably and rapidly developed a sense of easy, informal unity. Much of the credit for this went to the chairman. He had good relations with all the commissioners. Father Lévesque he had known only by reputation, but they became close associates, so that the recent tendency to refer to the commission as the Massey-Lévesque commission is not simply a bow in the direction of bilingual politics. Father Lévesque wrote to me that 'notre étroite collaboration à la Commission Royale a créé entre nous deux des liens d'une sincère et profonde amitié qui a duré jusqu'à sa mort.'[14] Vincent was conscious of his colleague's political vulnerability in Quebec, of the personal dilemma he would face in reconciling national convictions and provincial dogma. Father Lévesque described the delicate way in which Massey introduced the proposed recommendation for federal support of universities. Massey said: 'We are all agreed on this subject. But we realize that because of the special situation in Quebec, Father Lévesque will, as a consequence, face painful and hard opposition. As our mandate does not specifically request us to concern ourselves with this question and as we have always respected the particular responsibilities of each of us, I propose that we set aside this particular recommendation if Father Lévesque does not consent to it.'[15] Father Lévesque gave his consent 'même si j'entendais déjà éclater les tonnerres dans le ciel québécois.' Vincent and Father Lévesque kept in touch with each other after the commission's report appeared. Lévesque was close to the prime minister and was in a position to keep up a genial but determined pressure for the establishment of the Canada Council.

Massey had known Mackenzie since 1927. Mackenzie had then just returned from Geneva; there for two years he had been legal adviser to the International Labour Organisation but had decided that he wanted to spend his life in Canada and accepted an appointment at a reduced salary as associate professor of law at the University of Toronto. When Massey was preparing to go to Washington as Canadian minister he had interviewed Mackenzie as a possible first secretary. Mackenzie did not want to leave Canada and the interview, he concluded, had made it clear that 'temperamentally Vincent and I were not too compatible.' He was, in his own words, 'something of a rough diamond and Vincent "the perfect gentleman".'[16] But they had respect and admiration for each other, and they worked together easily and effectively on the commission.

Vincent had not known Hilda Neatby before her appointment. As the commission was taking shape he had seen that it would be important to have a woman as a member, given the keen interest of many women's organizations in the arts and the fact that many of the best artists were women (a considerable concession for a man not known for his feminist sympathies). If the woman also came from a region not yet represented, so much the better. Hilda Neatby was a representative of the prairies in a complete and striking fashion. Her family had come from England in 1906 when she was an infant and had experienced the ordeal of immigrant life on a prairie farm. Her attachment as a teacher had been to the University of Saskatchewan and its satellite, Regina College.

Her place in the commission, however, transcended these regional and minority accidentals. Massey had received strong academic recommendations on her behalf from Professor George Brown of the history department of the University of Toronto and no doubt from her former teacher at Saskatchewan, Frank Underhill, whom she revered. She was an uncompromising intellectual with a strong moral bias from her devout Presbyterian convictions, and she was a scholar who united a passion for exactness in detail with a capacity for bold and enlightening generalization. To Massey she became indispensable, and he was unhappy when she missed meetings where important decisions were to be made. For his last convocation as chancellor at the University of Toronto he proposed her for an honorary degree, explaining in his letter to Sidney Smith that 'her work as a member of the Royal Commission on Arts, Letters, and Sciences, made her a national figure.'[17] (She got the degree, and made the speech at the official luncheon preceding the ceremony.)

Vincent thus had close associations with three of his fellow commissioners and a friendly understanding with the fourth. This bade well for the principle the chairman had enunciated that there should be unanimity in final recommendations. Vincent was happy in his task and at ease with his colleagues. He was working with congenial people on topics that were large in scope and that had long engaged his attention. They were also topics that had an immediate and specific context. Although he had considerable facility in generalization, he was not at ease with abstract speculation and was happiest with orderly, methodical arrangements. In the internal discussions he welcomed extended discussions and encouraged individual views, but reminded his colleagues of the necessity for a final resolution of differences. He knew how to preside, wrote Father Lévesque, 'avec un main de fer dans un gant de velours.'

In general sessions, when delegations presented their views, the chairman took over responsibility for guiding the discussions. The stiffness of the official figure and the sober urbanity of the public speeches disappeared. He was relaxed, easy and friendly, particularly with nervous witnesses, tolerant of well-intentioned irrelevancies, adroit in bringing discussions back to the main point. He was aware of the nuances of cultural politics. I recall vividly an appearance before the commission on behalf of the Canadian Writer's Committee along with Frank Scott, poet, political activist, and constitutional theorist, and Len Peterson, dramatist and novelist. We represented a group of writers dissatisfied with the Canadian Authors' Association but anxious not to fragment the case for the writer. The chairman grasped the situation quickly. 'You represent,' he said quietly, with a smile, 'a tougher and more critical attitude towards writing in Canada than is found among our friends in the Canadian Authors' Association.' We modestly agreed with his summation.

The open sessions attracted a good deal of newspaper comment. A writer for the *Globe and Mail*, Harold Morrison, who had been following the sessions, was moved to write of the chairman's necromantic leadership: 'The 62-year old commission chairman wields his spellbinding art with a magician's skill ... only a spellbinder could promote such continuous harmony and goodwill throughout the hearing. There is never a heated clash or a bitter word over a controversial subject. Most witnesses appear eager to hold nothing back ... those hands and eyes appear to be significant tools in the spellbinding job. While the eyes penetrate, the long expressive hands that might have belonged to a concert pianist shape invisible things in the air.'[18]

From the very beginning of his chairmanship, Massey was determined to finish the report of the commission with dispatch. He realized that a long drawn-out investigation, so tempting in view of the vague and controversial nature of many of the questions to be addressed, would arouse scepticism in the public and indifference in the government. The announcement of the commission had been greeted with widespread interest; newspapers had given it a good deal of attention; it was important to capitalize on this mood, which might vanish as suddenly as it had arisen. Canada was not, after all, a country where speculation about the arts and education challenged the supremacy of politics, religion, and sports. At the first meeting of the members on 2 May 1949, he announced that he intended to give his full time to the commission and that in his opinion their work should be completed in approximately two years. It was a daunting timetable, but it was closely adhered to, despite Vincent's withdrawal from active participation for a period following the illness and death of Alice in July 1950. Vincent was working on proofs of the report in February 1951, and the final report was submitted to the prime minister on 1 June 1951. The speed with which the commission worked meant that it would not make heavy demands on the Treasury, since the major expenses were *per diem* allowances of the commissioners, and salaries for the staff, now expanded to include a small legal division with two officers, Peter Wright and Guy Roberge. The only conspicuous extravagance was the hiring of a private railway car for the extended trips to the west and east, an administrative convenience that greatly simplified travel arrangements and provided the commission with a mobile central office. The sums were not large by to-day's standards for royal commissions. The total expenses as reported in the public accounts of Canada for the years 1950 and 1951 were in the vicinity of $400,000. The chairman was paid $50.00 per day and the members $40.00. The legal officers, in accordance with the traditional (and mysterious) practice, were paid more handsomely – $125.00 per day.

The summer of 1949 was devoted to establishing an administrative structure for the commission, which was thought of from the beginning as an active committee with a life of its own independent, to a degree, from the public hearings. (When Hilda Neatby was first mentioned as a possible member she commented that, according to the inside gossip, the chairman had already made up his mind about the main issues – a cynical comment with a small, hard core of truth.) The commissioners decided on areas of specialization: television and radio were clearly Surveyer's primary concern, just as scholarships and research belonged to Mackenzie. The chairman, Neatby, and Lévesque would concentrate on the nature of a possible arts council and the state of the major cultural institutions. A system of advisory committees of external experts was established, each committee chaired by a member of the commission. Perhaps the most powerful was the one on federal scholarships, chaired by Mackenzie, and consisting of R.C. Trotter, a leading historian from Queen's; David Thomson of McGill and Leon Lortie of the University of Montreal, two scientists with wide interests, influential figures both in their own universities and in national councils of higher education; Vincent Bladen, an economist with a strong humanist bias and a deep interest in the arts; and C.J. Mackenzie, chairman of the National Research Council, another scientist with a liberal and humane view of scholarship and research.

A final part of the internal structure was the commissioning of specialized studies on individual subjects. There were forty of these special studies, from which a selection was published as a separate volume. At a late stage in its deliberations the committee realized that none of the special studies would come from either the Maritimes or British Columbia – an early indication of the ease with which a national body in the arts and letters could assume a central concentration of resources. 'The Commission agreed that a study on Handicrafts by an author in New Brunswick and another on the Indian Arts by someone in B.C. should, if possible, be prepared.'[19] In some cases, a special report was made by an expert. The most important was 'Aspects of Broadcasting in Canada,' prepared by Charles A. Siepman of New York University. Surveyer was concerned that a report by an academic would betray a bias towards government control and argued that the commission should hear from an American spokesman for the private stations, such as the president of the Columbia Broadcasting Corporation. The chairman turned a cold eye on the suggestion.

The commission considered two general political problems: what should be its relationship to the provinces, and what to the political parties? The first was an obvious question that confronted any federal body; the second was raised by an inquiry from the provincial CCF organization of British Columbia requesting permission to appear before the commission. That request was debated over several meetings. The first response was to refuse the CCF on the ground that 'briefs should not be accepted from political organizations as such.'[20] The federal leader of the party, M.J. Coldwell, protested and the commission agreed to reconsider its decision; discussions with the prime minister, however, led them to reaffirm their original decision. The provincial relationship was smoothly established with all provinces except Quebec by letters of explanation to the premiers. Duplessis rejected the commission with brusque finality. 'Nous respectons l'opinion contraire et les membres de votre commission, mais nous sommes d'avis que le mandat conferé à votre commission par les autorités fédérales se rapporte à des problèmes qui découlent de la juridiction exclusive des provinces, c'est-à-dire, à des problèmes éducationales. En conséquence le gouvernement du Québec est d'opinion qu'il ne doit pas acquiescer à votre mandat ni participer à son exécution.'[21] This was distressing, but not inhibiting. In Father Lévesque the commission had an expert in Quebec political warfare just as tough and shrewd as Duplessis himself. He advised the commission to insist on holdings its meetings at the University of Montreal and at Laval, where 'the friendly attitude of these two universities toward the commission would be a polite but serious blow to Mr. Duplessis in his own province.'[22]

The commission was overwhelmed with briefs. The country was honeycombed with organizations devoted to activities that came into its terms of reference. There were, for instance, sixty-five national bodies concerned with adult education alone, of which twenty-three elected to present briefs. Between August 1949 and the spring of the following year, the commission heard from about four hundred and fifty individuals and organizations, of which about four hundred presented briefs. It began its hearings with a long session, more than a month in Ottawa, devoted to the major federal agencies, concluding with four days on radio and television. Then began a systematic movement across the country, to the Atlantic and Pacific; on these journeys the emphasis shifted to regional activities. Back in central Canada there were extended stays in Toronto, Montreal, and Quebec, and a final return to Ottawa to consider the representations of the National Film Board. The commission paused, and then in early July of 1950 completed its survey with a visit to Newfoundland, an appropriately conspicuous arrangement for the newest province which had joined Confederation just before the commission was established.

In such a cloud of witnesses were several who were confused about the nature of the commission and a few who had meagre credentials for making a representation. The commissioners took a generous attitude towards these peripheral groups. Both the chairman and the secretary thought that the main deliberations required light relief. Day, for instance, wrote to Vincent about two unlikely candidates for attention: 'I recommend that the Commission give an audience to the World Calendar Association largely because of its amiable Canadian representative, one Arthur J. Hills, who I gather is an old acquaintance of Mrs. Massey and yourself. Mr. Hills in the introduction to his Brief, which he delivered in person, has, it seems to me, very ingeniously brought or contorted his representations so that they seem to be well within the Terms of Reference. I fancy that this will be as good a session as the one on Heraldry, and though it may not add much to the richness of Canadian life, it will I think add a great deal to the pleasure of the Royal Commission.'[23]

Under Massey's direction, the commission worked with purposeful intensity. There was, at the same time, a good deal of hospitality and relaxation. One minor crisis arose. Vincent reported that in Toronto he had to placate two of his colleagues, in all likelihood Arthur Surveyer and Hilda Neatby, who had accused Day of disloyalty. The 'disloyalty' arose from an incident during a social evening in Winnipeg when Day, fortified and inspired by a drink or two, gave an imitation of Surveyer in session. Surveyer was not present, but the host, unfortunately, was Surveyer's son-in-law, who was not amused. Nor was Hilda Neatby. But the commissioners usually maintained a tone of ease and even merriment, especially when they assembled at Batterwood. Day fondly recalls one Batterwood week-end when Massey read passages from the introduction to the section of the report on the mass media, in which the pre-radio, pre-film culture of the Canadian community was celebrated – the culture of the organist trained in the English tradition, of the rector or pastor who lectured on Browning, of the school concert or play 'with its light and colour, its tears and laughter, its triumphs and disasters,' of 'the editor of the local paper with his strong views on politics and on cigars, who in his young days had met Mark Twain.' These passages Massey grouped under the general designation 'lavender and old lace,' and he read them in his best Upper Canada-Balliol accents, with a tremor in his voice. Day, like Massey, wrote light verse. Massey has left no contribution from this period. Day's verses on the submission of the report to the King's Printer, 'Ballade de la commission royale,' provide a cheerful gleam among official documents and deserve a more formal recording.

> *We undertook our labours in the Spring,*
>   *Yet still we're toiling, through our second Fall.*
> *The briefs now have a somewhat hollow ring*
>   *Yes, even Special Studies slightly pall.*
> *Now when the summer birds no longer call*
>   *And mellow Autumn's had her annual fling,*

Our thoughts turn homeward to our fire-lit hall, –
  (But first we hail the Printer to the King.)

Ah, may the Muse smile on us as we sing
  Of Saskatoon, Victoria, Montreal,
Of Pullman cars, missed breakfasts, and the ring
  That summoned genial Gabriel to our call.
Sweet Muse, nod kindly from thy temple wall
  For soon now (D.V.) shall we broudly bring
To Thee our first-born volume – AND THAT'S ALL –
  (Resplendent from the Printer to the King).

'Let there be music!' – 'But the play's the thing!'
  'Museums!' – 'Painting!' – 'Look – our crumbling wall!'
'Films – more and better!' – 'Let us have less Bing
  Crosby and more of Bach – no soap at all!'
We've briefs from ballet dancers (short and tall),
  From music lovers (classical and swing).
We've drafted eighteen versions, we recall, –
  (and now it's yours, O Printer to the King).

                    ENVOI
Prince, we can see the writing on the wall.
  Alas, our grammar, spelling and the thing
Called syntax, – prithee, pardon us them all, –
  (And pin them on the Printer to the King).

When the report came from the King's Printer there was jocular comment on its predominantly red cover. Massey observed that, given the wave of anti-Red hysteria sweeping the United States in the wake of the McCarthy hearings, the commissioners might come under colective suspicion, particularly in Duplessis's Quebec. Day, who had guided the report through the press, had a verse response (this time, not his own):

When I shall die, I trust it may be said
His sins were scarlet, but his books were read.

Massey took great pains when the establishment of the commission was announced to dispel the popular notion that the commission was a high-brow conspiracy to direct support to cultural activities of interest only to a minority.[24] At a general press conference following the announcement, he deplored the use by journalists of the word 'culture' to describe the subjects with which the commission was concerned. This, he assured them, was to be a wide-ranging survey of human activities that give colour and vitality to human life, not a deification of the esoteric and the precious.

As soon as it began to hear representations from the public, the commission gave immediate credence to the chairman's insistence on the democratic approach. He and his fellow commissioners were receptive, prepared to listen sympathetically and to avoid any suggestion of schoolmasterly superiority. More important, the final report itself was characterized by a relaxed urbanity; it avoided a hectoring tone, and especially in the long first section, which summarized the representations, gave the impression of simply reflecting accurately what the commissioners had been told. That section concluded in this way: 'We are struck by the fact that those who appeared before us, whether representing one of the arts, the sciences, labour or the farm, spoke to us primarily as Canadians deeply interested in the entire scope of the vast inquiry which we ventured to undertake; in the hundreds of briefs which we received and in the thousands of pages of evidence which we gathered, we believe we have heard the voice of Canada. We should like to think that we have recorded and reproduced this voice as clearly and honestly as it came to us throughout our country from so many of our fellow citizens.'[25]

The assumption that the commission was not imposing an elaborate and impractical program on a recalcitrant country was carefully maintained. 'At the outset of the inquiry we were asked whether it was our purpose to try to 'educate' the public in literature, music and the arts in the sense of declaring what was good for them to see or hear. We answered that nothing was further from our minds than the thought of suggesting standards in taste from some cultural stratosphere.'[26] The commission did occasionally adopt a didactic tone, but it was always indirect and suggestive. One passage of the report, for instance, talks about 'a proper sense of values, moral and intellectual' encouraged by the study of the humanities, but the sentiment is expressed through an approving reference to the presentations of others: 'we were particularly struck by the earnestness and the acuteness with which those who are responsible, Protestant and Catholic alike, for the spiritual guidance of the Canadian people, discussed those matters, showing how fully aware they are that it would be difficult to maintain in Canada a proper sense of essential values, moral and intellectual, if we permit the study of history, of literature and philosophy to become neglected and debased.'[27] When the schoolmasterly tone emerges, it is always gently muted: with the proper attitude in teacher and taught, instruction becomes entertainment. The creation and marking of historic sites and monuments, for instance, must convey essential facts, but also stimulate thought, arouse wonder, and convey a sense of the reality of the past. 'We consider,' the commissioners concluded, 'the enjoyment of national history to be a form of entertainment not sufficiently familiar to Canadians.'[28] In other words, they say, 'we are not commending the study of history because it is good for you and will strengthen your mental fibres; we are presenting it to you as a means of expanding your range of pleasures.'

The commissioners resisted the temptation to lecture the country on the meanness of its financial support of the arts, letters, and sciences. It preferred the quiet thrust-home by the ingenious use of statistics that demonstrated the ludicrous inadequacy of the Canadian effort: 'the American Museum of National History employs more full-time scientists in its Insect and Spider Division alone than are employed in our National Museum as a whole,'[29] a fact, the commisioners remarked with ironical under-statement, they noted 'with interest.' The search for shocking and demeaning financial comparisons became a diverting activity. 'The combined annual revenue of all museums in Canada, public or private, would not pay the cost of one of the aircraft used in our transcontinental service.'[30] A recommendation to double the CBC revenue 'may seem to be a very large annual expenditure, but it represents less than a dollar a year for each Canadian, less than what is paid yearly in Canada for chewing gum.'[31] Such startling and humorous contrasts were preferred to a parade of statistics – an effective rhetorical principle, if a questionably sound use of statistics. The only statistical table in the body of the report was simple enough to carry a clear and mind-numbing message. In the year 1948, to take a single entry, English-speaking Canada produced fourteen novels compared to 1,830 in Britain and 1,102 in the United States; the statistics for poetry and drama and for general non-fiction were equally demonstrative, although the numbers for all three countries were much smaller.

In financial matters, the commissioners usually preferred to avoid exact figures and to speak in modest generalities. At their first meeting Massey insisted that they should avoid suggestions of financial extravagance in their recommendations and should be chary of setting up new organizations that would require special government outlays. As their deliberations moved towards a conclusion the commissioners were conscious as well of 'a darkening horizon in the international world'[32] and of the resulting budgetary demands for defence. In proposing a central arts council, they mentioned an 'expenditure of public money, not large in amount but wisely directed.'[33]

The style of the report is deceptively cool. It was designed to lead the reader gently and persuasively into the sympathetic consideration of fundamental questions. Massey, as we have seen, disdained the use of the word 'culture' and the word was rigorously excluded from the terms of reference and almost entirely excluded from the report. But it made its appearance when the commissioners wanted to indicate the highest reaches of artistic and intellectual activity, when they were designating the great masterpieces that had survived the scrutiny of time or the scholarship that had illuminated a part of man's history. Cultural life, in this high sense, they saw as manifesting itself in the work of individual artists and in the institutions that preserve and exalt this work – in universities, theatres, opera houses, libraries, and museums. It has a universal appeal, but it also has a specific national setting, and greatness in a nation was dependent on the quality and strength of its culture in this sense. The epigraph to the report from St Augustine's *The City of God* – surely the boldest epigraph to grace a government report – focuses the task of the commission: 'A nation is an association of reasonable beings united in a peaceful sharing of things they cherish; therefore to determine the quality of a nation, you must consider what those things are.'

The commission's terms of reference had a strong nationalistic emphasis. They began with a simple postulate: 'that it is in the national interest to give encouragement to institutions which express national feeling, promote common understanding and add to the variety and richness of Canadian life, rural as well as urban,' and concluded, 'it is desirable that an examination be conducted into such agencies and activities, with a view to recommending their most effective conduct in the national interest and with full respect for the constitutional jurisdiction of the provinces.' Vincent Massey accepted these terms of reference, indeed, had a hand in drafting them. The commission would give him the opportunity for which his whole career had been a preparation: to elucidate and to strengthen the cultural independence of Canada, without which both political and economic independence had an empty ring. His fellow commissioners went along with the nationalistic bias. It was, they were aware, susceptible to charges of chauvinism. In a retrospective article on the report, Hilda Neatby defended the national emphasis. She referred to the St Augustine epigraph. It left 'plenty of room for Canadianism, and none for Chauvinism.'[34] The commissioners raised the question not 'of Canadian culture but of culture in Canada.'

At the commissioners' third meeting on 20–21 June 1949, three months before they held their first public meeting, Massey outlined what he thought was the main question the commission must try to answer. He had always been impressed by the work of André Siegfried, the French historian and sociologist, who had made national psychology his peculiar specialty. In the early part of the century he had written a classic study of the race question in Canada, and in 1937 he had published a general study, *Canada an International Power*. The assertive title concealed some fundamental doubts about the survival of the nation. He argued that Canada's east-west axis, European in its orientation, was being overcome by the north-south axis, which commanded enormus economic power and was increasingly dominant in the cultural field. 'With an American culture whose centre of gravity lies outside Canada's frontiers,' he asked, 'is it possible to found a lasting Canadian nation?'[35] A favourable answer could be found in only one manner. 'It [Canadian nationalism] is mainly a political patriotism, and it would have to be supported by a culture to acquire the foundation it needs.'[36] Massey took the question and his reply as constituting the basic structure of the commission's report. The minutes of the meeting read: 'The main question to be answered had already been proposed by Mr André Seigfried. Could Canadian culture survive as an entity in view of the increasingly strong influences tending to unify the culture of North America? It was the view of the Commission that at the present time Canadian national feeling is stronger than it has been in the past, but also that the pressures upon Canadian life from abroad were also stronger.'[37]

Massey was largely responsible for the elucidation of the major question. It consisted of two chapters in the first section of the report, 'The Nature of the Task' and 'The Forces of Geography.' The second chapter confronted Siegfried's question. Canada shared with many other countries two conditions: a small population, clustered beside a much larger one. But there was a third and more significant condition – 'a majority of Canadians share their mother tongue with their neighbour, which leads to peculiarly close and intimate relations.'[38] The chapter becomes an exploration of American cultural influences. They are both benign and malign, and both kinds constitute a problem for Canadian survival. The benign influences – the generous support given by American corporations and universities to Canada's cultural activities, the easy absorption of Canadian scholars and artists into American society – blunt Canadian initiative and impede its independent growth. The malign influences – the result of the very size, diversity, and power of American society – saturate our popular culture and turn it into a copy of the American. The analysis is cool, objective, and unimpassioned, and here and elsewhere in the report does not justify the criticism of being anti-American.[39] The nearest approach to anti-Americanism was a quotation from an essay on philosophy that George Grant prepared for the commission. The essay is mainly an argument for the close interrelationship between philosophy and theology, which will, Grant predicted, result in the formulation of a rational faith. The enemies of philosophy in Canadian universities, he continued, are vocationalism and secularism; but there is a more formidable enemy, 'a barbaric empire which puts its faith in salvation by the machine.' In the light of Grant's subsequent writing, the capital of the 'barbaric empire' is in the United States. The report carefully avoids any such implication. The dominance of technology is a 'new problem which we share with all modern states.'[40]

There is no comparable analysis of the British influence on Canadian culture, and the criticism that the report showed a strong British bias, as least by implication, is sound. No doubt Massey (and the other commissioners less forthrightly) would have replied that this was simply reflecting a strong and healthy influence which was not oppressive, but stimulating. Robert Fulford has pointed out the dominance in recent years of the British expert – John Grierson in film, Celia Franca, Betty Oliphant, and Gweneth Lloyd in ballet, Tyrone Guthrie and Michael Langham in drama, Peter Dwyer in the administration of the arts,[41] and he might have added George Woodcock in literary criticism, and in humanistic scholarship, reaching back to the very beginning of the universities, a long list: Maurice Hutton, John Watson, George Paxton Young, J. Clark Murray, William Lyall, George Sidney Brett, Barker Fairley, Gilbert Norwood. Canada was not under pressure from British popular culture, and in the arts and letters, although the British influence was stronger than the American, it showed itself in echoes and accent rather than in direct imitation.

The answer to American and British influences is not to deny these, but indeed to accept the influence selectively and critically, and to attend to the nurture of our own culture, which, while absorbing American and European influence, will be distinctively Canadian. This Canadian nationalism permeates the introduction to the second section of recommendations. The prose here has an emotional eloquence not elsewhere attempted. The following passage embodies the propulsive ideas of the report:

The work with which we have been entrusted is concerned with nothing less than the spiritual foundations of our national life. Canadian achievement in every field depends mainly on the quality of the Canadian mind and spirit. This quality is determined by what Canadians think, and think about; by the books they read, the pictures they see and the programmes they hear. These things, whether we call them arts and letters or use other words to describe them, we believe to lie at the roots of our life as a nation.

They are also the foundations of national unity. We thought it deeply significant to hear repeatedly from representatives of the two Canadian cultures expressions of hope and of a confidence that in our common cultivation of the things of the mind, Canadians – French- and English-speaking – can find true 'Canadianism'. Through this shared confidence we can nurture what we have in common and resist those influences which could impair, and even destroy, our integrity. In our search we have thus been made aware of what can serve our country in a double sense: what can make it great, and what can make it one.[42]

Each of the activities the report examines is assessed in the light of this cultural nationalism. 'Canadian painting, through its honesty and its artistic value, has become above all the other arts the great means of giving expression to the Canadian spirit.'[43] The expression of the Canadian spirit does not imply an introverted mediocrity. In literature, for instance, 'it may be that the Canadian writer, whether in English or French, has not yet reached that level of universalism which would permit his work to awaken echoes outside our country as well as within it; he may still have some way to go before finding a Canadian cadence.'[44] National pride and a sense of unity, which are the political offspring of the arts, are most directly stimulated by national cultural institutions, of which the CBC is the prime example.

When Louis St Laurent established the commission, he and his cabinet colleagues were most immediately concerned about radio and television. Television in Canada was still only a delectable promise that, nevertheless, raised political and administrative problems far more complicated than those that radio had faced for more than twenty years. The commission responded by giving a high priority to consideration of these media. Arrangements were made for representatives of the Canadian Broadcasting Corporation and the Canadian Association of Broadcasters, which represented private stations, to appear both at the beginning and the end of the public sessions; and almost every organization that appeared had comments to make or careful briefs to present on the question of radio. Each of the two divisions of the report begins with a long section on radio (with a minor addendum on television), and the recommendations in this area had a planned prominence.

The essential features of the Canadian radio system – a mixture of public and private enterprise – had been established in 1936 by the Canadian Broadcasting Act, a bill introduced by the Liberals after their return to power. It had been preceded by the Aird commission of 1928 (called after its chairman, Sir John Aird, president of the Bank of Commerce) which had surprisingly proclaimed the principle of a publicly owned system that would eventually eliminate the existing private stations. The Canadian Radio Broadcasting Act of 1932 passed when the Conservatives were in power under R.B. Bennett, implemented the Aird report, reapproving the principle of public ownership but establishing a shaky and inadequately financed administrative structure. The act of 1936, which established the Canadian Broadcasting Corporation, made clear that Canada had one national system of radio broadcasting and that its newly created Board of Governors had the power as well to regulate the private stations.

Between 1936 and 1949 the concept of one publicly controlled system, devoted to national goals, blending entertainment and education with an emphasis on the latter, had begun to break down. The private stations grew in number, and some were permitted to increase their kilowatt power so that they could challenge the dominance of the CBC. With post-war industrialization and emphasis on mass consumer response, advertising found a congenial medium in radio and the private stations flourished accordingly. Moreover, during the war the CBC had made decisions about the broadcasting of political speeches that aroused genuine concern about its ability to preserve freedom of speech and to shield itself against government interference. It found itself at the centre of a series of controversies, no longer an institution beyond attack.

The principal attack was not on this point but on the concept of a single system. Spokesmen for the private stations (now speaking with the backing of a powerful organization, the CAB), argued that there were two systems in competition with each other, the private and public, and that it was grossly unfair for one competitor to regulate the other. The private stations, it was argued, were more in harmony with the spirit of a free, capitalistic society. They were unapologetically allied to advertising, and advertising, proclaimed Joseph Sedgwick, a prominent Toronto lawyer and a vigorous apologist for the private stations, 'caters to public taste' and 'has made radio in America the bright, topical, attractive entertainment that it is to-day.'[45] On a more solemn, ideological plane, the CAB contended that the private system was a hardier defender of freedom of speech than a system that, whatever its assertion of independence, was ultimately dependent upon the existing government.

The conflict between the CBC and private stations echoed a number of wider conflicts in Canadian society – between nationalism and continentalism, between a European and an American tradition, and, at another level, between those who thought that the mass media should set educational goals for themselves and those who accepted them as the darlings of entertainment; between those who believed in a certain amount of state direction and those who were content with the inscrutable dictates of the market place.

The conflict did not take a specific political form until the mid-forties. The CBC had been the joint product of the two old parties, and it had always had the enthusiastic support of the CCF. A series of inter-parliamentary radio committees had always reported in favour of CBC policy. But then the Conservatives began to echo the complaints of the CAB, some of whose members had close associations with influential newspapers. During a debate on the CBC in February 1944, John Diefenbaker declared: 'The broadcasting corporation is in the position of being both litigant and judge, both investigator and jury. It is in the position of being, as someone has said, a cop and a competitor.'[46] At the Progressive Conservative party's annual convention in 1947, the appointment of an external, independent regulating body became official party policy.

Against this background, the selection of the chairman and the commissioners who would review broadcasting policy struck the CAB as deeply prejudiced. Vincent Massey had been an active Liberal, and it could be assumed that the other academic commissioners had Liberal sympathies. The demolition of the Conservatives in the election of 27 June 1949, however, removed for the commissioners the unhappy prospect of a confrontation with a hostile government.

In representations before the commission, the defenders and the critics of the CBC were clearly demarcated. The defenders were the national organizations with educational goals, representing labour unions, farming communities, and the churches. They all relied heavily on a brief drawn up by the joint planning commission of the Canadian Association for Adult Education, which argued persuasively in defence of the CBC, emphasizing the contribution to general enlightenment in programs that dealt with social issues. The critics presented a solid phalanx from the world of business – the Canadian Association of Broadcasters, the Canadian Chamber of Commerce, la Chambre de Commerce du Québec, the Radio Manufacturers Association, the Association of Canadian Advertisers, and the Canadian Daily Newspaper Association. (Newspapers had become major owners of radio stations.) The commissioners, with predominantly academic ties, were thought with some justice to be sceptical of the motives of the business groups. Joseph Sedgwick characterized Vincent Massey: 'The fine flower of Toronto and Oxford, scholar, diplomat, man of affairs and culture – everything indeed but a man of business.'[47] Sedgwick might have added to his indictment that Massey had long been a sympathetic supporter of Alan Plaunt and Graham Spry, the leaders of the Radio League that was largely responsible for winning the initial battles for a public system of broadcasting.

It is likely that all the commissioners (with the exception of Surveyer) were deeply committed to the existing system of radio broadcasting. The evidence they heard did not shake that commitment; rather it reinforced it in every way. The commitment arose from certain general presuppositions that Massey and his three allies considered to be incontrovertible, and that emerged clearly in the first three introductory chapters and in the summary of evidence on broadcasting that followed. They were as follows: Canada came into existence as a declaration of political independence from the United States. To preserve that independence, Canada was prepared to make great economic sacrifices (e.g. the refusal in the era of railway construction to take the cheap way from Montreal to Winnipeg via Chicago, and the insistence on an all-Canadian railway). Now the preservation of independence has shifted from the political to the cultural. The temptation to take the cheap way out is even greater; we need simply to accept the bounty of the Americans, whose powerful radio stations can easily encompass their northern neighbour. But now we cannot rest with economic measures, especially negative ones.

The commissioners remind us, in the chapter on mass media, that culture must deal with the machine cautiously. In the nineteenth century culture was preserved by individuals – the church organist, the local librarian, the small-town editor, the teacher and professor, and by voluntary societies. The implication of this chapter, with its nostalgic evocations of a rich and colourful past, is that humane values must not be swept aside by the blind surge of technology. It is not sufficient to establish our own system of broadcasting; it must be a system of a certain kind – one that gives an important place to the individual artist, one that addresses itself to the strengthening of national ties and the elevation of public taste. (The latter goal is not self-righteous didacticism; it is based on the assumption that to teach and to delight are not antithetic but complementary.) These goals must not be left to private enterprise harnessed to the profit motive. The airwaves are not the preserve of individuals: they are akin to a public trust, and demand public supervision.

The question to be answered by the commission was this: has the CBC discharged its public responsibilities? The answer is a confident 'yes': the present system had succeeded to a remarkable degree.[48] This conclusion is offered in the first section on broadcasting, presumably a factual summary. In the second section, preliminary to the actual recommendations, the commissioners indulged in a mildly rhapsodic outburst. The CBC had become to them the great national hero, the red-cross knight who will overcome prejudice, bigotry, and debilitating self-gratification. The CBC 'has become,' we have found 'a source of pride and gratification to the groups most representative of Canadian listeners ... Radio has opened the way to a mutual knowledge and understanding which would have seemed impossible a few years before ... From Vancouver Island to Newfoundland and from the Mackenzie River to the border, Canadians have been given a new consciousness of their unity and of their diversity.'[49]

Measured against these accomplishments, the private stations had, according to the commissioners, failed dismally. Their cultural record was poor; their programming 'inexpensive and unimaginative'; they had joyfully embraced a strident commercialism. They were not concerned about the American invasion. Indeed, they welcomed it. Jack Kent Cooke, president of radio station CKEY, was blatant in his acceptance of American programming, and his statement no doubt went a long way to consolidating the commissioners' views. 'An American,' said Cooke, 'is basically the same as a Canadian ... motivated by the same impulsion, exposed to the same influences of literature, music, the theatre, movies, and radio. In the first place, what is wrong with American material? If we are ever to have a Canadian culture, it will come as the result of full exposure to what is undoubtedly the fastest rising culture in the world to-day.'[50] But the commissioners did recognize that the private stations served special community needs, and, by lending their facilities to CBC network programs, had often been 'complementary and supplementary to the CBC.'

The main broadcasting recommendations were a declaration of approval of the CBC and a summons to strengthen it. The Canadian Broadcasting Corporation should continue to be the governing body for the single, national system; it should, however, be enlarged and receive double its present income. Some sops were offered to the private stations: they should be given the right of appeal against 'substantial miscarriages of justice'; the term of their licences should be extended from three to five years; and there was acquiescence in the financial need for advertising.

The private broadcasters found more encouragement in Surveyer's 'Reservations and Observations,' which were largely concerned with radio broadcasting. (Massey had hoped that Surveyer's reservations would be confined to a sentence or two that could be incorporated in the text, thus avoiding the appearance of division, but Surveyer insisted on a full statement of his position.) Surveyer's main recommendation was that there should be created 'an independent regulatory body with authority and jurisdiction over the activities of both the privately and the publicly owned broadcasting and telecasting stations.' But he did not accept the soft commercial approach of the private broadcasters. He was deeply concerned about programming and quoted approvingly a comment by an American critic of his own country's approach to broadcasting: 'There is a determined effort to perpetuate the adolescent mind.'[51] B.K. Sandwell, who had served on the CBC, commented that Surveyer's board 'might easily be found chastising the private stations with scorpions where the CBC had used merely a rather light whip.'[52]

The two sections on television were slight and tentative. At the time, Canadians owned 25,000 TV sets, and Americans ten million. The threat of complete American domination was thus far greater, the commissioners pointed out, than it had been with radio at a comparable point in radio's development. Moreover, TV demanded large initial investments and a steady income to sustain programming. The easy answer to this was to accept a close association between TV and advertising, which could now tie the huckstering voice to colourful and arresting pictures. An ominous note crept into the report: Canada must move slowly and with great caution in this new and treacherous terrain. The report approved of the government's interim report entrusting development of TV to the CBC, which should not license private stations until it had its own national programs.

This was pre-McLuhan Canada, and the commissioners did not speculate adventurously about the effect of the new medium. They offered two percipient generalizations: that 'television may develop and come to concentrate on its more immediate popular capacities such as variety shows and sports and news actualities leaving more serious programmes to radio and films,' and that there may emerge 'from its confined limitations and advantages an entirely new art essentially distinct from both radio and films.'[53] The latter speculation hints at the McLuhan world, with no premonition, however, of television's power to create political icons that would reawaken the personality cult of an earlier time.

The report thus began with the most controversial subject and the one that aroused, at the same time, the widest public interest; it concluded with a proposal of a revolutionary nature. It was revolutionary, however, only in the Canadian context, for it had a successful precedent in Great Britain and its need had been repeatedly emphasized by many Canadian cultural organizations. The proposal was to create a body 'to be known as the Canada Council for the Encouragement of the Arts, Letters, Humanities and Social Sciences, to stimulate and to help voluntary organizations within these fields, to foster Canada's cultural relations abroad, to perform the functions of a national commission for UNESCO, and to devise and administer a system of scholarships.'⁵⁴

The commission had decided, in short, to recommend government patronage of the arts. The commissioners warmly endorsed the model of the British Arts Council, 'state support of the arts without state control,' and to realize this goal they placed great reliance as a council that would have no government representation and, indeed, no artists appointed simply for their eminence as artists, but would consist entirely of 'distinguished and public-spirited Canadian citizens properly representative of the cultures and of the various regions of Canada.' As soon as the council was established and the principal full-time administrative officers were appointed, it became clear that the council's wisdom and independence must be increasingly supplemented by careful procedures for making awards. An elaborate jury system was devised and implemented. This system was thoroughly in the spirit of the original recomendations. The Massey commissioners would, I am sure, have approved of the conclusion reached by the Applebaum-Hébert report some thirty years later: 'These carefully worked out decision-making procedures, with this system of checks and balances, are an attempt to ensure that the governing principle in awarding grants remains the excellence of the project or artistic activity. This system derives from, and is central to, the Council's statutory power to make its own program policy and granting decisions, and represents the essence of the arm's-length relationship between the Council and government.'⁵⁵

The commissioners believed that financial support need not smother the creative spirit provided it did not attempt to direct or influence. They were not impressed by the comments on state patronage of the arts prepared on behalf of the government by Cyrus MacMillan, who had in the twenties and thirties exercised an icy dominion over McGill University's English department: 'Literature at any time and in any clime is a gift of the Creator, developed by the copious industry of the fortunate individual to whom it has been given in trust. It is not the result of government aid or subsidy.'⁵⁶ On the other hand, they respected the warning given by Lord Keynes: 'The artist walks where the breath of the spirit blows him. He cannot be told his direction; he does not know it himself. But he leads the rest of us into fresh pastures and teaches us to love and to enjoy what we often begin by rejecting, enlarging our sensibility and purifying our instincts. The task of an official body is not to teach or to censor, but to give courage, confidence and opportunity.'[57]

Of the four activities assigned to the Canada Council (each in itself providing justification for a single body), the final activity – the devising and administering of a system of scholarships – was the most precise and the most demanding. The commissioners had in mind scholarships for individual artists and writers, but gave an equal weight to the needs of academics – the providing of post-graduate scholarships for scholars in the humanities who would eventually strengthen the teaching of the humanities in the universities. The commissioners were well acquainted with 'the plight of the humanities,' which was a favourite subject at the time for after-dinner threnodies and for solemn discourses at official university gatherings. Certainly the cure did not lie in the adoption by the humanities of the methods of the sciences, which would mean the abandonment of their traditional role. The role of the study of history, of literature, and of philosophy is to give 'a proper sense of essential values, moral and intellectual,' to help form (quoting now from the brief of the National Conference of Canadian Universities) 'the citizens with trained minds, liberal and informed opinions, good taste and critical judgment without whom a national civilization is impossible.' 'Faculties of Arts,' the report went on, 'offer a congenial atmosphere for the growth of the creative worker in music and the arts.'[58]

Nor did the cure lie in sudden measures of a sensational, quantitative nature, such as the suggestion of Cyril James, principal of McGill and the chairman of a university delegation appearing before the commission, that 'if there could be brought to various universities twenty first-rate teachers and scholars in the humanities, and if they could be paid perhaps $10,000 a year, a great advance would be a sure consequence.'[59] The Canadian universities had a long and honourable humanistic tradition, and could generate their own renewal from within, provided they were given the resources to establish strong graduate departments and to attract to them the best students.

At first the commission wanted to assign the awarding of postgraduate scholarships to a separate body, a National Council of the

Humanities and Social Sciences, quite distinct from the Canada Council, which was to be confined to the arts and letters. (This recommendation was adopted twenty-eight years later. The initial proposal was made by the commission at its meeting on 12 July 1951.) A few months later, Vincent raised some objection to the proposal: he was apprehensive about establishing another new body, which would, he thought, arouse government concern about administrative machinery and expense. 'On the other hand if we invited an existing body outside the Government mechanism to undertake this duty we would be conforming to the principle in which we all believe, namely, that voluntary bodies should as far as possible be used to assume responsibilities that can fairly and effectively be given them.'[60] Here, moreover, was a chance to direct some money to the impoverished universities. The obvious body for administering the scholarship system was the National Conference of Canadian Universities, which would now require a permanent secretariat that could be financed only by federal government funds.

The Massey proposal was not adopted. The award of scholarships in the arts and the humanities and social sciences remained with the council. But the Massey proposal brought into focus the whole question of the place of the universities in the commission's deliberations and proposals. The universities had not been listed in the terms of reference as 'institutions which express national feeling, promote common understanding and add to the variety and richness of Canadian life,' the areas assigned to the commission. Given the commission's proper concern with the humanities, however, the universities could not be ignored. Norman Mackenzie thought, indeed, that the commission should not content itself with an indirect, cautious approach, such as Massey suggested for the award of scholarships, but should press forward boldly on a wider front, despite his awareness of the sensitivities of the government about encroaching on provincial jurisdiction and the consequent danger of weakening the appeal of the report.

Certainly the prime minister, a lawyer from Quebec, was acutely aware of the danger. On the other hand, St Laurent was a staunch university man who had taught at Laval, and he was conscious that the universities were moving towards a deep financial crisis when in

1951 the special federal grants for veterans ceased. Mackenzie had a powerful intermediary in the prime minister's special assistant, Jack Pickersgill, who was sympathetic to the universities, fully understood the constitutional problem, and worked out a formula for aid that would make the federal government a *deus ex machina* and not a supreme busybody.[61] Pickersgill kept the prime minister informed about the 'university question,' and the prime minister, without giving specific authorization, acquiesced in the movement of the commission towards a frontal assault. When he was questioned in the House on 3 May 1951 about possible legislation for university aid, he recalled a comment he had made on receiving an honorary degree from the University of Toronto a few months earlier. In his speech of acceptance he had said, 'I think many of us recognize increasingly that some means must be found to ensure our universities the financial capacity to perform the many services which are required in the interest of the whole nation.' 'I then,' he told the House, 'turned to Mr Massey who is the Chancellor of the University, and expressed the hope that his commission would be able to help us find a proper solution of that difficult problem.'[62]

With the prime minister's benign (but unofficial) approval, the commissioners decided to look at the universities as cultural institutions that belonged centrally in their terms of reference. In effect, they resolved themselves into a second commission on the role of the federal government in higher education – the first time in the history of Canada that this question had been examined directly by a formally constituted body. Now that St Laurent was prepared to face the inevitable objections from Quebec, Massey had no hesitation in broadening the approach to the universities. He had begun his career as an academic and as he had once written to a host at a British college, 'I am always very happy to get back, even for a fleeting visit, to academic soil.'[63] His devotion to his two alma maters – Toronto and Oxford – was exceeded, but only slightly, by his devotion to the monarchy.

The commission, aware that it was concerned with the sciences as well as the arts and letters, presented, first of all, the general arguments for federal support that were always set forth in university briefs. Universities were, despite their provincial sponsorship, inherently national institutions, drawing students, especially at the postgraduate level, from all regions of the country, and contributing most of the professionals to federal government departments. But the commission came back repeatedly to another argument that was related to its essential concern for the development of a national culture. Universities were 'nurseries of a truly Canadian civilization and culture.'[64] On a practical plan, they were essential patrons, without which, in many parts of the country, musical, theatrical, and literary activities could not exist. At the highest level, they took the initiative in developing a national culture that was also part of an international culture of high standards and ancient lineage. The universities inspired departures in the report from the measured sobriety of the prose: 'Theirs must be regarded as the finest of contributions to national strength and unity.'[65] 'Without them culture in the sense of the full development of man's intellectual and aesthetic faculties would be in grave peril.'[66] 'There is probably no civilized country in the world where dependence on the universities in the cultural field is so great as in Canada.'[67]

The recommendations with respect to broadcasting, the establishment of the Canada Council, and financial aid to the universities were the three most important and controversial the commissioners proposed. Other recommendations – a new building for the National Gallery, the establishment of a number of museums with clearly defined responsibilities, the establishment of a National Library, clarification and strengthening of the National Archives and the National Film Board – were important also, but they seemed to emerge inevitably from a sober review of the current situation; they did not invite sharp controversy, although in some instances, as in the building of a National Gallery, they were consumed in apathy and endless delays.

Of the three major groups of recommendations, those on broadcasting were largely embodied in a new radio act, introduced six months after the report was received and subsequently passed by Parliament. But in the years that followed the world of broadcasting changed unrecognizably, and the report's discussion and recommendations now seem to belong to another era of comparative peace and simplicity. The concept of one national system disintegrated. The CBC held its own in radio as the national voice of authority and quality, but in television it found it increasingly difficult to rise above the discordant babble. The narrator in Saul Bellow's short story, 'Him with His Foot in His Mouth,' expresses the Canadian dilemma in a painfully lucid way: 'It's no easy thing to share a border with the USA. Canada's chief entertainment – it has no choice – is to watch (from a gorgeous setting) what happens in our country. The disaster is that there is no other show. Night after night they sit in darkness and watch us on the lighted screen.'[68]

The recommendations with respect to financial aid to the universities were of immediate concern to St Laurent and were the first recommendations of the commission to be accepted and implemented. The recommendations were that 'the Federal Government make annual contributions to support the work of the universities on the basis of the population of each of the provinces of Canada,' that these contributions 'be distributed to each university proportionately to the student enrolment,' and that 'all members of the National Conference of Canadian Universities be eligible for the federal grants.' These recommendations demanded a radical change in the attitude of the federal government towards universities. In the past, universities had been ill-favoured wards of the provinces dealt with arbitrarily and selectively; now the federal government created a second system of support that avoided interference and discrimination. When the Canada Council was created, the government added a second measure to its program of operating support – it set aside half of the entire Canada Council endowment, 50 million dollars, to be used for university buildings that were directly related to the teaching of the humanities and social sciences (chiefly libraries, facilities of the arts faculty, and residences). Much more was to be done in the future to meet the needs of the universities greatly expanded by the increase in enrolment and the urgency for advanced instruction and research, but the recommendations of the commission initiated the revolution in university support. By relating the activities of the universities to the entire cultural life of the country, the commission wrenched them from their constricted provincial context and gave them a national resonance.

If the commissioners were writing today, they would say of the

Canada Council what they said in 1951 of the CBC – 'Canadians have been given a new consciousness of their unity and of their diversity.' The Canada Council has worked in a more limited area – in literature, scholarship, and the arts – and often in association with the CBC. But it has had no need to be defensive towards American art and literature, for it is concerned with the best, and the best absorbs or ignores any national influence in accordance with its own inner logic. The council is not responsible for the advances in all the arts during the last thirty years – vast in quantity, impressive in quality – but, more than any other body, it created the atmosphere in which the advances could take place and it gave Canadians a relaxed pride in the accomplishments of their artists.

By 1957, all of the major recommendations of the report had been implemented. Only the recommendation on 'honours' (contained in a special report never released) had been ignored, but in 1967 (as we shall see) it was adopted in substance by the Pearson government. No other Canadian commission, before or since, has had such an immediate and transforming effect.

The question for the biographer is to what extent the report was a reflection of Vincent Massey. The answer, I think, is that popular perception was sound in calling it the Massey Report (although he would have warmly approved of the recent fashion of calling it the Massey-Lévesque Report). He was, as I have pointed out, a strong but flexible and urbane chairman who dominated the discussions and directed the progress of the commission. In the composition of the report he orchestrated the various themes and conclusions and left his impress on many chapters.[69] I think particularly of the chapter on the theatre, where the voices of the actor, the passionate play-goer, the organizer of dramatic festivals are heard in rapid succession or in happy fusion. The chapter parallels the special study on the theatre by Robertson Davies, which is a witty and eloquent dialogue between two Restoration figures, Lovewhit and Trueman, who display an extraordinary knowledge of the Canadian theatre. When Trueman says, 'Canada will not become great by a continued display of her virtues, for virtues are – let us face it – dull. It must have art if it is to be great, and it has more real vitality, in my opinion, in the art of the theatre, than in any other, sans music.'⁷⁰ The report picks up the idea and the observation, and provides a prologue for the Stratford Festival founded two years later. Massey had selected Davies, then the editor of the *Peterborough Examiner*, to write the piece on the theatre. Davies now became a member of the remarkable Massey court of young men who made up a glittering company (although occasionally guilty of lèse-majesté): Steven Cartwright, Ross McLean, Thomas Stone, Paul Martin, Brooke Claxton, Hume Wrong, Lester Pearson, George Ignatieff, Charles Ritchie, Douglas LePan, John Holmes, James Eayrs, William Kilbourn, Michael Pitfield.

The élitist impact of the major recommendations, despite the careful cultivation in the report of a democratic tone, reflected Massey's convictions and attitudes. Vincent had a strong ally in Hilda Neatby. A passage from her book *So Little for the Mind*, which came out two years after the report, expresses the élitist ideas behind it: 'Democratic society ... lives only on the creative efforts of the gifted few in all forms of endeavour, and on the ability of the majority in varying degrees to inspire, support, and use them. The society that supports it lives always on the brink of dictatorship from which it is saved only by cultivating a kind of fluid and voluntary aristocracy: an admission that freedom and equality are best retained by the fullest recognition of natural differences and the most complete utilization of natural "gifts".'⁷¹

The Massey-Neatby point of view is not a foreign importation, the offspring of Massey's anglophile sentiments. It is, as Carl Berger convincingly argues in his study *The Writing of Canadian History*, a persistent theme of leading Canadian historians: Wrong, Milner, Underhill, Lower, Innis. Underhill and Lower both hailed the report as a classic Canadian document. Underhill, as we have seen, had reservation about its attitude towards the United States, but he praised the commissioners for their thorough work. Lower's praise was undimmed by any reservations: 'The report of the commissioners is a classic document. The Canadian state now turns to the highest function of a state, building the spiritual structure (the word is not used in the religious sense) of a civilization, the material foundations of which it has already sturdily laid. If the builders can continue to be men and women of the combined vision of those who prepared this report, the work will go forward to brilliant achievement in future ages.'[72]

The report reflected Massey's Canadian nationalism, which, in his mind, did not conflict with élitism or with his vivid awareness that Canada had two cultures. Cultural nationalism would be the means of fusing the two cultures. 'We thought it deeply significant,' the commissioners wrote, 'to hear repeatedly from representatives of the two Canadian cultures expressions of hope and confidence that in our common cultivation of things of the mind, Canadians – French- and English-speaking – can find true Canadianism.'[73] This euphoric Candianism was carried over in Massey's first major speech following the publication of the report. At the Montreal Canadian Club on 11 June 1951 he declared that 'our work, and whatever may stem from it, rests upon the conviction that Canada is to remain an independent nation, and that in consequence it is the right and duty of our governments and of our citizens to do all that is possible under the law and under the constitution to strengthen our sense of Canadianism.'[74] He closed with a quotation supplied by Archibald Day, the classicist. It was from Thucydides, near the end of Pericles' funeral oration, and the audience was invited to make the imaginative leap from Athens to Canada

You must yourselves realize the power of Athens, and feed your eyes upon her from day to day, till love of her fill your hearts and thus ... all her greatness shall break upon you.

Everything about Massey's assignment was congenial to him. For thirty years he had worked under the shadow of Mackenzie King, and he had never been happy with the routine of trade and the gritty jargon of economics which made up an increasing proportion of the work of the diplomat. Now there was no menacing shadow; his political sponsors were benign. Culture had not yet become the 'cultural industry'; it was a subject for the historian and the literary critic, not for the makers of administrative and economic models. He was happy in his colleagues on the commission; Lévesque was the embodiment of the idea of the French-English entente; Mackenzie was a loyal colleague, genially persistent about his areas of interest; Surveyer was the most removed of the commissioners, but he was thoughtful and not intransigent. The strongest alliance was between Vincent Massey and Hilda Neatby. The lapsed Methodist who still believed in striving for perfection in this life was at home with the devout Presbyterian who placed her faith in the elect.

In the royal commission the man and the occasion came together perfectly. Massey had spent a lifetime preparing for what the report now urged. Part of its success, its tone of revolutionary élan, lay in the very barrenness of the cultural landscape it surveyed. But Massey knew that, cautiously and obscurely, changes had already begun, and that the function of the report was to bless and release the energies that awaited an authoritative summons.

CHAPTER SEVEN

Governor-General

To Canadians who still clung to the old imperial ties – their numbers reduced but their passionate convictions undiminished – Vincent Massey had failed to live up to his initial promise. By accepting the appointment of first minister to the United States, he had endangered imperial unity. Henceforth in Washington there would be a second, and potentially disruptive, spokesman for the Empire. His acceptance of the appointment of governor-general, the first native Canadian to occupy this august post, was a fundamental violation of the faith. The office had become inseparable from the imperial tradition, and even sturdy autonomists might have confessed to a preference for a noble lord dwelling within the penumbra of the royal family or, even better, a member of the royal family itself.

Vincent Massey had from an early age found a comfortable niche in the imperial tradition. His vice-regal associations had begun in 1911 when he was a young man who had just graduated from the University of Toronto and was preparing for Oxford, devoting his time to political causes like imperial federation and to the detailed planning of the new student centre for his alma mater. Lord Grey, the governor-general, was in his final year of a seven-year term but was still full of soaring plans and ideas for Canada. In his energy and his belief in Canada's enormous potential, he brought back the palmy post-Confederation days of Lord Dufferin and, like Dufferin, his imperialism translated easily into a form of Canadian nationalism. Young Vincent, aged 26, was a little condescending to the great man. 'He is,' he wrote in his diary after an initial meeting at Rideau Hall, 'a delightfully affable, democratic sort of man with boundless enthusiasm but rather a tactless and flighty mind.'[1] But Vincent was pleased and flattered when a week later, during a visit to Toronto, the governor-general sought him out, and discussed with him a battery of ideas, including 'Rhodes Scholarships, Commission Government in Cities, Town planning.' Certainly Grey impressed the young man with the importance of his office; beneath the ceremony and the decorous public statements, there was a lively mind and a delight in new ventures.

There is no record that Vincent ever met Grey's successor, the Duke of Connaught, the third son of Queen Victoria and Prince Albert, and the first member of the royal family to be governor-general. Vincent was out of the country or engaged in war work. For the first two years of the duke's term, he was a student at Oxford; and for the remaining four years he was a full-time employee of the University of Toronto and then on active duty with the army. With Connaught's successor, the Duke of Devonshire, an aristocrat from the pages of Trollope, with vast estates, a deceptively unimpressive appearance, and a concerned shrewdness, Vincent resumed his place in the vice-regal entourage. He was now a promising young civil servant in Ottawa, and he was about to take the place of his shy and withdrawn father as the head of the family and of the industry on which the family fortune rested. The Duke of Devonshire was the central figure on 11 November 1919, when Hart House, used by the army during the war, was presented to the university, and the governor-general laid the foundation stone of the memorial tower adjoining the main building. Later references suggest that Vincent had become a part of the vice-regal household. When the duke and duchess visited Chester Massey in Toronto, young Vincent took the duchess to an evening performance of a review by the celebrated concert group 'the Dumbells' that had turned war-time fame among the troops into general popularity. He later records attending 'a large family party' at Government House, where he noted especially a meeting with his old Balliol contemporary, Harold Macmillan, now an ADC to the governor-general, with whom he renewed his friendship.

Vincent was rapidly on familiar terms with Devonshire's successor, Lord Byng. The diary tells of intimate dinners at Rideau Hall and at the Massey home on Queen's Park in Toronto. Then as Vincent became a political figure of consequence, Byng turned to him for advice. In May 1925 Vincent recorded discussions with the governor-general about a possible extension of his term of office; and in the famous constitutional crisis of 1926, he steered a narrow course between loyalty to King and support of the governor-general's prerogatives.

Byng was the last governor-general to be appointed in a double capacity as an agent of the British government and as a representative of the Crown. In 1926 the new doctrine of the Empire, proclaiming equality of status among the dominions, who were 'united by a common allegiance to the Crown,' made the governor-general's office an inappropriate medium for intergovernmental business. Now these tasks were to be carried out by a British high commissioner in Ottawa. The question arose about how the governor-general should be appointed. Previously the initiative had come from the Colonial Office or the British prime minister, with the king or queen making the final appointment, and often putting forward successfully their own personal nomination. Lord Willingdon, Byng's successor, who had been the king's personal suggestion, thought that the new regime called for an even more direct role for the Crown. Willingdon wrote to the king's secretary, Lord Stamfordham: 'His Majesty should send out from England his own personal representative, or a man with whom he has some personal acquaintance, and to whom he can communicate freely, a man, in fact, whom he could trust to be his personal liaison officer in the particular part of the Empire where he is sent.'[2] But this high and dry doctrine was acceptable neither to the dominions nor to Great Britain. At the imperial conference of 1930, it was decided that the king should henceforth act on the advice of his dominion ministers, who would, however, have an informal consultation with the king before he made the appointment.

The new procedure obviously cleared the way for the appointment of a native as governor-general. Indeed, Australia had already recommended such an appointment before the procedure had been worked out, and the king, who had not been consulted, had agreed only with extreme reluctance. Canada moved more slowly. Mackenzie King, as we have seen, had in 1944 offered the governor-generalship to General McNaughton, but had then persuaded him to give up this office for a cabinet appointment. Otherwise King's proposals followed solidly in the imperial tradition: Buchan (who became Lord Tweedsmuir on appointment), the Earl of Athlone (both he and his wife were members of the royal family), and Lord Alexander (a noble soldier who, like Byng, was a Canadian war hero).

Vincent certainly approved of the new concept of the governor-general. It bestowed an immaculate royalism on the office and removed the last cluttering encumbrances of a colonial past. But he never showed any enthusiasm for a native appointment. From 1926 onward the question of a Canadian as governor-general became a subject for newspaper comment and editorials, with heated assertions on both sides. Vincent noted the controversy in a letter to Philip Kerr (later Lord Lothian) on 15 May 1928. His tone combined disapproval with a casual dismissal of the controversy as an ephemeral irritant. 'I notice that there has been much discussion in our House of Commons over the estimates for the rehabilitation of Government House and also for the establishment of a vice-regal residence in the Citadel at Quebec. This has precipitated a newspaper controversy over the Governor-Generalship, whether he should be a Canadian, and so on. I was amazed to see an interview given by Glazebrook, in which he expressed himself as overwhelmingly in favour of there being a Canadian at Government House. I do not think this represents the mass of opinion. I sincerely hope not, and the whole question is probably simply a passing flurry.' But over the next decade or two 'the flurry' became an established part of the political climate. Moreover, Vincent Massey's name began to be mentioned as a strong candidate for the governor-generalship. His years in London had given him a commanding imperial profile: he was seen to be an intimate of royalty and of the British political élite, and his adept use of radio on national occasions made his voice and his vibrant patriotism familiar to Canadians at home.

By the time he returned to Canada, Vincent had, in all probability, reconciled himself theoretically to the idea of a Canadian as governor-general and personally to his own elevation. His name now appeared regularly in newspaper discussions of the question. Even the staunch traditionalists admitted the strength of his qualifications, but pointed out that given his past allegiance to the Liberal party his appointment would politicize the governor-generalship. Vincent, for his part, was not worried by this argument. His active political career in the twenties and thirties seemed to belong to a distant past in which bitterness and disappointment had predominated over modest triumphs. During his years in England the breach between him and Mackenzie King had been widened. He became an admirer of George Drew who seemed to him to be far more urbane and informed than Mackenzie King. It was true that he still had close friends and protégés in the Liberal cabinet – Paul Martin, Brooke Claxton, Lester Pearson, in particular – but the bonds were not narrowly political.

Whether he still entertained some inner doubts about the wisdom of Canada's turning her back on a personal representative of the mother country, he recognized that the decision had now been made in the mind of the public and in the inner government circles. Louis St Laurent did not, like his predecessor, have bouts of sentimental nostalgia for English country houses and those who frequented them. He was a Canadian *pur et simple*, and the appointment of a countryman to the nation's highest post was the natural outcome of complete autonomy.

What was most important of all was Vincent's realization that Alice would rejoice in his election. This was really a double appointment, in which the wife, as so often in the past, would play a part no less important than her husband. And there was no doubt at all that Alice would be enthusiastic about the appointment, and would play her part superbly. Vincent could imagine the subtle transformations she would make in the furnishings of Rideau Hall, a responsibility undertaken by a long line of governor-generals' wives, often with more zest than taste, and he knew that, as always, he could rely upon her for frank criticism and for loyal support. After Lester Pearson had made the first approach to Vincent with the assurance that the government had no one else in mind and that, at the proper time, he would be formally offered the post, he confided the secret to Alice.

Five months later Alice, in the summer of 1950, died. A few months before, she had had a severe fall and had not been able to leave Batterwood. Her death was a sudden, devastating shock, although there had been signs of a steady decline. Her doctor, the distinguished Toronto physician Ray Farquharson, wrote to Vincent after her death: 'Her gradual downhill course since last winter made it more probable that the downward slope would be increased than it would level off in a plateau. I am satisfied that nothing could have been done to change it and I believe that it was better for her to continue with her interests and activities as long as possible. With your great help she was able to do so with enjoyment till near the end.'[3] Behind Alice's final illness lay the draining years of the war. Early in the war Vincent wrote to Raymond about her labours. 'Alice takes but little rest. She seems to get away with it although it worries me at times. I sometimes think she is rather like a bicycle that has to go at a certain pace or else it falls over.' When she returned to Canada, she was entering her seventies, but gave no indication of slackening her pace. When Vincent became chancellor of the University of Toronto, she was present at all the convocations over which he presided (and, on one occasion, upbraided him sharply for a momentary lapse in the ceremonial liturgy), and was present at most of the public hearings of the Massey commission, sitting to one side of the commissioners and following the proceedings with great intentness.

Alice was a woman of strong convictions and inflexible determination, and she pursued her goals with an intense, and somewhat narrow, concentration. But she had a warm, emotional nature, and was quick to recognize injustice and to help those in need. She gloried in the society of the great and the famous, but did not, for that reason, turn her back on those who were neither great nor famous. She valued the work of those who provided the basic pleasures and comforts of daily life, and she herself was proud to be known as a superb cook and an exemplary housekeeper. At the service in the little Anglican Church of St Marks in Port Hope, the casket was borne by old workers at Batterwood, and their faces showed deeply the sorrow they felt at her going.

Tributes to Alice came in great numbers from all over the world. I select two, one of the hundreds from Britain, one of the even greater number from Canada. The first is from Sibyl Colefax, their London hostess on so many occasions:

One just can't believe that Alice has gone – the utter desolation of that news today has left us all thinking of no other thing than of you Vincent. This sudden blow – surely it must have been that – and Alice more alive and vivid than almost anyone among our intimates. Oh, my dear, what can one say for you. Nothing but that we know your heart must be breaking and nothing can help now – cold hard courage to struggle on (don't I know what a struggle it is) and the knowledge that joy has gone out of life.

Only a year ago you were about to arrive. We had that heavenly drive down to Sonia's, the golden day and – delight at seeing you both there and later on – looking so well and full of activities – friendship – precious friendship as none knows better than I.

May your own high heart help you to face that desolation – none can help you – only feel every hour for the agony you must all be suffering.

The second is from Harold Innis, the great Canadian economic historian.

This is a very belated condolence letter and like all condolence letters can do little to comfort you. I did think however that you would be interested in a conversation which I had with Dave, the porter, on the chair car to Ottawa. He mentioned Mrs. Massey to say how much he had appreciated her kindness. Apparently both of you on your return from England went back via Ottawa to Port Hope and both recognized him. As he said, this meant much to him and I thought was a single beautiful tribute which would have pleased Mrs. Massey.

Shortly after Vincent had been approached by Lester Pearson about the governor-generalship, the high commissioner for Canada in London, Dana Wilgress, was asked to inform the king of his government's intention. Wilgress sent back a dispatch to Pearson: 'I said ... that we were contemplating a recommendation of a Canadian name to His Majesty. The King did not seem particularly surprised by this, and any uneasiness he may have felt was, I think, removed by my assurance that you would not naturally want to recommend anyone to him who was politically controversial in Canada, or likely to be unknown to him. I said that you had it in mind, though no decisions had, of course, been reached, recommending Vincent Massey. The King was obviously pleased about this possibility. You will be interested and amused to learn that almost his first observation when I mentioned Mr. Massey's name was, 'How is Mrs. Massey these days?'[4]

The king's words were more than a polite inquiry. He was reflecting the natural tendency to think of Alice and Vincent together – inseparable, each an essential support to the other. Several years later, when Vincent had been successfully established as governor-general, he was showing Harold Macmillan, now prime minister and on a Canadian visit, through Rideau Hall. 'Suddenly,' wrote Vincent, 'in the long drawing room he drew me over to a sofa and I sat down beside him. He was too moved to speak and the tears came freely. He then said that he couldn't help thinking of Alice and what it would have meant to have her here.'[5] The feeling that Alice was an inseparable part of Vincent's appointment as governor-general was general. It was strongly felt by St Laurent, himself a devout family man. He began to think that Massey could not carry out the duties of the governor-general by himself and that he should think of other possibilities. Alexander's term of office was extended twice, once in October 1950 until the spring of 1952, and then until 5 October – a recognition of Alexander's popularity in Canada, but also the purchase of time for reconsideration of his successor. Alexander's early departure at the beginning of 1952 to become minister of defence in the Churchill government forced St Laurent's hand, and on 14 January 1952, he telephoned Massey, who was in England, to tell him that he had been officially appointed governor-general.

Between 25 February 1950 when Massey was first approached and the actual appointment, there is some evidence that C.D. Howe, the most powerful and the best-known member of the Liberal cabinet, had been seriously considered for the post of governor-general.[6] In the spring of 1951 Vincent was in England chiefly to discuss the report on honours that his commission had been asked to prepare. In his audience with the king, the question of the governor-generalship came up, and Vincent commented that the king 'doesn't like the idea of Howe as being too political.'[7] Vincent, in the meantime, was resolving his own doubts. Lionel, not happy at his job in Massey-Harris, agreed to come as his father's private secretary. He and Lilias and their three small daughters would live in Rideau Cottage (actually a commodious Victorian villa), a stone's throw from Rideau Hall. They would provide a happy domestic background for the vice-regal duties, and Lilias could act as the governor-general's hostess. Vincent now believed that he could accept the appointment. Without Alice it would be difficult, but he was confident he could do it. When he saw the king and queen as governor-general elect, the queen commented, 'You are very brave, Mr. Massey, to take on this job alone.'[8]

Since the governor-general was now the direct, personal representative of the king or queen, his major task was to expound the theory of the Crown and to demonstrate its vitality in the life of the people over whom he presided. This was a task that Massey accepted with enthusiasm and untroubled conviction. After he retired, in a speech that he described as his final word to the nation or, as he put it, his 'swan song,' he devoted himself to an exposition of the meaning of the Crown, conscious that the doctrine was now being challenged or, worse, ignored.[9] He argued that in Great Britain the Crown had been the single most reconciling force, a benign principle of unity in a pluralistic democracy. The principle of unity had a human face: it was embodied in a man or woman, the head of a family that reached far back in time and yet presented itself to contemporaries with a homely familiarity.

Vincent spoke of the monarchy with deep feeling. He had a tendency to sweep all royalty into a charmed circle where they were endowed with a preternatural wisdom and a native shrewdness. This perception was often based on casual acquaintance. But this was not true of his feeling towards the British monarchy, which grew out of a personal association. King George v had personally appointed him as his ambassador to the United States, and during the war Queen Mary had been a familiar figure at Canadian celebrations. Of King Edward viii, whom Vincent had known since the early twenties, it was politic not to speak. His retreat from duty highlighted the achievement of his younger brother. To Vincent King George vi and Queen Elizabeth were the complete embodiment of the kingly ideal, combining dignity and probity with a simple but compelling charm. George vi had brought Vincent's career to a glorious conclusion with the bestowal of the Companion of Honour, in a special, personal ceremony, and he had welcomed him warmly to his post as governor-general just two weeks before he died.

Vincent served his entire term as governor-general as the representative of Queen Elizabeth II. During these years, she and Prince Philip twice visited Canada – on the first occasion to open parliament in October 1957, on the second to open the St Lawrence Seaway in the summer of 1959. They had been guests at Government House and for a brief relaxing time at Batterwood, following their official duties in 1959. In addition, Philip came twice on his own, in August 1954 and October 1958, to discuss the holding of a conference in Canada on problems of industrialization (the first conference sponsored by Philip had been held in Oxford).[10] The personal correspondence between Vincent and Elizabeth and between him and Philip is relaxed and informal. Vincent was at home with the young, particularly if, like these royal friends, they were handsome and spirited. There are suggestions of slight tensions with Philip when he became persistently aggressive at small points in official speeches, or succumbed to a black mood at an official act he disapproved of, as, for instance, a too zealous security arrangement.

The Crown had survived and grown stronger by the dedication and moral strength of those who had occupied the throne. It depended also on its own inherent power as a symbol that was at the heart of the national consciousness and that glowed most brilliantly on coronation days. Vincent had felt that glow at the coronation of George VI on 6 May 1937; he felt it again on 2 June 1953 as he presided at a national assembly on Parliament Hill, Ottawa, to coincide with the young Queen's coronation in London. He loved symbolism and ceremony – the colour and pomp, the assumption of a role, the careful observance of a procedure shaped by custom and sanctified by time. In his Toronto speech, he quoted with satisfaction some comments made in the British House of Commons by Clement Attlee, the prime minister (the implied statement was 'I am a dedicated socialist, but royal pageantry is part of our common life'): 'I think that public opinion to-day likes a certain amount of pageantry. It is a great mistake to make government too dull. That, I think, was the fault of the German Republic after the First World War ... the trouble was that they let the devil get all the best tunes.'

Such, then, were the justifications for maintaining an institution that had long ceased to exercise direct political power and seemed to most people indeed to exist in complete separation from the political process. In a later speech, Massey quoted with delight Goldwin Smith's cynical comment: 'Religious Canada prays each Sunday that the Governor-General may govern well, on the understanding that heaven will never be so unconstitutional as to grant her prayer.'[11] But the principal argument of defenders of the Crown (which Massey repeated) was that the Crown did exercise power almost always indirectly, but directly at certain extraordinary moments of crisis. Such a crisis occurs when the continuity of government is threatened, when, for instance, a prime minister resigns suddenly and unexpectedly and there is no obvious leader of the party to succeed him. (A British example is the response of King George v in April 1924, when the prime minister, gravely ill, suddenly resigned: Bonar Law was in no position to advise the king as to his successor. Lord Curzon during Law's absence had been acting as deputy prime minister, and Stanley Baldwin had been leader of the House of Commons. The king took the advice from a number of leading conservatives, but his decision to invite Baldwin to form a government was his own. He exercised his royal prerogative to maintain the continuity and stability of government.) There is also the royal prerogative either to refuse or to grant a request by the prime minister for the dissolution of parliament, whose wide incidence throughout the Commonwealth Eugene Forsey has carefully chronicled and analysed.[12]

But the real power of the Crown was, paradoxically, indirect and, to the electorate, largely invisible. The nature of that power is contained in a famous summary of the rights of the Crown by Walter Bagehot set down in his classic work, *The English Consitution* – 'the right to be consulted, the right to encourage and the right to warn.' For a British monarch, who had been carefully nurtured since childhood on the nature of the constitution and the relation of the Crown to it, who had often seen a succession of governments come and go, and who had established a reputation for wisdom and moderation, these rights could become genuine powers.

Massey's Toronto speech in 1965 was entitled 'The Crown in Canada,' and he was speaking, in large part, of the role of the governor-general. No governor-general was more aware of his primary status as the representative of the Crown, and embraced more enthusiastically the

simple proposition that his relation to his ministers was the same as
the monarch's relation to his ministers. Yet Vincent realized that there
were local circumstances that made it difficult for a governor-general
to act with full vice-regal authority. Much of the power of the Crown
arose from a fragile mystique that descended from a past that the
dominions could not share. Indeed, Canadian nationalism in the nineteenth and early twentieth century had grown on resistance to authority exercised by the mother country and had been nurtured by a
sturdy suspicion of class distinctions and aristocratic pomp, all associated in the popular mind with the Crown. But Massey believed that
these ideas were crossed by an instinctive royalism that had deeper
roots than anti-monarchist populist sentiment. 'A crown has continuously been a symbol of sovereignty in Canada longer than any other
nation except the Scandinavian countries.' This was a statement in a
little document on 'The Governor-General of Canada' that Rideau
Hall had prepared. The document went on to support this surprising
statement by pointing out that 'England abolished the monarchy from
1649 to 1660 during Cromwell's Commonwealth when Canada was
under the Kings of France.'

Vincent believed that the Canadian people would welcome vice-
regal pomp. The restoration of ceremony might be, he reflected, a
shrewd political move, a reassurance to imperialist critics that a Canadian as governor-general did not mean a break with tradition, that
Rideau Hall was not likely with Vincent Massey resident to become a
Jacksonian White House. Vincent brought back a number of traditions
– the wearing of the uniform prescribed for the governor-general
(fortunately her late husband's uniform presented to him by Lady
Tweedsmuir fitted him perfectly), the use at the opening of parliament
and on coronation day of the state carriage, with a mounted escort
from the RCMP (the carriage had not been seen since 1939, when it
was used by George VI and Queen Elizabeth), the daily parade of a
guard of the Royal 22nd Regiment when he was in residence at the
Citadel in Quebec. His emphasis on the Citadel was a part of his
traditionalist revival, as well as a recognition of the importance of
French Canada. It was a splendidly unspectacular building, actually
'the eastern portion of a long military Regency building of massive
stone construction, which dates from the early nineteenth century

and which also houses the officers' mess and commandant's residence of the Royal 22 Regiment.'¹³ But it had a superb view down the St Lawrence, and it had a comfortable snugness especially by contrast with the meandering amplitudes of Rideau Hall.

Vincent also made it clear that he wanted to retain the lady's curtsey to the governor-general, describing it as simply a continuation of a normal Victorian greeting. As he was travelling back to Canada to be sworn in as governor-general, he reports that Brooke Claxton, who was a fellow passenger, 'tackled me about the custom of curtseying to the Governor-General and urged me to abolish it. I said I disagreed and even if I thought it should be done away with, it shouldn't be the act of the first Canadian Governor General.'¹⁴ Vincent had a solemn satisfaction in noting when and how the ladies (inclusive of his three small grand-daughters) curtseyed. But it was not a subject to be treated with unvaried solemnity. He tells about a party at Clarence House in London when he was sitting at a table with the Queen Mother and other guests, including Danny Kaye, who was both guest and entertainer. Kaye turned to the queen when he was introduced to Vincent and said, 'Mam, you know he is the Queen in Canada – they curtsey to him!'¹⁵ Another widely accepted rule in royal protocol, he curtly dismissed. When he discussed the reception of royalty with the new prime minister, John Diefenbaker, he pointed out that the belief 'that you mustn't speak to royalty until spoken to' went out with Queen Victoria.

But ceremony and protocol were frail props to the office of governor-general. The major ceremonies took place in Ottawa and were seen and enjoyed by only a few. They were solemn and serious, and Vincent Massey always appeared on these occasions unsmiling and a little grim in his official uniform that seemed to have been fashioned for a taller and more robust figure. An exception was the governor-general's gift of a goat to the Royal 22nd, presented and received, solemnly in formal speeches in French by Massey and the honorary colonel, Georges Vanier. The goat took over in an unrehearsed finale: 'When officers had been marched off, the goat was produced from behind the stand. When he saw me he made a bound towards me, reared up and placed his hooves on my shoulders as if to say 'There's a chap I know' ... When the troops were in line again and the Royal

Salute was given and 'God Save the Queen' was played, the goat knelt down (I am afraid he also nibbled some grass).'[16]

It was easier for Massey to abandon formal protocol during the extensive tours to all parts of Canada. A certain amount of formal ceremony was observed – presentations of resolutions of loyalty by the mayor, solemn inspections of guards of honour, usually featuring boy scouts and members of the Canadian Legion, followed by inspections of notable industrial plants, hospitals, and schools. Vincent was always pleased when the mayor wore his chain of office, thus identifying him as a leading player in the little drama. At each stage there would be an exchange of speeches, informal and short, but cumulatively exhausting if a community insisted on a series of official events. Inevitably His Excellency was presented with an example of local creativity, rarely treasures to be preserved – 'a grim piece of local needle-work,' patriotic figures or resident animals roughly hewn out of wood – but Vincent managed to keep up a cheerful face and even to enjoy himself. The antidote to boredom was to concentrate on people. In visits to institutions, he always asked the administrator if he could concentrate on people rather than equipment. Inevitably there would be some saving incident that would break through the mechanical formality. He tells the following story about a visit to Vernon, BC: 'At the end of the line was a distinguished looking oldish man with a long, grey beard – apparently slightly deaf. As the young man making the presentations made clear to him that the Governor-General wanted to meet him, he shouted out 'Jesus Christ!' and leapt to his feet. After which I seized him by the hand and tried to relieve his apprehension!'[17]

Vincent showed an unexpected tolerance for the national saturnalia in which his office was inevitably involved (the exception being the Grey Cup, despite the association of the trophy with his revered predecessor; he disliked football, and disliked even more the surrounding Americanized rituals). He enjoyed himself greatly at the Calgary stampede and was pleased by the warmth of the welcome. During the parade he reports proudly that 'I was busy waving my white hat for the whole hour and a half or more.' He found 'the stampede less commercial than I thought it would be' and 'the atmosphere more true of the old ranch life and less affected by alien entertainment that

I imagined.'[18] Such festivals provided material for good-humoured mimicry. His scretary, Joyce Turpin (now Mrs Bryant), tells of his return to his private car at the end of a strenuous day at the stampede, and how with a few gestures and a slight change of expression he would transform himself into a shrewd, appraising cattleman.

Some of the visits he enjoyed most were completely innocent of ceremony. He tells of a visit to Juskatla logging camp in the Queen Charlotte Islands off the British Columbia coast and of how he had a drink with a famous camp superintendent, 'Panicky Bell.' 'Bell,' he wrote, 'was off duty and appeared very relaxed.'[19] Roy Jones, who was a vice-president of the Powell River Company, the owner of the camp, and was present at Massey's visit, provides a gloss on 'relaxed.' 'At noon "Panicky" made his appearance and, hitting the "G.G." on the back said "Have you seen enough of this horse-shit?" Massey, recognizing who it must be, came back with, "Well, Mr. Bell, what have you in mind?" "I thought that you might like a snort with old Panicky." "Mr. Bell, I would be delighted – but, gentlemen, no pictures please." Panicky pulled out two mugs from his mackinaw and a bottle. The Governor-General took a healthy drink eye to eye with Panicky who danced with glee, shouting "you are alright, you old son of a bitch." '[20]

Another sure source of enjoyment during the tours was the meeting with children, usually assembled in schools for the governor-general's visit. Both he and the children were sure of the ultimate message – the royal request for a school holiday that was always granted on these occasions. Vincent turned what could have been a flat statement into a dramatic performance, in which the children quickly sensed their part and joined in the fun. After his retirement, the National Film Board produced a film on Massey's work as governor-general. It began with an actual film of his appearance before a school audience at Georgetown, Ontario. 'School audiences,' he began, 'have an idea in their minds, that I'm going to do something which may be of some advantage to them.' When the children laughed, he commented soberly. 'I haven't the remotest idea what you're thinking about, no idea at all. What I really meant was, of course, that I want to give you, offer you good wishes for your work in school.' More laughter, which redoubled when Vincent added, 'that's what is closest to your hearts, I know.' Then he warily approached the expected announcement. He said that his predecessors had 'an old-fashioned idea of asking the mayor of the city or town if the boys and girls might have a holiday.' This elicited cheers. The announcement was clearly going to follow. 'I'm so glad,' he observed with schoolmasterly approval, 'that you have a feeling for history. And though,' he continued, 'we may read about these habits of governor-generals in the past, we've got to be modern and nowadays, the schools – and Georgetown, I am sure, is a very good example of this – are terribly attractive and people don't like being locked out of school to-day. You see, what I really ought to do, is to say to his Worship that if the boys and girls are really very good here, they might as a special privilege, as a very great privilege, be allowed to go to school on Saturday.' The children now realized that the comic drama was coming to an end. They laughed loudly and yelled in excitement. Vincent turned to the Mayor. 'Your Worship, it's not going down at all well. You can see that. Well, now let's get down to business.' Then followed the official request, which was received with unrestrained cheers.

In his ceremonial public life Massey gave great emphasis to French Canada. Shortly after he was installed in Rideau Hall, he asked a friend, Jean Sarrazin, to spend two weeks with him at Rideau Hall so that in daily conversation he could sharpen his French, grown a little flabby from long disuse. He seized every opportunity to emphasize French as an official language, insisting at the opening of parliament on making all the exchanges in both French and English (as well, of course, as the Speech from the Throne). In a speech at the Canadian Club in Toronto, where, given the locale, he felt he might be violating the law of innocuousness in vice-regal oratory, he urged English-speaking Canadians to learn French and criticized the arid methods of teaching the language in schools. Early in his regime he made a Quebec tour and, thereafter, numerous visits. He firmly established the Citadel in Quebec as the governor-general's alternate home, and made it during his residence a centre of Quebec social life. He got along well with the Quebec premier, Duplessis, his antagonist from royal commission days. He had strong support from Lilias, who quickly established an irreverent, bantering relationship with Duplessis. In an early visit to Trois-Rivières, Vincent received such an ovation at the city hall reception that Duplessis whispered to him as the cheers mounted in volume 'I hope you're not thinking of running against me in the next election.' But there were distressing pockets of French-Canadian nationalism, which Massey noted and then diplomatically ignored. At Victoriaville and Montmagny, teachers at the schools, run by the Frères du Sacré Coeur, led the students in the *salut au Drapeau* (always the provincial flag), and pointedly avoided any reference to the queen. One father spoke of the govenor-general's tours in the nine provinces and in the republic of Quebec.

The most highly publicized of the Massey tours was the tour of the far north. It was not a response to John Diefenbaker's vision of the north (this, the emotional core of Diefenbaker's first election campaign, came a year later), nor was it a proposal that originated with Massey himself. He had had, it is true, his own vision of the north as a shining frontier awaiting development. In 1939 he had written an article for the *Geographical Magazine* entitled 'Canada Looks North,'[21] in which he referred admiringly to Lord Tweedsmuir's 1937 journey to the far north. Tweedsmuir had reached the Arctic just above Aklavik and then had gone south-west into the unchartered areas of the Yukon. The deep impression that the north made on him was expressed in a highly emotional and dramatic way in his 'Canadian' novel, *Sick Heart River*, where the north is a source of congealing fear, 'a part of the globe which had no care for human life, which was not built to man's scale, a remnant of that Ice Age which had long ago withered the earth,'[22] and yet it provided a cleansing ordeal through which man could pass to a clear and saving vision. Vincent was not inclined to mystical reflections, certainly about the north, nor did he have Tweedsmuir's delight, nurtured by long and arduous walks in Scotland and by mountain-climbing in Switzerland, in tough physical challenges. But he greatly admired Tweedsmuir and thought of his concept of the governor-generalship as constituting a model.

The idea for the Massey tour was political, but of such a nature that it demanded a symbolic rather than a specific expression through normal channels. The nuclear stand-off between the Soviet and the Western powers had reached a stage where the chief American and Canadian fear was of enemy bombers with nuclear weapons approaching from the Arctic. As a result Canada and the United States had undertaken a joint defensive measure – a line of radar stations across the far Canadian north, the Distant Early Warning (DEW) line. The American contribution in manpower, technology, and resources was, of course, greater than that of the Canadian, and there was a natural tendency for American representatives to forget about Canadian territorial sovereignty. Vincent recalled his concern during the war about American aggressiveness in Newfoundland, Labrador, and the Yukon, and understood the renewed Canadian apprehensions. During the tour American representatives, both civilian and military, were members of the welcoming parties, but the chief Canadian representative, no matter how junior his rank, officially received the governor-general and his party. At Cambridge Bay, which had recently achieved prominence as a result of the DEW line, the party was met by Corporal E.E. Jones, member-in-charge, RCMP detachment, who presented Mr Herbert Donaldson, general superintendent, Northern Construction Company. Vincent commented, 'I liked the position which the RCMP holds in this settlement.'[23] Later on when the Canadian party was entertained at the Northern Construction Company's camp, they were shown a film about the DEW line, which, Vincent noted, 'was not overweighted in its reference to Canada – nor were the remarks by the American who introduced it.' Vincent heard that before the arrival of his party, there had been 'quite a scurry' to get a Canadian flag to fly beside the American. But this was the only approach to an incident. If, as Lionel wrote to a friend following his return from the north, the purpose of the whole venture was 'to let the Americans know that Canada owns the High Arctic,' that purpose was deeply interred in the governor-general's affirmations of Canadian-American amity and co-operation.

The political motivation was more, however, than an assertion of sovereignty, a polite reminder to Canada's powerful neighbour of geographic facts. It was also a reminder to Canadians that they possessed only a small portion of their own country, that the far north was not a frontier to be glimpsed briefly in adventure stories and then forgotten. The Department of Northern Affairs and National Resources had a vigorous minister, Jean Lesage, and a senior civil servant, Gordon Robertson, who could present the case for the development of the north vividly and compellingly. Robertson was chairman of a representative committee that charted the governor-general's tour, and worked out the program. For each stop a member of the department, Graham Rowley, co-ordinated the arrangements with the local representatives. He had studied archaeology at Cambridge, had engaged in independent research on Eskimo sites, and had travelled throughout the far north (parts of which he had been the first to explore). When the itinerary had been settled, there was a preliminary 'dry run,' during which Esmond Butler, the assistant secretary, was responsible for envisaging possible difficulties and devising schemes for overcoming them. Lionel Massey attended to a multitude of details, including a purchase of four and a half tins of tobacco of a rich and strong nature for the Eskimos, and three pounds of bulk sweets to be distributed by the Governor-General to children (obtainable, he pointed out to the comptroller, at Woolworth's on Sparks Street at 49 cents a pound).

The itinerary was far more ambitious than the one devised for Lord Tweedsmuir. It circumscribed the whole of the Northwest Territories, with a separate flight to and from the North Pole, taking off from the most northerly settlement, Resolute on Cornwallis Island. Tweedsmuir in 1937 could do only part of his journey by air. The Massey party travelled in the comparative ease of a TCA North Star. It was slow by modern standards, with a ground speed of 200 miles an hour; the continuous roar of its four engines gave a feeling of security, but seemed to assult the whole body. Earle Birney's description of the North Star's take off is suggestive of the plane in actual flight:

> *Snorts through four great nostrils Bellerophon's stallion*
> *roars him seven thousand strong*
> *trembles moves like a cloud on the runway. Wheels –*
> *charges the night.*[24]

The air flights were uneventful, except for the second landing at Frobisher Bay. 'As we approached Frobisher, visibility was greatly reduced by the presence of ice crystals – a sort of haze which is a phenomenon of the Arctic ... The pilot made one landing without success, circled and tried it again. This time we were only a few feet off the runway when he 'gunned' the engines and rose steeply ... on the third attempt, however, he made it – much to the relief of everybody. It was not a pleasant moment – landing down-wind in a heavy aircraft, on a shortish runway, is not a pleasurable experience!'[25] There were no other untoward incidents. Most of the flights were short – from two to five hours (except for the all-day flight to and from the North Pole). Still a 16-day tour of the high Arctic, with a continuous succession of meetings, ceremonies, dinners, and inspections of installations and equipment (a good deal of it outdoors in sub-zero weather) was a courageous undertaking for a man of sixty-nine, whose physical exertions for the last four years had been confined to walks in the Rideau Hall grounds. The Arctic could not, moreover, make available the usual vice-regal amenities. All the houses where he, Lionel, and Lilias (she was the only woman on the trip) stayed were without running water and plumbing in any form, and virtually without ventilation (the head of an American group said that he was too hot for three-quarters of the time, and too cold for the remaining quarter). At the various settlements, air bases and DEW line constructions would be at some distance from each other, and travel was by dog sled. Vincent, a great lover of dogs, welcomed this mode of travel. The dogs, however, disdained fraternizing with humans (at the end of one trip, the lead dog wandered into the living quarters, looked around haughtily, then happily rejoined his fellows outside). Vincent described 'a very rough journey of about one hour and a half. Most of the sleds upset, some of the dogs became detached and got fantastically interwoven ... the sleds, very rigidly constructed, when they dropped six inches or a foot from one level of ice to the next, gave one the sensation of having one's spine driven well up into the skull.'[26]

The governor-general's party included representatives of the Canadian, American, and British presses, photographers, and cameramen from the CBC and the National Film Board. As Raymond Daniell, the *New York Times* correspondent in Ottawa, remarked in a letter enquiring about press representation on the tour, 'it will be a very colorful and human story.'[27] The arrangements called for the full exploitation of the trip to the North Pole. When the plane reached the pole, it dropped from seven thousand to one thousand feet, and Massey placed on a shute a metal canister that had been carefully constructed at the National Research Council, and contained information about the trip in French, English, and Danish. There was a chance that at some future time it might arrive on the coast of Greenland, or Spitzbergen, or some other distant northern port. Massey then recorded a short message for radio. Romantic notions of the North Pole were reawakened 'as I look down on the polar ice, bright in the sun, which can now be seen night and day just above the Canadian horizon.'

The tour, thus widely publicized, no doubt aroused interest in the north, and may have unintentionally prepared the way for Diefenbaker's vision on the road to power. But it was perhaps more important for what it did for the public representation of Vincent Massey, governor-general. It helped to dislodge the image of the small figure in the strange uniform with the set, serious expression, presiding at Ottawa ceremonials. For Vincent, the tour itself was a discovery of individuals and people. When it came to explanations of the working of meteorological equipment or refineries, he had limited powers of absorption. He much preferred the meetings with the people who actually lived in the Arctic, particularly the Eskimos, who were the dominant natives at most of the settlements. A preliminary briefing thus described one group of Eskimos that made a special trip to meet the great man: 'The Iglielik Eskimos are one of the tribes least affected by civilization, and are as nice a people as one could hope to meet.' This judgment was abundantly confirmed. Vincent was charmed by the Eskimos, especially by the children, who had, he said, delightful manners. The Eskimos had a great self-confidence that the Indians lacked. At a drum dance at Aklavik, he remarked that the Eskimo dancers 'were sure of themselves, full of good humour – perfect extroverts. The Indians appeared to be inhibited, suffering from a sense of inferiority.'[28]

Besides the Eskimos and Indians, the most interesting people Vincent met were those who had become citizens of the Arctic. At Resolute it was Constable Gibson of the RCMP, a lieutenant-commander in the navy during the war, who became, in response to any given situation, midwife, teacher, magistrate, and government representative. At Aklavik it was Father Bénaimé, a Belgian by birth but a Canadian citizen, who had given his life to the Arctic – 'a most remarkable and magnetic person,' Vincent commented.

At Rideau Hall Massey's policy was to maintain the traditional pattern, but within that pattern to try to create an atmosphere of warmth and informality. Lester Pearson, ironically having argued in defence of the appointment of a Canadian, said that 'under the first Canadian Governor-General, there was an atmosphere rather more regal and formal than, say, under the Earl of Athlone, a member of the Royal Family.'[29] This was certainly not Massey's intention. He instituted a number of innovations that broadened the scope of entertainment. In his first year he invited groups of twenty MP's and senators to come to informal receptions, following official sessions, and provided transportation for them between Parliament Hill and Rideau Hall. This was designed to remedy a tradition whereby Rideau Hall was seen as a preserve of cabinet ministers, senior civil servants, and old Ottawa society, the ordinary MP being looked upon as a transitory intruder. He instituted informal dinner dances for young people and enlarged the scope of Christmas entertaining. Sunday evenings were usually set aside for informal dinners with friends, always followed by a movie in the private projection room, the title of which Vincent, a movie enthusiast, always noted in his diary accompanied by a phrase or two of critical assessment.

The image of Massey as cold and staid had considerable currency. Even *Saturday Night*, spokesman for the arts and of sweet, reasonable conservatism, had occasionally burnished the distorted public image. B.K. Sandwell, the cultivated and urbane editor for many years, had cast an amused eye on the Massey heritage, chiefly as embodied in Vincent Massey:

> Let the old world, where rank's yet vital,
> Part those who have and have not title.
> Toronto has no social classes,
> Only the Masseys and the Masses.[30]

But now two years after Massey's appointment, *Saturday Night* turned from poetic raillery to Billingsgate prose. The leading editorial of 13 November 1954, beginning with speculation about Massey's successor, moved into an attack on the incumbent. 'One more Governor-General as grey and remote as Mr. Massey will finish the job of making Canadians forget that there is such a thing as a royal deputy in Canada ... Mr. Massey undoubtedly performs his social duties at Ottawa with proper, if grim, dignity. Certainly he has been successful as a speech maker at gatherings on a rarified intellectual level. But as the Queen's representative to the people of Canada he has been a dismal flop.' The letter column of succeeding issues of *Saturday Night* had a number of letters of protest, including a heated one from Charlotte Whitton, the mayor of Ottawa, who had initially opposed Massey's appointment. Vincent was not deeply distressed by *Saturday Night*'s surly outburst. The magazine had recently been bought by Jack Kent Cooke, owner of a prominent commercial radio station in Toronto and a flamboyant opponent of public broadcasting. His representation before the Massey commission had not been enthusiastically received, and the subsequent report had drawn on some of his animadversions for its case against an unchecked commercialism. The words in the editorial were presumably those of the editor, Gwyn Kinsey, but the animus was that of the owner.

By the time the editorial appeared, Massey was confident he had given the public role of the governor-general the right emphasis – dignity and solemnity on formal occasions, relieved by a friendly democratic approach in his travels about the country and a readiness to recognize the ease with which the solemn could tumble into the ridiculous. Sometimes he led the way himself, as in his speech to the Press Gallery dinner, Ottawa, in the spring of 1956. This was an annual affair, by tradition irreverent and often rowdy, in which the leaders of the nation attempted to amuse and placate their severest critics. Massey, who always came at the end of proceedings, had agonized over each appearance, but had been uniformly successful, often aided by the dulness of those who preceded him. For the 1956 speech he reverted to an old idea he had used in the twenties as president of the Arts and Letters Club, and wrote his speech in rhyming couplets

> *I offer you a doubtful form of sport –*
> *The reading of my annual report.*

Four times we've met at this delightful meal.
Four times you've suffered from a grim ordeal,
For when you fondly hoped the bar to reach –
You've always had to listen to my speech.

He complained about his bondage to his 'advisers.'

Under their orders I can have no choice,
The country hears me as His Master's Voice,
Transmitting policies that are not mine,
I'm just an old Trans-Canada Pipe Line.

He speculated about one throne speech in a mixture of English and French.

If one could but exprimer les ideés
In one discours, but aux deux langues mêlées
We would avoir, as the discours went on,
A magnifique linguistic macédoine.

Unfortunately, he could bring no message from the Eskimos, whom he had recently visited;

From radio they have immunity
And adequate protection from TV.
Thus they are unaware of Davy Crockett
And have no knowledge of the guided rocket.[31]

The governor-general dealing lightly with himself was one thing; others dealing lightly with the governor-general was quite another – to the public, if not to Vincent. The students at McGill University, grown weary of stale American imitations, resolved in their annual review for 1957 to give it Canadian emphasis. *My Fur Lady* was a lighthearted but shrewd comment on the current cultural scene in Canada. A leading figure was the governor-general – not any governor-general, but specifically and unmistakably Vincent Massey. In his opening song, the governor-general bemoans his traditional role:

> *From Victoria to Gander*
> *I tend to vice-regalities,*
> *To quote Lord Alexander,*
> *I govern generalities.*
>
> *It's part of the vice-regal game*
> *To tour municipalities.*
> *At every stop I must declaim*
> *The same polite banalities.*

But now, the governor-general reflects, happier prospects open up: 'after six years they finally got around to doing something about my report.' He says to his admiring secretary that 'one day you and I will see them get rid of all these politicians and legislators, and let the Canada Council take over the country. After all, culture is the only thing that really matters in the long run.'[32] A reporter rhapsodizes about the governor-general: 'Here we are, in the presence of the Head of State, the living symbol of our nationhood, and its undying bonds with that great Commonwealth across the seas. Here's to that great lineage of Governors: Champlain, Frontenac, Montcalm, LaSalle, Pontiac ... ' The governor-general then explains that he has solved the problem of Canada's 'cultural identity.' He has established a 'Culturality Squad' that will quickly identify cultural characteristics. The squad is precious and very British.

> *Our hankies are made in the Burlington Arcade,*
> *And we go to Savile Row for our styles.*
> *We look queer in our caps,*
> *But actually, chaps,*
> *It's simply that we're Anglophiles.*

My Fur Lady was a sell-out at McGill, moved to the Stratford Festival (the first of the 'fringe' shows), then to Toronto, where it was equally popular, and opened in Ottawa in the fall of 1957. The authors were concerned when they heard Vincent Massey had ordered seats for the opening night, and disturbed, but unbending, when the Ottawa sponsors urged deletion of passages that were clearly inspired by the speeches and attitudes of the current governor-general. The sponsors obviously were ignorant of their man. On 4 October 1957 Vincent Massey noted in his diary that it was 'a crowded day on matters concerned with the Queen's visit,' but 'in the evening to see "My Fur Lady," the McGill musical comedy largely concerned with good witty satire at the expense of my office. Very sophisticated production. I enjoyed it immensely.' At the performance, any tensions that may have existed vanished when following the secretary's speech ('I still think you're the best Governor-General we've ever had'), the audience burst into applause.

The social event that bore most strongly the Massey imprint was the dinner on 1 July 1959, given officially by the queen, although devised and arranged by the governor-general. It came appropriately towards the end of his term and was a brief summary of his interests and activities. He had formulated the idea some months in advance and had discussed it with the prime minister, Mr Diefenbaker. It was to be a formal dinner with an informal spirit. It was to abandon protocol (protocol would have meant a concentration of the highest officers in the government, the judiciary, and the diplomatic service) and to draw its guests from across Canada. The guests were to represent all the principal endeavours of Canadians – business, labour, the press, the church, education, the arts, literature, agriculture, athletics, medicine. Only the prime minister (who warmly agreed with the idea) and Mrs Diefenbaker, and the leader of the opposition and Mrs Pearson would be there in their official government capacities. There would be no speeches (outside of a toast to the queen proposed by the governor-general, which consisted of four words – two in English, two in French), and there would be plenty of time afterwards for all the guests to talk to the queen and Prince Philip. Vincent Massey, who devoted a great deal of time to seating arrangements at formal dinners, strove for both easy compatibility and ironic contrast. Thus Robertson Davies listened with a novelist's curiosity to Madame Richard's problem in presiding over a house with six children, constantly reinforced by hordes of teen-agers anxious to get a glimpse of the great 'Rocket.' Christine Bissell found herself blessedly relieved of the need to discuss the problems of higher education. As the guests assembled, she met Mrs Penney, warm and witty, who came from Ramia, a little island off the coast of Newfoundland where she was president of a large fishing company. Vincent Massey had met her during an eastern tour, and described her as 'a remarkable woman, who runs the island like a feudal chief.' At dinner, Father Bénaimé, on the one side, Vincent Massey's great favourite from Aklavik, gave a lively, erudite discourse on the vintage of the wines that were served, and on the other, Mr Howard Hymas, a farmer from Rosebud, Alberta, described, with the aid of the abundant cutlery, the chuckwagon race at the stampede.

There is no doubt that Vincent Massey enjoyed his years as governor-general. Indeed, he revelled in them. The diary for those years is far more detailed than for previous years. He is now the relaxed observer, rather than the harassed diplomat striving to fit a multitude of obligations into a limited time, many of them rising suddenly and unexpectedly. Now all is planned in advance, elaborate briefing papers are prepared, and the actual events are carefully supervised by a solicitous staff. A certain blandness suffuses much of the diary for these years, and dominates the comments he makes about a succession of distinguished visitors. Rarely in any part of his diary did he give himself a licence for satiric comment. Foreign visitors who differed widely in personal qualities, some of them known for their asperity, are swept into a common pool of placid approval. Nehru 'has manners which are both distinguished and easy. A very civilized person indeed,' and Mrs Gandhi, his daughter, is 'a charming and intelligent guest.'[33] Montgomery 'spoke generously about everyone and showed immense knowledge, clarity of thinking and great qualities of character'; 'I was deeply impressed with Adenauer'; and 'Billy Graham was a pleasant, frank, unassuming young man – very sincere, obviously with a great deal of drive.'[34]

But there was one concern, obsessive and continuous, that shattered the blandness of Vincent's reporting of his governor-generalship. In August of 1954, Prince Philip was in Canada on a short visit and was staying with the governor-general at the Citadel. Then suddenly a pleasant, uneventful visit produced one of the great moments of Vincent's life. 'Before dinner H.R.H. and I had a talk by ourselves on the terrace. He asked me if I would accept the Garter. I was completely overwhelmed by the thought and told him that I hoped he would tell the Queen how touched I was ... What a wonderful idea it is! And how I would love to be able to accept the fabulous honour.' To Vincent, with his love of symbolism, his thorough acquaintance with the structure of the orders of chivalry, his reverence for any honour associated with royalty (and no honour could have had a more stirring royal resonance: the sovereign and senior members of the royal family were members, and St George's chapel, Windsor, the chapel of the Garter, had become the royal chapel also), the offer of the Garter was a glory he had not dared to contemplate. He would become a member of the highest order of chivalry in England – and the oldest order in the world (established in 1384). He would be the first person in the Commonwealth overseas to be honoured. If the Companion of Honour had gloriously terminated his years as high commissioner, the Garter would be a gleaming crown to his whole career. He was aware that the Garter had not always been highly esteemed. He knew Melbourne's rough jibe, 'I like the Garter. There is no damned merit in it.' As an avid reader of Trollope he doubtless knew the chapter in *The Prime Minister* in which the Duke of Omnium, the head of a coalition government, is urged to award the Garter to the Marquis of Mount Fidgett, simply on the grounds of 'wealth, rank, and territorial influence' and of his family's traditional entitlement to the award. But by 1954 the award of the Garter had become 'the unfettered gift of the Sovereign.'[35] George VI had taken a special interest in the order, and recent appointments had all been of men who had served during the war with unquestioned national acclaim – Mountbatten, Alanbrooke, Portal, Cranborne, Montgomery in 1946, with Anthony Eden and Winston Churchill following when they no longer held office.

Massey was acutely aware that the queen's offer of the Garter did not mean its automatic award. No one in Canada knew more than Massey about the tangled history of honours in Canada and the confusion over them that still prevailed. During its sessions, the Royal Commission on National Development in the Arts, Letters, and Sciences had been asked by the prime minister to add to their terms of reference 'honours and awards.' The report had been presented some months later. There had been no publicity, and St Laurent had shown no interest in discussing it, let alone implementing it. Its major recommendation was the establishment of a Canadian order to be known as the Order of St Lawrence, with five classes. The 'recommendations' had begun with the general statement that 'it is not our intention to recommend the revival of titles.' This implicitly ruled out the award to Canadians of the highest honours in the orders of chivalry, since these carried knighthoods with them. The Garter was not even mentioned in the report since all companions of the Garter, restricted to 24, automatically became knights.

Vincent hoped that, since there was as yet no fixed government policy, his acceptance of the Garter would be approved. He could be looked upon as being outside all recognized categories by reason of his vice-regal position. Moreover, it could be presented to the public as the queen's recognition of the services of one of her appointees, which carried with it only a non-hereditary title that did not run counter to official government policy. If the award were made by the queen during a Canadian visit, its special nature would be evident to the public and would cause no alarm. On the other hand, there were those, among them John Diefenbaker, who preferred the award to be made (if it were made) shortly after the end of the term of Massey's governor-generalship when he could receive it as an ordinary citizen. Under any consideration, Massey realized that he would need the prime minister's approval, and this would be in the broad sense a political decision. For six years Massey clung to the hope that permission would be given, especially after Diefenbaker, with his strong attachment to Great Britain, became prime minister.

From 1954 to the election of 1957 Massey's conversations on the subject of the Garter were with St Laurent. St Laurent was not a willing conspirator. He did not share Massey's deep love of Britain and royalty and he had difficulty in grasping why the Garter was of such transcendent importance to Massey. Moreover, in the matter of honours he stood in the shadow of Mackenzie King's obsessive opposition to any action – an opposition that King himself was able to overcome when, on his retirement, he was offered and accepted the Order of Merit. There were two faint rays of light amid the general gloom. St Laurent thought there was a possibility of Massey's accepting as a private citizen, and Pearson, with whom the prime minister had discussed the matter, thought that, in the matter of honours, the governor-general belonged to a separate category.

With Diefenbaker the atmosphere suddenly changed. When Massey raised the matter in an interview on 4 September 1957, the prime minister instantly responded with the enthusiasm of a fellow royalist. It was 'wonderful' and he would do all he could to facilitate it. Given a solid majority at the next election, which could not long be delayed, he would acquiesce without hesitation. He envisaged a solution that accorded with Massey's. He said 'that the Government should put itself on record as being strongly opposed to the revival of titular honours, but that an exception should be made for anyone holding the post of Governor-General. At this time the announcement of my K.G. could be made. This would link up the personal honour with the general subject, and prevent the public from getting the impression that my K.G. was the herald of a revival of titles.' 'His thinking on this subject,' Massey commented, 'is fresh and ingenious.'[36]

The election of March 1958 gave Diefenbaker a magnificently solid majority. 'Stability,' Massey mused, 'has come with a vengeance,' and he rejoiced in the added assurance the election gave to his hopes for the Garter. Diefenbaker now wavered. He thought it was necessary to have cabinet approval, and, to this end, Massey must see senior ministers – Donald Fleming, Sidney Smith, Gordon Churchill, Howard Green. Of these Howard Green was the only one adamantly opposed, on the grounds that the acceptance of the honour would do damage to Massey's high Canadian reputation. The prime minister began to think of a strategic withdrawal. If Robert Menzies, the retired Australian prime minister, came to Canada as Massey's successor, would Massey go to Australia as governor-general, where the acceptance of the Garter would raise no questions? Massey was not impressed by this elaborate evasion. Then came a blessed moment when Diefenbaker's consent seemed assured. On 16 May 1959, having just returned from England, he said to Massey that 'Slim's appointment [Field-Marshal Sir William Slim] left one vacancy, but this mustn't go into your diary or mine.' Massey could draw only one conclusion: that he was to fill that vacancy.

A month later, shortly before the queen arrived in Canada, Diefenbaker gave what Massey thought was final assurance. He said that the award of the Garter 'is something with which the Government has no concern and what she [the queen] does is her decision and we will take no action positive or negative.' Massey goes on to describe a scene that is rather similar to the one with Mackenzie King when he relented and gave his approval to the CH. ' "You mean to say that you will tell her you will stand aside and offer no obstruction?" ... "Well, Prime Minister, this is wonderful news." "Yes," he said, "that is what I shall say. Directly you cease to be Governor-General the announcement can be made from London." I shook him by the hand; I was quite emotional. I said "Now let me get this clear. You are going to tell the Queen that you have no objection to this happening?" "Yes." "Well," I said, "I deeply appreciate this – it means a great deal to me, as you know." He said, "I know it does." '37

This was the high point of Massey's expectations. From here on there was a rapid decine. The government was smothered in vexatious issues – a growing disagreement with the governor of the Bank of Canada, James Coyne, a hopelessly confused policy on Canada's role in northern defence, and the abrupt cancellation of a contract with A.V. Roe Canada for building an all-Canadian supersonic fighter plane, with the loss of 14,000 jobs. An election was drawing near, and Diefenbaker, faced with internal divisions, was in no mood to take on new issues, even a minor one, as to whether a governor-general should receive an honour from the queen and thereby acquire a title for his remaining years. Diefenbaker now began to emphasize cabinet solidarity, and Massey sensed gloomily that this meant ultimate refusal. He kept his faith in the prime minister, however, although he began in his diary to write of 'vacillation,' 'procrastination,' and 'political timidity.'

Massey left office on 15 September 1959. All across Canada there was a great outpouring of praise for the way in which he had transformed and strengthened the office. The Ottawa *Journal* urged that he be given the Canada medal (established in 1943 in recognition of 'meritorious service above and beyond the faithful performance of duties,' but never awarded). Massey speculated that the public response would provide a good background for a favourable decision on the Garter. He confided his problem to Robertson Davies, the editor of the *Peterborough Examiner*, and Davies, irritated by the government attitude, wrote a strong editorial. 'The Queen,' the editorial pointed out, 'had just given the Garter to Sir William Slim, on his retirement as Governor-General of Australia, and we think she would give it to Mr. Massey if there were reason to believe that such an action would be acceptable in Ottawa.' It was not a question of violating, but of accepting 'a reasonable exception to an existing policy ... Is the Sovereign to be allowed to say "thank you" ... or are we going to put on a holier-than-thou face and ask her not to smirch the lily whiteness of our egalitarian principles? Could anything be more provincial, more perversely colonial?'[38]

The Davies suggestion was not taken up. Early in June, Vincent discussed with Blair Fraser, one of the most influential journalists of the day, the possibility of a 'calculated leak,' which should be preceded by a direct question to the prime minister. But time was swiftly running out. On 13 June 1960, Vincent was informed by the queen's secretary, Sir Michael Adeane, that the prime minister had written to say that the Canadian government had advised her that 'a renewal of the practice of granting titles of nobility and knighthood to Canadians would not be appropriate.' Vincent, initially full of praise of Diefenbaker, was bitter about what he considered his cynical betrayal. Diefenbaker's defence of his decision in his *Memoirs* was, it must be granted, a piece of pious disingenuity. 'I personally was in the position,' he wrote, 'when I might have received high and prestigious honours, but I made it clear I could not accept them. For example, in 1958 when I was in Malaya, Prime Minister Tunku Abdul Rahman offered me his country's highest decoration. I automatically turned it down.'[39]

There could be no doubt about Vincent Massey's success in representing the Crown in Canada, in making it vivid reality in all parts of the country. He treasured most the comment, 'he made the crown Canadian,' which became, in the public eye, the great distinguishing mark of his régime.[40] Beyond his vice-regal function lay a second, more difficult role to define, ultimately more important than first – the exercise of political power, directly in certain crises, indirectly, through the right 'to be consulted' by the prime minister and the members of his cabinet, and to advise and to warn them about decisions and policy. Beyond the cabinet lay a national audience, where power of a more subtle kind, could be exercised, power that was never nakedly revealed and never rawly political. In these areas, Massey was even more successful than in the first.

The exercise of direct political power beckoned once to Vincent Massey and then providentially withdrew. The election of June 1957 immediately brought to mind the election of November 1925. Vincent Massey now contemplated a House of 112 Conservatives, 105 Liberals, 25 CCF, 19 Social Credit, 4 Independents. The earlier House had had 116 Conservatives, 101 Liberals, 24 Progressives, 2 Independents, 2 Labour, and had set the stage for Byng's controversial action – his refusal to grant King's request for a dissolution and an election and his acceptance of an identical request from Meighen a few days later. Massey was apprehensive. 'A Governor-General's nightmare ... The ghost of 1926 stalked about already.' Some liberal advisers, including Massey's close friend, Father Lévesque, thought that the Government should carry on and meet the House as it did in 1925.[41] Fortunately his hand was not forced. St Laurent had no intention of carrying on, and the Liberal party, recognizing that it must now find a new leader, was in no hurry to force an immediate election. Moreover the CCF members, unlike the Progressives, saw themselves as ideologically self-contained, and were not inclined to join forces with the Liberals to maintain the government. St Laurent resigned and handed over to Diefenbaker. There still remained a possibility that the governor-general would be called upon, in the event of a swift request for dissolution, to exercise more than ceremonial power. Professor Mallory points out 'that after the Canadian general election of June 10, 1957, there was a more general awareness that the Governor-General might have some constitutional responsibility in the succeeding months, and little disposition to denounce the prerogative as an imperial anachronism.'[42] But Diefenbaker waited until a dissolution was made inevitable by a sudden ill-considered Liberal insurgency. When Diefenbaker phoned Massey, who was then in residence at the Citadel, to request a dissolution, Massey insisted that 'it was important that it should not appear that they were dealing with so important a matter too casually'[43] and that the prime minister should come to Quebec to sign the formal notice. Diefenbaker agreed, and flew to Quebec the next day with two of his senior ministers, George Hees and Léon Balcer.

The traditions of the governor-generalship called for regular reports by the prime minister to the vice-regal representative. These could be superficial and routine or serious discussions of policy. All depended on the relationship between prime minister and governor-general and on the authority that the latter had acquired during his career. Massey had good relationships with both St Laurent and Diefenbaker. He was closer to St Laurent by reason of the extended network of associations he had formed with Liberals (several of whom became cabinet ministers) in his pre-diplomatic days and during the war, but he was (until the final Garter débâcle) more relaxed with Diefenbaker, who was less restrained and more disposed to open up general policy questions and to invite comment.

St Laurent became more and more depressed by the international situation, by what he felt to be Britain's rash reversion in the Suez crisis of 1956 to her old imperial ways, and by the bitter intransigence of the United States towards Russia and China. In one session with Massey 'he spoke of the shadow of a possible third world war which seemed to make so much unreal.' Massey offered some consolatory reflections – optimism based on the acceptance of a grim alternative. 'I said that I said to myself that it is necessary to choose between two points of view: (a) there is going to be a war and the end of the world will come. If this is true there is no point in doing anything. (b) one must have faith that civilization will survive and carry on accordingly. There is no middle course between these two outlooks.'[44]

During the fifties, Canadian-American relations did not follow an untroubled course. Massey, as a former minister to Washington, had several opportunities to play his vice-regal intermediary role. President Eisenhower came to Ottawa on a state visit in November 1953, and Massey found him 'a thoroughly likeable person ... warm-hearted, fair-minded, with great integrity'; and Massey returned the visit in May 1954, when he addressed the joint houses in Washington, an event, so he was told, that had even caused the adjournment of the McCarthy committee (later during a visit to New York, he spent hours before the television listening to the proceedings of the McCarthy committee with 'frightening fascination'). But beneath the calm surface of Canadian-American relations, there were strong and vexatious currents. When in July 1958 Eisenhower and his secretary of state, John Foster Dulles, came to Ottawa on a working mission, Massey was sympathetic to Diefenbaker's suggestion that Canada should raise the possibility of recognizing Red China, even though to the United States the very possibility touched on 'an exposed nerve.' Massey was also disturbed by the inflexible American attitude towards Russia. The U.S. regarded a more flexible attitude towards Russia as appeasement. 'They really are the slaves of words and phrases and the prejudices of the Pentagon can often outweigh the weight of the State department.'[45]

Foreign affairs was an area that publicly the governor-general never touched upon; and private conversations on this subject were simply a natural exchange of general ideas between men who could draw upon long experience. In public, the traditional area for vice-regal opinion and, on occasion, action was the pleasant and uncultivated hinterland of the arts and learning. I have pointed out that there was a long and impressive tradition in this area, and Vincent Massey was superbly equipped to continue and enhance it. But now there was a notable change in the cultural atmosphere. Formerly, the government looked on these vice-regal activities with the benign approval of an observer who need not fear his own involvement. But with the Massey report culture had become a political issue and its principal Canadian proponent was in a strong and invulnerable position to influence the legislative response. At the same time, Massey, who was, in the arts and education, Canada's leading benefactor and most accomplished advocate, recognized that much remained to be done in the voluntary field, and addressed himself to a number of artistic and educational enterprises.

The project that relied most on vice-regal initiative was an international festival of music and the arts. Its inspiration was a speech given on 18 December 1952 to the Canadian Club in Ottawa, in which Massey proposed a festival of the arts in the capital city. The proposal came at the end of a lively historical sketch of Ottawa in which Massey pointed out some similarities between Edinburgh and Ottawa: both were northern capitals built on sites of great natural beauty, and both were centres removed from the pressures of business and commerce, but attracting international attention. Ottawa was, of course, the much lesser part in the comparison, but still the comparison was valid, and the conclusion Massey drew that Ottawa, like Edinburgh, could support an international festival emerged convincingly. Having made the proposal, Massey withdrew, as his position decreed, and waited for developments. They came two years later in the formation of a citizen's committee to explore the idea. The governor-general, now working discreetly behind the scenes, arranged for an initial grant from the Massey Foundation and consulted international experts, Kenneth Clark in England, Rudolph Bing and Edward Johnson in the United States, Tyrone Guthrie and Robertson Davies in Canada, the former now established as the artistic director of the Stratford Festival, successfully launched in 1953. The committee brought in Ian Hunter, who had been the artistic director of the Edinburgh Festival, to do a survey and to write a report. It drew up a tentative budget and in May 1959 officially incorporated itself. But the great gap in the plans was the absence of a concert hall. The federal government, it was thought, was the main hope for funds, but the government was not responsive, especially after the election of 1957. While Ottawa pondered, others moved ahead, not only Stratford, but also Vancouver, which launched its own international festival in 1960. The Massey initiative expired, but was not without issue. The concert hall came in due time in a splendour not contemplated, and later, at least the outlines of an international festival.

Massey was closely associated with the Stratford Festival from the very beginning. When the founder of the festival, Tom Patterson, and the first president of the board, Dr H.A. Showalter, turned to him for encouragement and advice, they received both in reassuring abundance. Moreover, at a critical point, when a decision to go ahead with their plans hung in the balance, the board received a crucial grant of $10,000 from the Massey Foundation. Tom Patterson wrote to Lionel Massey: 'I can quite honestly say that the results of your call from Victoria did more than any other single thing to renew the faith that the Board of Directors have always had in the project. When word of an anonymous donation was received, one could almost see the life-blood rising in the prostrate body of the Festival!'[46] Massey attended the two magical performances with which the Stratford Festival opened, *All's Well That Ends Well* and *Richard III*, and in subsequent years attending the festival was always a priority.

In literature, Massey took one initiative, rather modest and unimaginative beside the festival projects. He brought together a group of writers at Rideau Hall for an informal week-end of discussion. The representation was strongly on the side of journalism and history: Bruce Hutchison, George Ferguson, Gérard Filion (plus a contingent of seven journalists from Ottawa), Arthur Lower, Donald Creighton, Frank Underhill were participants; Hugh MacLennan, who had been consulted on this project, and Robertson Davies were the only writers not primarily concerned with journalism and history.

Throughout his regime, Massey maintained a wide association with cultural organizations – the National Gallery, with its new director, Alan Jarvis, a Canadian Rhodes scholar who had had a lively career in England in administration and the arts and who was able, by a mixture of authority and bravado, to make the Gallery front page news (Vincent Massey approved highly of Jarvis, except when he made sharp comments on the gallery display of Queen Mary's quilt); with the Dominion Drama Festival which had once been his responsibility and which still called upon him for the resolution of particular problems; and, indeed, in some degree, with almost all the organizations, federal and provincial, concerned with the arts and education. One personal association outside the conventional structure of the arts was with the American entrepreneur Joe Hirshhorn, who had made a great fortune in Canada in uranium, and had assembled a large collection of modern art, a part of which he exhibited at a special show in the National Gallery. Massey found Hirshhorn 'a fabulous character, utterly candid, very outspoken and extremely discerning in what he said. His language was that of a N.Y. East Side Jew and he was careful to explain at one point that he came from the gutter in Brooklyn and left school at nine. He had a deep interest in the arts and considerable knowledge. He is critical of Canada's failure to take "culture" seriously. He was with me for an hour and twenty minutes. We got on extremely well; he asked me to call him "Joe." '[47] Hirshhorn wrote in equally complimentary terms to Massey: 'most of the men and acquaintances which I have met in Canada have not been touched, or have not sought a cultural life, or as I use the phrase "an inner life". That part of living seems to have passed them by, or they have pushed it aside. And meeting you was refreshing and thrilling. Culture comes naturally to you and aesthetics is evidently part of your nature and make-up. I must confess that it is good to know there are some people in Canada who have the "feel" for the better things.'[48]

Vincent Massey's main influence on the cultural life of Canada came through the pressure he exerted on the prime minister for the implementation of the central recommendation of his report – the establishment of a federal body, the Canada Council, that would receive its financial support from the government and its direction from an independent board. St Laurent was known to be less than enthusiastic about the council. It was one thing to direct tax money to the universities that were essential parts of the social structure; it was quite another to direct tax money to writers, musicians, actors, and ballet dancers who were not essential and were frequently eccentric and subversive. At first St Laurent pleaded the pressures of other legislation and, in particular, his long absence, shortly after taking over, on a world tour. But by January 1955, when the preliminary draft of the Speech from the Throne did not mention the Canada Council, Massey abandoned his vice-regal imperturbability. When pressed, the prime minister revealed that his inactivity was based on political convenience: the Canada Council would be an added irritation to an unfriendly Quebec, and, besides, there were few votes in the rest of Canada to be won by its establishment.

Massey sprang to the attack. 'I expressed my disappointment over the omission of any reference to the Canada Council. He proceeded to explain why it had been left out. It was thought that it might have an unfortunate effect on the present issue between Ottawa and Quebec. I said that it was impossible to placate Duplessis. The P.M. agreed but said that more moderate opinion might be affected adversely if they thought that the Canada Council was a centralizing instrument. We talked about it at some length and I expressed the deepest regrets. I said it would disappoint many to feel this project dropped. The P.M. suggested that those interested would not be very numerous. I said that their importance could not be measured by numbers or by material strength; they were the people who had been heartened by the P.M.'s university speeches. Those who would be pleased and encouraged by what has happened would be *Saturday Night*, the *Montreal Gazette*, the *Vancouver Sun*.'[49] St Laurent was unmoved by the exchange. The final version of the Speech from the Throne was, according to Massey, 'a dreary document with nothing new, no imagination and reflecting no boldness or courage,' and the prime minister 'seemed shrouded in an impenetrable veil of politeness.'

But by the fall of 1956, St Laurent's whole attitude had changed. He was buoyant and full of bold plans, among which was the introduction of legislation to establish the Canada Council with an endowment of $100,000,000. Massey had had some influence after all. He had enlisted the help of Father Lévesque who could speak to St Laurent as an old friend and compatriot. Lévesque spoke to others, particularly to C.D. Howe, who was lukewarm about the Canada Council and reinforced the prime minister's doubts. On one occasion Massey arranged for Lévesque to sit beside Howe at a Rideau Hall luncheon, with whispered instructions 'to soften him up' – an exercise fitted to Lévesque's blending of charm and persuasiveness.[50] There was another more humdrum reason for the prime minister's conversion. Jack Pickersgill suggested that he announce that the $100,000,000 came from an estate tax windfall – $50,000,000 from each of the estates of Sir James Dunn and Isaac Killam – and thus give the plausible impression that the council, with its airy schemes, was costing the ordinary taxpayer nothing.

The formation of the Canada Council was announced on 12 November 1956 in a speech given by the prime minister to a meeting of the National Conference of Canadian Universities. The inaugural meeting took place on 30 April 1957, with Brooke Claxton, the newly appointed chairman, presiding. Vincent Massey opened the meeting. Claxton's speech of thanks went far beyond the usual civilties. It was a finely fashioned statement of the dominating role that Massey had played in the cultural revolution that began in Canada in the twenties:

throughout his busy life the Right Honourable Vincent Massey extended to the arts, humanities and social sciences a great part of his efforts, of his interests, of his fortune. It is perhaps not too much to say that in these fields he did more than anyone else in Canada. Indeed a list of his contributions to these important subjects is almost a catalogue of all of them that we have in Canada to-day. But probably more important even than the material assistance so imaginatively planned and carried out was the way in which he took a personal interest in the people doing the work. The interest and encouragement continued as it has been over the years has meant much more to the hundreds of our artists and writers, workers and scientists he has met, known and helped than even the material aid given by foundations, or the Massey Foundation itself.[51]

Claxton closed his remarks by asking Massey 'if you would do us the honour of accepting this invitation to be the Patron of the Canada Council.' Massey was deeply moved by the whole occasion. Lionel wrote, 'I must say the G.G. was more excited and emotional on this occasion than at any other time he has been to the Parliament Buildings, including the annual opening! His brain child is now in being and functioning.'[52]

For the remainder of his term Massey kept in close touch with Brooke Claxton and the affairs of the council. When Diefenbaker came to power, Claxton wondered whether, as a Liberal stalwart, he should submit his resignation. Massey argued strenuously and successfully in the negative: to resign would be an admission that the chairmanship was a political appointment. Claxton asked for advice on specific matters of policy. He wondered, for instance, if the Canada Council should give money to accompany the governor-general's awards for literature. Massey thought they should, and action was taken (attached to Massey's letter on the subject is an article by Earle Birney in which he had argued that Canadian writers found it difficult to be published, both in Canada and the United States, because of an assumption that readers would not be interested in Canadian themes or backgrounds).[53]

One institution dear to Massey, the CBC, engaged his vice-regal attention. It had been vindicated in the Massey report and sent off to fulfil its public mission. But the private commercial lobby was strong, and St Laurent, irritated, as all politicians (especially those in power) are, by criticism of government-supported agencies, was not a strong ally. Diefenbaker, who was not sympathetic to the CBC, was even more sensitive to such criticism. Massey was apprehensive about the appointments to the new commission on radio and television that was contemplated. He was greatly relieved after a long conversation with the Chairman, R.M. Fowler, who came to see him, presumably on his own initiative. 'He couldn't have been sounder on radio and T.V. in Canada. He and his colleagues are fed up with the campaign of the commercial stations.'[54]

To the general public, who did not participate in either national or local ceremonies and were, of course, unaware of the covert political influence that the governor-general could exert, his influence was confined to the speeches that he gave, and only then if they were broadcast or were controversial enough to be reported by the press. The governor-general could, if he were so disposed, confine himself to the obligatory governor-generalities and carefully avoid any speaking engagement that might elicit remarks of an even faintly arresting nature. It would be difficult to recall a speech by Alexander or Athlone that had been memorable either for individuality of expression or sprightliness of ideas. It had been different with Tweedsmuir. He was an accomplished speaker who clearly enjoyed himself on the platform, and occasionally entered territory from which governors-general were traditionally banned. In this matter, as in others, Massey saw Tweedsmuir as a model. But he believed that as a Canadian of wide experience he could, even more than Tweedsmuir, speak directly to Canadians on serious subjects without being accused of patronizing them or of clouding his vice-regal eminence.

The opportunities for making serious speeches were, for Massey, numerous. At the beginning of his term he was still a university chancellor, and he had been before his appointment a lively and well-informed chairman of a commission that explored issues of wide interest. He had become the great national adviser, the recognized seer on education and the arts – on, in general, the spiritual state of the nation. He had no intention of abandoning this role on becoming governor-general. It give him, indeed, greater scope than he had ever had and greater immunity from criticism. As high commissioner in London during the war, his speeches had inevitably been part of the war effort, and he had preserved in book form only his brief, hortatory excursions. As minister in Washington, he had had many opportunities to speak at universities, but these were usually convocations, which could be constraining, ceremonial occasions. Now a whole host of institutions, organizations, and clubs were available, and he could choose those that would welcome a serious discourse.

For this task he would need a good deal of help. He did not have Tweedsmuir's easy facility. Colonel Willis-O'Connor, for twenty-five years the principal ADC at Rideau Hall, thus described Tweedsmuir speech preparations: 'He wrote his speeches entirely himself. No ghost-writing for him! He dictated, read and corrected, had it re-typed, read it carefully again, and laid it away. On the day it was to be delivered, he got it out, went over it again and handed it to one of the aides to pass on to the press. Many a time I have held a speech in my hand following him as he talked, and discovered that he was practically word perfect, that he could hardly have stuck more closely to the material if he had been reading it.'[55] Massey was not averse to using a speech-writer especially when the occasion called for tested political generalizations, as in his address to the Congress of the United States. In most cases, however, it was a question of a co-author, not a speech writer. His usual procedure ensured that the speech when finally given was his own. He would begin work on it several months before it was to be given. Either he or his co-author would set out a general approach and the principal ideas; the co-author would do then most of the research, and would prepare an initial draft often in skeletal form; he and the co-author would meet, and discuss and rewrite the text; and Massey would then prepare the final version. The co-author worked on the long speeches on serious topics to be delivered, usually to professional audiences. Lighter speeches demanding a personal touch – for instance, all the speeches at the Press Gallery dinners – Massey wrote himself. The co-author had to be a person of wide scholarship and demonstrated ability as a writer who was congenial to Massey and who liked working with him. Massey was fortunate in having such a person. She was Hilda Neatby, his colleague on the royal commission.

In the work on the commission, Hilda Neatby and Vincent Massey rapidly formed a firm alliance. He came to depend on her in the making of all major decisions and was reluctant to act unless she was present. Her share in the formulation of the report and its actual composition was great. Another bond developed during the work on the report. For some years Hilda Neatby had been actively concerned with the state of primary and secondary school education. She had been disturbed by the shortcomings of students entering university – their inability to write clearly and simply, their narrow base of reading, their non-intellectual attitude, their contempt for the scholarly virtues of contemplation and private study. She attributed this malaise to the spread of a superficial progressivism, fueled by the apostle of democracy, John Dewey (she referred to Dewey's version of democracy as 'equalitarianism'), and by the spread of a professional bureaucracy enamoured of the machinery of organization. Primary and secondary education as a provincial responsibility were severely excluded from the commission's terms of reference. But in the consideration of the universities, especially in the passages on the humanities, they could not be ignored. Two startling sentences briefly opened up the vista of the educational wasteland through which Hilda Neatby had despairingly wandered. 'In high schools, we are told, pupils often receive no adequate preparation for serious work, and on this point representations from high school teachers themselves and from university professors are in general agreement.' 'We learn from the Humanities Research Council that it is now difficult to secure qualified persons to teach humanities in the high schools.'[56] Obviously, a study of this whole area was crucial in any general treatment of education and as a specific background to the report. Massey encouraged Hilda Neatby to undertake the task as a separate project, and offered to find financial support for it. She accepted, and with a grant of a little over $2,000 from the Massey Foundation secured research and secretarial support. The result was *So Little for the Mind*, published in 1953, two years after the issue of the report, the major contribution in Canada to the great educational debate that had inspired a succession of books in Britain and the United States.

As usual, Massey was not content to be a passive giver. He read and commented on the chapters as they were written; he gave advice on publishers (Canadian publishers were so tied up with the educational establishment that they drew back from Professor Neatby's uncompromising and acerbic prose); and soothed her fears that his connection with the book would become known and would arouse a controversy about vice-regal indiscretion. When Hilda Neatby sent Massey a copy of *So Little for the Mind*, she concluded her letter with this sentence. 'I am, as always, deeply grateful to you for having asked me and enabled me to write the book.'[57] In a subsequent letter, she emphasized a quality that characterized Massey's cultural benefactions – sensitivity to a situation, confidence in his own judgment, and a determination to see a project carried through. She wrote: 'I am increasingly impressed with the importance of your original contribution – the conviction which, I understand you maintained over a considerable period, that the thing must be done, and that you were determined to do all in your power to further it. That quality of imaginative comprehension of a "situation" (these wretched educators have killed so many useful words) and, if I may say so, faith in your judgment on it, is one which I admire very much.'[58]

It was during the long correspondence on *So Little for the Mind* that an understanding was arrived at by which Hilda Neatby became Vincent's assistant in the preparation of speeches (in fact, as I have noted, his co-author). At first, Vincent had in mind a young man who would do the research work and make preliminary drafts of routine speeches, and would, presumably, be attached to Rideau Hall. But after some preliminary work on early speeches, Miss Neatby began to think that she would like to continue on a permanent basis. She had a number of formal reasons for her decision. 'I appreciate fully the valuable work that you are doing and will do, and also the strain involved. I should be happy to think that you will allow me to help you as a public service without any particular feeling of personal obligation.'[59] She points out that they have already worked together successfully on the commission, and that they share a common educational background in the study of history. But the real reason is that she greatly enjoys working on the speeches. They provide more latitude than he had thought at first for the expression of ideas. 'I have realized increasingly how interesting and important the whole problem is; I mean the problem of saying things appropriate to a Canadian in your position, and yet things that will be useful, and that are really characteristic of yourself.'[60] The process of distance can be resolved easily; she could come to Ottawa at regular intervals, and for periods of two or three days, so that they can confer on the final text. He need have no concern about abdicating his final responsibility. 'I think that no one who considers this would doubt that the speeches which I help you with are your speeches, that they say what you want said, and that it happens that I have a special advantage in helping you say what you want to say in the way you want to say it.'[61]

Hilda Neatby became as essential to the governor-general as she was to the chairman of the commission. The diary records ten visits of Hilda Neatby during Massey's tenure of office – to Rideau Hall (when she stayed in the city), to the Citadel, and to Batterwood. The visits were always for two or three days, and during this time no other engagement was permitted to intrude. She insisted that there should be no working sessions on Sunday, and in a letter to Lionel explained why she made this request. 'I do not want to be disobliging, but for me to plan routine work on Sunday is undesirable from every view point. My idea of a good week-end is to use the mind on Saturday and Monday and let the subconscious operate on Sunday – and it generally does! This is, I am afraid, a worldly way of explaining what, to me is not entirely a worldly matter ... You will find this difficult to understand, but your great-grandfather to whose generation I really belong would have understood quite well.'[62]

Hilda Neatby was a strategist as well as an active participant in the Massey speaking program. The Canadian Manufacturers' Association would not, she thought, welcome any of Massey's typical excursions into the arts or education. She recommended a glance at industrial design as 'the saving grace in an almost inevitable mountain of platitudes – mixed metaphor – an altar to truth on the summit of a mountain of flattery might be better.'[63] On the other hand, a speech to the National Council of Women should be longer than the usual offering, and far more serious since 'women, as you know, have far more endurance than men and they like to be taken seriously.'[64]

Her contributions, however, were usually directed to the substance of a speech. Massey had a clear idea of what he wanted to say, and Hilda Neatby supplied illustrative ballast and, on occasion, a complete version that would be modified only slightly. Occasionally, indeed, her Sunday ruminations supplied ideas that would not have occurred to Massey. She was a devout (but not unquestioning) Presbyterian, and she found it impossible to discuss human goals and aspirations without introducing religious ideas. Massey had discarded his early evangelical Methodism and had joined the Anglican church, more for aesthetic and social than for theological reasons. He had shown no inclination to raise religious questions except in a perfunctory way on ceremonial occasions. Hilda Neatby lectured him gently on his reluctance 'to be theological, philosophical, or professional which makes it extremely difficult to say anything significant' to certain audiences.[65] Massey capitulated and in speeches to audiences with strong religious associations (alumni of the Collège de Montréal, convocation of St Francis Xavier University, Montreal Council for a Christian Social Order, Canadian Jewish Congress) he raised philosophical and theological questions. He referred on several occasions to an idea that Hilda Neatby had stressed in *So Little for the Mind*, the divergence between faith and reason caused by the refusal of science to accept the possibility of a framework of meaning and to insist on looking stoically into an abyss of darkness. The framework of meaning would come from the contemplation of the infinite and the mystical, which would be powered sometimes by religious faith, sometimes by the study of the great works of the human imagination. Hilda Neatby pursued her argument even in the narrow medium of the telegram. From Saskatoon to Antigonish came this arresting message: 'Suggest strengthening science section with Gilson stop far from keeping away from science a truly religious mind should do its utmost to follow it in its progress as the most perfect homage rendered by nature to its creator psalm eighteen one this has never been more true than in our own days at a time when astro physics is beginning to reveal to us the prodigious dimensions of the world we are in Hilda Neatby.'

The speech to the Canadian Jewish Congress, 'The Mission of the Jews,' moved on a less theoretical plane and did not require Miss Neatby's ministrations. The first section dealt with the great contribution of the Jews to the universal frame of reference – the concept of one God and one moral order – and the second, with the holocaust, 'the most hideous crime that human history records,' 'the greatest case of moral retrogression that the world has known.' 'No human being can contemplate it without a personal sense of shame.' We cannot look upon the holocaust as a 'a kind of sterile crime'; we cannot leave 'the iniquity in oblivion'; it is a terrible reminder of the active spirit of evil in the world.'[66] In his speech of thanks, Rabbi Reuben Slonim said: 'In the vocabulary of our tradition there is a signal designation reserved for spirits great and noble, of whatever faith they be. They are called Chassidas Umoth Ha-Olan, "the pious of the nations of the world", and their status in the aristocracy of the elect is of the highest. The address of the Governor-General of Canada establishes him firmly among the foremost of that illustrious company.'[67] The governor-general was no doubt touched by this glowing eulogy; the diplomat may have winced.

When a selection of Massey's speeches as governor-general was published in 1959, it received, particularly for such an unpromising genre, a generally enthusiastic reception. Certainly it enjoys an untroubled eminence among collections of public speeches by Canadians. The prose is simple and direct, but rises occasionally to an arresting phrase or a vivid compressed generalization. The humorous touches are unforced and were, undoubtedly, given Massey's dramatic skills, effective when delivered on the public platform. In his brief introduction, Massey did not mention his co-author; she would have been horrified if he had. In retrospect, the speeches might be looked upon as a series of commentaries on the Royal Commission on the Arts, Letters and Sciences by two of the commissioners.[68] They underlined a number of propositions upon which the report of the commission rested: that, to determine the quality of a nation, you must consider the things it cherishes; that the quality is most clearly perceived in the work of the scholar and the artist; that Canadians recognize this in theory and are now prepared to recognize it in practice.

CHAPTER EIGHT

Patriae profuit

When Vincent Massey's term as governor-general came to an end in 1959, he was seventy-two years old. The years had dealt kindly with him. The face was a little more gaunt, the eyes less penetrating, the carriage not as erect; the voice was still a fine instrument, low-pitched and resonant. Had he chosen the stage, he would now have been in the prime of his profession, playing elderly men of a reflective and didactic temperament. He remained spare and active. A love of food constantly sharpened by dining in high places had not added an ounce of weight, and he had survived with undimmed faculties a continuous succession over the years of cocktail parties and formal dinners preceded by aperitifs, followed by liqueurs, and agreeably punctuated by sherry, wine, and champagne. He had had no serious illness since his long bout with typhoid fever as a young man. At Rideau Hall he had suffered from bursitis in one shoulder and arm. He had had some minor urological surgery and was told that he faced another operation to relieve his bursitis. (The operation was performed in early August 1960; he required a month for convalescence, but suffered no serious after-effects.)

Physically and mentally, he felt that he could continue to lead an active life. There would, of course, be more time for his family, but the family associations had, in recent years, narrowed considerably. Since Alice's death, he had seen less and less of her family. Maude Grant had been the great link, but she was now in failing health, and her voice, once warmly encouraging or healthily critical, was growing faint. When he had gone to see her two years before, 'it was,' he wrote, 'sad to see how much she had failed'; she died in February 1963. His closest friend from childhood days, his cousin, Ruth Tovell, who was his only durable associate with the other main branch of the Massey family, died in September 1961. He had lost touch with the second generation of relatives. When a young lady from the CBC came to see him in connection with the queen's visit, he was delighted to discover that she was a relative. She was Susan Fletcher, a daughter of Dorothy Goulding, his cousin. 'I had never met her before,' he wrote, 'but found her most attractive. It is a pleasure to discover nice cousins!'[1] He continued to see Raymond, a permanent resident now in Beverly Hills, but only on special occasions. Raymond was present at his installation as governor-general. In his memoirs Raymond tells with relish of how, drawing upon his knowledge of formal military costumes that he had worn in films of high romance, he had been able to instruct his brother in the technique of donning his vice-regal uniform.[2] A few months after his installation, Vincent had made a special trip to Toronto to see Raymond in a reading by a drama quartet of Stephen Vincent Benet's *John Brown's Body* at Massey Hall, and later Raymond and Dorothy had spent a week-end at the Citadel. On visits to London, Vincent saw Raymond's two children by Adrianne Allen, Anna and Daniel, both rapidly establishing themselves on the London stage. He also kept in touch with Geoffrey, Raymond's son by his first wife, now an architect in Vancouver, and a recently appointed trustee of the Massey Foundation.

The family at Batterwood – and then only at intervals and for a few days at a time – was confined to Lionel and Hart, their wives and children. Hart had married in 1947. His wife was Melodie Willis-O'Connor and they had a son, Jonathan (Melodie had a daughter, Caroline, from an earlier marriage). Melodie's father had been an ADC at Rideau Hall for twenty-five years, and she may well have sensed in Hart a fellow deviate from the paternal tradition. Although they lived in Ottawa after Hart's graduation in 1951, they rarely attended formal events at Rideau Hall. As Hart wrote to his father, 'I am not, as you may perhaps have noticed, a fervent royalist – in fact as far as these matters are concerned my attitude could be said to be relaxed!'[3] But there was no break between father and son. They saw each other for long talks, and Hart and Melodie were guests at Vincent's informal

Sunday evening entertainment – a dinner followed by a movie. Hart was not given to emotional displays, but he could show his affection in acts. Vincent was deeply moved when on one 20 February the whole family – Hart, Melodie, Caroline, and Jonathan – came to wish him a happy birthday and brought as a present a golden retriever puppy. A few years later the puppy achieved great fame as Duff, the governor-general's dog, who had proudly and delicately carried the queen's purse during a stroll in the Rideau Hall gardens. Hart moved ahead rapidly in his profession; by the mid-fifties he was active as one of the designers of the new Carleton University campus. Vincent was proud of his success, and respected his professional opinions, even though those opinions had long since passed far beyond Vincent's Georgian orthodoxy.

After leaving Rideau Hall, Lionel spent the next year at Batterwood, helping his father to get re-established and considering his own future prospects. He had been a resourceful and efficient administrative officer, and had fully satisfied the demands of a most exacting chief. Some of the tensions he had felt working under the parental eye had been misread by the press as a testiness and an arrogance that were completely foreign to his nature. Both he and his father realized that the seven years at Rideau Hall constituted a sharp break in his career, and made his next move difficult and unpredictable. Vincent was greatly concerned about Lionel's future, and sent out a letter to influential friends about the excellence of Lionel's work at Rideau Hall and the broad preparation it gave for a variety of responsible positions. Eventually Lionel got a job that was congenial to him and satisfactory to his father. It was director of administration of the Royal Ontario Museum, at that time an integral part of the University of Toronto. Vincent thus described the job – a little grandiosely – in a letter to Hilda Neatby: 'He is on a parity with the Director and the post he occupies is a newly created one.'[4] Lionel and Lilias left Batterwood and moved to a house in Toronto.

Vincent was as deeply indebted to Lilias as he was to Lionel, even more so, for she worked directly on stage. In 1955 she had had a serious breakdown from which she eventually made a complete recovery. Hilda Neatby, who was devoted to her and Lionel, wrote to

Vincent with discerning affection about Lilias' illness. 'She pays too much for an apparently easy and effortless charm.'[5]

Lilias and Lionel had three girls – Jane, Evva, and Susan – close together in age, who, in pictures taken at Rideau Hall and Batterwood, look like a demure set of triplets, in defiance of their individual and assertive ways. Vincent, whom the girls knew as 'gaudy' – their version of grandfather – had an affectionate understanding of the children's world. On one occasion, a Rideau Hall bulletin solemnly declared that 'His Excellency will receive Master Jonathan Massey who will remain to tea.' Vincent thus described the audience. 'Had a pleasant hour with Jonathan. A good deal of talk about Indians; showed him my Indian head dress upstairs.'[6] The years and grandfatherly responsibilities, however, brought problems. At Batterwood he was without vice-regal defences, and his day-care communiqué had a quiet air of desperation. 'More often than not since returning from England have had the three girls reinforced for about ten days by Jonathan on my hands at Batterwood. On the whole they were pretty good responding to criticism, but with Jonathan a fourth member of the party the element of "showing off" appeared (Jonathan cock among the hens and Jane the oldest) and things were more difficult. Before they all left I had really enough.'[7]

Despite this familiar grandfatherly lament, Vincent enjoyed the opportunity at Batterwood to come close to his family. But it was a limited exposure to only the most immediate members, and left plenty of time for other activities. His own personal security and comfort were assured by the continued service of Mircha as steward and valet and of his wife, Anna, cook and housekeeper. To his great relief, his secretary at Rideau Hall, Joyce Turpin, decided to leave Government House and to come to work for him. She came in October 1960 just as Vincent was turning his attention to his book of memoirs and a number of important speeches. She was a splendid secretary, and also a friend who knew his idiosyncrasies, took a lively interest in the work he did, and enjoyed the vigour, softened by humorous self-deprecation, with which he did it. His family established, his household organized to his satisfaction, he could now turn his mind to a growing cluster of interests. Like a Henry James' character in *The Bostonians*, his 'nature was pitched altogether in the key of public life.' The pomp and colour had gone, but he could continue some of his activities in a more relaxed way.

Almost immediately there were tempting opportunities. In May of 1960 he had met Diefenbaker at a social gathering in London prior to the marriage of Princess Margaret and Anthony Armstrong-Jones, and the prime minister had suddenly made a surprising proposal. Would Massey undertake a one-man royal commission to examine the problems of Canadian magazines in relation to American competition? 'If you did,' Massey reported him as saying, 'we would accept your recommendations without question and put them into effect.'[8] This was a problem at the very heart of Massey's deepest concern. But at the time he set the invitation aside as a casual exchange, an unpremeditated outburst that, like the prime minister's optimism about the Garter, could not be taken seriously. Diefenbaker, however, followed up the exchange with a formal letter, closing on an organ note of solemn praise. 'Because of your great interest in this subject, the experience you have gained and the thought you have given to problems related to the development of a Canadian national entity, my colleagues and I believe that, if a Royal Commission is to be established, there is no Canadian better qualified than yourself to serve as its Chairman and to guide its work. By doing so, you would make another notable contribution to the interests and progress of Canada.'[9] But Massey was unmoved. He was still smarting from the Garter débâcle. He declined in a rather perfunctory letter, giving as his reason 'that I have a number of commitments which would leave me too little time for the work which the hardship of a Royal Commission would involve.'[10]

Most of the commitments he had in mind were of a personal nature and were bound up with the revival of his pre-war love affair with English high society. But there was one immediate commitment of increasing weight. Before he left Rideau Hall, he had accepted the chairmanship of the council that was to plan the Duke of Edinburgh's second Commonwealth study conference in Canada in 1962 on industrial problems. When the prime minister's letter arrived, he had been asked to be the main speaker at the opening session of the conference – a task which called for a comprehensive and accurate purview of Canada's development both as a political state and as an industrial power. He accepted the task,[11] and later in the year he responded favourably to another imperial request. The vice-chancellor of Oxford, A.P. Norrington, invited him to give the Romanes lecture for 1961, his predecessors during the previous ten years including Sir Lewis Namier, Sir Kenneth Clark, Sir Thomas Beecham, and Lord Adrian. The prospect of following in such a succession – and at Oxford – was irresistible. Another formal commitment came two years later. On 22 May 1964, the Honourable Paul Martin, the minister for external affairs, announced that Massey would be the president of the third Commonwealth education conference to be held in Ottawa from 21 August to 24 September 1964. He would be expected to make the opening speech.

These three speeches called for early, careful preparation on the model already worked out when he was governor-general. He could no longer fall back on Hilda Neatby's help. They continued to correspond, and she still provided ideas and made critical comments on early versions of his speeches. But for each of these speeches he needed constant consultations and the discreetly anonymous help of a specialist co-author. He took good advice about expert help. For the Romanes lecture he had James Eayrs, professor of political science at the University of Toronto; for the Duke of Edinburgh's conference, William Kilbourn, a professor of history at McMaster University; and for the education conference, Michael Pitfield, an Ottawa civil servant attached to the office of the governor-general. All these followed in the Massey tradition of brilliant young assistants.

Massey's career on the public platform effectively came to an end in 1965. All the main speeches of this post-vice-regal period were published in that year by Macmillan of Canada under the title *Confederation on the March: Views on Major Canadian Issues during the Sixties*. The subtitle is not accurately descriptive. The only speech directed to an immediate issue was his convocation speech at Carleton University in May 1963, in which he made his strongest plea for bilingualism and his sharpest criticism of anglophone lethargy and insensitivity towards the French language. Otherwise the speeches are discursive and reflective, looking back on the past, deriving general conclusions from the historical record and the inescapable facts of geography. They have a strong political and social emphasis; he is concerned with the nature of the Canadian state and its position in the Commonwealth. The cultural development is mentioned, but only casually and almost apologetically. In his longest survey of the Canadian scene, one short, perfunctory paragraph is devoted to cultural affairs. 'We have not, until the revolution that has just begun to overtake us at mid century, been much concerned to foster the arts. But it is true that in the past decade, there have been some hopeful developments. A few years ago a public body was set up free of governmental interference and with a substantial endowment for the purpose of fostering scholarship, the arts, and literature. Of our marked progress in these fields, the Canada Council is both a symbol and an incident.'[12] No doubt the political and social emphasis is a reflection of the anticipated interests of the special audiences he addressed. But when in his final speech, what he called his 'swan song', he had complete freedom to choose his subject, he again came down heavily on a political and social theme – 'The Crown in Canada.'

These final speeches lack the emotional involvement, the passionate conviction touched with humour, of the speeches he gave during his governor-generalship. He is not dealing with what he is really most interested in and most at home with – the centrality of literature and the arts in the making of a nation. His political and social analysis, moreover, does not have the buoyant optimism of *On Being Canadian*. The emphasis is now on a capacity for compromise and a talent for tolerance. If we lack a revolutionary past and a sprightliness in creating national heroes in the American fashion, we have compensating virtues in a canny empiricism and a respect for authority. The Commonwealth, too, is not seen in a theatrical light. It is not really a political entity, not an alliance for power, but an act of will, a shared experience, a spiritual reality. There is a hushed, religious atmosphere about his treatment of the Crown, which is at the summit of both the nation and the Commonwealth. His 'swan song' is a tone poem to the Crown as a centre of moral permanence in a world of uncertain and shifting values.

The mood of the speeches – realistic, cautious, conservative – reflects, no doubt, the conclusion of an old man reflecting on a long career. They are of a piece with his autobiography, which was written between 1960 and 1962.

The autobiography was his *magnum opus*, certainly in length, over 500 pages. It is graced with a Shakespearean quotation for a title, more splendid to the ear than satisfying to the mind.[13] Massey could draw upon diaries continuously kept since undergraduate days, although often baldly factual and brief. The London years were, however, richly documented, and, with the help of James Eayrs, he was able to present a detailed and coherent picture of the drift to war, as seen from the point of view of an unapologetic appeaser. But he made little use of the non-political correspondence, much of it with students, friends, and artists. In the final section dealing with the years after his return from London, he seemed reluctant to go below the surface, as if, having taken the vow of discretion as governor-general, he was under a moral obligation to continue observing it on retirement.

Both the critical and popular reception of *What's Past Is Prologue* had an underlying current of dissatisfaction. Miss Turpin prepared an elaborate analysis of critical comments, dividing them between 'pro' and 'adverse.' Often the two kinds of comment occurred in the same notice, occasionally in the same paragraph. Here are some examples she uncovered: 'style laboured – felicity with words throughout'; 'students will probably find little to provoke serious thought – invaluable aid to our understanding of Canadian History'; 'variety and snobbishness – becoming modesty'; 'self-effacement – personal and provocative views.' The flattering comments often seem to be based on admiration for what the man has done rather than on the book he has written.

The reticence that irritated a good many readers was, to a certain extent, imposed by circumstances. He could not describe the report on honours (which was signed by all the commissioners), since, for some reason, it was considered confidential. He could not talk about the Garter, since the queen's secretary thought it was a private matter between the sovereign and the recipient. But these are comparatively minor items. The problem is much more basic. In his concern with establishing the character of a tolerant, objective, self-deprecating observer (the very model of a classical diplomat), and in emphasizing tradition, custom, and ceremony, he gave an impression of staid conservatism and he slowed the movement of his narrative. Hilda Neatby put it with flattering subtlety in her low-keyed review: 'the reader can see as the underlying theme of the book the writer's conviction of the importance of the symbol as explaining the truth, as revealing the truth, as truth itself ... all of which might become a little stuffy in action as narration without the simplicity and sense of humour which pervades the whole narrative.'[14]

The hard fact is that 'the simplicity and sense of humour' were not strong enough to save the book from dulness. Massey was ignoring the real source of his strength – his capacity for personal, unorthodox innovation and his dogged persistence in realizing his goals. In his review of *What's Past Is Prologue*, Frank Underhill spoke disparagingly of the autobiography: 'the constant reiteration of Massey's reverence for inherited institutions and habits, his fondness for ceremonies and rituals that emphasize one's connections with the past.' 'His real contributions,' Underhill went on to say, 'spring from the fact that he is so individual in his qualities, so unlike what we are apt to think as the typical or ideal Canadian.'[15] These qualities appear at their best in his personal enterprises, chiefly those connected with education and the arts – Hart House, Hart House Theatre, the Hart House Quartet, the Dominion Drama Festival, the celebration of Canadian painting, the chairmanship of the Royal Commission on National Development in the Arts, Letters, and Sciences, the demonstration of what a Canadian governor-general could be and do, and most immediately, Massey College. These give the key to the real Massey and would have provided the substance for a dramatic narrative. In his formal reflections he chose to downplay these qualities and these subjects, and his autobiography struggles for life in an atmosphere of pallid remoteness.

The retrospective and solemn review of the past in his speeches and autobiography received, as it were, its official endorsement in a flood of honours that swept over the retired governor-general. High schools and at least two universities – Royal Military College and the Hebrew University in Israel – named buildings after him.[16] He added substantially to his roster of honorary degrees and to his honorary memberships in learned societies; he was one of the first recipients of the Canada Council medal, awarded for distinguished work in the arts, humanities, and social sciences (fellow recipients were Wilfrid Pelletier, Healey Willan, A.Y. Jackson, Marius Barbeau, Lawren Harris, Ethel Wilson, E.J. Pratt, Abbé Groulx, and Mrs Brooke Claxton (accepting for her late husband)); he received the Canada-Israel Friendship award in 1962. The climactic honour was the award, presented personally by the queen in the summer of 1960, of the Victoria Chain. It did not have the resonance and the popular fame of the Garter, but, to the initiate, it had an even greater cachet. Since its establishment by Edward VII in 1902, there had been only seventy awarded; Vincent Massey was the twenty-first living recipient, half of them royal heads of state. An old English friend wrote to him: 'Has not H.M. cocked a magnificent snook at Mr. D? Has she not given you something much rarer and more distinguished than the Garter? Even more personal a mark of favour from the Sovereign?'[17]

When we turn from the writer and speaker to look at Vincent Massey, citizen and country gentleman, the atmosphere changes radically. He has returned to the enthusiasm of his youth; he is now Underhill's innovator pursuing new ideas and projects with a dogged determination, reactivating his role as a concerned philanthropist. Since the major project of Hart House, which had been launched by Vincent when he had just graduated from the University of Toronto some fifty years before, the Massey Foundation had contented itself with small ventures supported by the annual income, which, under the sober ministration of the National Trust, did not respond adventurously to the market. In 1937 Vincent, who exercised a personal control over the foundation, had offered to build and equip a concert hall in Ottawa if the government would make available the land. But Mackenzie King, to whom the offer was made, did not respond and the offer died. Shortly after Vincent became governor-general, he began to think of a second major venture by the foundation, which would take the form of a building and would be a memorial to his wife. It was now possible for all the foundation trustees to meet – in addition to Vincent there were Lionel, Hart, Raymond, and Geoffrey. There were several meetings in 1954, but this yielded only a list of possible projects.

In a letter to Raymond, 1 April 1957, Vincent reviewed the suggestions that had been made. There were four possibilities, two in Ottawa, two in Toronto. The Ottawa projects were a building for cultural purposes, based on a small theatre, and a house in Ottawa 'in which a certain number of young men would live for a year or so, half English-speaking, half French-speaking, for the purpose of learning each other's language.' But 'the building for cultural purposes,' given the change in popular attitudes, might well come from other sources, and the bilingual house would pose difficult organizational problems. The Toronto projects were an Upper Canada College chapel and 'a residential hall at the University of Toronto giving to, say, 50 residents, a life similar to that of an Oxford or a Cambridge college.' Both of these projects were implemented, and the Upper Canada College chapel became the memorial to Alice. Initially, Vincent thought that 'the residential hall' had insuperable problems. There was a serious financial problem. 'To do this properly would cost a great deal, apart from the building. There would have to be some endowment, providing at least for the salary of the Head, and I don't think we could manage it.' As a governor of the University of Toronto, Vincent knew about the difficulties of fitting a new college into a university with a federated system. On the whole, he was inclined to think that the 'scheme involves very complicated and possibly insurmountable difficulties.'

A few months later, the residential hall had become the firm choice of the trustees, subject to the working out of a satisfactory agreement with the university. Massey discussed the project with me in June of 1957. I was then president of Carleton University, but I had worked with Massey on a few matters when I was in the president's office at the University of Toronto. The project was now to be associated with the graduate school. This gave a specific definition to the idea, and related it formally to fundamental changes in the University of Toronto. It was another example of Massey's sensitive response to a specific situation. He was not, by disposition or experience, disposed to give emphasis to post-graduate studies in a university. His years both at University College and Balliol had left him with the enduring impression of the college as a community of undergraduates, who, in J.H. Newman's words, had found 'a second home not so tender, but more noble and majestic and authoritative.'[18] There, learning was only one of several graces that the college nurtured. But his work on the commission had made him acquainted with the need for graduate schools as nurseries for university teachers and as the source of the ideas upon which an increasingly complex society depended. No doubt Hilda Neatby, a fine research scholar herself, had demonstrated the ease and versatility that came with the full mastery of a specific subject. His ideas on the new college were still, however, vague and unformed, and seemed to waver between Balliol and All Souls as models. But he had gained the assent of his fellow trustees and he was now prepared to approach the University of Toronto, which, at the time, during the interregnum between Sidney Smith and the appointment of a successor, meant, in effect, the powerful chairman of the board, Eric Phillips.

After several conversations with Phillips and later in 1959 with the president, during which general agreement was reached, Massey addressed a formal letter of intent for transmission to the board. The letter emphasized the increasing importance of graduate education, and the need to give the students 'fitting living accommodation, and a sense of their common purpose and the responsibilities which, by reason of their advanced work will rest upon them.' The proposed institution would be an attempt to satisfy the need, but only for 'a few men of special prominence' (a residential college, it was assumed, must be confined to one sex, and Vincent never had any doubt about which sex should have the priority). The letter raised the vital question of financial responsibility: 'The University should exercise some measure of control over the scale of charges for rooms, meals etc. in the college. These would be entirely reasonable because, should the college be operated at a loss, there would be no source from which the deficit could be defrayed except the University itself.'[19]

The Board of Governors did not receive the offer with unbridled enthusiasm. They sensed a danger in assuming financial responsibility for a building and an organization for which they had not been responsible. But Phillips assured the members that they need have no apprehension, and that the university, in accepting the proposal, would be acting in its own interests. A public announcement of the university's acceptance of the gift was made on 19 December 1959; it was hailed as an imaginative acquisition that would never have been financed by the state or by a public appeal. The final agreement between the foundation and the university did not come until 5 January 1961. The university was to make available a central site, to maintain the fabric of the building, supply the services, and 'supervise the financial arrangements of Massey College and pay and discharge from time to time any deficits arising from its operation.' The governing body of the college would be made up of senior fellows, members of the teaching staff, and laymen with an interest in higher education, with the president of the university and the dean of the School of Graduate Studies ex-officio members. The first master would be the joint selection of the university and the foundation, but his successors would be appointed by the senior fellows, subject to approval by the university. The agreement was followed by a bill introduced in the provincial house by the premier, Leslie Frost, which established Massey College as a private corporation.

For some time Vincent had had a firm conviction who the first master should be. It was to be Robertson Davies, at that time publisher and editor of the *Peterborough Examiner*. He had known Davies in England when he was a student at Balliol. During his years at Rideau Hall, he had turned to Davies for advice on a number of matters – the Dominion Drama Festival, a proposed Ottawa festival of the arts, and the dilemma of the Garter. In education and literature, Davies had, like Massey, an English bias, but there was no taint of colonialism in his attitude.[20] He was a Canadian whose affection for his country enabled him to accept its defects as well as to embrace its virtues. He was now established as a public figure, and this appealed to Massey, who did not admire cloistered virtues. His scholarship, demonstrated in early Shakespearean studies, had since been enriched by plays that had been widely performed, a witty and satirical diary, three comic novels that evoked memories of Leacock and Peacock, and a highly individual collection of critical pieces on a wide range of subjects. When Massey first approached him about the mastership he was teaching part-time at Trinity College, University of Toronto, and becoming acquainted with a society whose more interesting citizens he was later to designate as 'rebel angels.'

Davies had some reservations about the agreement with the university. Would not the university's responsibility for a deficit lead to penny-pinching by the college authorities in an effort to avoid university interference; or, if an actual deficit occurred, would not the university gradually assume control? Davies was not only a man of letters, but a businessman who, in the classic phrase, 'had met a payroll.' Massey's initial reluctance to be concerned with the yearly operations disappeared. 'We were able,' he wrote, 'to relieve Davies' worries about the independence of Massey College, which must be assured by monies from the Foundation paid to the corporation operating the college.'[21] Davies was now ready to accept the appointment, which was announced on 1 February 1961. Until the building was actually constructed, he was to be known as master-designate. When two years later he and his wife moved into the master's house (which flanked the college entrance), they brought the college to vivid life. Brenda Davies was a warm and charming hostess; she was sensitive to the velleities and obsessions of academic life (here displayed in their purest and most concentrated forms), but the demands of diplomacy never dulled her native wit and exuberance. Davies persuaded his secretary – Moira Whalon – to leave Peterborough and a newspaper office for Toronto and academia. She very quickly became a central person in the college – a dean of students without seeming to be one. And in Colin Friesen Davies found a financial officer for whom the bottom line always included the academic health of the college.

Davies entered upon his administrative duties with enthusiasm and vigour. There were numerous theoretical matters about the governance of the college to be settled. The first meeting of the master and fellows took place on 24 November 1961 in the senate room of the main administrative building of the university, Simcoe Hall, and Massey commented that 'one felt that the college had really come into being.'[22] There were also continuous and passionate meetings about every detail of the college furnishings. Vincent saw in the college a chance to implement fully his conviction that the physical surroundings have a profound effect on attitudes and manners. Massey College was to be the complete embodiment of his aesthetic faith. Colour and form were to spell out an attitude towards life. This must not be confused with luxury, Massey pointed out, which was often vulgar and ostentatious. He was irritated when much was made of the invitation to twenty of the world's leading silver designers to design the college silver. The winning design by Eric Clements of Birmingham, England, he pointed out, was one of extreme simplicity.

The design of the building itself had been determined by the foundation trustees at an early stage of their deliberations. Vincent would have been happy with a traditional design, say a Georgian building to provide an appropriately modern contrast with the Gothic of Hart House and to harmonize with St Hilda's College immediately to the north. But the two architects on the foundation, Hart and Geoffrey, were adamant about the necessity of a contemporary design and they prevailed. The trustees agreed to a competition between four leading Canadian architects who had demonstrated their skill in contemporary design – John Parkin, Arthur Erickson, Ronald Thom, and Carmen Corneill. The decision would rest mainly on the architect's success in embodying the concept of the college: a community of scholars concerned with the inner life of the mind, but not cut off from the outside world; a constant reminder, particularly in the communal areas, that beauty and truth were intertwined. Ronald Thom's design was chosen in October 1960, and construction of the building was begun a year later.

The Thom design was brilliant in conception and successful in execution. The college looked inward to its quadrangle and to the individual houses grouped around it, each joined to the other, but separated internally, and with separate entrances. Indeed the inward look was accompanied by what seemed like an almost calculated affront to the outside world in a blank brick wall. (The immediate outside world – one heavily travelled east-west thoroughfare, and a road leading to the football stadium – invited this treatment.) The quadrangle opened up beautifully, with a concentration at the south end of a tall, ingeniously geometrical bell tower, and the upper part of the dining-room (really a great hall), with its series of tall, thin windows, creating at night a diadem of light. The internal walls of the rooms repeated the external brick, and lent a touch of almost medieval asceticism. But all the materials – wood, stone, plaster, brick, and bronze (the commercial age of iron and glass was rejected) – had a warm and richly textured effect. As an English critic wrote, 'the trustees asked for a building that would be eminently functional, eminently sturdy, and eminently beautiful, and that is what they got.'[23]

Before and after the completion of the building in the late summer of 1963, there were two characteristically Massey ceremonies. The first was the laying of the corner stone, which took place on a bright, sunny day in May 1962. The ceremony had been delayed in order to fit into the program of Prince Philip, who had come to Canada to preside over his second conference on industrial problems in the Commonwealth. To signalize the royal occasion four trumpeters in full-dress military uniform sounded a fanfare. The audience was made up principally of the representatives of the thirty-five members of the Commonwealth attending the conference, prefiguring the international character of the future college. The second ceremony on 4 October 1963 was the official opening of the college. It took place in the great hall before an audience made up of the first group of junior fellows and the full complement of senior fellows.

The first ceremony was public and solemn; the second was private and irreverent. The first was Massey the royalist and lover of ceremony; the second was Massey the actor and fantasist. The first was prologue, colourful and simple. The second was masque, complex and artful. The second opened quietly with an urbane speech by the founder in which he thanked those who had helped to bring the college into being. Robertson Davies followed in a more robust vein, personal, packed with witty metaphors. He elaborated the idea that as a writer he wore a hair shirt that would constantly rescue him from any smug satisfaction in his new academic eminence. Suddenly, just as he was saying, 'I have brought my hair shirt to Massey College and I shall continue to write here,' there was a disturbance at the back of the hall, and, while the audience looked on apprehensively, a junior fellow, Robert Dinsmore, advanced towards the lectern, shouting,

> *Cease and suspend this endless flow of tripe.*
> *May I come forth?*

At this point all the speakers began to use verse. The junior fellow announced himself as *terrae filius*, son of the earth, the licensed critic of the establishment. He then proceeded to repeat all the harshest criticism of the college:

> *Curios you've made us; post-graduate specimen slides.*
> *Snobs you have made us too!*
> *We study with too much luxury for comfort.*
>
> *We're expected to work at a hive of activities*
> *While the Queen Bee, broad-bottomed, bearded, benign,*
> *Sits manorially elegant.*

(Each of the participants was responsible for his own verse; and there was no prior consultation.)

Terrae filius then appealed to Mr Massey, who as the visitor of the college was charged with the task of resolving conflicts that would not yield to parliamentary procedures. After some admonitory words, the visitor ordained that *terrae filius* join the master and him at the high table.

> *Despite his gay, his Latin Quarter airs*
> *He'll find himself commingling with the Squares.*
> *Yet thus will strife and turmoil find surcease,*
> *As this begins a lasting reign of peace.*

They drank in amity from the founder's cup, as the bell in the tower rang solemn approval.

The masque was a genial anticipation of the confrontation between students and administrators that would riddle the campus during the sixties. In his final arbitration, the visitor spoke with some personal heat of the mood of the students – a mood that he found harsh and absurd:

> *The men for whom you speak with so much passion –*
> *Angry young men – theirs is the current fashion*
> *Of mutiny, revolt, their anger spent*
> *To liquidate the damned establishment.*

As the audience left the hall to have refreshments below, Raymond

Massey, smiling broadly, said to me, 'I don't think such an opening could have taken place at any other college in the world.' I agreed.

Between the two official ceremonies, there was one event of a less formal nature that bore the Massey imprint. Throughout his life he had always had good relations with those who worked for him in practical ways – the employees in the Massey Harris plant, the farmers at Batterwood, the attendants at legations, and now the craftsmen and workers in the construction of Massey College. If there was a feudalistic touch about his concern, it was nevertheless genuine and warm. When the building was completed, he had a party at the college for the workmen and their wives. 'I was impressed,' he wrote, 'by the fact that men engaged in the construction of the building have a very real sense of pride in what they have done ... a man who had worked in the factory which had made a lot of the furniture for Massey College commented on the fact that there had been 6 or 8 designs before we got the chair we wanted – he respected that.'[24]

During the first few years, the college was harshly attacked. Three general points were made. It was élitist – presumably the mediocre and the sub-mediocre should have been preferred to the best students. It was imitative of English models, a legitimate point, although a good model, in education as in the arts, is not to be despised, provided room is left for adaptation and revision. Most cogently, the college was a male chauvinist creation. Hilda Neatby, in congratulating Vincent on the College, observed with gentle irony: 'No doubt you will go on to establish one for the women whose presence in the university precincts you value so much.'[25]

During the remaining years of his life, the college was always a central concern for Vincent Massey. He greatly valued his election as visitor, an office that never fortunately made administrative demands on him, but that he, in a highly personal way, defined and enlarged. It was his custom to stay at the college on visits to Toronto and, then, he liked to join the junior fellows in the common room for a drink and talk. Once, it is recalled, he began to reminisce about his days as high commissioner. The fellows were fascinated, but he suddenly stopped, looked a little embarrassed, and said, 'But gentlemen, I am boring you.'

Batterwood – with its extensions in Toronto, Ottawa, and Montreal, and beyond, in Washington, New York, and the Caribbean – provided a full and varied life. Toronto was chiefly Massey College, but it was also the university. He attended board meetings at the university regularly, and took great satisfaction in his status as the senior governor. The problems of Massey College alerted him to the wider problems of the college system in a university burdened with a much heavier enrolment than had ever been anticipated, and tempted to make mass economies. His was the decisive voice on the board for an extension of the undergraduate college system, even though it meant the abandonment of a neat, economical plan for mass residential accommodation. His was also the decisive voice that preserved the name of 'Innis' for one of the new colleges, in the face of a stolid tradition that it was invidious to name a building after an academic, no matter how distinguished. Massey also resumed his interest in Upper Canada College, now engaged in a costly rebuilding program. With the reactivation of the Massey Foundation, he had much to do with the National Trust, which looked after both the Foundation and his own financial affairs. He was elected to the board of National Trust, and attended their meetings regularly. Wilmot (Bill) Broughall was the officer in the National Trust who looked after the Massey affairs, and he became an indispensable ally in the college project. Broughall was an astute and cultivated man of affairs, whose sombre appearance masked a rich and allusive wit. He became a trustee of the foundation, and brought an independent, informed voice to the family councils.

Some of the vice-regal glow still remained. Massey was invited by his successor to state functions at Rideau Hall. On 30 January 1965 he gave the speech on Churchill for the national ceremony of mourning in the Hall of Fame in the Parliament Building. It was a short speech conceived of as a prose poem (an idea suggested by Michael Pitfield) and he was pleased by the warm national response it received. The Queen Mother stayed at Batterwood on two occasions, and Vincent gloried in this mark of royal recognition from one whom he looked upon as an old and intimate friend (sentiments that the Queen Mother warmly echoed in her letter of thanks).

Vincent had made new friends during his governor-generalship, chief among them Aird and Honor Nesbitt of Montreal. Aird Nesbit was a prominent Montreal business man; his friendship with Massey grew out of his early work as an honorary aide to the governor-general. The Nesbitt's home in Montreal was a relaxing retreat, and they were happy companions on various trips. Old friends from his years in London and Washington – Frederic Hudd and Tommy Stone – came to stay with him. In New York, Whitney Shephardson, a Balliol compatriot and for many years a senior officer in the Carnegie Corporation, was his host; and in Washington, Charles Ritchie, now the Canadian ambassador, was happy to welcome his old chief. Admiration and affection for Massey always glowed through Ritchie's critical estimate.

For four successive years, in March and April, he stayed with Ronald and Marietta Tree in their beautiful palladian house at Heron Bay, Barbados. He had known Ronald Tree in England, when he was for many years an MP holding various positions in the coalition government. After his marriage to Marietta Endicott Fitzgerald, a member of an old New England family, he sold his magnificent Georgian home and estate, Ditchley Park, and established himself in New York and Barbados. The house in Barbados, built of silver white local coral stone, was always full of guests, political associates of Marietta, who was a social activist and a prominent figure in the Democratic party, actors, writers, financiers from both Europe and America. But the atmosphere was always benign and relaxed, and Vincent, besides lively conversation and revelry, could look forward to a regimen of 'sand, sun, and croquet.' Sometimes he would go on to stay with James and Trini Duncan, old friends from Massey-Harris days, who were now living in Bermuda.

But life in Canada, with its pleasant extensions in the United States and the Caribbean, did not satisfy Vincent Massey. He never forgot that England was his second home, indeed, in some respects his first, for on taking up his residence there he had found an ease and satisfaction that he had not yet experienced in his native land. His English visits in retirement became more numerous, and had a hectic quality about them, as if he were trying to revive the life he had known and had lost – an enchanted maze of luncheons and dinners with important people who were close to the highest sources of information, of great evenings at the theatre, and, best of all, of long, leisurely week-ends at country houses, where nature and human artistry were superbly blended. The diary for the English visits is honeycombed with the famous in politics and the arts, referred to with the casualness of long acquaintance. 'Bobbety and Betty' are the Marquess and Marchioness of Salisbury; 'Harold and Dorothy' are the prime minister and his wife; 'Sidney and Mary' are the Earl and Countess of Pembroke; 'Anthony and Clarissa' are the Earl and Countess of Avon. Vincent Massey, aged seventy-four, revelled in the ceaseless round of social activities. He wondered at his own staying power. 'I don't know how long I could keep up with this life which is as enchanting as it is exhausting, although I feel very well. I was called out of my bath by the telephone three times. I couldn't accept the invitations.'[26]

At his London club a fellow member referred to him as the débutant of the year. It was a discerning comment. He had been a widower now for ten years. His marriage had brought him great strength and happiness. He was not conscious of age, of any diminution in body or mind. Perhaps he should marry again. An old English friend 'was disturbed that I contemplated living alone at Batterwood and urged me to marry.'[27] Perhaps, Vincent reflected, she had in mind someone in England.

Vincent Massey's name had once been associated with Baroness Ravensdale, spinster daughter of Marquess Curzon, viceroy of India, 1898–1905, foreign secretary, 1919–24, and almost prime minister in 1923. That was in 1952, when he was in England preparing to return to Canada as governor-general, and the press across Canada reported the likelihood that he would wed Baroness Ravensdale in England and have a short honeymoon in France, before he returned. The rumour was based on the frequency with which they were seen together during Massey's English visit. A sedulous reporter might have provided a more extensive background. Irene Ravensdale ('Ravensdale' was a subsidiary title obtained by her father which would pass from one generation through the female line; Curzon had three daughters, and no son) had been a friend of the Masseys during the war years in London. Like them she was living in the Dorchester hotel, having been bombed out of her London house. Vincent and Alice found her a congenial guest at luncheons, an impression not dulled by the fact that she was the daughter of the great proconsul, a man of protean and caesarian talents who had missed achieving the highest office by the very excess of his virtues. She was, also, a woman of independent means, having inherited a substantial life income from her American grandfather, a Chicago millionaire. When the Masseys met her she had given up a life of conspicuous pleasure, devoted to horses, parties, and occasional liaisons. She had espoused a social gospel, had organized, for instance, a conference in the Albert Hall, chaired by Sir Stafford Cripps, on 'The Church in Relation to Society,' and was an active relief-worker in the air-raid shelters in the east end. Vincent kept up his friendship with her after he left London and she visited him later on at Batterwood.

In 1960 it was Irene's younger sister, Lady Alexander Metcalfe, who aroused speculation in London that she and Vincent might marry. 'Baba,' as she was known, does not appear in the war diaries. In 1927 she had married Major Edward Metcalfe, who bore the unhappy sobriquet of 'Fruity,' and was a close friend of the Prince of Wales. Baba too had an extensive background in the activities of an affluent and morally untroubled society, and her affairs were said to encompass an impressive variety of the great and the famous. Both she and Irene had been deeply disturbed when their brother-in-law, Oswald Mosley, had been imprisoned during the war as a threat to national security, and they had worked sedulously and successfully through the highest channels to have him released.[28] In 1960, when Vincent saw her frequently, she was a widowed fifty-five, youthful and handsome, and, like her sister, active in social work.

The speculations about Vincent and Baba were well-founded but came to nothing. After 1962 the English scene became for Vincent more a pleasant backdrop than one of which he could feel himself a part. He was, in a sense, repeating the 1946 crisis of national allegiance, and making another and final decision for Canada. This time the decision had a strong personal and private accent.

In the fall of 1962, Vincent was working on the early sections of his book. His diary reminded him that in the summer of 1911 when he was a recent graduate at the University of Toronto and in the summer of 1912 when he was returning from his first year at Balliol, he had spent some time at a cottage on Georgian Bay built by a prominent Toronto business man, Archibald Hamilton Campbell, and then presided over after his death, in a strong matriarchal way, by his widow. He recalled meeting four young girls, ranging in age from three to ten, the daughters of Mrs Leighton McCarthy, who was the youngest daughter of Archibald Campbell. The oldest girl was Leigh, aged 10, who was now Mrs Leigh Gossage. He arranged a meeting to talk about those distant days. Mrs Gossage recalled the summers at Languissa (as the cottage was called): 'I can vividly remember each incident, especially you and Herman Boulton demonstrating the fireman's lift, the knitting lesson with you, etc. They were happy days with such good people. I won't be returning until the year after next, but you must come and revisit the old place. She is little changed and loves to have her old admirer's return.' Mrs Gossage ended the letter, 'After so many years it was delightful seeing you again.'[29]

They saw a great deal of each other in the following years. In February of 1964 Leigh Gossage visited Batterwood for the first time, and from then on she was a frequent guest. After her first visit she wrote, 'How delightful to have found an old friend again, thank you for making it possible. I loved being with you and thought Lionel and Evva very charming and patient with 'the old folkes'. Make sure that your help take good care of you, so that I may come again.'[30] Leigh Gossage now became Vincent's constant companion. They went to social evenings at Massey College and to the Stratford Festival; they explored the area around Grafton in eastern Ontario where the Masseys had first settled; he visited her on her birthday at their country home, taking with him an Italian enamelled bowl as a present. Following his farewell speech on 'The Crown in Canada,' on 8 February 1965, she held a celebration in her Rosedale home, and the atmosphere was warm and domestic. When in the summer of 1966 Hilda Neatby came to spend a few days at Batterwood, she met Leigh Gossage and obviously knew of their marriage plans. 'I was particularly happy to meet Mrs. Gossage and to be able to share with you your hopes of continued happiness together in the future. She is indeed, as you told me, a gifted and charming person, with much good sense, and a sense of humour, and great kindness – all this and beauty too – what more could one want. I shall be so happy to learn that all has gone as you both hope. And what makes me very happy is that I believe with her encouragement you may feel able to do even more of the work for our country that you do well.'³¹

Leigh Gossage's family background was similar to Vincent's. Her grandfather on her mother's side, who arrived in Canada from Scotland in 1845, had, like Hart Massey, made his way by his own efforts, and by the seventies was the head of a prosperous lumber business. Again like Hart, his public efforts were devoted to education and religion; he was a leader in the founding of the Anglican College, Wycliffe, and he was involved in the launching of two private schools, Ridley and Havergal. Leigh's father, Leighton Goldie McCarthy, was a prominent lawyer and in the forties became the Canadian ambassador to Washington. But she protested that she had none of Vincent's wide cultural interests. Her talents were practical and managerial (her father used to refer to her as 'Mrs Bossage'). They had met on a common ground of memories: he, of the charming little girl who had attached herself to him; she, of the young man, unpretentious and full of high spirits; and fifty years later, those memories had found a vital re-embodiment.

It was difficult for them to work out definite plans. Leigh Gossage had been long separated from her husband, but there were problems in obtaining a divorce. Then, shortly after they met, the tranquil life of Batterwood was tragically disrupted.

On 27 July 1965, Vincent was visiting Lionel and Lilias in their Toronto home when Lionel was suddenly taken ill and collapsed. He was taken to hospital and died the following day. It was a shattering blow. There had been no immediate warning, although doctors were always apprehensive about the after-effects of serious war-time operations performed in prisoner-of-war camps. The immediate cause of death was a cerebral haemorrhage. Vincent was desolate. Lionel had always been very close to him. Vincent and Alice had thought of him constantly during the long agony of his wounding and imprisonment. At Rideau Hall he had been Vincent's daily associate, and in recent years he had thrown himself with great zeal into implementing his father's plans for Massey College.

Now a sharp division was arising among the trustees about the financing of the College, and, without Lionel's support, Vincent found himself in a minority. The question before the trustees was whether Massey College should receive an endowment from the foundation that would yield enough to cover the shortfall (or most of it) between residential revenue and expenses. Vincent had originally ruled out an endowment as too crippling to the foundation, but had accepted a pledge to pay the college deficits for five years. But already in 1965, the master was convinced that this was a poor solution. It encouraged penny-pinching in the budget in order to keep the deficit at a minimum. It discouraged any change or innovation, and the master was determined to run an academic college and not a residential hall. He had, for instance, placed great emphasis on the library and an accompanying bibliographical centre. These were services of value to the university as well as to the college, but they demanded additional resources. Broughall was Davies' resolute ally. He warned about a university take-over in the event of too large a deficit, and in a letter to Hart he reminded him of his family's full commitment to establishing, guiding, and shaping the college. They have, he pointed out, personally controlled the choice of every piece of material that went into the college, decided on its constitution, chosen the people who would direct its affairs, given it their family name, and appointed members of the family as senior fellows. Moreover, he argued 'it is well within the means of the Foundation to provide financial independence for the College and still have an amount which will be quite adequate for the purposes of a family foundation.'[32]

Hart was not impressed by the last argument. He wanted the foundation to retain a sufficient balance to finance another major project. A substantial endowment for Massey College would eliminate this possibility. Vincent finally came around to the Davies-Broughall point of view, influenced greatly in his decision by the enthusiasm of Leigh Gossage for the college. In the past he had personally determined foundation expenditures, and now the official legal advice was that as the sole remaining trustee of his grandfather's estate (from which the foundation derived) it was entirely within his power to direct the objects of the foundation. Accordingly in January 1966 a special fund was established of $1,250,000 (called the Quadrangle Fund), the income from which was to be placed at the disposal of Massey College. This gave the college an additional fixed income, which went a long way to closing the gap between expenditure and revenue. At the same time the university's agreement to pay for the use of academic accommodation in the college further improved (although it by no means resolved) the college's financial situation. The decision to set up the fund caused much bitterness in the Massey family. There was justice and strong emotional conviction on both sides, and the dispute was not lightly set aside. It brought great strain to Vincent's final years.

At the beginning of 1967 Vincent was in good health. In 1963 he had had some heart trouble and had been told to slow down. In the fall of 1966 he had had a bout of influenza. But he had fully recovered, and was now prepared for a vigorous centennial year.

Professor Derick Breach, now in the department of mathematics at the University of Canterbury, New Zealand, a junior fellow at Massey College in 1967, was one of a group of four fellows to bring greetings to Vincent Massey on his eightieth birthday, 20 February 1967. Vincent, as the years went by, was not enthusiastic about birthdays and discouraged celebrations, but Moira Whalon, the college secretary, had cleared the way and he was prepared for the deputation. At Batterwood he presented an unfamiliar figure to the fellows, who were accustomed to seeing him cross the college quadrangle, dressed in a heavy black greatcoat and a black homburg. Now he was wearing a brown tweed jacket, fawn trousers, an open-necked shirt and a silk cravat, and his manner was equally informal. The fellows sent greetings from the college, and presented him with gifts: a small wooden plaque on which the college coat of arms had been painted and an etching by a contemporary Canadian artist. Then Breach produced a large box which he said was a case of Mr Massey's favourite champagne. Massey was obviously puzzled by the choice of such a resplendent gift, but laughed with delight when he saw the champagne was twelve bottles of beer – his favourite tipple. He then gave his guests a glass of sherry, and they chattered easily for a short while. Massey said he had just taken out Marshall McLuhan's *The Gutenberg Galaxy* from the local library, and asked if they had difficulties with the elliptical McLuhan style. He was comforted to find that he was not alone in his difficulties. When they announced their intention of leaving, he said they must have another glass of sherry. Breach, who was driving, declined. Massey said with mock severity, 'That's too bad, then, you'll just have to go without,' and he filled up the glasses of the others and his own.

As the centenary celebrations approached, Massey became greatly concerned about the failure to implement the recommendations in the special report on honours and awards that his royal commission had made. There had been no response from the governments of St Laurent and Diefenbaker; indeed, the report had never been made public and seemed to be regarded officially as a dangerous document full of explosive implications. When Pearson became prime minister in 1962, Massey hoped that action would be taken. In February 1966, Pearson asked him what changes he would make if he were drafting a new report. In substance, no changes, Massey replied, and then proceeded to offer the prime minister a number of debating points when legislation was put forward. He pointed out that the proposed honours were non-titular, that such honours would go chiefly, as in Great Britain and France, to people 'in very modest walks of life'; that fear of social or political influence in the selection of names would be overcome by the use of a non-political selection committee; and that an honours system, far from being divisive, would contribute to a sense of national unity. Massey met with a representative of the prime minister's office on several occasions to discuss the details of an honours system. In the event, the Government established a simple version of the commission's proposals, the Order of Canada instead of the Order of St Lawrence, with three categories instead of five. The announcement was made in July 1967, and Massey was one of the original thirty-five companions appointed to 'Canada's highest decoration ... made for outstanding merit of the highest degree, especially service to Canada or to humanity at large.' He received the award from the governor-general, Roland Michener (who had been appointed following Georges Vanier's death in March 1967), in a ceremony at Government House on 24 November 1967.

A second centennial of great interest to Massey was Expo – the world exhibition in Montreal – which he viewed as a delighted spectator. He spent a week in September 1967 seeing the pavilions, concentrating on two or three each day. One of the protocol officers who accompanied him, a young man named Conrad Black, remembers a curious incident. Vincent Massey at first declined to enter the American pavilion on the grounds that he strongly disapproved of American policy in Vietnam, but finally relented when it was pointed out that such an action by a former head of the Canadian state would create publicity embarrassing to his own government. (Perhaps Vincent Massey wanted to reassert the family's liberal tradition in the face of Raymond's TV appeals on behalf of Goldwater in the election of 1964.)

The centennial year was a happy one for Vincent Massey. The last important recommendation of his royal commission had been effectively implemented; the success of the Expo – a fusing, as it was said, of English technology and French artistry – seemed to remove, for the time being, the sullen threat of separatism. When the queen and Prince Philip came as centennial guests, Vincent met them at a number of state events and, on one occasion, had the kind of intimate chat with the queen that always gave a special glow to his monarchical sentiments. He had acquired an almost hieratic position in the Canadian consciousness. Peter Newman concluded a cross-country series of interviews with provincial premiers and other key figures with a lengthy two-part interview with Vincent Massey. 'If any man,' Newman began, 'through his life and times personalizes the very best that is Canadian, it is Vincent Massey.'[33] In the interview, Massey replied to questions with unusual vigour, candour, and assertiveness. He seemed poised for another lengthy period as a senior adviser to the Canadian nation. It was not to be.

The year ended with his death. It was not the peaceful going of an old man who had run his course; it was a sudden, tragic end to a career that still retained its characteristic drive and sense of purpose. At the end of September, he had accepted an invitation of Dorothy and Raymond Massey to spend Christmas with them in Hawaii. A week or so later he changed his mind, and he announced that he had decided to go to London. Hart and Melodie were going to London over the Christmas holiday, and he would keep in touch with them in London. He arranged to hold the usual Christmas gatherings for the Batterwood staff early in December, and he left for London on

12 December. His valet, Mircha, was unhappy and apprehensive about the trip and made a final effort to dissuade him from going. Mircha realized that the miasmal mid-December London weather was a threat to a man of eighty who a year ago had had a debilitating bout of influenza.

For the first week in London, Vincent followed the usual pattern – luncheons, dinner parties, the theatre, and late retiral. Then he fell a victim to an influenza epidemic, and was told by his doctor to remain in his flat for several days. He was alone in the flat (Hart and Melodie were living some distance away), and he arranged for a nurse to stay with him. Then pneumonia developed, and he was taken to the King Edward VII hospital. Leigh Gossage, who had been in daily touch with him by telephone, arranged for Mircha to fly to London on 27 December. Mircha saw him on the afternoon of his arrival. 'Never had I seen a man so terribly altered within such a short space of time! His face was ghastly pale and it was obvious that he was extremely weak. But he looked very pleased to see me and said quietly, "It's so nice of you to have come."'[34] Mircha phoned Mrs Gossage to report on Mr Massey's critical condition, and she flew over the following day. Later on that day when Mircha returned to the hospital, he found Mr Massey asleep, and a large box of flowers lying unopened on the table. When he woke up, 'I told him,' Mircha wrote, 'that they had just arrived and asked if he would like me to read the enclosed message. The flowers were from the Queen Mother, who sent her best wishes for his recovery. Before he fell asleep again, he said faintly, "Lovely, Mircha, lovely. She is a very gracious lady."'

Leigh Gossage stayed with him overnight. Hart and Melodie joined her in the morning. At 10 a.m. on 30 December 1967 he slowly and peacefully stopped breathing.

The state funeral in Ottawa took place on 4 January. A second service was held at St Marks Church in Port Hope on 5 January. Eight Massey College junior fellows – four were from foreign countries (Japan, Nigeria, Ireland, and Iran), four Canadians represented different groups within the College – were pallbearers. The congregation was made up of senior and junior fellows of the college, members of the Massey family, old friends and neighbours, and they together created an intimate, familial atmosphere that was moving and comforting. Vincent Massey was buried beside his wife and his son, Lionel, in the St Marks churchyard. On the flat, grey stone, which in the spring would almost disappear in the grass, was this inscription:

Patriae profuit

He was useful to his country

A Note on Sources

In my first volume I described in some detail the Massey papers in Massey College on which my biography is based. The diary ends in 1965, two years before Massey's death, and is sketchy for the previous six years. For the period 1952–59 (the Rideau Hall years), however, the diary is unusually detailed. For the war years, Vincent Massey's papers are supplemented by his wife's voluminous papers, also in Massey College, which constitute in themselves the basis of a separate study of her many activities during the war.

In the Public Archives of Canada, the W.L. Mackenzie King papers are still central to this volume – MG 26J – especially the Primary Series Correspondence (J1) and the Diaries (J13). The W.L. Grant papers (MG3 D59), especially Alice Massey's letters to her sister, Maude Grant, have important material for the period 1935–46. The St Laurent papers (MG 26) are particularly useful for the material on Lord Alexander's extension, Massey's appointment, and St Laurent's ideas on the nature and responsibilities of the governor-generalship. The Massey papers contain Massey's correspondence with prominent contemporaries such as Brooke Claxton, Lester Pearson, and Lord Tweedsmuir.

The Public Archives of Canada has the record of the sixty-five meetings of the Massey commissioners, beginning on 2 May 1949 and ending on 26 July 1950 (RG 33, 28, VR/a). A record of public hearings is in RG 33, 28 V39. All of the 460 briefs to the commission are in the Massey papers.

The chapters 'Appeasement' and 'The Masseys Go to War' draw heavily on material in the Public Records Office, Kew, London, England. The crucial material is the record of the meetings of the high commissioners (DO121/6/7/9/11/12/13/14/15) from 8 September 1939 to the end of the war. The minutes have enough detail to bring out the interplay of personalities and the emergence of leadership. There is a great deal of additional material in the

Public Records Office that illuminates the role of the high commissioners and the relations between Great Britain and Canada.

The university archives in the Thomas Fisher Rare Book Library of the Robarts Library, University of Toronto, contains most of the material about the founding and early history of Massey College.

The following abbreviations have been used:

WLMK   King papers
WLG   Grant papers
WPP   *What's Past Is Prologue.*

Quotations from Primary material, unless otherwise identified, are from the Massey papers in Massey College.

Notes

CHAPTER ONE

1 John Herries McCulloch in *Scottish Daily Express*, 15 February 1938
2 Quoted by Peter Oliver, *G. Howard Ferguson: Ontario Tory* (Toronto: University of Toronto Press, 1977), p. 378
3 *Ibid.*, p. 414
4 *Ibid.*, p. 413 (quoted from the Toronto *Globe*, January 1934)
5 3 February 1936. WLG vol. 43
6 Massey Diary, 21 January 1936
7 *Ibid.*, 24 January 1936
8 4 January 1937 WLG vol. 43
9 Massey Diary, 16 October 1924
10 *Ibid.*, 3 November 1936
11 *Ibid.*, 26 November 1936
12 10 December 1936. WLG vol. 43
13 Massey Diary, 6 December 1936
14 Massey Diary, 7 December 1936
15 Sir John W. Wheeler-Bennett, *King George VI* (London: Macmillan, 1958), pp. 300, 304–5
16 This is from an 'Ode for the Coronation of Their Majesties, May 12, 1937,' by Osbert Sitwell. The full text is given by Wheeler-Bennett, *ibid.*, p. 314.
17 Massey Diary, 1 April 1937
18 To Maude Grant, 14 June 1937. WLG vol. 43
19 Massey Diary, 12 May 1937
20 14 June 1937. WLG vol. 43
21 To Massey, 29 May 1939

22 H.C. Osborne to Massey, 28 June 1939
23 Shuldham Redfern to Massey, 20 July 1939
24 To Lord Tweedsmuir, 20 October 1939
25 18 April 1939. WLG vol. 42
26 Massey Diary, 2 May 1939
27 28 February 1936
28 9 June 1936. WLMK, vol. 223, p. 191841
29 King Diary, 22 October 1936
30 To Maude Grant, 30 January 1937. WLG vol. 43
31 Robert Rhode James, ed., *Chips: The Diary of Sir Henry Channon* (London: Weidenfeld and Nicolson, 1967), p. 232 (entry for 23 January 1940)
32 Massey Diary, 13 November 1938
33 Kenneth Clark, *Another Part of the Wood* (London: John Murray, 1974), p. 212. The following six pages are devoted to Sybil Colefax.
34 Thomas Jones, *A Diary with Letters, 1931-1950* (London: Oxford University Press, 1954), p. 318 – Violet Markham to Thomas Jones, 24 February 1937.
35 26 May 1939
36 Massey Diary, 11 October 1938
37 To Maude Grant, 15 February 1937. WLG, vol. 43
38 Massey Diary, 10 February 1938
39 Massey Diary, 3 February 1938
40 *Life in the English Country House* (New Haven: Yale University Press), 1976, p. 310
41 (New York: Popular Library, 1976), p. 185
42 Massey Diary, 1 July 1939
43 14 June 1937. WLG vol. 43
44 The phrase is Jones's in the introduction to *A Diary with Letters*, p. xxxv.
45 Irving Abella and Harold Tropur, *None Is Too Many* (Toronto: Lester and Orpen Dennys, 1982), p. 48. The relevant sentence is: 'Vincent Massey, prominent scion of the wealthy Massey family, had in fact become a fringe member of the aristocratic, largely pro-German and anti-Semitic [Cliveden] set' – an indictment by hazy association.
46 Quoted by Richard Griffiths, *Fellow Travellers of the Right* (Oxford University Press, 1983), p. 285. Cockburn's autobiographical volumes were gathered into one volume under the title *I, Claud* (Penguin Books, 1967). He is a diverting and witty writer, and discusses with

untroubled candour his joining the Communist party in the late thirties and leaving it after the war. The *Week* was mimeographed and consisted of a few pages of distilled news and gossip. It first appeared in the spring of 1933, had little initial impact, but rapidly gained subscribers. Cockburn writes proudly, 'The *Week* was one of the half-dozen British publications most often quoted in the Press of the entire world. It included among its subscribers the Foreign Ministers of eleven nations, all the Embassies and Legations in London, all diplomatic correspondents of the principal newspapers in three continents, the foreign correspondents of all the leading newspapers stationed in London, the leading banking and brokerage houses in London, Paris, Amsterdam, and New York, a dozen members of the United States senate, twenty or thirty members of the House of Representatives, about fifty members of the House of Commons and a hundred or so in the House of Lords, King Edward VIII, the secretaries of most of the leading trades unions, Charlie Chaplin and the Nizam of Hyderabad.' (*I, Claud*, p. 141) While still producing the *Week*, he became foreign editor of the *Daily Worker*. After the Nazi-Russian pact, the *Week* was closed down by government order. He writes with objectivity about the phrase 'the Cliveden Set.' He realizes that there was no such set. 'The phrase went marching on because it first had dramatized, and now summarized, a whole vague body of suspicions and fears.' (*Ibid*, p. 180)

47 *A Diary with Letters*, p. 173
48 Massey Diary, 7 March 1936
49 Donald McLachlan, *In the Chair: Barrington-Ward of the Times, 1927-1948* (London: Weidenfeld and Nicolson, 1971), p. 215. This is an excerpt from Barrington-Ward's diary.
50 *Winds of Change, 1914-1937* (London: Macmillan, 1966), p. 115
51 W.L. Burns, *The Dictionary of National Biography 1951-60* (Oxford University Press, 1971), p. 805
52 *Halifax* (London: Hamish Hamilton, 1965), p. 320
53 Massey Diary, 26 March 1936
54 *Ibid.*, 7 April 1936
55 *Ibid.*, 17 November 1937. The last phrase has been added in handwriting. It is a little difficult to know what Massey meant by 'the reactionary wing in the cabinet.'
56 *Ibid.*, 2 February 1939
57 *WPP*, p. 286

58 Charles Edward Lysaght, *Brendan Bracken*, (London: Allen Lane 1979), p. 183. The quotation is from the diary of General Raymond E. Lee, US military attaché in London during the blitz.
59 *Another Part of the Wood*. See the chapter 'Innocents in the Clover,' pp. 211ff.
60 George Bernard Shaw, *Geneva, Cymbeline Refinished, Good King Charles* (London: Constable and Company, 1946), pp. 121–2
61 Massey Diary, 15 December 1938
62 *WPP*, pp. 10, 11
63 Massey Diary, 30 July 1936
64 The speech, which exists in mimeographed form, was given in London on 15 May 1939 to the Georgian Group.
65 Lawrence Jones, *An Edwardian Youth* (London: Macmillan, 1956), p. 41
66 Vincent Massey's eulogy of the country house as great civilizing force is in *WPP*, p. 115. He quotes from H.G. Wells to support his case, but omits Wells' major point that 'through the curiosity and enterprise and free deliberate thinking' of country house gentlemen 'modern machinery and economic organization have developed ... It is the country house that has opened the way to human equality, not in the form of a democracy of insurgent proletarians, but as a world of universal gentlefolk no longer in need of a servile substratum. It was the experimental cellule of the coming Modern State.' H.G. Wells, *Experiment in Autobiography* (Toronto: Macmillan, 1934), p. 105. Presumably this was not an outcome that Massey either perceived or approved.
67 Massey Diary, 27 February 1936
68 *A Diary with Letters*, p. 291 (from a letter to Lady Grigg, 8 December 1941)
69 Nancy Mitford, *Love in a Cold Climate* (Penguin Books, 1980), p. 298
70 Massey Diary, 21 June 1939
71 William Maxwell Aitken, Baron Beaverbrook, *Friends Sixty Years: Intimate Personal Relations with Richard Bedford Bennett, Viscount Bennett of Mickleham, Surrey, and of Calgary and Hopewell, Canada* (London: Heinemann, 1959), p. 40
72 *Ibid.*, p. 121

CHAPTER TWO

1 17 June 1936
2 30 December 1937
3 In a letter to Susie Buchan (Lady Tweedsmuir), Alice wrote: 'Do you

remember Stephen Tallent's title for one of his pamphlets when he was on the Empire Marketing Board "The Projection of England"? In our very humble way I feel that the projection of Canada is our job here.' 30 April 1936
4   The quotations from Lovat Dickson are from a letter that was part of a memorandum submitted to Massey, initialed F–H (Frederic Hudd, chief Canadian trade commissioner in the United Kingdom). The memorandum is undated, but was written before Lovat Dickson sold his own publishing firm and joined Macmillan. This took place in 1939.
5   6 July 1937
6   *Wilderness Man: The Strange Story of Grey Owl* (Toronto: Macmillan, 1973). The quotations are from two passages describing Grey Owl, one on pp. 4–5, one on p. 234.
7   Massey Diary, 10 December 1937
8   *Wilderness Man*, p. 251
9   13 February 1938
10 Eric Brown to Sir Alfred Thomas, 16 October 1936. Sir Alfred was organizing an exhibition of 'artists of the British Empire Overseas', which was to be a coronation event in May 1937, and Brown was dissatisfied with the amount of space allotted to Canada. He pointed out that 'at the Wembley Exhibition of 1924–25, Canada was granted space in the Fine Arts Building equal to that of all the other Dominions together.'
11 *Augustus John* (New York; Holt, Rinehart and Winston, 1974), p. 462
12 24 July 1938
13 10 November 1938
14 The carbon copy of the letter, dated 5 April 1939, does not indicate the name of the correspondent. In all likelihood, it was Roy Gilley, assistant warden.
15 7 July 1939
16 9 November 1936. Max Patrick subsequently taught English at various American universities. His special field was seventeenth-century English puritanism on which he published extensively.
17 Saul Rae joined the Department of External Affairs in 1940, and had a long and distinguished career in the department, culminating in the sixties and seventies with a succession of ambassadorial appointments.
18 *Pat Moss: Canadian and English Letters 1924–1936* (Toronto: University of Toronto Press, 1940), p. 380 (to his mother, 2 February 1936)
19 2 June 1936

20 *Both Sides of the Street* (Toronto: Macmillan, 1983), p. 97
21 Massey Diary, 11 July 1931
22 *Ibid.*, 5 December 1930
23 Robert Speaght, *Vanier: Soldier, Diplomat, and Governor General: A Biography* (Toronto: Collins, 1971), p. 43. The letter was written 30 September 1915. Vanier had been briefly out of the line and had visited the French countryside.
24 *Ibid.*, p. 174
25 *Ibid.*, p. 161
26 The memorandum is undated and unsigned, but the internal evidence points clearly to Pearson and to a date either late in 1935 or early in 1936.
27 1 March, 1936. WLG vol. 43
28 *Mike: The Memoirs of the Right Honourable Lester Pearson*, vol. 1 (Toronto: University of Toronto Press, 1972), pp. 104–5
29 *Ibid.*
30 PAC, 29 August 1935
31 *Ibid.*, 22 December 1935
32 2 December 1938
33 Thomas Wayling to Vincent Massey, 28 January 1938
34 3 March 1938
35 31 January 1938
36 3 February 1938
37 14 January 1938
38 *Ottawa Citizen*, 29 December 1937
39 External Affairs dispatch, 1 February 1938
40 John Buchan to Vincent Massey, 5 January 1938
41 14 November 1935
42 14 April 1938
43 31 July 1937
44 20 October 1938
45 31 May 1937
46 Toronto *Mail and Empire*, 27 August 1935
47 7 January 1936
48 King Diary, 23 October 1936
49 29 October 1938
50 *A Hundred Different Lives* (Toronto: McClelland and Stewart, 1979) p. 248
51 George Grant to Vincent Massey, 31 June (in all likelihood, 1939)
52 Kenneth Bell to Alice Massey, 16 August 1938

53 June 1936, p. 301

CHAPTER THREE

1 PRO DO/156/6109H/354, Archer to Batterbee, 28 May 1936
2 A. L. Toynbee, ed., *British Commonwealth Relations* (Oxford University Press, 1934), p. 189
3 Peter Oliver, *G. Howard Ferguson: Ontario Tory* (Toronto: University of Toronto Press, 1977), pp. 423–4
4 King Diary, 30 October 1936
5 14 March 1936, WLMK, vol. 205, p. 111559
6 Massey to King, 9 January 1936
7 Telegram 119, 9 May 1936. WLMK vol. 223, p. 191788
8 Massey Diary, 11 May 1936
9 Telegram 167, 10 May 1936. WLMK vol. 223, p. 191791
10 The account is written by Massey in pencilled long-hand, presumably for his own satisfaction. It is dated 19 September 1938, and is headed 'The High Commissioner's Office in the Crisis of 1938.'
11 Massey Diary, 16 September 1938
12 The Massey comments are taken from an entry in his diary that covers the period 30 June – 6 July when he was in Geneva.
13 *In Defence of Canada: vol. 2, Appeasement and Rearmament* (Toronto: University of Toronto Press, 1965), p. 40
14 *WPP.*, p. 233
15 Quoted by Eayrs *in Defence of Canada*, vol. 2, p. 53 (from the official report of the proceedings of the conference)
16 This and the preceding two quotations are from a letter from Pearson, 16 July 1939.
17 David Carlton, *Anthony Eden: A Biography* (London: Allen Lane, 1981), p. 151
18 Quoted from Thomas Inskip, Diary, in Joe Garner, *The Commonwealth Office 1925–58* (London: Heinemann, 1978), p. 137
19 Cecil Edwards, *Bruce of Melbourne: Man of Two Worlds* (London: Heinemann, 1965), p. 87
20 *The Commonwealth Office*, p. 138
21 Quoted in Gilbert Martin, *The Roots of Appeasement* (London: Weidenfeld and Nicolson, 1966), p. 90
22 2 December 1935
23 In *The Liberal Way* (Toronto: J.M. Dent, 1933), p. 137
24 'Canada in the World,' *Ibid.*, p. 63

25 *Ibid.*, p. 65
26 *Ibid.*, p. 87
27 *Ibid.*, p. 89
28 *The Liberal Way*, p. 137
29 The speech was given to the Kiwanis international convention in Toronto, 12 June 1935.
30 In William Lyon Mackenzie King, vol. II (University of Toronto Press, 1976), p. 191
31 (New York: Charles Scribner's Sons, 1936).
32 *Ibid.*, pp. 103–4 (Act II, scene ii)
33 Carlton, *Eden*, p. 45
34 Quoted by Alan Bullock, *Hitler: A Study in Tyranny* (Penguin Books, 1962), p. 322
35 Massey Diary, 10 December 1935
36 *Ibid.*, 19 December 1935
37 *Ibid.*, 20 December 1935
38 *Ibid.*, 25 December 1935
39 Carlton, *Eden*, p. 79
40 Massey Diary, 14 March 1936
41 Review of *Searchlight in Spain* by the Duchess of Atholl in *The Collected Essays, Journalism and Letters of George Orwell*, ed. Sonia Orwell and Ian Angus (New York: Harcourt, Brace, 1968), vol. I, p. 345
42 Massey Diary, 22 November 1936
43 Carlton, *Eden*, p. 92
44 Massey Diary, 21 November 1935. Massey made this entry in his diary after an early interview with Baldwin. He would still have held this appraisal two or so years later.
45 Carlton, *Eden*, p. 115
46 Anthony Eden, *Facing the Dictators* (Boston: Houghton Mifflin, 1962), p. 577. This is from a minute that Eden wrote about Lord Halifax's proposed visit to Germany in November, 1937.
47 Martin Gilbert, *Winston S. Churchill* (London: Heinemann, 1976), vol. 5, *1922–1939*, p. 903
48 Massey Diary, 21 February 1938
49 *Ibid.*, 25 October 1938
50 *Ibid.*, 15 March 1938
51 *Ibid.*, 14 September 1938
52 The picture appeared in the *Illustrated London News*, 8 October 1938
53 Massey Diary, 4 October 1938
54 1 November 1938

55 15 November 1938
56 Massey Diary, 15 March 1938
57 To the Hon. W.A. Buchanan, 16 May 1939
58 *The Roots of Appeasement*, p. 84
59 Massey Diary, 18 August 1936
60 *Ibid.*, 16 February 1937
61 To Maude Grant, 26 February 1937. WLG vol. 43
62 Quoted by Richard Griffiths, *Fellow Travellers of the Right: British Enthusiasm for Nazi Germany, 1933–39* (Oxford University Press, 1983), p. 223
63 King Diary, 26 June 1937
64 *Ibid.*
65 *Ibid.*
66 Quoted in Gilbert, *Churchill*, vol. 5, p. 777. Baldwin made the remark to a parliamentary deputation presenting a case to accelerate armament, 24 July 1936.
67 Obituary, *The Times*, 6 September 1975
68 Griffith, *Fellow Travellers*, p. 153
69 *Ibid.*, p. 223
70 6 April 1937
71 (London: Methuen, 1939). The book was first published in 1937. A supplementary chapter was added in 1939, bringing the summary of events up to June 1938
72 Keith Feiling, *The Life of Neville Chamberlain* (London: MacMillan, 1946), p. 328.
73 G.M. Young, *Stanley Baldwin* (London, 1952), p. 124
74 Gilbert, *Churchill*, vol. 5, p. 626
75 Arthur Bryant, ed., *Speeches (1937–1938) by the Rt. Hon. Neville Chamberlain* (London: Hutchinson, n.d.), p. 84
76 PRO DO 121/4 Letter form Gerald Campbell to the Duke of Devonshire, Dominions Office, 7 October 1938
77 Massey Diary, 28 September 1938
78 Eayrs, *In Defence of Canada*, vol. 2, pp. 76–80
79 *Mike* (Toronto: University of Toronto Press, 1972), vol. 1, p. 130
80 Garner, *The Commonwealth Office*, p. 89
81 PRO DO 121/4
82 Massey Diary, 16 September 1938
83 *Diaries and Letters, 1930–39*, ed. Nigel Nicolson (London: Collins, 1969), p. 354
84 14 September 1938

85 13 October 1938
86 Editorial, *Globe and Mail*, 25 October 1938
87 *Evening Telegram*, 28 October 1938
88 *Too True to be Good, Village Wooing, On the Rocks* (London: Constable, 1934), p. 23
89 Ibid., p. 168
90 Pp. 258–60
91 *Too True to be Good*, p. 145
92 Quoted in Ronald Steel, *Walter Lippmann and the American Century* (New York: Random House, 1981), p. 330
93 Massey Diary, 25 October 1933
94 In Gilbert, *The Roots of Appeasement*, p. 163
95 In Thomas Jones, *A Diary with Letters, 1931–1950* (London: Oxford University Press, 1954), p. 390
96 3 Feb., 1939. WLMK vol. 274, pp. 231616–2
97 *None Is Too Many* (Toronto: Lester and Orpen Dennys, 1982), p. 30. My summary of Canadian immigration policy is largely derived from the first chapter of this book.
98 25 November 1938. WLMK, vol. 255, p. 217567
99 Telegram 269 to External Affairs, 27 November 1938. WLMK vol. 338, p. 217619
100 2 December 1938

CHAPTER FOUR

1 23 April 1941. WLG vol. 42
2 *The Heat of the Day* (New York: Alfred A. Knopp, 1949), p. 100
3 *Ibid.*, p. 99
4 Massey Diary, 9 September 1940
5 *The Siren Years: A Canadian Diplomat Abroad* (Toronto: Macmillan, 1974), p. 73
6 29 March, 1951. WLG vol. 41
7 Massey Diary, 9 September 1940
8 *Officers and Gentlemen* (London: Penguin Books, 1964), p. 9
9 Massey Diary, 14 October 1940
10 *Ibid.*, 16 April 1941
11 *Ibid.*, 15 September 1941
12 Ritchie, *The Siren Years*, 73
13 'Mr. Massey suggested that houses demolished by bombs should be cleared rapidly, as they had a depressing psychological effect; he

suggested that either persons rendered unemployed by the raids, or the army, should be used for this purpose.' Records of meetings between the secretary of state for dominion affairs and dominion high commissioners, PRO DO 121/6 (28 September 1940)
' In a discussion on the recent fire bombing Mr. Massey asked that it should be represented to the appropriate authorities that valuable records belonging to public institutions (such as those destroyed at Trinity House) should be removed from places of danger.' *Ibid.*, 3 January 1941
14 *Triumph and Tragedy* (Boston: Houghton Mifflin, 1953), p. 39
15 23 June, 1944. WLG, vol. 41
16 19 March 1945
17 Massey Diary, 2 September 1939
18 *Ibid.*, 13 October 1940
19 *Ibid.*, 10 November 1941
20 *Ibid.*, 15 April 1941
21 *Ibid.*, 18 April 1941
22 The phrase is from a poem by Ted Hughes, 'Under the Hill of Centuries,' in *River* (London: Faber & Faber, 1983), p. 36.
23 The letter was from Toby Low, and was dated 31 May 1941. Eden sent it on to the Masseys on 25 August. It is in WLG, vol. 41. Low reported that the odds against the British were 22 to 1.
24 13 June 1944. WLG, vol. 41
25 Massey Diary, 18 August 1943
26 Alice Massey quoted this in a letter to Maude Grant, 15 January 1942. WLG. vol. 42
27 Churchill, *Triumph and Tragedy*, p. 276
28 This account is drawn from two sources, the first in Vincent Massey's letter to Maude in WLG, vol. 41 (9 January 1945) and the second from Major Johnson's account as reported by Massey in his diary for 3 April 1941, as well as my own experience. 'I happened at the time to be a short distance from the airfield where Hart was wounded. My regiment, the Argyll and Sutherland Highlanders of Canada, of which I was intelligence officer, had withdrawn briefly to billets to the town of Reijen in Holland. On New Year's morning, which was bright and clear, we watched with amazement German fighters in considerable numbers putting in an attack on an objective nearby, but still pleasantly outside our concentration area (with 'amazement' because we had rarely seen German planes since landing in Normandy in late July).'

The regimental history reports the incident laconically: 'Low-flying attacks in considerable strength were delivered against the Gelse Airfield just south of the Battalion position, and vehicles on Maple Leaf route between Breda and Tilburg were strafed, although without any particular effect. The attack was not accompanied by any ground effort. It had some effect and did a certain amount of damage, but by 1000 hours had been completely driven off with heavy loss, as squadron after squadron of avenging Spitfires and Typhoons roared in upon the German forces.' *The Argyll and Sutherland Highlanders of Canada (Princess Louise's) 1928–1953*, compiled by officers of the Regiment, 1953.

The wonderful new substance was, in all likelihood, heparin that had been developed at the University of Toronto by Dr Charles Best.

29 21 February 1945. WLG, vol. 41
30 26 September 1939
31 To Miss A. Bushell, 27 January 1942
32 Sir Edward Peacock to Vincent Massey, 10 October 1941
33 1 June 1944
34 Massey Diary, June 17 1937
35 PRO CAB 21/873 (Memorandum of High Commissioner for the UK to the Right Hon. The Viscount Cranborne, Secretary of State for Dominion Affairs, 21 February 1941)
36 Massey Diary, 23 August 1941
37 *Ibid.*, 4 September 1941
38 Telegram, 23 December 1943, WLMK, vol. 47
39 Massey Diary, 11 May 1944
40 2 June 1944
41 Quoted by J.L. Granatstein, *A Man of Influence: Norman A. Robertson, and Canadian Statecraft, 1929–68* (Ottawa: Deneau, 1981), p. 29
42 Quoted in *Ibid.*, p. 74
43 Massey Diary, 25 August 1941
44 *Ibid.*, 13 February 1940
45 To Vincent and Alice Massey, 1 April 1942
46 To Lester Pearson, 25 June 1941
47 Massey Diary, 2 March 1944
48 16 July 1942. WLG, vol. 43
49 *The Commonwealth Office, 1925–68* (London: Heinemann, 1978), p. 197
50 Massey Diary, 15 May 1940
51 *Ibid.*, 26 July 1943
52 PRO DO 121/10, 4 January 1941

53 *Ibid.*, 18 November 1941
54 Massey Diary, 7 December 1936
55 In his broadcast to Canada, 28 June 1941, Massey paid this tribute to Churchill: 'it is not only in his faith in victory but in his will to victory that Mr. Churchill stands as a great leader for a great moment. No one could more splendidly embody the fighting spirit of the British race.'
56 Massey Diary, 14 April 1942
57 PRO DO 121/6, Record of Meetings between the Secretary of State for Dominion Affairs and Dominion High Commissioners, 13 September 1939
58 Massey Diary, 10 September 1939
59 *Ibid.*, 29 July 1942
60 This was reported by Leonard Brockington after he had returned from his lecture tour. *Ibid.*, 21 June 1943
61 *Ibid.*, 8 December 1942
62 PRO DO 35/1010 WN 1/55 (Letter from Brendan Bracken Minister of Information) to Clement Attlee, (Dominions Office)
63 PRO DO 121/12, 21 August 1942
64 PRO DO 121/12, 9 June 1942
65 PRO DO 121/14, 28 November 1944
66 Massey Diary, 21 January 1945
67 PRO DO 121/14, 18 September 1944
68 PRO DO 121/13 27 October 1943
69 Massey Diary, 27 April 1940
70 *Ibid.*, 23 June 1940
71 C.P. Stacey, *Canada and the Age of Conflict*, vol. 2, *1921–1948* (Toronto: University of Toronto Press, 1981), p. 300
72 Massey Diary, 11 November 1940
73 *The Siren Years* (Toronto: Macmillan, 1974), p. 145
74 Martin Gilbert, *Finest Hour: Winston Churchill, 1937–1941* (London: Heinemann, 1983), p. 958
75 Massey Diary, 30 December 1940
76 Irving Abella and Harold Troper, *None Is Too Many* (Toronto: Lester and Orpen Dennys, 1982), p. 100
77 PRO DO 121/13 13 February 1943
78 Bernard Wasserstein, *Britain and the Jews of Europe 1939–1945* (London: Clarendon Press, 1979), p. 194
79 Abella and Troper, *None*, p. 527
80 PRO DO 121/15 12 May 1941

81 Abella and Troper, *None*, p. 80
82 PRO DO 121/11, 6 February 1941
83 PRO DO 121/14 10 August 1944
84 PRO DO 121/9 16 July 1941
85 Eric Koch's *Deemed Suspect* (Toronto: Methuen, 1980) gives a detailed account of the affair.
86 Massey Diary, 12 October 1939
87 *Ibid.*, 26 July 1940
88 6 January 1945
89 16 March 1942. WLG, vol. 42
90 *The Reckoning* (London: Cassell, 1965), p. 70
91 PRO DO 121/6, 16 September 1939
92 Massey Diary, 23 September 1939
93 King Diary, 9 March 1946. King inaccurately refers to Eden as foreign minister. At this time he was secretary of state for dominion affairs.
94 Cecil Edwards, *Bruce of Melbourne* (London: Heinemann, 1965), p. 281
95 *The Times*, 8 May 1946
96 Gilbert, *Finest Hour*, p. 670
97 PRO DO 121/9
98 Massey Diary, 9 July 1941
99 13 September 1941
100 PRO DO 131/27, 30 June 1941
101 Massey Diary, 6 January 1941
102 *Ibid.*, 1 November 1939
103 Quoted by C.P. Stacey, *Official History of the Canadian Army in the Second World War*, vol. I: *Six Years of War: The Army in Canada, Britain, and the Pacific* (Ottawa: Queen's Printer, 1955), p. 214.
104 Massey Diary, 31 March 1943
105 *Ibid.*, 14 January 1942
106 C.P. Stacey makes some caustic comments on the luxury of Army HQ in his lively autobiography, *A Date with History* (Ottawa: Deneau, 1982), p. 166.
107 *Ibid.*, p. 76
108 Massey Diary, 24 May 1940
109 *Ibid.*, 18 January 1940, 30 August 1941
110 *Mike*, vol. I, p. 163
111 Douglas LePan, *Bright Glass of Memory* (Toronto: McGraw-Hill Ryerson, 1979), pp. 24, 51
112 Massey Diary, 11 March 1941

113 *Ibid.*, 14 September 1942. When Mackenzie King saw Dieppe on 18 August 1946, he wrote in his diary, 'I really felt as though the men who had planned that raid ought to have been cashiered. It did strike me as the most impossible of all places to attempt to effect a landing. It was sending men to certain death without a ghost of a chance.'
114 Massey Diary, 10 July 1943
115 To Norman Robertson, 10 April 1943
116 Massey Diary, 23 October 1941
117 This is based on a conversation with Carl Schaeffer, which took place appropriately in a room in the Art Gallery of Ontario devoted to contemporary Canadian art.
118 To Marion Buck, 14 December 1945
119 25 October 1939
120 10 November 1939
121 Massey Diary, 11 December 1939
122 To Lady Minto, 21 December 1939
123 To J.M. McConnell, 12 January 1940
124 To Maude Grant, 14 July 1940. WLG, vol. 42
125 Massey Diary, 12 April 1940
126 *Ibid.*, 10 March 1940
127 This is from Repton's prospectus, written in his own hand, in the possession of the family at Garnons.
128 Lieutenant McDougall became the first director of the Institute of Canadian Studies and a professor in the Department of English at Carleton University. He made available excerpts from the letters he wrote to his mother, Mrs. R.J. McDougall, during the year when he was a resident at Garnons. This is from a letter written on 27 December 1942.
129 *Kilvert's Diary*, ed. William Plomer (London: Jonathan Cape, 1940), vol. III, p. 160 (entry for 6 April 1875)
130 Kitty Earp is now Kitty de Cheveigné. After the war she married a member of the French resistance. They lived in Canada for a number of years. Mrs Cheveigné now lives in southern France. She reached back in memory some forty years and gave me a frank and full account of her years at Garnons, upon which I have drawn freely both for detail and for general ideas. I am immensely indebted to her.
131 29 October 1944
132 Of the hundreds of 'thank you' letters, I selected one that had a good

deal of detail, and was written with care and thoughtfulness. This letter, which follows, came from Brian Dickson, a lieutenant in the Royal Canadian Artillery. He is now the Chief Justice of Canada.

'Dear Mrs. Massey:
Thank you for one of the most enjoyable three weeks I have ever spent. Since returning to my Regiment from Garnons feeling fit enough to engage the Germany Army single handed, I have done little except sing the praises of the Massey Foundation Convalescent Home for Officers, of its beauty and its comforts. Before being sent there I had, of course, heard a number of glowing reports of Garnons so that the anticipation was considerable. But in this instance the pleasures of realization far exceeded those of anticipation.

I would very much like to detail the many things that contributed to the pleasures of my Garnons sojourn. But they are almost innumerable, the riding, the golf, the weekly expeditions to historic spots, the library, the musical facilities, all these and many more. There would seem to be something there to appeal to even the most jaded taste; one is free to pursue whatever appeals to him in the quiet atmosphere of home, and I can assure you that this is very much appreciated. I at least was able to forget for the time being that the world seems full of evil forces, tyranny and oppression, fighting and bloodshed. I also must mention how I enjoyed the opportunity to meet and discuss subjects of mutual interest with the officers, senior and junior, of other regiments, and to learn through them of the exploits of mutual friends in other branches of the Canadian Army and in the other services.

After leaving Garnons, perhaps more than while actually there I was struck by the thought and organization which have gone to make the Home what it is, and the contribution which you and Mr. Massey must have made in this respect. I can't tell you how the officers look forward each weekend to your arrival, those whom you have met on previous weekends and those who have not yet enjoyed the privilege and pleasure of your acquaintance. Although they may not mention it, all appreciate more than I can say, the interest which you have in their welfare, and what you have done and are doing to make the period of their convalescence something to remember.

Now I am back with the Regiment and have heard about all that my friends have been doing during the past month, and acquainting them with the details of some of my travels. It is good to see all the officers and men again and to return to the work which we are doing here, good work and intensely interesting. I am sorry to have missed the past month but that couldn't have been avoided and now as I try to make up for the time lost, I will have many grand memories to reflect upon.

Thank you again Mrs. Massey for Garnons. The three weeks I spent there couldn't have been more enjoyable. I hope that some time in the not too distant future I may have the pleasure of meeting you at the Officers Club in London.
Very Sincerely,
Brian Dickson

133 *The Siren Years*, p. 62
134 Massey Diary, 4 August 1941. For much of the detail in this account of Garnons, I am indebted to the present incumbent, Sir John Cotterell, and Lady Cotterell. My wife and I visited Garnons in October 1983, and were given a warm welcome. All our questions were patiently answered; we dined royally but informally, and we were taken on a tour of the estate. Much of the land was sold to pay succession duties, and after the war the main section of the house was torn down. Sir John and Lady Cotterell live in the west wing, which is spacious enough to permit the retention of many of the pictures and books from the old house. Nothing has altered the superb view. Sir John was five years old when the war broke out, and during the war years the family occupied an Elizabethan manor house some distance from Garnons. He does not, of course, have vivid memories of the Canadian invasion, but has preserved pictures and mementoes of these years.
135 The letter is undated.
136 To Vincent Massey, 29 October 1945
137 *The Siren Years*, pp. 10–11

CHAPTER FIVE

1 26 February 1946. WLG. vol. 41
2 *Ibid.*, 15 February 1946
3 13 July 1945, WLKM G26 J8, vol. 27
4 Massey Diary, 12 March 1946
5 Marjorie McFarland, 'Canada's Churchill,' *Living Age* (April 1941), pp. 141–3: 'If Canada ever comes seriously to feel the need of a strong

National Government, Vincent Massey, now High Commissioner to the United Kingdom, might be the only man of sufficient stature in the Canadian political scene to fill the role of Churchill' (p. 143).
6 Empire Day broadcast, 3 July 1944, reported in *The Times*
7 11 March 1942
8 *Evening News*, 23 January 1941
9 *Telegraph*, 11 March 1942
10 9 July 1942. For the text of the broadcast see *The Sword of Lionheart* (London: Hodder and Stoughton, 1942), pp. 33–5
11 *The Siren Years* (Toronto: Macmillan, 1974), p. 52
12 *Telegraph*, 1 November 1943
13 26 June 1943
14 14 April 1946
15 To Vincent Massey, 16 May 1941
16 14 October 1943. WLG, vol. 41
17 To Vincent Massey, 1 March 1945
18 18 February 1941
19 14 May 1945
20 To Viscount Lee, 7 June 1945
21 Kenneth Clark's version of the appointment is different: 'I will not describe the events that accompanied my leaving the Gallery, except to say that my successor, who had been appointed solely on my recommendation, refused to come and see me.' *The Other Half*, (Toronto: Longmans Canada 1977), p. 78. The Massey papers have several letters about the appointment from various trustees and give no indication of a director-sponsored *fait accompli*.
22 7 June 1946
23 The two phrases in quotation marks are translations of a Latin inscription at the entrance to the room.
24 Massey Diary, 1 November 1944
25 23 May 1945
26 Massey Diary, 27 July 1945
27 To Maude Grant, WLG vol. 41 (undated but late 1944 or early 1945)
28 Massey Diary, 26 July 1945
29 13 March 1946
30 King Diary, 20 April 1946
31 *Ibid.*
32 *Ibid.*, 6 March 1946
33 *Ibid.*, 22 May 1946
34 Massey Diary, 21 May 1946

35 King Diary, 22 May 1946
36 Massey Diary, 22 May 1946
37 King Diary, 22 May 1946
38 8 February 1946. WLG, vol. 41
39 28 February 1941
40 Massey Diary, 3 December 1943
41 *Ibid.*, 18 February 1943
42 17 May 1944
43 Stanley McLean, who had been active from an early point in supporting Massey for the chancellorship, gave a long, detailed account of this second campaign in a letter to Vincent Massey, 26 November 1944.
44 18 October 1944
45 'Raymond writes that he is becoming an American citizen in order to join the US army. I am really shocked to hear that he is becoming an American. I can't get over it.' Massey Diary, 1 June 1942. Apparently Raymond had contemplated the move in 1942, but delayed it until he had returned from Canada.
46 Raymond Massey to Vincent Massey, 30 August 1943
47 Massey Diary, 5 March 1944
48 24 April 1944
49 Vincent thus reported an after-dinner speech in London by the American movie actor Adolph Menjou: 'The words came in a torrent, a mixture of personal vanity, Anglo-American sentimentality and American Imperialism.' Massey Diary, 19 July 1943. He accepted an analysis of US attitudes given by the historian John Wheeler-Bennett: 'a most depressing account of the American scene – anglophobia, isolationism, no passionate interest in the European war, growing reaction in domestic politics etc. etc. He said quite definitely that it was the desire of official Washington, including Americans of varied types of mind, to detach Canada from the British Commonwealth in order to make her more amenable to American influence.' *Ibid.*, 2 July 1943. A brief portrait of a popular visitor is in Massey's anti-American manner. 'Went to a cocktail party given by Wendell Wilkie, the Republican candidate in the recent US election. His visit seems like an extension of his election campaign and his sitting room at the Dorchester was like a campaign committee room – henchmen and secretaries receiving above while the Great Man shook hands with everyone, greeting them with automatic affability and no knowledge whatsoever who they were.' *Ibid.*, 30 January 1941
50 *Globe and Mail*, 8 October 1946

51 Speech to the Canadian Club, Toronto, 17 November 1947
52 *On Being Canadian* (Toronto: J.M. Dent & Sons, 1948), pp. 13, 124
53 To Vincent Massey, June 1947
54 15 August 1947
55 The honorary graduands were Harold Dodds, president of Princeton University, who represented the humanistic tradition in higher education; Sir Alexander Cadogan, for many years permanent under-secretary of state in Great Britain, representative of the British civil service tradition of scholarship and objectivity; Rt. Hon. Thibaudeau Rinfret, chief justice of Canada; the Reverend Monseigneur Ferdinand Vaudry, rector of Laval University, representatives of the French-Canadian devotion to law, education, and the Church; Lord Beaverbrook, Mrs Ogden Reid of the New York *Herald Tribune*, and George McCullagh, publisher of the *Globe and Mail*, all representing the power of the press in a good cause – the promotion of allied unity in the war.
56 Inaugural address
57 12 November 1946. There was a happy outcome to this impasse. Nicholas Ignatieff succeeded Bickersteth as warden. He was ideally suited to the job, and his untimely death in 1952 was a shattering blow to Hart House and to the university.
58 Eric Phillips to Hon. Paul Martin, 31 August 1949
59 To Henry Borden, 2 June 1944
60 29 September 1947
61 PAC, St Laurent Papers, MG 262, vol. 222, 5 November 1948

CHAPTER SIX

1 Massey Diary, 6 January 1949
2 *Ibid.*
3 18 April 1946, WLMK, MG 26J4, vol. 306, C242–455
4 19 March 1949
5 *Debates, House of Commons*, vol. CCLXVI (1949), p. 46
6 *Minutes of Proceeding and Evidence of the Speech Committee on Reconstruction and Re-Establishment*, 21 June 1941 (Ottawa: King's Printer)
7 *On Being Canadian* (Toronto: J.M. Dent & Sons, 1948), p. 60
8 26 February 1949
9 21 March 1949
10 18 March 1949

11 Quoted in 'The Fight over Father Lévesque,' *Maclean's* 1 July 1950, p. 51
12 26 June 1950
13 26 April 1949
14 To Claude Bissell, 15 April 1977
15 *Ibid.*, (my translation)
16 Norman Mackenzie to Claude Bissell, 12 July 1976
17 31 December 1952
18 *Globe and Mail*, 24 August 1951
19 Minutes of the 34th Meeting, 13 January 1951. The minutes for the meetings of the commission are in PAC RC 33, 28, vol. 1A.
20 Fourth Meeting, 1 August 1949
21 The letter (to Vincent Massey, 21 September 1949) is one of a number of preliminary documents to the minutes of the commission's meetings.
22 René Garneau to Vincent Massey, 27 September 1949
23 9 March 1950
24 A good many English-speaking Canadians would have agreed with Duplessis, whose sentiments about the commission were described approvingly by his biographer, Conrad Black. 'Duplessis considered it [the Massey commission] as a growth not only of Vincent Massey's aerated patronage, not only of Georges-Henri Lévesque's insolent priesthood, but a new endeavour by the federal government to pose as Santa Claus with money that rightfully belonged to the province in a jurisdiction where the province had exclusive rights.' Black makes this comment about the commission's proposals for the universities: 'What started as yet another of Vincent Massey's lofty but inoffensive cultural gestures became another political Armageddon.' *Duplessis* (Toronto: McClelland and Stewart, 1977), pp. 481–2
25 *Report of the Royal Commission on National Development in the Arts, Letters, and Sciences 1949–1951* (Ottawa: King's Printer, 1951), p. 268 (henceforth referred to as *Report*)
26 *Report*, p. 5
27 *Ibid.*, p. 150
28 *Ibid.*, p. 346
29 *Ibid.*, p. 89
30 *Ibid.*, p. 93
31 *Ibid.*, p. 293
32 *Ibid.*, p. 274
33 *Ibid.*, p. 372

34 The article appeared in the *Tamarack Review*, vol. 1 (Autumn 1956), pp. 37–47. It is reprinted in *So Much to Do, So Little Time; The Writings of Hilda Neatby*, edited and annotated by Michael Hayden (University of British Columbia Press, 1983). My quotation is from the reprint, p. 289.
35 (London: Jonathan Cape, 1937), p. 245
36 *Ibid.*, 247
37 PAC, RG 33 28 vol. 1A, Minutes of the Third Meeting, 20–21 June 1949, p. 18
38 *Report*, p. 11
39 Frank Underhill thought that a strain of anti-Americanism was the main weakness of the report. After praising the commissioners for 'their thorough work in searching out and assembling the relevant facts, their imaginative grasp of their subject, their masterly presentation of a programme of action,' he went on to scold them for their anti-Americanism. 'What we need, we, the minority of Canadians who care for the culture of the few, is closer contact with the finest expressions of the American mind. The fear that what will result from such contact will be our own absorption is pure defeatism.' 'Notes on the Massey Report' in *In Search of Canadian Liberalism* (Toronto: Macmillan, 1960), p. 213. The original article appeared in the *Canadian Forum*, August 1951. No member of the commission, certainly not Vincent Massey, would have disagreed with Underhill.
40 The Grant article appears in *Royal Commission Studies* (Ottawa: King's Printer, 1951), p. 132, and is quoted (with some minor deviations from Grant's text) on p. 272 of the *Report*. Grant, who was at the time professor of philosophy in Dalhousie University, was a junior in the field, and I recall hearing lively protests against his choice as Canadian spokesman from Professor Fulton Anderson, a senior member of the philosophy department at the University of Toronto.
41 'The Canada Council at Twenty-five,' *Saturday Night*, March 1982, p. 37
42 *Report*, p. 271
43 *Ibid.*, p. 211
44 *Ibid.*, p. 226
45 Quoted by Frank W. Peers in *The Politics of Canadian Broadcasting, 1920–1951* (University of Toronto Press, 1969), p. 354. The quotation is taken from an article by Joseph Sedgwick in *Saturday Night* (2 November 1942), pp. 18–19. I am greatly indebted to Peers' book for

my brief summary of developments in broadcasting politics prior to the appointment of the Massey Commission.
46 Quoted by Peers, *Canadian Broadcasting*, p. 361
47 Quoted by Peers, *Ibid.*, p. 424
48 *Report*, p. 28
49 *Ibid.*, pp. 279–80
50 PAC RG 28, vol. 39
51 *Report*, p. 397. Surveyer was quoting from Gilbert Seldes, *The Great Audience* (1950).
52 Quoted by Peers, *Canadian Broadcasting*, p. 427
53 *Report*, p. 304
54 *Ibid.*, p. 377
55 *Report of the Federal Cultural Policy Review Committee* (1982), p. 54
56 PAC RG 33, 28, vol. 1A, p. 5
57 Quoted in the *Report*, p. 375
58 *Report*, p. 167
59 PAC RG 33, 28, vol. 1A, Minutes of the 46th meeting, 20 June 1951
60 To Norman Mackenzie, 15 September 1950
61 Pickersgill writes: 'I recall pointing out to Larry [Mackenzie] that a per capita grant based on the provincial population would serve as a rough measure of equalization since, generally speaking, the poorer provinces had fewer students in proportion to their population. But I insisted that the stronger argument was that such a formula would be entirely automatic and could not possibly be construed as discriminating among provinces or institutions, and that any other formula was certain to be attacked as an invasion of provincial jurisdiction.' To Claude Bissell, 10 March 1979
62 *Debates, House of Commons*, 3 May 1951, p. 2633
63 To A.A. Hall, 22 February 1938
64 *Report*, p. 143
65 *Ibid.*, p. 132
66 *Ibid.*, p. 352
67 *Ibid.*, pp. 354–5
68 Saul Bellow, *Him with His Foot In his Mouth and Other Stories* (New York: Harper and Row, 1984), p. 53
69 The wide discussion of the report in the press inspired a revival of articles on the Masseys as Canada's royal family. In a bold journalistic exercise, Pierre Berton saw the Report as the summation of the family virtues: 'The now famous Report bears the unmistakeable im-

print of the man for whom it is popularly named: Vincent Massey, a lean, ascetic figure with the hands of a concert pianist, the long melancholy features of a Savonarola. The head of the Massey dynasty, he is also the product. If his fine Canadian hand is to be seen throughout the Report's four-hundred pages, so are the shadowy hands of his father. The showmanship of his Uncle Walter is in the gay cover and the journalistic turn of phrase. The religion of his father Chester is in the quotations from the evangelical saints, Paul and Augustine. The stern sense of detail of his aunts Lilian and Susan is in the personal choice of typeface and careful redesign of the coat of arms. The practical business sense of his great-grandfather Daniel is in the recommendations. And the Made-in-Canada approach of his grandfather Hart is in the entire venture.' 'There'll Always Be a Massey' in *Maclean's*, 15 October 1951, p. 8
70 *Royal Commission Studies*, p. 390
71 *So Little for the Mind*, (Toronto: Clarke, Irwin, 1953), pp. 47–8
72 The Massey Report' in W.H. Heick, ed., *History and Myth: Arthur Lower and the Making of Canadian Nationalism* (University of British Columbia Press, 1975), p. 124. The original article appeared in the *Canadian Banker*, vol. 59 (winter 1952), pp. 22–32.
73 *Report*, p. 271
74 *Montreal Daily Star*, 11 June 1951

CHAPTER SEVEN

1 Massey Diary, 7 May 1911
2 J.R. Mallory, 'The Appointment of the Governor General: Responsible Government, Autonomy, and the Royal Prerogative.' *Canadian Journal of Economics and Political Science*, vol. XXVI no. 1 (Feb. 1960), p. 99. The date of the letter is 17 June 1930.
3 25 August 1950
4 15 May 1950. PAC MG 20, vol. 12
5 Massey Diary, 25 October 1957
6 In their biography of C.D. Howe (Toronto: McClelland and Stewart, 1979), pp. 258–60, Robert Bothwell and William Kilbourn present a different story of the appointment of the first Canadian governor-general. According to them, St Laurent discussed the governor-generalship with Howe in the spring of 1950. The implication is that Howe accepted – subject to having enough time to resign from

parliament and purify his image as a tough party man. Alexander left earlier than expected, and St Laurent (reluctantly, it would follow) appointed Massey who, the authors say, had 'practised the vice-regal arts on a small scale at his country estate outside Port Hope, Ontario.'

The story encounters the fundamental difficulty of reconciling St Laurent's sensitivity to public opinion and to legal niceties with Howe's robust image as political warrior and arrogant partisan. After Massey's appointment, St Laurent wrote as follows to Ross Macdonald, Speaker of the House, and a man widely spoken of as a possible governor-general: 'But I am sure you would be the first to agree that in recommending a Canadian for the first time, the utmost care had to be taken to avoid even the unjustified suggestion that the appointment was a reward for party loyalty,' 23 January 1952. PAC MG 26, vol. 105. St Laurent's words to Macdonald apply *a fortiori* to Howe.

It is difficult to believe that St Laurent talked to Howe about the governor-generalship in the spring of 1950, as Bothwell and Kilbourn suggest. The proposal to Massey had been made on 25 February 1950, and the king had been informed of Massey's probable appointment on 12 May 1950.

7 Massey Diary, 25 March 1951
8 *Ibid.*, 26 January 1952
9 The speech was delivered at a dinner held in Massey's honour by the Canadian Club of Toronto on 8 February 1965. The speech exists in the Massey papers in at least five drafts. There is accompanying correspondence with Robertson Davies and Michael Pitfield, who read and commented on the text.
10 Philip's visits *solus* on business was an important royal departure. Vincent wrote to Maude Grant about the first visit. 'The tour worked out as it was planned and will, I think, be a very important precedent, showing that a member of the Royal Family can visit a Commonwealth country for a specific purpose with a minimum of formality and without spending more time than can be allotted to a given visit.' 18 August 1954
11 The quotation occurs (p. 1) in Massey's Romanes lecture at Oxford, 1 June 1961, which was issued as a pamphlet by Oxford University Press in the same year.
12 Eugene A. Forsey, *The Royal Power of Dissolution of Parliament in the British Commonwealth.* (Toronto: Oxford University Press, 1943). The copy in the Massey Library has a book plate 'Rideau Hall, ex libris.' It

was apparently compulsory reading for governors-general. Forsey had tutored the Massey children in the summer of 1924. Following Alice's death, he wrote a warm letter of sympathy to Vincent.
13 R.H. Hubbard, *Rideau Hall: An Illustrated History of Government House, Ottawa, from Victorian Times to the Present Day* (Montreal, London: McGill-Queen's University Press, 1977), p. 167
14 Massey Diary, 16 February 1952
15 Danny Kaye succeeded Charlie Chaplin as Vincent Massey's favourite movie actor. Later on he attended a Danny Kaye show at the Canadian National Exhibition and entertained Kaye at Batterwood. 'Kaye was in tremendous form,' Vincent reported. 'Indulged in a little gentle leg-pulling, e.g. when I referred to my 'actor brother' he said, "it sounded just as if I had said my 'gangster brother.' *Ibid.*, 24 August 1958
16 *Ibid.*, 10 October 1955
17 *Ibid.*, 16 May 1953
18 *Ibid.*, 9 July 1956
19 *Ibid.*, 14 July 1956
20 W.C.R. Jones to Claude Bissell, 7 May 1984
21 Vol. VIII, no. 6 (April 1939), pp. 371–86
22 (London: Hodder and Stoughton, 1941), p. 241
23 Massey Diary, 26 March 1956
24 'North Star West,' *Collected Poems* (Toronto: McClelland and Stewart, 1975), vol. I, p. 156
25 Massey Diary, 20 March 1956
26 *Ibid.*, 21 March 1956
27 To Lionel Massey, 9 December 1955
28 Massey Diary, 31 March 1956
29 *Mike: The Memoirs of The Right Honourable Lester Pearson* (Toronto: University of Toronto Press, 1975), vol. III, *1957–1968*, p. 224. I suspect that this may have been editorial speculation. I was a visitor at Rideau Hall in the spring of 1952 – my first visit, and, in prospect, rather intimidating. My most vivid memory is seeing Lester Pearson wander in out of the night unannounced, and of him and Vincent Massey standing at the entrance, talking like old-time neighbours, before Pearson, who was out for a stroll, casually left. This was hardly a regal and formal atmosphere.
30 'On the Appointment of Governor-general Vincent Massey, 1952' in *The Blasted Pine*, selected by F.R. Scott and A.J.M. Smith (Toronto: Macmillan, 1957), p. 59

31 'A Play to The "Gallery," ' in *Speaking of Canada* (Toronto: Macmillan, 1959), pp. 210–12
32 These words may well have been written by Timothy Porteous, later the director of the Canada Council.
33 Massey Diary, 22 December 1956
34 The comments are from *ibid.*, 15 April 1952, 18 April 1952, and 3 October 1955.
35 John W. Wheeler-Bennett, *King George VI* (London: Macmillan 1958), p. 756
36 Massey Diary, 5 October 1957
37 *Ibid.*, 15 June 1959
38 18 January 1960
39 *One Canada* (Toronto: Macmillan, 1976), vol. II, p. 58
40 *WPP*, p. 516
41 Massey Diary, 11 June 1957
42 Mallory, 'The Appointment of the Governor general,' p. 106
43 Massey Diary, 1 February 1958
44 *Ibid.*, 4 January 1955
45 *Ibid.*, 18 March 1959
46 14 May 1953
47 Massey Diary, 14 February 1956
48 29 February 1956
49 Massey Diary, 4 January 1955
50 The story is told by Douglas Fullerton in his *Quebec: Voyage of Discovery* (Toronto: McClelland and Stewart, 1978), p. 33
51 *The Canada Council: Opening Proceedings* (Ottawa, May 1957), p. 4
52 To Ian Hunter, 2 May 1957
53 *Mayfair* (February 1953). Birney said 'yes' to the question 'Does Canada owe its writers a living?'
54 Massey Diary, 15 November 1956
55 *Inside Government House, as told by Colonel H. Willis-O'Connor to Madge Macbeth* (Toronto: Ryerson Press, 1954), p. 79
56 *Report of the Royal Commission on Arts, Letters, and Sciences*, p. 162
57 20 October 1953. During his term as governor-general, Hilda Neatby always addressed Vincent Massey as 'Your Excellency.'
58 29 December 1953
59 22 November 1953
60 15 September 1953
61 13 January 1952
62 22 May 1953

63 30 October 1955
64 12 January 1956
65 7 April, 1953
66 *In Speaking of Canada*, pp. 200–1
67 *Canadian Jewish Congress Bulletin* (Montreal, December 1953), p. 4
68 Michael Hayden in *So Much to Do, So Little Time* (University of British Columbia Press, 1983) gives an interesting account of the relationship between Vincent Massey and Hilda Neatby, based upon material in the Saskatchewan archives. The Massey papers have 126 letters from Hilda Neatby to Massey, almost all hand-written, which, I presume, are not in the Saskatchewan archives. There are only a few letters from Vincent Massey to Hilda Neatby in the Massey collection, most of them dating from post-governor-general days.

CHAPTER EIGHT

1 Massey Diary, 22 May 1959
2 Raymond Massey, *A Hundred Different Lives* (Toronto: McClelland and Stewart, 1979), pp. 337–9
3 February 1965
4 31 January 1961
5 24 January 1955
6 Massey Diary, 16 February 1955
7 *Ibid.*, 23 August 1961
8 *Ibid.*, 9 June 1960
9 30 June 1960
10 8 July 1960
11 Massey no doubt was impressed by the comments of R.M. Fowler, president of the Canadian Pulp and Paper Association, and a leading business man in the conference council. After discussing possible speakers for the conference with others, he wrote to Massey that 'their opinion was unanimous that you would be the best choice for a main speaker from Canada at the conference. It is appropriate that the chairman should make such a speech. You bring to it great prestige as a former Governor-General. More important, you have seen Canada and its industrial scene as no other living Canadian has done. And you are an accomplished speaker' (27 June 1960). Vacy Ash, president of Shell Oil Company of Canada and as vice-chairman of the Edinburgh Conference, its effective administrative head, strongly supported Fowler. 'I am absolutely clear in my own mind that the only possible

speaker for our Canadian host-nation address is yourself. As Governor-General you have an absolutely unique knowledge of the country from coast to coast and border to border ... Finally and most important, you will bring to it the wisdom, thought and feeling which it has been a great privilege to me to learn to appreciate from my association with you in this venture' (22 June 1960).

12 'An Introduction to Canada,' in *Confederation on the March* (Toronto: Macmillan, 1965), pp. 22–3. This is the address at the opening session of the Duke of Edinburgh's Second Commonwealth Study Conference, 15 May 1962.

13 The quotation is from *The Tempest*, act II, scene i, l. 247. The words are in a speech by Antonio, Prospero's villainous brother, who has supplanted him as the Duke of Milan, and is now trying to convince Sebastian, brother of Alonso, King of Naples, that he too should murder his brother and inherit the crown. Antonio is pointing out how recent events are a 'prologue' or a preparation for these designs, and that the future is now in their hands. It's difficult to see how a quotation from a Shakespearean villain at his most transparently evil accords with the mood or the intent of Massey's book.

14 *Queen's Quarterly*, vol. 71 (summer 1964), p. 71

15 *Globe and Mail*, 5 October 1963

16 Royal Military College named its new library after him. Massey opened the building on 4 November 1960, and, at the same time, received an honorary degree. The reception centre in the Jewish National Library at the Hebrew University was also named after him.

17 Alesta Widdenburn to Vincent Massey, 23 July 1964

18 *The Office and Work of Universities* (London, 1856), p. 353

19 To Eric Phillips, 14 December 1959

20 At this time Davies wrote a letter to the *Guardian*, in response to a reference by one of its correspondents to Canada as a 'cultural backwater.' After speaking of Canadian achievements in music and the production of Shakespeare, he went on to say, 'It would not become me to take up the cudgel for Canadian authors, though they are well received in the United States, in Germany, and the low countries, and of course in France. But I foresee that a genius may arise in Canada so overwhelming that even Britain will have to acknowledge him – of course after the post-mortem cooling off period you insist upon in the case of Ibsen, Chekov, and other outsiders.' The letter was quoted in the *Toronto Daily Star*, 12 August 1961. Davies had been writing some articles for the *Star*.

21 Massey Diary, 1 February 1961
22 *Ibid.*, 24 November 1961
23 Peter Collins, 'Home for Scholars,' in the *Guardian*, 28 November 1963
24 Massey Diary, 13 September 1963.
25 1 July 1960
26 Massey Diary, 12 May 1960
27 *Ibid.*, 27 April 1960. The old friend was Ava Waverley, widow of Viscount Waverley, more familiar as John Anderson, chancellor of the exchequer in Churchill's war-time government.
28 These two paragraphs rely on Nicholas Mosley's two autobiographical books, *Rules of the Game* (London: Fontana/Collins, 1982) and *Beyond the Pale* (London: Secker & Warburg, 1983). Nicholas Mosley's mother was Cynthia Curzon (Curzon's second daughter, always known as 'Cimmie' to her family) who married Mosley at the beginning of his political career and died in 1933 when her husband was beginning his rapid descent into fascism and his affair with Diana Guinness, whom he eventually married. When Mosley was imprisoned, his aunt Irene was declared the guardian of his children.
29 4 October 1962
30 4 February 1964
31 2 August 1966
32 5 November 1965
33 *Toronto Daily Star*, 25, 27 February 1967
34 This account is from an unpublished account by Miroslav Stajanovich of his life with Vincent Massey.

Index

Adaskin, Harry 42
Adeane, Sir Michael 268
Aird, Sir John 221
Alba, Duke of 87
Alexander, Lord 173, 201, 244, 277
Allen, Adrianne 67–9
Anderson, Fulton 338n
Andrew, Geoffrey 66
Applebaum, Louis 227
Archer, Norman 73
Ash, Vacy 344–45n
Asquith, Margot (Countess of Oxford and Asquith) 17–18
Astor, Lord 102
Athlone, Earl of 240, 277
Attlee, Clement 80, 125, 163, 246

Bagehot, Walter 247
Balcer, Léon 270
Baldwin, Stanley 83, 87, 94, 96, 247
Balliol College 170–1
Balogh, T.H. 171
Barbeau, Marius 293
Barrington-Ward, Robin 22–3, 136, 139, 171

Baum, Gregory 135
Beaverbrook, Lord (Max Aitken) 32, 50–1, 146–7, 152–3, 162–3, 336n
Beaver Club 151–3
Bell, 'Panicky' 251
Bénaimé, Father 257
Bennett, Richard Bedford 32–3, 74, 150–1, 221
Berger, Carl 227
Berle, Adolf, 130
Berton, Pierre 339–40n
Bessborough, Lord 200–1
Bickersteth, Burgon 46, 47–8, 191–2
Bieler, André 198
Bing, Rudolph 272
Birney, Earle 197–8, 255, 276
Bissell, Christine 263
Black, Conrad 311, 337n
Blackstone, Milton 41–2
Bladen, Vincent 209
Blair, Charles 103
Blume, Helmut 135
Bone, Muirhead 147
Bothwell, Robert 340–1n
Bowen, Elizabeth 108

Bracken, Brendan 27, 98, 189
Brandeis, Louis 105
Breach, Derick, 309–10
Breadner, Air Chief Marshal 115
Brett, George Sidney 219
British background 1935–39: international affairs 6; temper of society 6–7; role of the social hostess 15; place of the country house 17–19; creation of Dominions Office 79–80; foreign policy under Baldwin 83–7; foreign policy under Chamberlain 87–91; analysis of 'appeasement' in British foreign policy 90–1; British sympathy with German grievances 91; British visitors to Hitler 92–3; belief that world war meant destruction of European civilization 96; opposition to appeasement 98–9; praise of dictators 101; attitudes towards Hitler's persecution of the Jews 101–3
1939–47: the London blitz and the V-1's and V-2's 107–8, 111; the collapse of the Greek front 112; German offensive, January 1945 115; military disasters 1942, 126; American criticism of British colonial policy 124; wartime attitude towards the Jewish question 133; Labour victory in election of July 1945 171–2
Brockington, Leonard, 129
Brooke, Sir Alan 144
Broughall, Wilmot 302, 308
Brown, Eric 42, 44

Brown, George 206–7
Bruce, Herbert 63, 178–9
Bruce, Stanley 76, 80, 98, 124–5, 127, 137–8
Butler, Esmond 255
Butler, Robert Austin 26–27, 88, 171
Byng, Lord 54, 238–9, 240

Cadogan, Sir Alexander 336 fn.
Cairns, Hugh 36
Callaghan, Morley 38
Campbell, Archibald Hamilton 305
Canadian Authors' Association 208
Canadian background: early history of high commissionership in London 49; ambiguity in the function of high commissioner 73–4; Canadian attitude towards Italian aggression 1935, 74–5; foreign policy attitudes 80–2; acceptance of appeasement 99–100; government policy on Jewish immigration 103–4; Canada and the cold war 186; Canadian Broadcasting Corporation 220–6, 231–2; the new status of the governor-general after 1926 239; the political role of the governor-general 269; election of June 1957 269; election of June 1958 266
Canadian Broadcasting Corporation 220–6, 231-2
Canadian Council of the Arts 199
Canadian Officers' Club 153, 162–3
Carnegie Corporation 198–9
Cartwright, Stephen 197
Chalmers, Floyd 49, 100
Chamberlain, Neville 87–90, 95, 96

Channon, Sir Henry ('Chips') 15
Churchill, Gordon 266
Churchill, Winston 9, 81, 88, 96, 111, 126–7, 136, 139, 163, 264, 329n
Claxton, Brooke 61, 62, 71, 99, 195–6, 234, 241, 249, 275–6, 293
Clark, Gregory 152
Clark, Sir Kenneth 27–8, 43, 148–9, 167, 168–9, 272, 334n
'Cliveden set' 20–1
Cockburn, Claud 21, 318–19n
Cody, Henry John 63, 176–7, 179–81
Coldwell, M.J. 210
Colefax, Sybil 16, 242
Connaught, Duke of 238
Connolly, Cyril 28
Cooke, Jack Kent 225, 259
Corbett, E.A. 118
Corbett, P.E. 82
Corneill, Carmen 298
Cotterell, Sir John and Lady 333n
Cotterell, Sir Richard 154
Coyne, James 267
Cranborne, Lord 25–6, 80, 98, 124, 125–6, 171, 264
Crawley, Alan 205
Creighton, Donald 273
Crerar, General Harry D.C. 130, 141–2
Crerar, Thomas 103
Cunard, Lady Emerald 15
Currie, Sir Arthur 176
Curzon, Lord 304–5
Curzon, Cynthia (Lady Oswald Mosley) 346

Daniell, Raymond 256
Davies, Brenda 287

Davies, Robertson 233–4, 262, 268, 272, 273, 296–7, 299, 345n
Day, Archibald 202, 211–13
Devonshire, Duke of 238
Dewey, John 279
Dickson, Brian 332–3n
Dickson, H. Lovat 37, 39
Diefenbaker, John 222, 249, 262, 265–8, 269–71, 288, 310
Dill, Sir John 112
Dinsmore, Robert 299
Dodds, Harold 336
Dorchester Hotel 108–9
Drew, George 177–8, 179–80, 189, 241, 253
Dufferin, Lord 237
Duguid, Colonel Archer Fortescue 147
Dulles, John Foster 271
Duncan, James 49, 303
Dunn, Sir James 275
Duplessis, Maurice 203, 210–11, 252, 257
Dupuy, Pierre 131–2
Dwyer, Peter 219

Earp, Kitty (Mrs de Cheveigné) 157–8, 331n
Earys, James 78, 97, 234, 287, 291
Eden, Anthony 25–6, 79, 84, 85, 86, 88, 98, 113, 133, 137–8, 264
Edwards, Air Vice Marshal 144–5
Eisendrath, Maurice 102
Eisenhower, Dwight 271
Erickson, Arthur 298
Ervine, St John 38

Fackenheim, Emil 135
Fairley, Barker 291
Falconer, Sir Robert 106

Farquharson, Ray 241–2
Federation of Canadian Artists 199
Fennell, A.B. 179–80
Ferguson, George 273
Ferguson, Howard 5, 24, 49, 73, 74–5
Filion, Gérard 273
Fleming, Donald 266
Fletcher, Susan 285
Forsey, Eugene 247, 341–2n
Fowler, R.M. 277, 344n
Franca, Celia 219
Frankfurter, Felix 105
Fraser, Blair 268
Friesen, Colin 297
Frost, Leslie 296
Fulford, Robert 219
Fullerton, Douglas 343n

Gamelin, General 131
Gandhi, Mrs Indira 263
Garneau, René 203
Garner, Joe (Lord Saville Garner) 80, 98
Garnons 154–9, 162
Gelber, Lionel 105–6
George, Lloyd 92–3
Gossage, Leigh McCarthy 306–7, 312
Goulding, Dorothy 285
Gouzenko, Igor 186
Graham Billy 263
Grant, Alison (Mrs George Ignatieff) 66, 87, 116
Grant, Charity 66
Grant, George 116–18, 191, 218–19, 338n
Grant, Margaret (Mrs Geoffrey Andrew) 66
Grant, Maude 66, 196

Green, Howard 266
Greville, Maggie 15–16
Grey, Lord 237–8
Grey Owl (Archie Belaney) 39–40
Grierson, John 219
Grove, Frederick Philip 38
Groulx, Abbé 293
Guinness, Diana 346n
Guthrie, Tyrone 219, 272

Halifax, Lord (Edward Wood) 24–5, 92
Hambourg, Boris 184
Harris, Lawren 199, 200, 293
Hart House 190–2, 238
Hart House Quartet 41–2, 183–4
Hees, George 270
Hendy, Philip 169
Herbert, Walter 200
Hess, Myra 167–8
Hiller, Tristram 112
Hirshhorn, Joe 273–4
Hitler, Adolf 84, 85–6, 88–9, 90, 91–3, 95, 135
Hoare, Sir Samuel 84
Hoeniger, David 135
Holgate, Edwin 45
Holmes, John 234
Howe, C.D. 244, 340–1n
Hudd, Frederic 52, 303
Hunter, Ian 272
Hutchison, Bruce 273
Hutton, Maurice 219
Hymas, Howard 263

Ignatieff, George 234
Innis, Harold 234
Inskip, Sir Thomas (Viscount Caldecote) 79, 125

Jackson, A.Y. 45, 200, 293
James, Cyril 228
Jarvis, Alan 273
John, Augustus 43-4, 147
Johnson, Edward 272
Jones, Roy 251
Jordan, William 110-11, 124

Kaye, Danny 249, 342n
Kennedy, Joseph 127, 186
Kent, Duke of 45
Keynes, John Maynard 92, 168
Kilbourn, William 234, 289, 340-1n
Killam, Isaac 275
Kilvert, Francis 156-7
King George V 247
King George VI 10-11, 40, 245, 248
King, William Lyon Mackenzie: refuses Massey's request to purchase a London residence for the high commissioners 13; praises the Masseys' work in London 13-14; defends Massey's work in London against attacks 60; criticizes Raymond Massey's style of living 68; deprives Massey of any role in international affairs 76-8; visits Hitler 93; rejoices in outcome of Munich meetings 96-7; maintains belief in appeasement until outbreak of war 97; his malevolent view of Massey expressed in interview 17 June 1937 119; improved relations between King and Massey during the war 120-2; retrospectively enraged on learning about Massey's role in initiating the British Commonwealth Air Training Plan 137-8; considers Massey for governor-generalship in 1944, but offers post to McNaughton 172-3; King's dislike of Massey revived 173-4; first opposes, then consents to, Massey's receiving CH 174-6; offers Massey lieutenant-governorship of Ontario 175-6; declines Claxton's suggestion that Massey be put in charge of government agencies concerned with the arts and communication 195-6; does not respond to Masseys offer of a concert hall for Ottawa 293; bitter about Dieppe 331n
Kinsey, Gwyn 259
Koch, Erick 135
Koldofsky, Adolphe 42
Kreisel, Henry 135

Lamb, Henry 148
Lambert, Norman 61
Langham, Michael 219
Lansbury, George 92
Lapointe, Ernest 104
Lascelles, Sir Alan 174-5
Laval, Pierre 84
Law, Bonar 247
Lee, Arthur (Viscount Lee of Fareham) 167
LePan, Douglas 143, 164, 201-2, 234
Lesage, Jean 254
Lévesque, Georges-Henri 203, 204, 205-6, 209, 211-12, 235, 269, 275

Levey, James 36
Levy, Kurt 135
Lewis, Wyndham 147
Lindsay, A.D. (Lord Lindsay of Birker) 171
Lippmann, Walter 101–2, 105
Livesay, Dorothy 205
Lloyd, Gweneth 219
Lorne, Marquess of 200
Lortie, Leon 209
Lothian, Lord (Philip Kerr) 21–2, 92, 94–5, 128
Lower, Arthur 234–5, 273
Lyall, William 219

Maisky, Ivan 94
Markham, Violet 16–17, 128, 159
Martin, Paul 62, 234, 241, 282
Massey, Alice Parkin: early life in England 4–5; comments on coronation ceremony 10; describes English aristocratic society 14, 18; criticizes Oxford Group 20; relations with Pauline Vanier 53–4; praises Lester Pearson 56; comments on Frau von Ribbentrop 92; experience during air raids on London 109, 111; her account of Lionel's return from prison camp 114; her pride in Hart 116; her account of George Grant's war experiences 117; welcomes Canadian war artists 149; her central role in the organization and administration of 'auxiliary services' 149–50; conflict with R.B. Bennett about the role of women's organizations 150–1; discovers building for the Beaver Club 152; Canadian Officers' Club, her creation 153; administers Garnons 154; her dedication to her war work 159–60; regrets failure of Canadian press to recognize Vincent's appointment as chairman of the National Gallery 167; resents King's offer to Vincent of lieutenant-governorship 175–6; comments on poem by Earle Birney 198; her delight in the prospect of going to Rideau Hall 241; her death 241; tributes 242–4
Massey, Anna 285
Massey, Arnold 66–7
Massey, Arthur 66–7
Massey College 294–301, 307–9
Massey, Daniel 285
Massey, Denton 66
Massey, Dorothy Ludington Whitney 68–9
Massey, Hart 69–70, 110, 114–16, 145, 172, 182, 285–6, 311–12
Massey, Jonathan 285, 286
Massey, Lilias (Mrs Lionel Massey) 172, 182, 244, 254, 255, 276, 286–7
Massey, Lionel 46, 69–70, 112–14, 182, 244, 255, 276, 286, 307
Massey, Melodie (Mrs Hart Massey) 285, 311–12
Massey, Raymond 67–9, 182–3, 301
Massey scholarships 47
Massey, Walter 66
Massey, Vincent: early career: education and official appointments 3; marriage to Alice Parkin 4–5

High commissioner to London, 1935–39: appearance and speech 4, 5, 6; attends accession council for George VI 7; approves Baldwin's handling of abdication of Edward VIII 8; rejoices in succession of George VI 8–9; role in the visit of the King and Queen to Canada in 1939 10–11; establishes London residence 12–14; analysis of his anglophilia 29–31; receives honorary degree at Oxford 31–2; comparison of his anglophilia with that of R.B. Bennett 32–3; his insistence on Canadian autonomy 35–6; self-appointed Canadian cultural attaché in Great Britain 37–49; as spokesman for Canadian business and trade 49–52; relations with senior officers, Georges Vanier and Lester Pearson 52–7; answers complaints about the operation of Canada House 58–61; returns to Canada 1936 and 1937 61–2; Canadian correspondents 62–4; comparison of John Buchan and Vincent Massey 64–5; relations with members of the Massey family 66–7; relations with Raymond Massey 67–9; delight in London appointment 70–1; his varied experience in international affairs 72–3; decides to meet with fellow high commissioners 75–8; speaker on behalf of Canada at League of Nations (July 1936) 78; confined to minor committees of League of Nations (September 1936) 79; ideas on foreign policy 81–3; attitude towards Spanish Civil War 86–7; supports Chamberlain's policy of appeasement 88–90; sympathy for Germany and criticisms of French vindictiveness 92; invited to visit Hitler but King forbids him to accept 92–3; attitude to Russia 94; influence of Lord Lothian 94–5; impressed by Robert's book, *The House that Hitler Built* 95; abandons hope of settlement with Germany 97; his views on appeasement shared by Dominions Office and fellow high commissioners 98; attitude towards Jewish immigration 104–5

The war years 1939–45: in London throughout the war, resident of Dorchester Hotel 107–11; concerned about destruction of works of art during air raids 110–11; Lionel's wounding, imprisonment, and eventual release 111–14; Hart's career in the air force, his wounding and recovery 114–16; concern for Alison and George Grant during the war years 116–18; improved relations during the war with Mackenzie King 118–21; establishes good rapport with Norman Robertson 121–2; as principal participant in meetings of the high commissioners 124–5; criticism of Churchill's war leadership 126–7; increasingly critical of American policy 127–30; responsible for Brockington's appointment in the Ministry of Information as adviser on Empire affairs 129; responsible for Pierre Dupuy's appointment as envoy to Vichy 131; concerned about fate of allied refugees 133–4; joins with other commissioners to urge clarification of war arms 136; major role in the launching of the British Commonwealth Air Training Plan 137–9; takes leading part in arrangements for the evacuation of British children 138–40; as principal liaison officer between the military and the Canadian government 141; relations with Ralston, Crerar, and McNaughton 141–4; protests against various actions of British government – leasing of Newfoundland bases to the USA, shackling of German prisoners after Dieppe 145; initiates and organizes scheme for Canadian war artists 146–9; part in organizing and directing 'auxiliary services' – Beaver Club, Canadian Officers' Club, and Garnons 151–9; decision to resign as high commissioner, March 1946 163; his reputation in England as public speaker 163–5; publication and reception of a selection of his London speeches, *The Sword of Lionheart* 165–6; his collection of modern English paintings exhibited at the Tate Gallery, April 1946 166; appointed trustee of British National Gallery, 1941, chairman, 1943 166–9; vice-chairman of committee on preservation and restitution of art treasures appropriated by the enemy 169; chairman of committee to examine functions of the National Gallery and Tate Gallery 169–70; chairman of committee to consider the state of Balliol College 170–1; receives CH 173–5; declines offer of lieutenant-governorship of Ontario 175–6

Canadian years 1946–67: approached to accept presidency of the University of Toronto 178; elected chancellor of the University of Toronto 179–81; goes on national speaking tour 185–9; asserts post-war strength of Great Britain 185; argues against Canada's joining Pan-American Union 185; anti-Americanism 186, 187; advocates patience in dealing with USSR 186–7; his cultural nationalism 187–8; publishes *On Being Canadian* 185, 187–8; his activities as chancellor 189–93; accepts chairmanship of the Royal Commission on National Development in the Arts, Letters and Sciences 195; his high qualifications for the chairmanship of the commission 197–8; approached about governor-generalship, February

1950 201; has major responsibility for selection of commissioners 202; an expert chairman of the commission 207–8; entertains the commission at Batterwood 212; anxious to avoid a high-brow attitude in the commissions's deliberations 214; his concern with the cultural independence of Canada 217–35; his devotion to the universities 230; his dominating role in the commission 233; the commission a summation of his life work 235–6; his vice-regal associations 1911–52, 237–9; early protests against the appointment of a native governor-general 246; his views on the nature of the Crown 245–8; relations with Elizabeth II and Prince Philip 246; revival of vice-regal pomp 248–9; his tour as governor-general 250–2; his deep concern for Quebec and the use of the French language 252; his tour of the far north 253–7; criticism of Massey as governor-general 258–9; his use of light verse in his speech to the Press Gallery 259–60; delights in his portrayal in *My Fur Lady* 260–2; the Queen's dinner of 1 July 1959 262–3; the offer of the Garter and the government's eventual decision to decline the offer 263–8; views on foreign affairs while governor-general 270–1; his support of cultural activities 273–4; his active lobbying on behalf of the Canada Council 274–5; Brooke Claxton's tribute to Massey at the inaugural meeting of the Canada Council, 30 April 1957 275–6; advises Claxton on Canada Council matters 276; his speeches as governor-general 277–83; greatly indebted in his speeches to Hilda Neatby 278–81, appearance and health in 1959 aged 72 284; the Massey family 285–7; his last public speeches 288–90; his autobiography, *What's Past Is Prologue* 211–3; awards and honours 292–3; planning and building Massey College 294–301; his service to the University of Toronto 302; his return to England 303–5; plans to marry Leigh Gossage 306–7; Lionel's death, 27 July 1965 307; problems in financing Massey College 307–9; his 80th birthday 309–10; the implementation of the recommendations in the commission's report on honours 310; death and funeral 311–13

Melbourne, Lord 264
Menjou, Adolph 335n
Menzies, Robert 266
Metcalfe, Lady Alexander 305
Michener, Roland 301
Milne, David 61, 147
Minto, Lord 200
Montagu, General Price 147–8
Montgomery, Lord 264
Morrison, Harold 208
Moss, Pat 48–9
Mountbatten, Lord Louis 264
Mulock, Sir William 176, 179–80

Murray, J. Clark 219
Mussolini, Benito 85
My Fur Lady 260–2

MacCarthy, Desmond 28
McCarthy, Joseph 270–1
McCarthy, Leighton 123, 307
McConnell, J.M. 151
McCullagh, George 178, 336n
McCurry, H.D. 147, 196
Macdermot, T.L. 62–3, 202
MacDonald, Malcolm 75, 78, 80, 85, 123, 133
Macdonald, Ross 341n
Macdonald, Wilson 197
Macdonnell, J.M. 196
McDougall, Robert L. 155, 331n
McFarland, C. Frank 41
Mackenzie, C.J. 209
Mackenzie, N.A.M. (Larry) 203, 204, 205, 206, 229, 235
Mackintosh, W.L. 168
McKinnon, Hector 168
McLean, Ross 57–8, 234
McLean, Stanley 180
Maclennan, Hugh 202
McLuhan, Marshall 226, 309
MacMillan, Cyrus 227
MacMillan, Sir Ernest 200
Macmillan, Harold 23–4, 98, 171, 238, 244
McNaughton, General A.G.L. 140, 142–4, 172

Naegale, Kaspar 135
Neatby, Blair 83
Neatby, Hilda 203, 204, 206–7, 209, 217, 234, 236, 278–82, 301, 344n
Nehru, Jawaharlal 263

Nesbitt, Aird and Honor 302
Nevinson, C.R.W. 147
Newman, Peter 311
Newmark, John 135
Newton, Eric 43, 166
Nicolson, Harold 98–9, 92
Norwood, Gilbert 219

Ogilvie, Will 148
Oliphant, Betty 219
Orpen, William 147
Orwell, George 86

Paget, Sir Bernard 144
Parkin, John 298
Pasmore, Victor 166
Patrick, Max 47, 321 fn.
Patterson, Tom 272
Peacock, Sir Edward 51
Pearson, Lester: early career and relation with Massey 55; joins office of the high commissioner 55; argues for central position of the high commissioner 56; writes a memorandum on British-Canadian relations 56; in 1938 appointed counsellor 56; his assessment of Massey in his autobiography 56; present at League of Nations discussions of sanctions against Italy 74; in 1939 reports on 'mess' in Department of External Affairs 79; has reservations about appeasement 97–8; leaves London 1941 to become minister-counsellor in Washington 122; correspondence with Vincent Massey 123; appointed ambassador to Washington

123; compares Massey and McNaughton 143; responsible for inclusion of Canada in the official announcement of invasion of Sicily 146; under-secretary of state for external affairs 185; September 1948, minister of external affairs 187; letter to Pickersgill about Massey 193–4; enthusiastically supports Royal Commission on National Development in the Arts, Letters and Sciences, and Massey's appointment as chairman 176; asks Massey, on behalf of the PM, to consider appointment as governor-general 201; with Martin and Claxton, gives strong cabinet support to Massey 241; comments on the atmosphere of Rideau Hall during Massey's régime 258; as PM introduces legislation on honours system based upon Massey's recommendations 310; as Rideau Hall neighbour 342n
Pelletier, Wilfrid 293
Penney, Mrs Marie 263
Percy, Eustace (Baron Percy of Newcastle) 24, 189
Peterson, Len 207
Petherick, Major Maurice 165
Phillips, Eric 189–90, 192, 295
Pickersgill, Jack 193, 196, 275
Pitfield, Michael 234, 299, 302
Plaunt, Alan 63, 223
Porter, John 205
Portal, Sir Charles 264
Porteous, Timothy 343 fn.
Pratt, E.J. 38, 293

Price, Nancy 38–9
Prince Philip 246, 263–4, 299

Queen Elizabeth 245, 248, 302
Queen Elizabeth II 246
Queen Mary 161–2

Rae, Saul 47, 321n
Ralston, J.L. 140–1, 148
Ravensdale, Irene 314
Reith, Lord 192–3
Ribbentrop, Joachim von 92
Riddell, W.A. 74
Ritchie, Charles 109, 110, 131–2, 159, 164, 234, 303
Robbins, John 202
Roberge, Guy 209
Roberts, Stephen H. 95, 101
Robertson, Gordon 254, 5
Robertson, Norman 79, 111, 121–2
Roche, Mazo de la 38–9
Rogers, Norman 130
Rowley, Gordon 255
Royal Commission on National Development in the Arts, Letters and Sciences: its background 195–200; role of the governor-general in culture 200–1; appointment of secretary, Archibald Day 201–2; appointment of the commissioners and their special interests and qualities 202–7; its efficiency 208–9; administrative structure 210–11; relation with political parties and provinces 210–11; variety of briefs and witnesses 211–12; the commissioners relax 212–13; non-didactic nature of the report

214–15; use of statistics 215–16; culture as the highest reaches of artistic and intellectual activity 216; the nationalistic tone 217–18; American cultural influences 219–19; the British cultural influence 219; examination of radio broadcasting and the position of the CBC 220–6; consideration of TV 226; recommendation of the Canada Council 226–9; financial support of universities 229–31; implementation of the report 231–3; élitist nature of the report 234–5
Rundle, W.E. 59

Salter, Sir Arthur 116
Sandwell, B.K. 106, 196, 225–6, 258
Schaeffer, Carl 149
Scott, Frank 207
Sedgwick, Joseph 222, 223
Shaw, George Bernard 28, 101
Shephardson, Whitney 303
Sherwood, Robert 83
Showalter, D.H.A. 272
Sickert, Walter 166
Siegfried, André 217–18
Siepman, Charles A. 210
Skelton, O.D. 35, 48, 74, 79, 118
Slim, Sir William 266
Slonim, Rabbi Reuben 282–3
Smith, George 63
Smith, Goldwin 247
Smith, Sidney 178, 181, 189–90, 207, 266
Sowby, C.W. 190

Spence, James 58
Spry, Graham 223
Stacey, Colonel C.P. 148, 330n
Stajanovich, Anna 182
Stajanovich, Miroslav 182, 287, 312
Steer, Philip Wilson 166
St Laurent, Louis 184–5, 220, 229–30, 241, 265–6, 269, 270, 274–5, 310, 340–1n
Stone, Thomas 303
Surveyer, Arthur 203, 204, 209, 225–6, 236
Sutherland, Graham 166

Thomson, David 209
Thom, Ronald 298–9
Toronto, University of 71, 178, 179–81, 189–93, 294–301, 307–9
Towers, Graham 168
Tovell, Harold 189
Tovell, Ruth 66, 285
Toynbee, Arnold 92
Tree, Ronald and Marietta 303
Trevelyan, G.M. 173
Trollope, Anthony 264
Trotter, R.C. 209
Turpin, Joyce (Mrs Bryant) 251, 287, 291
Tweedsmuir, Lord (John Buchan) 60–1, 64–5, 240, 253, 277

Underhill, Frank 207, 34, 273, 292

Vanier, Georges 53–4, 249, 310
Vanier, Pauline 53
Varley, Frederick 147
Vimy Ridge Memorial 35–6
Voaden, Herman 199

Watson, John 219
Waugh, Evelyn 109–10
Whalon, Moira 297
Wheeler-Bennett, John 335n
Whitton, Charlotte 259
Wilgress, Dana 243
Wilkie, Wendell 335n
Willan, Healey 293
Willingdon, Lord 239

Willis-O'Connor, Colonel 278
Wilson, Ethel 293
Wimperis, Harry and Grace 109
Wright, Peter 209
Wrong, George 61, 234
Wrong, Hume 57, 122
Wynwood, Elizabeth 199

Young, George Paxton 219